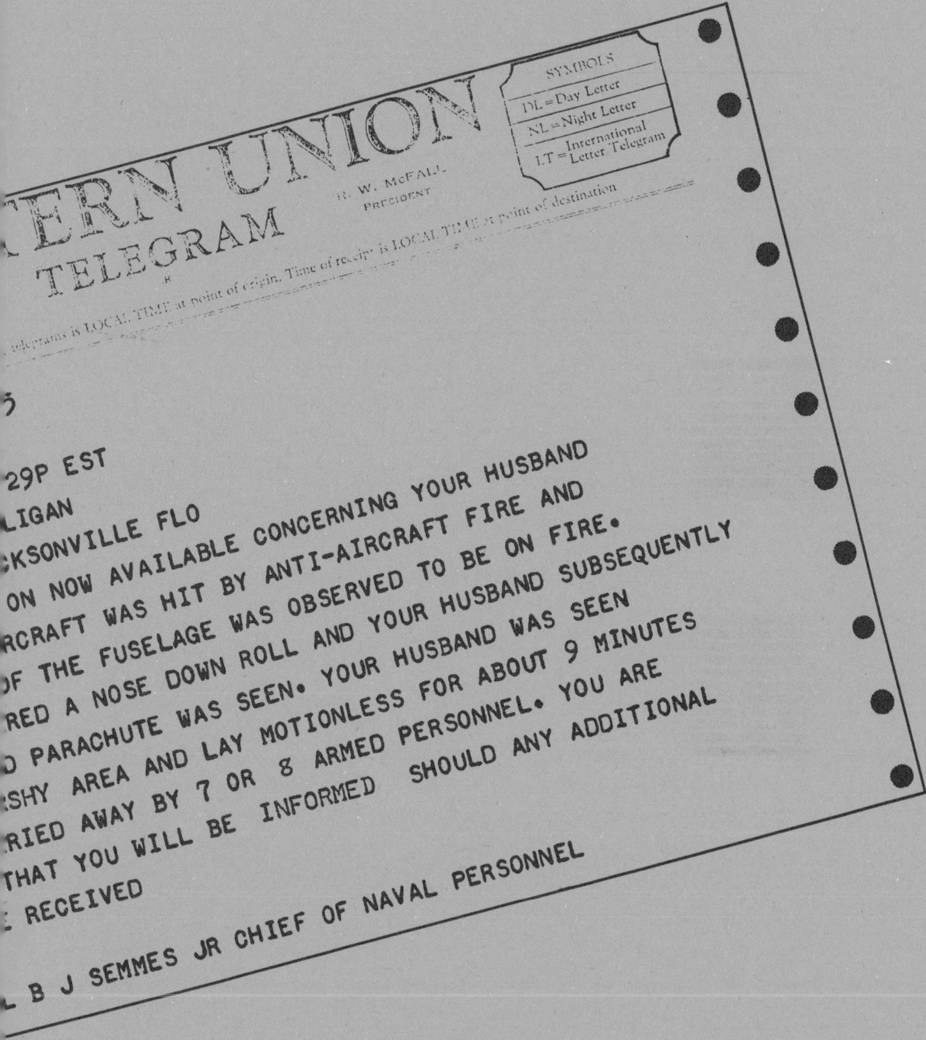

TERN UNION TELEGRAM

R. W. McFALL·
PRESIDENT

SYMBOLS
DL = Day Letter
NL = Night Letter
LT = International Letter Telegram

Telegrams is LOCAL TIME at point of origin. Time of receipt is LOCAL TIME at point of destination

29P EST

LIGAN

CKSONVILLE FLO

ON NOW AVAILABLE CONCERNING YOUR HUSBAND
RCRAFT WAS HIT BY ANTI-AIRCRAFT FIRE AND
OF THE FUSELAGE WAS OBSERVED TO BE ON FIRE.
RED A NOSE DOWN ROLL AND YOUR HUSBAND SUBSEQUENTLY
PARACHUTE WAS SEEN. YOUR HUSBAND WAS SEEN
SHY AREA AND LAY MOTIONLESS FOR ABOUT 9 MINUTES
RIED AWAY BY 7 OR 8 ARMED PERSONNEL. YOU ARE
THAT YOU WILL BE INFORMED SHOULD ANY ADDITIONAL
RECEIVED

L B J SEMMES JR CHIEF OF NAVAL PERSONNEL

THE HANOI COMMITMENT

By James A. Mulligan
Captain, U.S. Navy (Retired)

Published and Distributed by

RIF Marketing
912 Five Points Rd.
P.O. Box 3055
Virginia Beach, Virginia 23454

3rd Edition

Manufactured in the United States of America

Library of Congress Catalog Number: 81-90096

Mulligan, James A.
   The Hanoi Commitment

ISBN 0-9606000-0-0

Dedicated to
Louise and our six sons
and to all those American fighting men
and their families who paid the price
of Vietnam.

Captain Jim Mulligan
USS Enterprise Off Vietnam
Yankee Station 1965

TABLE OF CONTENTS

1971

1972

1973

1966

THE ENTERPRISE

Sunday was not a day of rest on the *ENTERPRISE* cruising on Yankee Station near Vietnam on the 20th of March 1966. A late switch in the flight schedule caused me to miss the usual Sunday 0900 Catholic Mass followed by breakfast in company of Father Ed Gallagher, formerly of the Diocese of Boston, then the Newport Navy Hospital, and now with the sea going Navy. Drawn together by origin and heritage we had become fast friends during the past six months since we first met on *ENTERPRISE.* He was a first tour chaplain new to ways of the carrier and I a seasoned 4th tour Naval Aviation Commander with twenty years of service. From the first minute I liked him and immediately decided I would do all in my power to bring him up to speed on the ways of carriers and their personnel and operational problems.

For his part he offered the stability of a man of God who had his feet on the ground. He knew life's full score, yet could accept the waverings and vicissitudes of man, the fallen creature struggling ever to be better than he was, but often losing. You could sum him up by saying that he was a man of great faith who understood the strengths and weaknesses of military men, and accepted them as they were. I knew he was a winner from the moment we met and I liked him and we were friends.

The order, "Pilots man your aircraft," came via the intercom and was immediately verified by the teletype. As I rushed headlong to the elevator I bumped into Father Gallagher who was making his way rapidly toward the Ready Room. "Where are you going?" he asked. "I thought you weren't scheduled and would be at 9 o'clock Mass." "Last minute switch," I said. "I'll catch Mass tonight. I'll be back a little after 11 a.m. See you then for breakfast." "Okay," he replied. "See you then. God bless."

The 0900 launch was routine. I would make my usual "hands off the stick" cat shot after verifying both internal and external trim tab indicators. At the cat officer's launch signal my Douglas A4C Skyhawk, heavy with extra fuel tank and two multi racks loaded with 500 lb. bombs, bowed gracefully as the catapult cable pulled first down, then rushed forward to lift off speed in only two hundred feet.

Slammed back into the seat, I sat immobile under the force of the acceleration until I left the rising deck a few knots above stalling speed, and dipped slowly towards the undulating movements of the tranquil South China Sea. Making a smooth clearing turn I accelerated under the thrust of 100% power, tapped the brakes, raised the gear and milked the flaps up in a manner so as not to cause any unnecessary loss of precious altitude. "703 airborne, switching tactical," I called flipping from UHF land launch to the more practical tactical squadron common frequency.

Reaching climb speed I pulled the power back to 98%, leaving the additional 2% available to my permanent wingman Ken, and Ralph the 3rd man in the flight who had launched after me. With this 2% they would be able to gain on me prior to my initiating a rendezvous turn. With any luck and proficiency they would catch me on the straightaway as I climbed out heading for the coast of North Vietnam. I'd make a 360 degree orbit for them at fifty miles if they weren't hooked on in formation. Time and fuel is precious in combat and expediency in rendezvous is like an added insurance policy or money in the bank.

But not so today. As expected Ken my regular wingman hooked on, but our third man, new to the squadron and combat was a trifle slow. This forced me to make the rendezvous orbit. While it only took an additional four minutes I was displeased and resolved to let him know about it in the debriefing. I had second thoughts immediately, as I recalled that he indeed was progressing faster than normal in the ways of combat carrier aviation. I can afford to forget this one but I'll keep an eye on him to insure he moves up a little faster next time, I thought. I didn't know that there wouldn't be a next time, that for me this time was my last carrier launch, that in a matter of a few short minutes my carrier flying career would terminate abruptly. But that was still ahead of me.

Once joined, we proceeded toward the coast of North Vietnam heading for a point south of Vinh where my target was allegedly located. I say allegedly because in my own mind there was serious doubt that the target we briefed for actually did exist. Our target assignments came from a computer sheet compiled in Saigon or Washington by Intelligence types charged with target assignment. On previous flights, I had been assigned small bridge interdiction targets over dirt roads crossing small streams only to find on my arrival at the aim point, that the bridge wasn't there. In such instances we would crater the road at the aim point hoping to cut it in two so it would not be usable at least for some hours. No matter how many craters we made in a dirt road they always were filled in and repaired by the next morning. I used to think that the North Vietnamese had thousands of men assigned to road repair, and they did.

That Sunday morning's target looked like it could be another of those intelligence, "by guess and by God," assignments made up from a questionable map showing a small estuary of water meandering up close to a small winding dirt road. On the map the road crossed the top of the estuary. Ergo a bridge must be there!

The air intelligence briefers didn't have a picture of the target which led me to believe that it would be another ficticious assignment. When I questioned them they agreed with the possibility of my assessment. "If there's no bridge, cut the road at the bend where the target is suppose to be, and we'll at least slow down some of the damn road traffic that's moving south on it every night," the senior briefer said. "And by the way, late yesterday the Air Force reported they thought a SAM missile site came up once or twice with their acquisition radar, somewhere south of Vinh. You better keep your eyes open for it. We haven't found one there yet, but you can never tell. Be careful!"

That's all I need, I thought, take a flight of three A4 Skyhawks into a possible hot SAM (Surface to Air Missile) area trying to find a bridge that possibly doesn't even exist. What the hell is this war coming to?

The introduction of the SAM threat added a new variable to the target problem. It required an alternative to our usual method of attack, which was to come in at 20,000 feet, look over the target area, let down to 10,000 feet on target acquisition and make a normal bombing run of 45 degrees of dive with bomb release at 4,500 feet and pull out level by 3,000 feet. This tactic would make us sitting ducks for any SAM site in the area.

The best alternative in such a SAM environment in early 1966, was to make a low level run in below the parameters of the SAM acquisition radar, and approach the target at 100 feet above the ground on the run in line. At a predetermined spot we'd pull up into a sharp climbing attitude visually acquire the target and roll in on it from above 5,000 feet using a 30 degree dive with release between 2,800 feet and 3,000 feet. After bombs away pull out by 1,500 feet, jink by using sharp evasion turns to throw off the SAM threat, and then push over for the deck going out at 100 feet above ground level as fast as possible until you were in a safe area or over the South China Sea.

This entire evolution was a maneuver that required professional skill at its highest. It was well within our capability, and had become routine during our four months of aerial combat over North Vietnam.

"We'll do a low level run in and pop up here for our attack," I briefed Ken and Ralph. "To make it easy I'll get the Willy Fudd's to give us a steer for this point on the coast line, where we'll enter at 100 feet at 465 knots. We'll be only two and a half minutes from pullup so the navigation will be easy. Since I'll be able to see the estuary on pull up, I can get a fast check to see if the bridge is actually there. Regardless of whether it's there or not we'll aim for this point of the road as our target. After release, jink. Keep me in sight as I make a left turn out, and we'll come back the same way we went in only faster. When I'm over the coast line I'll come back to 96% climb power, and you guys hook on as I climb heading back toward the ship. Any questions?" There were none.

"One more thing, keep your SAM warning system on and if you get a warning light or hear a warning tone he'll be locked on me and firing. Look for the missile lift off, lots of dust and flame. If you see the lift off, the SAM site becomes your target. Roll in on him and drop everything on one pass, and be sure to mark your map accurately showing his exact position. After your drop, jink extra hard and get flat on the deck as soon as possible. I don't want to lose a wingman to some damn Russian missile crew. Stay on tactical channel and holler like hell till we get joined up over the water, and then I'll make a report to the ship."

"One final item. We'll keep our zero delay lanyards to our parachutes and ejection seats hooked up from launch till after we're out safely from North Vietnam, and we'll set our bombing switch before we cross the coast line on the way in."

Getting a steer from the Willy Fudd electronic aircraft crew would be easy. Those pilots flew night and day, running up and down a coastal electronic barrier patrol set up to protect the fleet and intercept all returning aircraft. They were bored stiff with the war. When I asked the Fudd pilot if he could pick up my flight on his radar and vector us to our coastal penetration point, he gave an enthusiastic, "Hell yes!" reply. My squadron, "The Roadrunners", shared the same Ready Room facilities with the Willy Fudd crews, so we were on very friendly terms. "We'll monitor you on your squadron tactical frequency after take off, and then we'll vector you to coastal penetration. You can be sure we'll hit it right on the money," he said. "Thanks," I said. "That will make the navigation easy, and we won't waste any time getting into the target."

We were flying in a loose vee formation, Ken on my right wing and Ralph on my left. I leveled off at 18,000 feet as we headed toward North Vietnam at max cruise power. The Skyhawk was a great little attack aircraft. It had plenty of power and maneuverability, and flew like a hot little sports car rather than a truck. It was fun to fly, and for a war like the one in Vietnam, it was very cost effective. You could buy four Skyhawks for the price of one Phantom.

The weather was beautiful. High thin patches of cirrus dotted the dark blue sky. Visibility was unlimited and I could see the North Vietnamese coast ninety miles ahead. It was hard to believe that such a tranquil scene would become a combat arena in only a few minutes, with diving aircraft raining death and destruction on targets below. Targets that might be heavily defended with anti-aircraft flak that would dot the blue sky in dark bursts of puffs, anyone of which could mean the end of the flight, and the end of a career, or even the end of a life.

Whatever the outcome, it always happened fast. There were no lingering slogging battles in the air. You went in fast and out faster if you were smart. There were no multiple bombing runs, just one pass on the target. You better do the job right the first time, or you'd come back again tomorrow, and the next day, and the next, until the job was done.

"Don't duel with flak or mess with missiles" was the rule. Hanoi had a prohibited flight area with a radius of 25 miles, while Haiphong had a similar, though smaller 15 mile flight restricted zone. Within these areas were the best targets in the whole damn country. We couldn't even fly in these areas, never mind bomb those targets. So the watch word for all pilots was, "Be careful there isn't a damn target out of these areas that you should bust your ass for!"

"Hey X.O., this is Fudd One — flash your parrot for confirmation," a loud clear voice said over the tactical squadron common frequency.

"Rog," I replied as I hit my IFF (Radar Identification Friend or Foe) transmitter to flash. "We gottcha X.O.," said Fudd One, "Steer 278 to penetration point. You're about twelve minutes out now."

Everything was normal. I scanned my flight instruments, then visually checked each wingman. "Bogey's ten o'clock high," Ken called out. I immediately sector scanned this area but it took me at least ten seconds before I had them in sight. It was a flight of four Phantoms from the previous launch returning for recovery. They're late I thought, must have stayed too long looking for the target, or took too long getting joined up after their attack run. I could see their jet exhaust now. The F4 was a smoker, it left a trail of exhaust that was visible for a long way. I was glad the A4C didn't smoke. It was a damn hard plane to see even after you were used to looking for it. A low visibility profile was a big advantage over the few defending MIG's that North Vietnam had.

Ken has the best set of eyes for a wingman that I've ever seen, I thought. Early on, in a previous Mediterranean deployment, I had become acutely aware of Ken's talent for picking up other aircraft visually. I made him my permanent wingman in the Med, and he stayed on in that position in combat. With his eyes and my experience we made a helluva fine section. I couldn't have a better combat wingman than Ken. He had learned the tricks of the trade fast. He was aggressive, yet calm and competent in times of stress. Above all else he was loyal. He had as much respect for me as a senior aviator as I had for him. He never questioned my decisions or ability in the air, and I always felt that in the clutch I could count on him to be where he was supposed to be and to do what had to be done. This mutual respect and confidence had been successful for us so far in the North Vietnam air war. We had hardly been scratched in over eighty missions. "Roadrunner flight check all switches on, except master arm," I said, visually setting all my bomb station intervelometer and bomb sight settings.

I then looked over to Ralph on my left wing and gave him the move to right echelon by pumping my right arm up and down. Ralph immediately responded to my signal and slid gracefully across until he was in position on bearing and distance on Ken's right wing. We were 150 feet apart, close enough to look good in formation, but far enough apart so that I had room to maneuver without fear of a mid-air collision or without excessively fatiguing the wingmen who would tire quickly if they had to fly a close parade position. In combat you wanted all pilots to be alert, yet loose and relaxed until the final moment of actual engagement with the enemy. At that time, the adrenalin pumped by the stress of combat, would serve to keep us all in a super alert and responsive state.

No matter how many combat hops you flew, you never relaxed in those last minutes before bombs away. It was always like waiting for the bell to ring for round one. A little nervous tension, a few butterflies and then the adrenalin as you rolled in and dove on target. Then you settled down to the business at hand. A smooth run in on dive angle, making corrections, drop on altitude and airspeed, observe everything; flak, missiles, pull out, turn, jink, look for MIGS, look for wingman, note target damage if possible, note everything mentally. It was all over so fast. Then rendezvous, check each plane over for damage, and head for home to get back on time and turn the planes around for another launch and another strike. The entire flight from launch to recovery took generally only a few minutes over two hours, but were we tired and keyed up by the time we were safely back on *ENTERPRISE.* An ordinary flight from a carrier is a thrilling experience, live combat just adds to the thrill.

It's time to start down, I thought. By tapping the top of my instrument console with the palm of my right hand I signalled Ken and eased in forward trim lowering the nose in a graceful descent aimed at the intersection of the waters of the South China Sea and the coast of North Vietnam. I couldn't quite make out the coastal penetration point, but knew it was ahead of me and close to my present course.

"X.O. what's your run in course line?" called Fudd One. "Two eight zero true," I replied. "Rog! you're right on course for the penetration point, we'll vector you to hit the point so that you're on the run in course line. Standby for vector." "Rog, Fudd One. Will you give us a time hack as I cross the point please?" "Wilco X.O. vector 260." I dropped the left wing and smoothly turned left and rolled out on 260. "Steady on 260," I reported, continuing our descent heading for the coast in point.

As the air speed increased during the descent I retrimmed with increased left rudder tab to keep the Skyhawk on a perfectly balanced flight path. It's a real smooth tranquil day, I thought as I scanned the horizon, my instruments, and then my wingmen. Both of them were in perfect position, on bearing and distance in a loose combat right echelon and their aircraft looked normal. Over the years I had trained myself to always closely observe a wingman or leader's aircraft for telltale signs of some potential malfunction, looking for smoke, or oil leaks, or hydraulic leaks, which would indicate trouble. You didn't have to be a military aviator for long, before you realized your life and safety depended on a great many people, anyone of whom could make an error with disastrous personal consequences. As a result pilots flying in formation were part of a mutual protection society, each one looked out for the other to the best of his ability.

We were passing through 5,000 feet when Fudd One vectored me right to a heading of 280 degrees. "Steady on 280," I transmitted, rolling wings level. "Roadrunner flight, check your switches and set master arm on," I called, simultaneously rechecking my own switches and setting the master arm switch on.

"You're right on course and two minutes from hack time," said Fudd One, "Roger," I replied as we were passing through 3,000 feet. Ah, there it is, I thought as I made visual contact with the check point I had selected for coastal penetration.

"Good work Fudd One. You've got me right on the money," I transmitted as I made a smooth slow pull up to ease the rate of descent and level off at 500 feet. "One minute to hack time," called Fudd One. I made one last visual check of Ken and Ralph and gave them a thumbs up, signaling all's O.K. and then eased toward the water until I leveled off at 100 feet. The red warning light of the radar altimeter flickered on and off to let me know my exact altitude above the sea. I checked to see that I had 98% RPM power set, leaving the extra 2% for Ken and Ralph to play with. "Standby X.O., ten, nine, eight, seven, six, five, four, three, two, one, hack," called Fudd One as I crossed the green coast line, on course and indicating 465 knots. I hit the stop watch and only had two and a half minutes until I reached the pull up point.

The flat green and brown earth flew by. Rice fields, trees, dirt roads, native hooches all blended into a myriad stream of scenic panorama. Each second I covered a little more than 770 feet as I attempted to hold perfectly to course. The late winter air was still and cool enough that the usual bumpy turbulence caused by the uneven heating of fields and ground and woods was missing. At 100 feet there was no perceptible wind, and the air seemed perfectly still as I rushed headlong toward the target.

My eyes scanned the short horizon along my course. I searched for land marks to guide my way. I looked for evidence of opposition to my thrust: firing troops, a flak site, a truck park, moving vehicles or any other information with military significance. But there was nothing! I didn't even see a peasant or a buffalo in the fields.

The roads, the term is loosely used in North Vietnam to describe the primitive meandering of cart trails unknown in America except in the wilderness and depths of rural underdevelopment, were barren of traffic.

The earth ahead suddenly undulated as I flew headlong into a series of small rolling hills. I tensed and eased the stick to follow the contours as closely as possible to the 100 foot clearance. There was a large clump of trees, then a flat valley filled with rice fields and then a dirt road cutting across directly in front of my path.

The sudden movement of ant-like creatures ahead caught my eye as they scurried for cover near the road's edge. It was a column of troops! There were hundreds of them! They were stretching up and down the road as far as I could scan. They looked battalion size or larger. The flashes from their upturned firing sticks told me they were shooting at us. It was one and a half minutes to pull up when bang! A loud impact slammed into my silvery Skyhawk. I'm hit! You lucky bastards!, I thought.

Immediately the stick froze like it was buried in concrete. It wouldn't budge, as I instinctively pulled back trying to gain altitude and freedom from the threatening earth only 100 feet below me. A super shot of adrenalin raised my reactions and sensory perceptions to an almost super human state. Time stood still as I hit the electrical elevator trim override and my Skyhawk's nose raised slowly and smoothly just in time to keep me from slamming into a tree-studded rolling hill which was rushing at me. I pushed the throttle forward to 100% power. Whew! That was close. I've got to get some sky and turn this bird back for the water, I thought. Then hitting my radio transmitting switch I tried to call out my predicament to Ken and Ralph. But no luck, Ken was already transmitting and cutting me out. "X.O. I have you pulling up about one and a half minutes too early," he said. "We've got about ten more miles to go."

I released the trim tab override when the nose of my Skyhawk showed 30 degrees nose up on my gyro horizon indicator. Almost immediately as Ken was speaking a flak warning light flicked on illuminating my console and caused my heart to skip a beat. When it rains it pours, I thought.

Boom! A burst of flak went off at 11 o'clock slightly ahead of me. Wham! My Skyhawk shuttered as I took a hit in the engine somewhere aft of the cockpit.

"He's hit! He's on fire!" screamed Ken over the radio as my cockpit filled with dense black smoke. My SAM-2 warning light came on followed by a SAM warning tone indicating a missile had been launched. The engine started to come apart and all the fire warning lights came on and slowly faded out as I lost the electrical system. The radio died as Ken repeated, "He's on fire! Fir-re-re-re!" The stick was still unmoveable as I climbed straight ahead unable to turn.

Wham! I took a hit in the nose and something came through the instrument console and slammed into the escape and evasion radio which was strapped to my torso harness across the front of my chest. The sledgehammer-like blow to my chest knocked the wind out of me and left me stunned, gasping for breath and aching from pain and almost senseless.

But man's quest for survival is not easily overcome, and in seconds I regained my mental faculties sufficiently to analyze my situation and assess the possibilities.

I couldn't see the console because of the black smoke that filled the cockpit, the heat was getting intense and the muffled explosions from the engine told me that the end was near. I was hurting from the blow to my chest. All I could think of was, turn for the sea and safety, but the stick still wouldn't budge and I was helplessly just along for the ride in my disintegrating Skyhawk.

One last chance, I thought, as I instinctively reached forward and pulled the hydraulic control disconnect cable which would place me in manual flight control operation. The Skyhawk reacted immediately by snapping into an uncontrolled spin. I made one last effort to move the stick without avail. Uncontrolled, in a spin, at unknown altitude, on fire, and hurting badly I reached blindly for the face curtain with my right hand. The force of the spin prevented me from getting my left hand to the curtain so I pulled the face curtain with one hand and activated the automatic ejection seat system. Time stopped as I heard the rocket attached to the seat fire. The seat lifted gracefully, almost in a slow motion manner. The canopy left the aircraft and I heard the zero delay lanyard pulling out the chute as I entered into the violent wind stream spinning and flailing, like a rag doll tossed in the middle of a tornado. Slung into unconsciousness by the force of the instant opening of the chute, I hung limp and floated deathlike towards the ground below, oblivious to my condition and circumstances.

WELCOME TO NORTH VIETNAM

It was like a dream as I returned from the black of complete unconsciousness. First came the ooze of gray and the sound of a whispering movement of air as I felt that I was being transported from one state of nature to another, from the natural to the supernatural, a journey of my soul I imagined. I couldn't see. I knew who I was, but nothing more, nothing of my present situation or the circumstances that brought me there. Had I died? Was I on my journey to the hereafter? I sensed movement in space, a floating sensation that I couldn't recognize. I could hear the soft whistle of the wind like that which you hear in a stand of pines on a warm spring day. And the gray got brighter but I still couldn't see. Then the whistle of the wind was interrupted by the sounds of spit, spit, spit, flickering in the background but increasing in tempo and intensity. Then the gray turned to blue, and I could see. First the sky, then the blue water of the sea on the horizon not too far away. I was falling, swaying, floating alive in a chute as I regained my senses. Spit, flick, spit, "My God the little bastards are shooting at me." My left arm was on backwards and dangled limply. Swing the chute, I thought as I pulled on the right risers with my good arm to get the chute swaying and make myself a more difficult target. How high I was I don't know. I saw the sea and safety but it was beyond my reach. I pulled again to help oscillate the chute, the noise of gun shots grew clear and the earth rushed up at me, and suddenly I hit ground going backwards but relaxed. The sounds ceased and the color went from blue to gray to black and I returned to dreamland, oblivious to all that was going on around me.

I don't know how long I lay unconscious in that rice paddy. At the time I came to, it seemed I was unconscious for only a brief time after striking the earth, (years later, in another land when free again, I learned that I lay still and death-like for fifteen or twenty minutes and in fact was never seen to move by my loyal wingman, Ken).

It was the roar of his Skyhawk that awakened me finally to my senses. I was flat on my back, in a foot of muddy rice water when I heard his engine roaring only a hundred feet or so above my head and to my left. He dropped his left wing and it was Ken in the cockpit. We were eyeball to eyeball as he rushed by. I raised my right arm with a thumbs up, but he was gone and never knew that I was alive and had tried to signal him.

He was gone, but his place was immediately taken by a strange looking military oriental who hovered in front of me waving some type of Chinese burp gun. I was captured before I could even move. No escape and evasion techniques here, no jungle survival test to meet. Only surrender, a fait accompli beyond my control.

I struggled to my feet wobbily, removed my helmet, undid the quick release connections to the chute risers. The chute itself lay flat in the paddy water deflated and limp. I unzipped my torso harness and I pulled the shoulder section of the torso harness with my good right arm, shimmied out of it as it slid to my knees with the weight of my survival radio and escape and evasion kit. Unencumbered, I slogged slowly ahead in the rice paddy mud heading in the direction indicated by my captor. I was wearing only my khaki flight suit and boots. In minutes we were joined by others shouting and yelling as they saw he had captured their prey.

I hurt all over. My left arm, on backwards, hung uselessly at my side. My rib cage ached constantly, probably from the sledgehammer-like blow I had received in the cockpit. I limped badly as my left hip and thigh were damaged in the flailing ejection, and subsequent landing. My neck was stiff and sore as I moved my head. But I was alive!; alive because the automatic Douglas Rapec ejection seat had worked as advertised, with no help from me except when I initiated the firing action. In other times and other wars I would not have been as lucky and so well protected by technological innovation. But I was alive and that was enough to help me overcome the pain of my injuries at least for a few minutes until the excess of excitement and adrenalin wore off.

At the edge of the field the earth rose a few feet above the rice paddy; topped with small stone and gravel it made a path large enough for a buffalo-drawn cart. I had strained painfully forward and mastered the incline from the paddy to path, and now limped along more slowly as fatigue set in. I was still under the prodding of my burp gun-carrying captor. He was determined to keep his claim and his gutteral jibberish seemed to keep others who eagerly joined our ragged parade at a distance behind him and completely away from me.

In this manner I led the way, alone, followed by him, and then by the ever increasing numbers behind him. By the time we reached a small town we had acquired a large flock of inquisitive followers of all sizes, shapes and ages, and all of them Asian I noticed!

In the center of town, fronting a crude square, a wooden frame building stood like a house with a store front and porch. I was ushered up the porch stairs, pushed into a large empty room, and made to sit in a corner facing my captor who still retained control of what obviously was the greatest prize in his life: ME!

One by one within minutes the apparent village elders and leaders came into the room. When the last arrived, and they numbered five, the obvious leader instructed my armed escort to stand guard on the porch and keep the local populace out in the parched earthen square.

The group of elders held a meeting concerning my disposition for some minutes. They spoke in Vietnamese and I couldn't make out a thing they were saying. When the leader spoke some sentences, and they nodded their heads, I knew some decision had been agreed to.

One of them came close to me and pointing his finger said in very broken English, "Yoo our no pryson er of wah — yoo our crimeinal of wah." Which I translated that they didn't consider me a prisoner of war but a criminal.

"Bullshit!" I said, but he didn't understand the meaning, or even the inflection of my voice.

As they gazed at me, one of them showed great interest in my Rolex watch and my gold wedding band. After a few words to the group he received some agreeing head nods and proceeded to remove my watch, my wedding band, a small silver chain with medal and dog tags around my neck. He found my wallet with Geneva Convention I.D. card, fifty dollars in crisp American greenbacks, and a rosary as he search the pockets of my flight suit. In seconds the booty was divided among them never to be seen again by me or the Vietnamese authorities. These little bastards are all corrupt, I thought as I saw my possessions sliding secretly into their dirty pockets.

The porch guard banged on the door and shouted something. The leader of the elders replied and the door was thrown open. In came two men who were obviously medics. They hovered above me and motioned for me to stand up. I arose in pain, my left arm dangling. One of them inserted a sharp knife through my flight suit, and my skivvy shirt and proceeded to cut them loose from the upper part of my chest and shoulder. The suit fell to my ankles as they looked at my left shoulder and arm which was reversed and out of the shoulder socket. They spoke in Vietnamese to the elders, and motioned me to sit back on the floor.

"You bad injure. You go hospital, Hanoi," said the only English speaker giving me a clue to my eventual destination.

The medics prepared a large syringe and gave me a shot in the left arm, I assumed it was morphine or some form of pain killer for in minutes the pain was gone. Lying me on the floor one medic placed his foot on my chest, and then took my left arm through a series of 360 degree revolutions until he was satisfied that he had accomplished his objective. He mumbled in Vietnamese, and the other medic made a sling for my arm and placed it gently and secured it to my body. They indicated that they had done all they could, and that I should keep the arm in the sling. Then they left. As they went through the doorway I could see that a large, hostile crowd had gathered in the square outside the porch. It looked like a lynch mob in a western movie and I knew all too well who the intended victim was.

One of the elders looked at my flight boots and took a fancy to them. He removed the boots, had me get out of what was left of my flightsuit and left me dressed in socks, skivvy shorts and dangling skivvy shirt. I didn't know it then, but that was all I would have covering me for the next three weeks.

The noise from the mob increased and the elders, nervous about this turn of events, convened a quick meeting to decide what to do.

After a brief discussion the head man went out on the porch and began to address the crowd. At this time two of the other older men ushered me to my feet and hustled me out a back door into a garden growing with corn. They had me stoop and run forward through the garden and behind a fruit tree grove to a wooden house which belonged to one of them.

I was led through a kitchen area occupied by four or five elderly women who were engaged in some cooking and meal preparation, and then into a back bedroom.

The room had an old brass bed, a chair and some dilapidated bureaus. A spotted mirror hung on the wall alongside a picture of Ho Chi Minh, that was the centerpiece of the room's decor.

They sat me on the chair and left me there in view of the women who seemed curious, yet sympathetic to the human misery that sat before them. I was exhausted and drained, and as time wore on the pain returned to my arm and shoulder. I must escape somehow, I thought. I've got to get to the coast, but I wasn't sure which way it was or how far. Save your energy, rest, escape; that was my game plan. But each second I hurt more and more, and grew weaker in body and confused in mind.

I was kept in that room for a couple of hours that extended through the Vietnamese siesta time of which I was yet unaware. Soon after the clanging of some primitive wake-up gong, called a tocsin, several militia men entered the house and made signs that I would be moved to another location.

They removed the sling the medics had made for my arm and blindfolded me with it. Taking a piece of rope they tied each of my wrists, first the right, then left and with the excess rope they made a leash that would serve to pull me along and guide me in the direction they wanted me to go. Because of my large nose a small gap of light was visible, and I could see my feet and the ground around them if I kept my head pointed down. It was just enough to permit me to keep from falling as I moved ahead, but I could see nothing else. I felt like a cow with blinders on being led to slaughter.

They led me for some time along dirt pathways strewn with buffalo dung which I stepped in more than once. My feet covered only with socks became tender and sore from the many stones and pebbles that I stepped on. I hobbled and limped at whatever pace they set, and though I often stumbled and faltered, I never fell.

I could hear the noise of a crowd ahead of me. Soon our pace increased, and I was led down a gauntlet of angry men, women, and children all shouting in Vietnamese jibberish. They proceeded to pelt me with sticks, stones and fists from all sides, and I reeled and stumbled from one side of the gauntlet to the other. I suppose I went a distance of fifty yards in this manner, and then I was led off the pathway and up a small hill and made to stand on a mound of freshly dug earth. A Vietnamese man made a haranguing speech and railed in tones that were unmistakable in their hostility towards me.

As I looked down at my feet I suddenly saw that the earth I stood on came from a newly dug hole. My God, it's a grave, the little bastards are going to execute me, I thought. The speech reached a crescendo and the violent reaction of the crowd told me the moment of truth was at hand. This is it, what a way to go, I thought. Suddenly my thoughts were interrupted when I heard in broken English, "You no die today, Yankee," and I was led away and shoved into a nearby vehicle under the blows and tugs of the irate Vietnamese crowd.

Someone had hold of the dangling end of my blindfold and it pulled off as I fell in the back seat area of a carryall jeep. The driver started it and the vehicle lurched through the parting crowd as a middle aged military man slid into the other front seat and slammed the door.

From my position in the back I could see out of the front side windows and the windshield. The remainder of the area surrounding me was enclosed in canvas. I assessed my physical condition. My arm was useless and dangled. Both hands were still tied and I could see welts and scratches from the blows I had received from the crowd. I ached all over but the thought occurred to me that my physical pain was not as intense as my sense of loss, as I realized for the first time that because of my physical condition there was no chance of escape. I had read somewhere that the pain of loss is the greatest that man can suffer. Suddenly in my agony and despair I realized the truth of this statement. I thought of my wife and my children, my parents and my country, and I wondered if I would ever see them again.

The vehicle drove in second gear as it meandered up and down the rough dirt roads. I tried to keep a sense of direction and was able to tell by the sun's position that we were moving more or less north and then east. I was sure we weren't too far from the coast, maybe ten miles or less I thought.

We drove about a half hour at ten or fifteen miles per hour and we made enough jogs and turns that I thought we were no more than eight miles from where I was captured when suddenly I saw my first indication of twentieth century civilization. Two power lines came out of some trees to a pole and then down from the pole came a large cable that ran across the dirt road in front of us into a well camouflaged area behind a man-made wall of brush and trees. I could see where vehicle tracks turned off the road and entered into this area. The cable that led to the same spot had boards on each side of it as it went across the road. These were obviously placed there to keep passing vehicle wheels from running over the cable. I wonder what the hell they have way out here that needs such a power source, I thought.

As we passed the area of concern I saw a large truck van that was well hidden. My vehicle proceeded one hundred yards ahead and turned into a wooded covered clearing and lurched to a sudden stop.

I was let out on the passenger side and made to stand facing the canvas covering the rear side of the carry-all. My captors replaced my blindfold, spun me around three times and led me forward by the rope which dangled from my left arm. As I moved forward I reeled off the front fender and knew that I was heading away from the vehicle facing in the direction that it was parked. This placed the camouflaged area of the power cable behind me and to my right. I tried to keep track of my movements, because I felt I had seen something that was of military significance even if I didn't know what it was.

I estimate we walked over gravel-like paths through rice fields for about a half a mile before we came to our destination. My feet were sore from stones and dirty from buffalo dung that oozed between my toes. I had already worn away the bottoms of my socks along the ball and heel of my feet so the socks afforded little protection or comfort.

I was placed in a peasant hut built in the shade of some large trees on a slight incline overlooking some rice paddies. On entering, my blindfold was removed, and I was led to a primitive couch next to a window overlooking the fields. The room had a makeshift wooden floor and a large bed covered with a two-man mosquito net. In an adjacent room was an open hearth and dirt floor. An old woman was brewing tea and cooking some kind of greens that I had never seen before. She was being assisted by a very young and very pregnant girl who I assumed was her daughter or daughter-in-law.

Exhausted from the events of the day, I dozed in a sitting position draped over the arm rest of the couch for support, and always under the gaze of one or the other of my captors.

I awoke with a start to see the old woman standing before me. She offered me a cup of hot tea, and flashed a look of womanly compassion at my painful physical condition. I accepted with a polite thank you, savoring each sip as it passed over my dusty and parched lips and soothed my dry throat.

It must have been late afternoon, maybe about four p.m. The sky over the rice paddy was mostly blue with high thin cirrus patches silhouetted against the heaven.

Suddenly a group of young men, twenty to thirtyish, and dressed with sufficient parts of uniforms that I knew they were military, came into the house to gaze at me. One of my guards indicated by his hands that I had been shot down by them. I guessed they were from the flak site. They seemed more curious than hostile and one of them puffing on a cigarette offered me one. I accepted eagerly for at the time I was a heavy smoker and had not had a cigarette since I left the ready room for launch that morning.

The young men seemed to be in a joyous mood as they viewed what was probably their first American. I felt like a fallen eagle, captured and caged, now only the object of human curiosity. I think they were surprised at my age, I was close to forty. They seemed to defer to my condition as a military man even though my appearance in torn skivvies gave me no military image. I had finished the cigarette and sat immobile on the couch looking first at the young group of viewers and alternately out the window at the surrounding countryside. What the hell's gonna happen now, I thought.

Suddenly, from a short distance away I heard the loud roar of a surface to air missile lifting off its launcher. The men scattered and ran for the door. A second missile roared off seconds after the first. My God, it's a SAM site! The damn thing was here after all, I thought.

The roar of the missiles had barely died when I heard a flight of very low flying jets pass directly overhead. One of the guards grabbed a blanket and threw it over me to prevent me from seeing outside. The young military men were yelling and shouting and running when a string of bombs went off and hit the ground probably less than a quarter of a mile away.

That was it. One pass then get out fast. I heard the jets roar into the distance, until the sound of their engines completely faded away. Then the countryside returned to normal, quiet and serene.

The guard removed the blanket and nothing had changed except all the young military men were gone. The old woman kept on cooking as if nothing had happened. The young pregnant girl, stirred by the excitement, held her stomach and grimmaced indicating her delivery time was close.

Off in the distance I could hear the cries of excited Vietnamese, probably coming from the missile site or what was left of it.

It had been an exciting day for me. First I got shot down by the Vietnamese, then I got bombed by the Americans near a SAM site. I hoped they put the site out of action for good and wondered if the attacking planes were from *ENTERPRISE.* I thought they probably were but never did find out.

When darkness came the guard put my blindfold on and led me on a long trek in a general direction away from the SAM site. We walked for almost an hour. One guard led me by the excess rope that was still tied to my hands like a leash, and the other guard took up a position at my heels. I continually stumbled and stubbed my feet on rocks and other obstructions that littered the primitive pathways. In the rougher terrain the man following me steadied my body and kept me from falling by holding my right upper arm. Through the blindfold came traces of light which told me both captors had flashlights to help guide their way. It didn't help me though as the blindfold and the darkness prevented me from even seeing my toes. My feet ached and my left hip was in constant pain as my limp became more apparent by the minute. My pace slowed and this caused the guard leading me to grow angry and tug harder on the rope as he tried to get me to move faster. His accomplice pushed me from behind but the effort was fruitless and served only to cause me to lose my balance completely and pitch forward into the underbrush alongside the pathway. I hurt like hell all over and I was very angry, enough so that my captors decided to be more gentle and lead me at a slower pace once they had me on my feet and headed in the proper direction. Finally we arrived at a road that had heavy vehicle traffic. It's Route 1 I thought, the main thoroughfare in North Vietnam. In a few minutes a vehicle pulled up beside us, and I was hauled through the passenger door and pushed into the rear section. I sat on the floor alongside of the man who had been leading me. My rear guard got in and sat beside the driver and we lurched off heading north. Though I couldn't see I believed that I was in the same type of vehicle that had delivered me to the SAM site. Probably the same one.

We'd only gone a few miles when the driver turned off Route 1 and took a meandering rough road that I thought could not possibly be paved.

I tried to make myself as comfortable as possible but the trip was tortur-
ous as the truck bumped up and down, lurched and swayed from side to
side in a series of shaking and shuddering movements that threw me up
and down and slammed my sore hip and leg. I bounced off the side of the
truck and was able to grasp a part of the metal side to help hold myself in
a steadier position. While this good fortune helped keep me from being
thrown around it did not stop me from bouncing on my fanny on the metal
floor as we hit pot hole after pot hole. This son of a bitch must think he's
riding a bronco in a rodeo, I thought. Finally the road smoothed, and in a
few minutes I could hear people talking and bicycles passing. We drove
very slowly and then pulled to a smooth stop off the street.

The passenger door opened. We exited in reverse order from our
entrance. I could hear the murmuring of many voices. A large crowd of
people must be near me, I thought. My captors led me as before, one in
front pulling and giving me directions via the rope leash and the other
behind me occasionally pushing on my right shoulder. We walked a very
short way and went into some type of structure. I could hear hundreds of
voices, talking in Vietnamese jibberish.

I thought that something big was about to happen. My pulse increased and the adrenalin started pumping through my system. The pain
faded away and was replaced by excitement and unknown fear. I didn't
know what big event was going to happen but my sixth sense told me
that I would be a prominent part of the action, no matter what it was.

I was not long in finding out. My captors quickly removed my blindfold and passed the rope leash from my left wrist to another man who
seemed to be in charge of the event. I could see that I was in an entrance
way to some sort of arena. He pulled on the rope and led me towards the
lighted area. As he entered at a brisk pace I was limping and hobbling
behind him. My God, I'm in a circus arena, I thought. It was a large round
tent-like building but made of wood. The roof seemed seventy or eighty
feet in the air. It was supported by large telephone poles lashed together
forty feet or more in the air with large steel bands at the overlap. The
poles continued upward another thirty or forty feet from the overlap to the
wooden roof. High on some of the poles were large white lights which
illuminated the center ring of the arena. Rows of wooden bleacher seats
ringed the whole building from the edge of the ring to a flat round wall that
reached to the edge of the roof. It was a large structure, which seemed
primitive because of the absence of structural steel girders. It held several thousand spectators, and had more than eighty rows of seats. And it
was jammed pack full!

I was paraded around the earthen big top circle. The crowd was
hushed from their loud excited babbling to a murmur and then went to
dead silence. In my torn skivvy shirt and loose hanging shorts colored
brown by the mud from my rice paddy landing, I made a pitiful sight. My
left arm dangled uselessly. I limped badly, and I was cut and scratched
from the previous treatment I had received from the earlier mob. Around
and around and around I was led in repetitive circles of the arena's
perimeter. Finally, the leader went to the center of the ring, and indicated

I should sit down on the dirt beside a large wooden box on which stood an ancient microphone attached to some antiquated public address system. I complied willingly, I was exhausted.

My host mounted the box and began to address the crowd. They gave him their absolute attention, so much so that except for his soothing voice you could almost hear a pin drop. I gazed at the crowd as he spoke and I could see sympathy in their eyes as they saw the pitiful condition that I was in.

As the speaker went on, his voice grew in volume and intensity and speed. He spoke loud rapid sentences in Vietnamese and pointed his arm at a section of the crowd and some from that section would respond and shout, stand and raise their fists at me. He went around in this manner for eight or ten minutes and by the time he was through he had the whole damn crowd on their feet shouting, yelling, waving fists at me and making other threatening gestures.

He made me rise as the crowd screamed in unison, "Boo down! Boo down! Boo down!"

I didn't understand what they were screaming. "Boo down!" he said, "Boo down!" He got off the box and stood next to me and bowed to the crowd. "Boo down!" he said. "Boo down!" My God he wants me to bow down to that crowd I thought as the meaning finally came through to me. "Bullshit!", I said. "Screw you! I don't bow down to anyone, prisoner or not!"

"Boo down!" he repeated. I shook my head no and he understood me. Immediately he grabbed the rope attached to my left wrist and dangling arm and pulled as hard as he could towards the circus ring's earthen floor. The pain in my broken shoulder and chest surged and tears came to my eyes. No, I shook to him. He retorted with another massive pull on the rope attached to me. "Boo down!" I was on my knees now crying openly from the pain. I got up and shook no again. Once more he pulled and that effort exerted on my broken and twisted body was too much for me to stand and with tears flushing down my face I begged him to stop. "Boo down!" he said and went to pull on the rope but I bowed down. Broken and hurt, I had just received my first lesson in the North Vietnamese humane treatment of POW's which was based on pain and Pavlovian conditioning. I would see much more of these methods in the years ahead.

My captor led me around the ring and stopped me in front of each section and invited me to "Boo down" and I promptly complied. By the time we had circumvented the ring the crowd was nothing more than a violent mob, screaming for blood and revenge. I was the Christian that had been thrown to the lions, and I didn't know if I would be eaten or not.

Suddenly my ring master made a dash for the exit ramp dragging me on behind. As we rushed to exit some of the crowd gathered before us angry and screaming. When he forced his way through them they pummeled me with fists and covered me with spit. If there was an ugly American in North Vietnam I knew it must be me.

After the pushing and scuffling we were outside moving next to the building towards a vehicle that I immediately recognized as the one I had been taken to the SAM site in. The driver dropped a half burnt cigarette and leaped in and started the engine. My two captors from earlier took charge and shoved me through the passenger's door and into the rear compartment. One jumped in beside me as the other slid into the front seat and slammed the door. We were off in a lurch and left town a helluva lot faster than when we entered. The angry crowd chased vainly after us.

Though I was exhausted, hurt and in pain, I was glad to be alive and happy not to be blindfolded. I peered out ahead as the vehicle meandered about until we finally came to Route 1. The stars were out and it was cold and clear. I could see the Big Dipper and Polaris ahead of us. I knew that we were definitely traveling north.

On Route 1 the southbound traffic became very heavy. Trucks of all forms and shapes and sizes were heading south loaded with men, equipment and supplies. I couldn't believe the amount of traffic. I'd been on night road reconnaissance truck interdiction hops, and very rarely could I find a target on the road at night.

The vehicles were all heavily camouflaged with tree branches and netting. Each vehicle had special shields on the lights so that the lights themselves would not be visible from ahead and above by aircraft. The road seemed to have traffic directors located one or two miles apart. I noticed there was some type of electrical line connected to poles that ran along the side of the road. I could see something like a box on the poles every half mile or so. We were passing by one of these installations when I heard a loud clicking sound, like a metal switch making an intermittent connection. This sudden noise caused the driver and passenger to get excited. He pulled the vehicle over under the first available tree, cut his engine and we just sat. I noticed that all traffic was stopped. Nothing moved and Route 1 had the appearance of being completely empty of vehicular traffic. The passenger stepped out and stood with the door open staring into the heavens. He suddenly started shouting in Vietnamese and pointed overhead to the north.

Almost immediately I could hear the roar of searching jets. Must be a road recce flight, I thought as their engines faded into the distance. Suddenly the clicking started again only in a different sequence and tempo. The guard climbed into the passenger's seat as the driver started us moving once again.

My Lord, these little bastards have themselves one helluva fine system for moving right under our noses down Route 1. They had just reinforced the doubts that I had about our inability to stop truck traffic by flying night visual recces with jets like the A4 or F4. This type of mission had always been the hardest and most frustrating for me to fly, particularly at night. I guess this feeling of futility arose because in my heart I knew that the advocates of air power's ability to stop the movement of troops and supplies were unreal, and they were only kidding themselves and our political leaders who unfortunately were conducting their idea of an air war based on this false premise. We need a massive technological advance for air power to accomplish this task: a sophisticated radar system with moving target indicators accompanied by an area saturation bombing system. That combination might be quite effective, I thought but the effort we were making in 1965 and 1966 to hook up jets with multi bomb racks loaded with 250-pound bombs and some flares and then limit the whole system to the capability of the human eyeball at night was ridiculous. My first hour of travel up Route 1 was vindicating my previous deepest misgivings about our air war effort. It looks like it's going to be a long war, I concluded.

We continued north and passing us going south was a stream of traffic that seemed never ending. I was amazed at the size of this effort and could only think of how naive those reports were which bombarded the American people with the idea that the hostilities in South Vietnam were just an internal revolution fired by the efforts of a dissident peasantry. What a crazy war. Here was a massive invasion from North Vietnam and it was the best kept secret in the world. The world press not only believed it but spent most of their effort defending and building up the reality of this grand hoax. Seeing is believing and what I saw that night confirmed my own belief that the Communists were at it again in another aggression against the rights of man, and of course conducted in a shroud of liberation for the oppressed and down trodden masses, whose ultimate "liberation" would only result in the loss of what few freedoms they ever had. "By their deeds ye shall know them." You'd think the free world would have learned this lesson by now after all the previous examples we've had since the 1917 October Revolution. In my heart I knew Vietnam was the right place for the right war, but I also felt that the free world and our own people wouldn't have the guts to fight it properly. Johnson wants to twist their arm and not really pay the price, but that's a disastrous policy. The Communists are tougher than that. The only thing they really understand and respect is pure brute force. As these thoughts ran through my mind my morale sank as the fruits of the bitter sense of loss overcame me. I was a prisoner and there wasn't a damn thing I could do about the war one way or another. I must survive to live and fight another day, I thought.

We were proceeding northward covered by a row of protective trees which hid the road from aerial observation when suddenly we stopped in a long line of waiting traffic and waited for a half hour or so in the darkness. I could see trucks ahead and hear the Vietnamese drivers talking to one another. Suddenly the high pitch tempo of their excited voices told me they were concerned about some threat. I was looking northward at the dark sky over the column of stationary vehicles when a string of night illumination flares started going off a few thousand feet in the air. The North Vietnamese were very excited and their voices reached a feverish pitch when the noise from the roar of an oncoming jet aircraft inundated all other sounds. The roar from the first aircraft had hardly abated when it was replaced by the roar of a second, and then a third plane and a fourth and a fifth. They were overhead about ten or fifteen minutes, flying in an elongated circular search pattern. As the first flares died out they were replaced by a string of flares covering the same general area. The search continued but no bombs dropped. Finally the muffled roar of exploding bombs some miles north of us told me they had found a target or perhaps were just dropping on the road in a frustrated attempt to have some effect on the road traffic. They flew off in the distance and I never did find out the extent or even the cause of their effort.

Within minutes the ragged column of vehicles started and began heading north. We drove only a few hundred yards when suddenly we came out of the tree cover and onto a long bare stretch of road that went between diked level rice paddies. As we came to the edge of the tree cover there was a military-manned check point. Each vehicle was stopped and the driver interrogated. When our driver replied to them, one opened the passenger door and shined a light on me and my accompanying guard sitting in the rear compartment. He looked me over, said something in Vietnamese, laughed and slammed the door shut.

There was no oncoming traffic heading south as we rapidly moved over the open stretch of road and I thought this strange. We went about four or five miles in this fashion, bumping along the often repaired road. The clear area ended and we passed another military check point and were once again under the protective cover of overhanging trees. A long column of vehicles was stopped at the check point, obviously awaiting the vehicles coming north to pass through the open stretch before they could resume their trek south.

Clever people, these North Vietnamese. In their own primitive way they were dealing quite effectively with our supposedly sophisticated air threat to their ground supply system.

Our truck turned right off Route 1 and meandered in the darkness for about a mile before it came to its destination, obviously a familiar stopping place for the driver. We pulled to a stop next to a primitive house. I was led into the main room which had some elderly occupants sitting before a fire. My presence seemed routine to them. I was given a cup of tea and on finishing it was put into a corner of the room, given a rough blanket and told to sleep. A guard positioned himself between me and the door. Every part of my body hurt from head to toe. I was exhausted. The warm tea soothed my discomfort and I dropped off into a deep sleep.

Day number one in North Vietnam was over for me. I never dreamed it would be followed by 2521 more days.

HEADING NORTH

I awoke, startled, at a very early hour by a cock crowing out his challenge against a distant foe, who took it up in strident reply. It was an annoying, audible battle, reminiscent of earlier ones that I had heard as a young child while on vacation at my grandparents' home in the country.

My mind was fuzzy, I sought to put into perspective all the events of the previous day. My body was being overwhelmed with pain and exhaustion. The adrenalin and morphine had long ago worn off, and I was settling down to the physical and mental agonies of being the injured prisoner who was fast losing hope in his ability to affect his own fate. Escape becomes more remote with the passing of time, I reflected mentally. Deep in my heart I already knew that all was lost for me. My physical condition was bad and would become markedly worse without immediate medical attention. I was on the way to Hanoi, and nothing would happen to me medically until I got there, and maybe even then it wouldn't do any good. I'm helpless and things are hopeless, I thought, God help me!

My captors stirred, as the predawn darkness gave way to the early morning light. Soon they were up and moving with the rest of the rising household who were preparing for the day's labors. I couldn't make out any of their jibberish but it was obvious they were saying their goodbyes to close friends or family. In minutes I was hustled into the back end of the vehicle and we were off again meandering through a rural road system that was as primitive as any I had ever seen or imagined. I tried to keep track of the vehicle's movements, but after a while I gave up and settled down to the simple conclusion that we were more or less moving northward and were somewhat close to the coastline, for every once in a while I could see the waters of tidal flats and their seashore inhabitants: gulls and sandpipers.

We drove about two hours before the vehicle stopped alongside a sandy mound that appeared to be brick and reinforced. I was ushered out of the truck and led into a cavern area which had a large wooden green door, hinged so that both sides could swing open. Once inside I guessed that it was an old French ammo storage area, bricked from floor to wall to ceiling. The door was slammed shut and a bolt lock squeakily slid into its place. I was firmly locked in.

The outside light that entered through cracks in the door and the two-inch opening under it was sufficient for me to make out the entire outline of the room. It was a dank place, damp from moisture and smelled musky. I could see wet spots on the brick floor from drips of water falling off the red brick ceiling. Along the walls were damp spots that oozed with green moss. The floor was littered with human feces giving testimony to its local use. It smelled to high heaven. After inspecting the entire area and concluding there was no way out, except from the way I came in, I settled down in the driest and cleanest area to await whatever fate had in store for me.

No position I assumed was comfortable for more than a few minutes before it became unbearable. As time wore on I thrashed about, and lost more and more control over my body and mind. I was like a wounded unattended animal whose condition will only deteriorate with time. My sight was becoming blurry as I lapsed into a state of semi-hallucination.

My ears rang with the din of emotional anxiety and frustration. I heard nothing from the real world except the squeals from a flock of passing domestic geese. Then silence, and once again I was engulfed by the weird imaginary sounds that were conjured up from within my own brain and which I could not shut out or reduce in volume. I'm losing my mind, I thought in a rare rational moment. I needed medical attention, but none was forthcoming, at least on this day.

At noon the large door suddenly swung open, and I was handed a small bowl of rice and greens along with a cup of tea. The door closed and I tried to eat the main course, but its taste was so bitter and unfamiliar that I gave up and resorted to finishing the tea and that portion of the rice not affected by the greens. The warmth of the tea soothed my pain and I dropped off into a deep slumber. I awoke to the clanging of a distant tocsin which signalled the commencement of the Vietnamese siesta. Time stood still, engulfed in an eerie atmosphere of absolute silence. I flopped on the brick floor and returned to an imaginary world of dream, half asleep and half awake, my mind so confused that I could no longer distinguish the real from the unreal. I fantasized my plight in a series of well planned but totally imaginary escapes. I awoke finally from this mental stupor when the door was flung open. I had lost all concept of passing time.

What the hell's gonna happen now, I thought, as an unfamiliar Vietnamese man of about fifty entered, with the burst of bright sunlight. He motioned me to stand and follow him out to a waiting carry-all vehicle that was parked alongside. I must be out of it, I thought, I didn't even hear it drive up.

It was mid-afternoon. The sun shone brightly on a blue balmy day spotted only by whisps of high thin cirrus. A militarily dressed driver opened the rear door and pushed me into the vehicle. He closed the door, and both took their positions in the front seat. In a moment we were off in a bouncing start. These little monkeys aren't even smart enough to know how to use the clutch properly, I thought as we lurched and jumped from gear to gear under the control or lack of control of the novice driver.

My hands were tied as before but I was not blindfolded, though I could see that it was ready and available next to the windshield. We drove on winding dirt roads that seemed to go nowhere. I saw little human activity except for an occasional peasant urging on a water buffalo plowing up a rice field. After about an hour we came to an inhabited area, probably the outskirts of a large town. Just past the intersection of a major crossroad the vehicle pulled up to a primitive bus stop shelter that was empty. I was let out and told to sit on the wooden bench at the rear of the shelter out of view of any passersby.

We stayed there for more than an hour and I watched a parade of ancient jalopies of various sizes and vintages, most of which looked like they were on their last mile, pass by. They were filled to overflowing with militia, peasants, and children hanging on for dear life as they reeled and bounced over the bumpy road before me.

My physical condition seemed suddenly to deteriorate from its already poor state. My head hurt and a fever was overcoming my body. My ears began ringing incessantly. I lost and regained my senses as my mind flew back and forth from reality to hallucination. Of all my pains, it was the sense of loss that hurt the most. I had noticed in previous hours that the bodily pain I suffered moved from one segment of my body to another. First it was the broken shoulder, then the cracked ribs, then the hip, then the neck, then combinations of them, until finally I was just one big bundle of pain. I could stand all this physical torment until my mind centered on thoughts about home and country and family, my wife, my children. Then in my agony I realized the truth of the statement that the greatest pain is the pain of loss. Somewhere in my childhood or in my years of education I had heard or read this. Now it came back again and again to haunt me and taunt me into the depths of despair. I marveled at how my body shifted the burden of pain from one area and appendage to another. I can survive the physical torment, but can I survive the mental torment of the pain of loss, I thought. It was a challenge I would have to take up each day I was in North Vietnam, and it was still only day number two of my captivity.

A large truck half filled with Vietnamese soldiers pulled into a sliding stop before me. Under the direction of a lieutenant, six of them surrounded me, led me to the truck and then lifted me horizontally and slid me onto the metal floor. The civilian who had been my guard handed over the khaki cheese cloth which was originally used as a sling for my left arm. One of the army men immediately wrapped it around my forehead several times and I was blindfolded. They sat me against a fifty gallon drum tied next to the rear left wheels, and we were off once again, bouncing and bumping. I was jammed between the drum and the tailgate, and steadied myself to the best of my ability between them by pushing alternately on one and then the other as my body was tossed around by the rough ride.

I placed my head on my knees and gradually eased the blindfold above my nose until I could see the floor of the truck and my feet. Pleased with my success at being able to see a little, I was careful to hide this new found ability from my captors. If I have to walk I ought to be able to see enough to keep from stumbling and falling, I thought.

The truck drove till dusk and then pulled to a stop. I was lifted out horizontally and placed on my feet, then led a few hundred yards to a building. Once inside my blindfold was removed and I could see that I was in a wooden frame house whose floors, except in a bedroom, were dirt. An old woman was cooking over an open wood fire while several old Vietnamese men chatted and smoked their pipes at a rickety table. One of the army men stood guard over me at all times. I noticed that they all had some type of firearm. The lieutenant had a handgun; most of the others had rifles and two of them had burp guns of Chinese vintage.

The lieutenant seemed to know the inhabitants. The rest of the soldiers seemed unfamiliar with the surroundings. One of them lit a cigarette, and in a moment of kindness offered me one. I accepted gratefully and enjoyed a long lingering smoke, making each drag last as long as possible. The smoke quenched the hunger pains in my stomach, and I felt somewhat relieved from my physical miseries.

We stayed over an hour and it was totally dark when I was again blindfolded and led back to the truck, lifted aboard and placed in my previous position as we got underway for our journey northward. It wasn't long before we were back on the main road. From the sound and amount of traffic I surmised we were on Route 1 again.

I could hear the occasional clicking from the air attack warning system, which I had observed the previous night. The traffic seemed heavy in both directions as we went from check point to check point, sometimes stopping for ten or fifteen minutes and sometimes even longer. We made progress in our intended direction but at a snail's pace. Our longest wait occurred at a ferry.

After a prolonged wait our truck was driven over a crude wooden approach and was firmly on board amidst the yelling and shouting by those in charge of the operation. I couldn't see, but from the amount of turmoil I heard, it must have been a complicated evolution in a primitive and makeshift transportation system. Once underway, from the sounds of the engine, I guessed we were being propelled by some form of outboard motor. The ferry rocked and swayed and I hoped that the damn thing would make it to the other side before tipping over. The journey took about ten minutes; another fifteen or twenty minutes transpired before we were safely docked and on terra firma.

Our trip continued at a good pace for thirty minutes before we pulled off the highway and parked. Once the engine was off I could hear the voices of other Vietnamese, and every few minutes I heard another vehicle drive up, cut its engine and stay with the rest of us. I couldn't see, but felt that most of the soldiers had gotten off the trucks and were milling around the parked vehicles socializing with their fellow cohorts. I could smell the smoke from the Vietnamese cigarettes and I longed for just a drag. My stomach was empty and filled with a gnawing sensation. I must be having withdrawal pains from no smoking, I thought. I made myself as comfortable as possible between the tailgate and the fifty gallon drum and dozed off into slumberland.

I don't know how long I slept before I was suddenly awakened by shouting and yelling. I heard someone in the truck with me jump out onto the ground. Then it came. First the roar of an attacking jet as it pulled out of its dive and climbed back into the heavens, and then in a few short seconds a string of bombs went off all around me. The light from the exploding bombs pierced my blindfold before the deafening noise reached my ears and the concussion rocked the truck. I hunched over in a ball and plugged my ears with my fingers, but it was to no avail. I must be in a truck park and our guys have found it. The bombs rained around me, and I could hear the screams and curses of the Vietnamese who had taken refuge beneath the trucks. I couldn't tell how many planes were in the attack, but I thought there were more than the usual three assigned to a night road recce mission. Probably two groups, the first found us and called the second flight in to help out.

They bombed for about fifteen minutes, and from my position in the truck I could tell they had zeroed in on their target. Some of the bombs hit close and the truck rocked back and forth from the concussion and was peppered with bomb fragments I heard striking the metal sides.

Then it was over as the noise of the last jet faded into the distance. The Vietnamese began scurrying around in obvious mad confusion. I raised my head and lifted the blindfold in time to see several burning vehicles a short distance away. Soldiers began climbing frantically into the truck, so I returned the blindfold to its previous position and maintained my spot between the drum and tailgate. One of them shook me to see if I was alive. I grunted and moved enough to indicate I was unhurt. The engine started and as the cab door slammed shut, we were off in a mad dash for safety. I could hear the excited Vietnamese talking nervously to each other as we reeled and lurched down the road. We hit the highway and must have been first for I couldn't hear any other moving vehicles. My Lord, I thought, when the chips are down I'd rather be lucky than good — just like Lefty Gomez used to say. Tonight must have been my lucky night.

We rolled rapidly down the road for a half hour, and then pulled off into a side road and continued on our way until we reached our destination for the night. I was lifted out of the truck and led into another Vietnamese house. My blindfold was removed and I was placed under guard in a corner and told to "seep, seep," which I understood to mean sleep.

The adrenalin from the night's excitement had temporarily restored my mental alertness. Stark terror will scare you sober and there was no denying that the truck park bombing raid had had its effect on me. I was so damn glad to be alive I had forgotten my physical injuries and pain.

When dawn broke the soldiers rose from their makeshift sleeping quarters on the floor and headed for the truck. One stayed behind and kept me under guard as the truck drove off. We stayed in the house alone for about an hour, when a Vietnamese militia youth came in and spoke to my captor. After a short exchange I was ordered to follow the young militiaman out of the house and down a winding pathway through a rice paddy. He walked rapidly. I hobbled to keep up under the prodding of the armed guard who took up the rear.

We walked for a couple of miles passing homes and curious Vietnamese peasants and children, who ran out to gaze at the captured American. Finally we turned into a small grove of trees and entered a small Vietnamese house well sheltered by the overhang. I was led into a long rectangular room which contained besides a fireplace, a rough wooden table, three chairs, a homemade double bed and a picture of Ho Chi Minh hung on an otherwise bare wall. My captor took me to the end of the room and made me sit on the wooden floor in the corner, away from the open paneless windows and well removed from the only doorway. He took up a position on a chair beside the table so that he could scrutinize my every movement.

From time to time he was joined by other Vietnamese men who seemed to just wander in to see his prisoner. After looking me over they would engage in a brief conversation, sit for a few minutes, and then just as suddenly as they appeared, up and leave.

After a couple of hours passed, I started to have bladder pains and felt a sudden urge to urinate. I indicated my predicament to the guard, and he led me out of the house, so that I might relieve myself. When I got outside I was besieged by a group of thirty or forty children who were aware of my presence and were curious, as you would expect children to be in such a situation.

They taunted me in their childish manner delighted at being able to take advantage of a disarmed enemy of the people. Some of the braver ones got close enough to pelt me with small stones as I urinated on the Vietnamese countryside. "Piss on you guys," I said as I completed my mission. My guard finally chased them away in anger and led me back into the house.

My physical condition grew worse and I lapsed into senseless hallucination. Half alive and half dead I was in a never, never land getting further and further from reality as the hours passed.

During the siesta session time, a strange looking male human came in with a long water pipe. He popped some black seeds into it and lit it. After a few puffs he reeled away only to return at odd intervals to repeat the process. The guard didn't seem to pay any attention to him, and his actions seemed to indicate he was a permanent fixture in this house. I guessed that he was smoking some kind of opium or oriental drug because his eyes looked bleary and he seemed addicted.

In the late afternoon, about an hour before sundown, our guide returned, and I was led out as before with him leading, then me and finally the armed guard taking up the rear.

My feet were swollen, bruised and bleeding from all the walking I had done on gravel and stone paths. The bottoms of my athletic socks were worn away. My arm hung uselessly, both hands still tied loosely as before. My skivvy shorts and shirt were dried mud brown in color.

We walked till after dark over rough paths, through rice fields and thin covered wooded areas. Finally we came to the main paved road, and took up our position along side it to wait for transportation.

After a lengthly wait, the truck and soldiers who had deposited me that morning pulled up, and I was lifted aboard as before. Once back in my position between the tailgate and the fifty gallon drum, I was again blindfolded. The truck took off with a sudden jerk as we resumed our journey. Exhausted from the events of the past two days and suffering intense pain all over, I finally lost complete control of my senses and passed out.

I must have been semi-conscious at times for I remember hearing Vietnamese music and people talking in that foreign tongue. I kept dreaming that this whole series of events had happened to me before, in another place, in another time, in another life. The dream was so real I still recall it. I was a prisoner, a prisoner for years as a galley slave, shackled to the oars of a trireme slave boat. I dreamed I was in that state for years, but then somehow I survived it and was free. Now I was starting all over again, on a journey as a prisoner that would last for years. Not again I thought, not again. Why me, why must I go through this ordeal once more. What did I do to deserve this punishment? The eerie music filled my head and nothing made sense, and the dream repeated itself again and again, and I sobbed in my despair at the thought of my loss.

Suddenly I awoke and my head cleared when I heard in clear English, "Lieutenant, tell that queer guard of yours to keep his hands off my balls, or the next time I'll belt him!"

It's an American, another Yank in the truck with me, and I came back into the world of reality.

"Hey Yank," I said. "Yah," he replied. "I'm Jim Mulligan, Commander Jim Mulligan from the *ENTERPRISE.*" I had barely gotten the words out, when from directly opposite me, I received a vicious kick square in the middle of my rib cage. The force of the blow and the excruciating pain sent me back into unconsciousness.

I came to sometime later bouncing on the floor of the truck between the tailgate and fifty gallon drum. I dragged myself up to a sitting position and tried to cushion the blows from the erratic bounces the truck was taking. I could tell that we were in very hilly country on a winding road that seemed to challenge the driver to his utmost, as he whipped the wheel and shifted frantically from one gear to another. We slowed to a crawl on the steep inclines and accelerated like hell on the way down. The driver managed to hit every pot hole and bump on the road, and I was punished viciously bouncing first off the tailgate, then the drum, then the floor.

We came to a sliding halt at the bottom of the ride. The cab door slammed shut as the driver exited. He lowered the tailgate and pulled me to the ground feet first, yanked off my blindfold, stuffed it in his army shirt pocket, grabbed the dangling rope from my left arm and led me staggering into a farm house well lit by several oil lamps.

There were about a dozen Vietnamese women in the room along with a couple of young men. All looked to be in their mid twenties. I was pushed up against a bare wall and turned so that they could scrutinize me. Obviously I was a prize of some value and curiosity. The women chattered about my plight and condition in Vietnamese, laughing and giggling at this broken down male American, clad only in torn skivvies and socks standing before them. One of the bolder ones came next to me and suddenly put her hand in my fly opening, grabbed my testicles and massaged them and my penis. The others laughed and giggled at this maneuver. When my body failed to respond to her ministrations, she spat in my face, let go of my genitals and said, "Ancien! Ancien!" in disgust. I remembered ancien was the word for "old" in French.

One of the women brought me a small bowl of greens to eat. I was hungry, so I tried to eat them but they smelled of urine and the taste was so bad that my stomach rejected it and I retched and gave up on it completely. The driver was angered at this turn of events and led me back to the truck, replaced my blindfold and assisted, by another Vietnamese, heaved me unceremoniously into the truck, raised the tailgate and set it in place. I could hear the women giggling and laughing all the while.

I wondered what happened to the Yank I had heard. He wasn't in the truck. We started up the rugged mountain road once again, and I passed out from exhaustion and pain.

When I came to I heard a large number of Vietnamese voices. The truck was crowded with people. I dragged myself into a sitting position between the tailgate and drum.

The ropes on my wrists must have worked loose while I was unconscious and tossing about the bouncing truck. I felt I could release them completely and began to investigate this possibility. One of the Vietnamese must have noticed my efforts for suddenly the loosened ropes were grabbed violently and pulled excessively tight and knotted firmly to each wrist, to such an extent that both hands ached and soon lost all feeling.

I heard a train running alongside the road on which we were traveling. We must be nearing some type of urban civilization, I thought, just before I passed into unconsciousness once more. When I came to, I felt someone's hands manipulating my testicles and though I had lost all feeling from my wrists down, I angrily pushed at my provoker. He ceased his actions under the stern disapproving voice of a Vietnamese who must have been aware of his attempts. These bastards are all queer, I thought. The truck rolled on until finally as dawn came and the light penetrated my cheesecloth blindfold, it pulled to a stop. I could hear the loud volume of a Vietnamese sound system blaring forth oriental music completely foreign and distasteful to my ears. Someone released the tailgate, and I heard them fill a container from the fifty gallon drum alongside of me. I immediately recognized the smell of gasoline and assumed that we were making a routine gas stop, only we were our own self contained gas station. Smart people these North Vietnamese.

The position of the blindfold was such that with a little effort I could see a little of what was around me in the truck. I saw a man covered with bandages who obviously had suffered bad burns on his head and arms. He was immobile and seemed to be asleep. He wore a khaki flight suit. So there are two of us now, I thought.

As the fueling progressed, a large group of Vietnamese were attracted to the truck because of the prisoners it was carrying. They gathered to see the side show, and I was probably the most prominent part of it since I was awake and moving.

One of the soldiers decided to entertain the onlookers at my expense. He pulled the ropes tied to my wrists and put a container underneath the wrists and began pouring raw gasoline on the ropes over each wrist. The pain was unbearable, and I writhed in agony as the gas ran over my raw flesh. The onlookers applauded with glee, and my tormentor continued his actions until the ropes were thoroughly soaked with gasoline. When he finally stopped, the pain was so intense I sobbed uncontrollably in my agony and passed out.

I remained out of my senses and never again returned to reality during the remainder of the trip. I was more dead than alive and ranted and raved completely out of my senses, oblivious to whatever else was going on around me. I dreamed that I was a prisoner on a galley slaver. The pain of loss tormented me in my nightmarish dreams. I felt I was dying, and cried out in vain for a priest. I was completely out of my head undergoing an eerie experience that I felt I had been through before.

THE HANOI HILTON

I seemed to be slowly awakened from a frightening dream. I couldn't see and I didn't know who I was or where I was. My head hurt from a blow I had received. I felt a bump on my head and it was wet and sticky. Gradually, I regained more of my senses, and realized I was flat on my back, lying on a hard surface. My disoriented body felt like it was moving up and down. I'm on a ship, I thought. I felt dizzy and confused. I opened my eyes but I couldn't see. Suddenly I realized that I was blindfolded. I had difficulty breathing as the blindfold had slipped over my nostrils. I needed more air but I kept gagging more and more in a self induced panic. I struggled to a knee crawling position and started to move. I had no plan of action. I had to do something or I would certainly suffocate. I couldn't feel anything with my hands from the wrists down. They were paralyzed from the gasoline soaked ropes which had shrunk tighter as they dried, and cut deeper and deeper into my flesh, stopping all circulation.

I crawled and reeled a few feet and suddenly hit my head against a hard surface wall. The blow stunned me temporarily as my panic to do something about the gagging blindfold urged me on my unreal journey. I traveled along the wall and ran into a vertical obstacle. It was some type of pipe. I felt it with my head and forearms and decided to struggle to my feet. Once erect I felt a horizontal obstacle about three feet high from the floor. I leaned against it and with my forearms finally was able to determine it was some type of crossbeam.

The blindfold, though securely tied, dangled behind my back so that I could feel it brush my buttocks. I tried to maneuver the dangling end into my hands and arms, but still was unsuccessful after many frantic efforts. Exhausted and near suffocation, I leaned against the crossbar and rested and tried to think of a way out of my predicament. I was getting weaker and was probably hyperventilating, which only made matters worse.

I finally figured that I should try to wrap the dangling end of the blindfold around the crossbar in front of me, and then I would have a better chance to pull it from my head. I leaned back and surged forward snapping my head and right shoulder to throw the dangling end over the cross bar. On the third attempt I succeeded. The end of the blindfold fell across the bar in front of me. I dropped to a kneeling position and allowed the loose end to dangle closer to the floor. Then I pushed my forearms under the bar and managed to get the end of the cheesecloth wedged between them. Gently I arose and pulled the cloth around and over the top of the crossbar and let it fall again. I sank slowly to my knees and gently felt for the blindfold once again with my forearms. When I had successfully locked it in place, I pulled back on the blindfold with my head. The blindfold was tight, but I finally managed to pull it loose before I fell backwards to the floor. I could breathe and I could see.

To my surprise I was not on a ship but rather in a cell located in a stone building. I had no sense of balance and I sat down on the concrete floor with my back resting against the concrete wall. While resting I assessed my situation. The first thing I noticed was a pool of dried blood on the floor where I had been lying.

The room was bare except for a personal convenience bucket which served as the toilet facility, two wooden bunks about six feet long and three feet wide on each side of the room, and two reed Vietnamese sleeping mats which are the standard mattresses in that primitive land.

The solid door was covered with metal and painted black. In its center was a peek-in sliding window secured by five vertical bars and an outside solid cover which allowed the guards to inspect the cell without having to enter it. The large window at the end of the room, opposite the door, was barred from one side to the other with heavy vertical irons, about eight inches apart. A heavy wire mesh screen was wired to the window bars preventing entrance to birds and bats, and the exit of rodents.

Outside the window, I could see a high brick wall topped with sharp glass bottles, imbedded in the concrete, to prevent anyone from going over the top. Some bare electrical wires ran above the top of the wall as a further deterrant to escape. I was sure they were live. I had seen an exact duplicate of this wall around the city jail in Cannes, France a year earlier, so I was convinced I was located in an old French bastile.

Outside the wall, I could see a large tree with large branches situated in front of a mansion-like structure, which was topped with the traditional red tile roof. Between the branches and the house, I could see enough sky to know that it was late in the day. As I viewed the outside scenery I saw sparrows. They looked to be English and I took that to be a good omen. When my curiosity regarding my immediate surroundings had been saturated I decided to make a closer inspection of my physical condition and make an assessment of my position as a prisoner.

I was in bad shape. My mind was fuzzy and unclear. I could remember who I was and when I was captured and some of the events of the trip north, but I had no idea where I was, or what day it was. My guess was that I was in Hanoi. I could hear the horns of vehicles and bike traffic outside the walls in the street.

My body was racked with pain. Both hands were purplish blue from the wrists down. The ropes cutting into my wrists were so tight that they had buried themselves in my flesh causing large festering infections which oozed green pus. The sight and stench was enough to turn my stomach. My left arm still dangled uselessly from the shoulder socket. My ribs ached. I had cuts and bruises over my body from the beatings given by the crowds and the hours I spent bouncing around the back end of the truck. My left hip pained enough that I walked with a distinct limp. My feet were swollen and bloody from the miles I had walked. I was alive but that was about all. I needed medical attention but I knew none would come until after I had been put through some form of interrogation. I was surprised to have come this far without being interrogated. According to the POW training book it was long overdue. In survival school they told us that prisoners would be interrogated as soon as possible after capture.

Night comes fast in the tropics and the cell darkened quickly. I sat on the floor and waited to see what was going to happen next. Suddenly, a small electric light came on over the center of the door. The illumination from it was so weak that I could barely make out the outlines of the cell. I sat in a stupor, oblivious to everything that was going on. I'm more dead than alive, I thought. My fingers were swollen blue and made my hands look like a mass of purplish blue meat. I made a pitiful sight, a broken man in spirit and body.

I was tired, so I struggled to my feet and staggered to the bunks. The crossbar that traversed the width of the room three feet above the floor required that I bend down and crawl under it. This was another painful and slow occurring experience which required both mental and physical effort in order to be accomplished. Perseverance won out and I was finally able to slide my body onto the reed mat which covered the uneven planked bunk. Immediately, I left the real world and fell asleep or passed out into unconsciousness.

A loud rumble from the heavens returned me to reality. The wind began to blow furiously, lightening flashed and claps of thunder crashed through the sky and rolled and rolled thunderously into the night. Suddenly the torrential rains hit, adding a final act to one of the wildest shows of nature that I had ever witnessed. Then the temperature dropped sharply as the wind whistled a cold blast into my cell. The storm was over in about thirty minutes. I concluded that I had just witnessed the passage of a rapid moving cold front. I don't know what the temperature was but winter was definitely back as I sat shivering on my bunk.

The only cover available in the cell was the other reed mat on the opposite bunk. I got up from my bunk and retrieved this mat with difficulty, and returning with it I used it as a blanket. It wasn't much but it was better than nothing. I was shaking and shivering but managed to doze off into an uncomfortable slumber.

I awakened when I heard the iron bolt slam against its stay. The cell door was flung wide open and two Vietnamese soldiers came in. The first wore a two-pocket khaki coat that buttoned down the center with six buttons, he looked more official than the other khaki shirted man who was holding a ring of keys.

"Get up, come here," said the official looking man who obviously was in charge. I blinked my eyes and struggled to my feet. Then I limped forward, painfully bent down to pass under the crossbar and then staggered forward towards him. He spoke in Vietnamese and the key guard stepped forward, grabbed the dangling rope from my left wrist and led me out of the cell with his boss taking up the rear.

Coming out of the cell we turned left, passed two more cells and walked into another small hallway. We made a right turn into an outside courtyard, went twenty feet or so, made another right turn and walked into a hallway which led to a large room situated on the right side of the hallway.

The room was dimly lit from the outside hallway light. I was led into the darkness and told to sit on a small stool, that I could barely see. Once I was firmly on the stool, the key guard released the rope and turned on two bright spotlights which blinded me for minutes. I tried to keep the light from my eyes with my raised arm, but it was useless. Heat from the bulbs warmed my shivering body. As my eyes adjusted to the situation, I could see seated at a table before me five Vietnamese, one was the man of authority who had spoken to me in my cell. Later on in my captivity I learned that the POWs had named him "Rabbit." Alongside Rabbit and to his left sat "Mickey Mouse," who later claimed he was the camp commander. Next to him sat a man from the general staff who was known as "The Pro," because he spoke excellent English and seemed quite sophisticated and adjusted to western ways. Then came "Cat," the infamous "Major Buy," who was on the general staff and in overall charge of activities concerning American POWs. Finally there was a short stubby man with bad teeth, dressed in civilian clothes. He sat on the extreme left as I faced them, and he was top dog of the interrogation team for the others all deferred to him.

The Vietnamese watched me squirm unsteadily as I sat on the stool and tried to maintain my balance. Rabbit began the interrogation by saying, "You must remember that you are not a prisoner of wah — you are a crimeinal of wah in the eyes of the Vietnamese people. You must obey all the regulations of the camp if you expect to receive the human treatment offered by our people. You have bombed churches, pagodas, schools, hospitals and have killed many of our own innocent women and children and old folks, therefore, you must repent of your crimes and confess them to the world and the American people. You American aggressors must pay for your crimes against the Vietnamese people."

"Bat shit!", I replied curtly.

"You must answer all the questions of the camp authorities," Rabbit went on. "My name is James Alfred Mulligan, Jr., Commander, U.S. Navy, serial number 504324, born on 27 March 1926," I responded as clearly and distinctly as I could under the circumstances, and according to the Code of Conduct. "You are impolite, you have bad attitude, you have no rank in Vietnam, you are crimeinal of wah," Rabbit angrily retorted.

I sat in silence and glared as best I could at them. Cat said something in Vietnamese and Rabbit spoke again. "We know you are from the nuclear carrier *ENTERPRISE*. We know all about *ENTERPRISE*. We know everything. We have many other American crimeinals from the *ENTERPRISE*. The Vietnamese people will punish them all, you are all bad men." The pro looked up and said in perfect English, "We don't need military information about the *ENTERPRISE* from you, we have it all in here," as he patted a stack of documents that were on the table in front of him. Almost as an aside he said, "Does the executive officer, Captain Forrest Peterson spell his last name with an EN or an ON?" "I'm not sure," I replied, and with the state of mind I was in, it was a pretty truthful statement.

I was becoming mentally confused and physically groggy as I sat on the small stool under the bright lights. Suddenly I lost my balance and fell to the floor with a crash. The key guard, who was nicknamed "Pig Eye" by the POWs, ran forward and hauled me up back on the stool again. The panel of observing Vietnamese officers seemed amused at my plight.

Though I hurt all over, the strongest pain seemed to localize around my wrists which were now burned raw from the gasoline soaked ropes. I was half out of my mind again as the adrenalin acquired by fright from my new circumstances of initial interrogation wore off. I looked directly at them and said, "I am an American Prisoner of War and I demand medical treatment for my wounds, as guaranteed by the Geneva Convention." It was a statement not well received by my captors.

"Keep sil-lent, you are crimeinal of wah, you have no right to make demands of Vietnamese people. You will receive the human treatment when you admit your crimes to the Vietnamese people and to the world," said Mickey Mouse who was annoyed at my outburst. "You have no rights here, you must not be impolite to the authorities of the Vietnamese people and the people's army. You must answer all the questions of the authorities. You must obey all the regulations of the camp. When you do this you will receive the lenient and human treatment from the Vietnamese people. If you disobey, if you resist us, you will die like dog!" continued Mickey Mouse. Rabbit then said, "Moo lig gun, you are Commanda of U.S. Navy, you are high rank but we have many prisoners here, many have more rank than you. Do you know Col-lo-nel Risenor, Commanda Stockdale or Den-tone? They are here. They receive the human treatment. They have seen the error of their ways. They repent their crimes. They and all the others. You will read their documents — you will see for yourself. They know that the puppet Johnson has deceived the American people and the world. They have seen the hatred in the hearts of the Vietnamese people against the crimeinal American a-grease-ors."

"How is Denton," I asked. "He is in good health. I see him often in another camp," replied Rabbit. "Do you know him?" "Yes, we have served together before," I answered. "Ah," said Rabbit, "if you keep the regulations of the camp you may be permitted to be with him."

"How is Alcorn?" I asked. (LTJG Wendall R. Alcorn, from my squadron VA-36, had been downed just before Christmas 1965 on the power plant strike near Haiphong. We didn't know if he was dead or alive.) "Alcorn, Alcorn?" said Mickey Mouse who seemed perplexed by the name. Rabbit said something to the others in Vietnamese and turned to say scornfully, "Oh him! He is here." "Is he injured?" I asked. "His health is good," Rabbit replied. Thank God I thought. Baby Ray, (Alcorn's squadron nickname) must be giving the Vietnamese fits, they don't like him at all.

When Alcorn was downed, we had absolutely no information to indicate he was dead or alive, he was designated Missing In Action. Each member of his family had maintained written contact with a different member of the squadron hoping for some news. I corresponded with his mother and more than anything else, I wanted to know if he was alive and a prisoner. Now that I had found out, I could not let her know.

I must be careful, I thought, they've got me talking already. Remember name, rank, serial number, date of birth, that's all. Don't get tricked by them.

The Pro interrupted my mental reverie. "Where were you captured? What was your target? When were you shot down?" He rattled off in quick succession.

I remained mute. I didn't answer. Rabbit got excited. "Moo lig gun you are impolite. You must answer all of the questions of the authority. Do you understand?"

I gave name, rank, serial number and date of birth once again. The Vietnamese conferred in their native tongue. Finally Rabbit said, "You will stand attention on the wall and my guard will punish you if you fail to obey. You are very sick man. You will not receive the human treatment when you have bad attitude. You will get nothing until you are polite and repent your crimes."

He spoke a few words in Vietnamese to Pig Eye then they all left. The short man with bad teeth went first, followed by Cat, the Pro, Mickey Mouse, and finally Rabbit.

I was sitting on the stool alone in the room with Pig Eye. There was something about him I didn't like. He looked like evil personified, the type that enjoys inflicting pain and misery on others, I thought. I later learned that he was the professional torturer of that jail, and he had only recently put on an army uniform in place of his civilian attire. It was wartime now and he was in the Army.

Pig Eye came over to me, grabbed the dangling rope from my left arm and pulled it vigorously leading me to the wall. The pain increased. I moaned and sobbed. He pushed me against the wall, went back to one of the interrogators chairs, sat down and lit a cigarette. Then he waited.

I stood groggily against the wall. I was exhausted completely. My mind was running wild. I tried to concentrate but I couldn't. The ropes caused me terrible pain. God I'll be paralyzed if they don't get them off soon, I thought. I couldn't believe what they had done to me. In survival school training, POWs were subjected to physical pain and discomfort, but there you knew it would end. No one would go too far so you resisted until they didn't want to take any more chances, and then they'd let you loose. You felt good because you stuck it out, (some guys quit in the middle of training), but that was only playing games, getting you ready for the real thing. Well this was the real thing and it was a helluva lot different. No games here. These bastards didn't really care if you lived or died. They made their own rules, Geneva Convention, Bah! It meant nothing to the Vietnamese. That's the kind of stuff the State Department people write up and believe. It's ok to write those rules as long as you don't have to personally get involved in the game.

My ordeal was for real. I was at the absolute limit of my physical resistance. My mind was so muddled I was like putty, ready to be fashioned into whatever shape my masters wanted. I was a slave. A man without freedom who is no longer a man, because his own destiny is in the hands of others. I was broken, my spirit no longer willing to resist, my body no longer able to resist.

Pig Eye knew my condition. He must have seen it hundreds of times before. He hastened my surrender when he pulled on the rope and pushed me roughly back on to the stool. More than an hour must have passed since I was placed against the wall.

He opened the door and spoke loudly in Vietnamese. Mickey Mouse came in and said, "Moo lig gun you have come to see things our way. You will answer the questions of the camp authorities, you will obey all the regulations of the camp. Only then will you receive the human treatment, only then will you receive the medicine from our doctors."

The others came in a few minutes and took up their same positions at the interrogation table.

"Untie the ropes," I pleaded, "untie the ropes." "I will have my guard remove the ropes when you tell me that you will read the statement on the document we have prepared for you. You will make the recording and confess your crimes to the American people and the world," said Mickey Mouse. "Take off the ropes," I begged, "please take off the ropes. I can't stand it anymore. I'm done. I'm finished. I'll do what you want, but please take off the ropes."

Pig Eye responded to the order to remove the ropes. He tried to undo the knots but they were too imbedded in flesh to come loose. After some minutes of trying in vain he went out of the room and returned with a sharp knife. "Moo lig gun we are sorry but our guard must try to cut away the ropes. We do not want to injure you any more so please do not move." Pig Eye worked carefully and coolly. I tried not to show the added pain I received from his efforts, but I was unable to control my sobs. He finally cut through the ropes on my left hand, peeled them from the deep grooves imbedded in my flesh and pulled them off. Some pussy skin dried to the ropes pulled off and the festering sores started to bleed. He repeated his efforts on my right arm and the sequence was repeated.

When the ropes were at last removed the pain became bearable. I could feel the blood trying to work its way back down my hands, into my fingers. Both hands tingled and became warm. I felt heat in them before any form of feeling returned. I had no manual control of my hands or fingers. They were completely numb.

"We have prepared for you a document to read," said Rabbit as he placed a typewritten sheet of paper face up on the table in front of me. I leaned over and slowly read what was typed.

It was a statement saying that the war was illegal and unjust, that the United States couldn't win, that the best way to end the war was for the U.S. to stop the bombing and withdraw its troops and that I repented my crimes and begged forgiveness from the Vietnamese people. It was written as a piece of propaganda. While it didn't sound like something an American would write or say it could have been produced by a Yank in Hanoi who was writing general statements for the North Vietnamese.

Rabbit said, "You must confess your crimes and repent like the others. Read for yourself the confessions of the other American crimein-als," as he put several sheets of paper containing purported statements from other POWs before me. I glanced at them only to get the names so I'd know who was alive and a POW. I assumed the statements were forced or fake. Each had a heading which read, "Statement of _____ ; Lt. Colonel Risner, Commander Stockdale, Lieutenant Commander Shumaker, and Lieutenant Alvarez were the ones he picked out of a larger pile to show me. They were all bullshit statements to me.

When Rabbit was satisfied that I had seen enough, he swept them back into his pile and said, "You must make the recording of the statement we have prepared for you."

They plugged in an old large tape recorder and put a microphone in front of me. I started to read the statement but had a hard time for my mind was fuzzy and in addition to the unintentional mistakes, I tried to make some intentional ones in pronunciation and inflection.

Rabbit was dissatisfied at my effort and made me repeat the process several times. I was exhausted and getting more tired every minute. It was late, way after midnight I guessed.

Suddenly Rabbit spoke to the others and then he sent Pig Eye on an errand out of the room. Pig Eye returned in five minutes and had a large bucket half filled with thick black coffee and a two-pound brown bag filled with sugar.

Rabbit filled a cup three quarters full, added enormous amounts of sugar and told me to drink. I couldn't hold the cup in my hands so finally Rabbit held the cup to my mouth and I gobbled it down. He repeated the process with a second cup which went down like nectar.

I was thirsty and couldn't remember the last time I had eaten or had something to drink. The hot coffee and sugar was like a shot in the arm. My mind cleared, I came fully awake and alive.

Rabbit decided to add something to the end of the statement which said I would like to play some part in ending the war. Satisfied with his addition, he had me read the statement for a recording. The results were successful, even though I tried to mess it up enough for Americans to realize that something was not normal. I didn't have to repeat the performance again.

The Cat said something to the short stumpy Vietnamese who must have been the ultimate authority in the group. The man replied with a wave of his hand towards Mickey Mouse. Mickey Mouse spoke, "I am the camp commander of this camp, I will have for you the regulations of the camp which you must follow. If you do not follow the regulations of the camp my guard will punish you."

"You must now stand and bow to the authorities before you return to your room. You must remember to be polite and bow to all the Vietnamese army men and people. You greet everyone with a bow. Do you understand?" I nodded and said softly, "Yes, I understand." Mickey Mouse motioned for me to stand. I did and simultaneously all the Vietnamese stood up. "You may go back to your room. Follow my guard," said Mickey Mouse. I bowed politely and they smiled at my easy acquiescence. They didn't know I had learned to bow on my very first day in North Vietnam. I could not forget that initial lesson in bowing based on Pavlovian conditioning.

Pig Eye led me back to the cell, slammed the door and bolted it tight. I made my way to the bunk, passing under the crossbar painfully. The full impact of the night's activities hit me all at once, "I'm broken," I cried. "I'm a traitor. I've disgraced my family, my country and myself." I despaired at being alive and cursed the effectiveness of the automatic ejection system. I would have been better off if I had never gotten out of the plane I thought. I was crying softly in despair. I hurt from head to toe. I looked at my raw pus covered wrists. Maybe I'll die from blood poisoning, I vainly hoped.

It was the lowest point in my entire life. I had nothing. I had lost everything, even my self-respect. "Lord forgive me. Please Lord, help me," I cried as I dropped off into a sound sleep, the tears still running down my cheeks.

A TRIP TO THE HOSPITAL

I awoke ashamed of the previous night's activities and shivering from the wintry air that was blowing through the cell. I had to urinate. The urge was compelling so I struggled from the bunk and under the crossbar. The swelling in my fingers was reduced. I had some feeling and was somewhat able to manipulate both hands. This capability was still marginal but even the slight improvement in my condition was mentally reassuring. I massaged my hands gently and lifted the loose cover from the portable toilet facility. Though my urge to urinate was strong I produced only a very small stream of urine which was deep orange in color. I was totally dehydrated, hungry, thirsty and cold. I couldn't remember when I had last eaten, or when I had something to drink prior to last night's coffee. I tried to figure out what day it was, but was unable to. While I remembered some particular events of my journey to Hanoi, clearly the major portion was lost in mental amnesia. It seemed like a long time had passed since my shoot down and capture on 20 March, but I had no idea how many days or weeks had passed by since that day.

I noticed the air was much colder the closer I was to the concrete floor, so I made my way back to the wooden bunk, and sat in the corner of the bunk, trying to stay out of the cold wind blowing in through the large open barred window. I put a reed mat over myself for protection. It wasn't much good but it was better than nothing.

I sat shivering. My teeth chattered and chills ran up and down my spine. Suddenly I heard a door being unlocked or unbolted, then footsteps and someone was at my cell door. He opened the small window, peeked in and left the way he came. In minutes he returned, unlocked my cell and entered carrying a bowl of soup and a half a loaf of French bread. He reached in over the crossbar and set them down on the bunk. He returned to the hallway and I could hear him ladling something from a bucket. When he entered the cell he had an Asian looking tea pot, about a one quart capacity in size, a cup and a stubby metal spoon. He placed these on the bunk next to the bread and soup and in sign language told me to eat. Then he left, slamming the cell door shut and bolting it securely.

I immediately started to eat some of the soup. It was hot and was made up mostly of some type of greens that I had never seen before. My finger coordination with my spoon was bad and I spilled soup on my skivvy shirt as I drooled, managing to miss my mouth. God I'm clumsy, I thought. I ate ravenously until the bowl was half empty. I tried to eat some bread. It was fresh but the crust was hard and bruised my mouth so I dipped it in the remaining soup broth. I finished eating the bread in this manner, and then cleaned up what was left of the soup. My bowl was empty but I was still hungry.

I filled my cup from the contents of the spouted pot and discovered it was dark unsweetened tea. I didn't particularly like tea. As a youth that's all we drank besides milk. Tea always ran through me like a sieve. It was a strong diuretic to my body system. In cold weather I used to have a mental saying for myself, "Take tea and pee". This same thought now flashed through my mind. I'm in luck. Maybe the tea will get my kidneys working well again. I forced myself to drink every last drop in the pot and felt bloated but content.

The key guard came to see if I was finished eating. He removed my soup bowl and spoon, saw that I had emptied the tea pot so he took it, filled it, and returned it to me. My body was warmed from food and drink. My mind became much clearer and I could think and concentrate.

I looked at my wrists, raw and pussy and infected from the gas soaked ropes and decided that I must try to cleanse them some way. I remembered learning in a survival primitive medicine course that human urine could be used to clean infected wounds. I had to urinate badly, so I made my way to the bucket and directed the hot stream of urine on the infected area of each wrist. The urine was still orange but the color was weaker. The passage of the hot urine washed off some of the infection and relieved some of the discomfort. I went back to my bunk and poured a little tea over both wrists to clean off some of the urine smell. I was careful not to use much tea in this cleansing process. The infections were obviously extreme. I decided I would urinate on them whenever I had the chance. The tea will cleanse my kidneys and then the urine will cleanse my wrists. I didn't even blink at making this mental decision. I've got to survive. It's the only way to go, I thought.

I forced myself to drink most of the tea, saving only a small portion to rinse off after urinating on my wrists. In the cold weather, the tea ran through me quickly. I waited as long as I could and repeated the urination and wrist cleansing process again. I noticed the orange color was even more faded so I felt relieved about my physical improvement. Drink all you can, I thought, and eat, get in shape, you don't know how long you're going to be here. I was tired so I crawled back on the bunk and fell asleep between the two reed mats.

It seemed that I had been sleeping only a short while before I was awakened by the noise of my cell door being unbolted. Pig Eye, the guard from last night's session came in and motioned for me to get up. He came towards the crossbar as I arose and he raised it at one end and pointed to two small semi-circular indentations and by sign language told me to put my wrists and forearm in each. When I understood what he wanted, I complied and bent forward over the crossbar when he lowered it. I was left in a half standing bent over position with my arms in shackles. He checked to see that there was no way I could get my hands and wrists loose from this restraint and left as noisily as he had entered.

I wonder what the hell this is all about, I thought. The wind whistled through the window and under the door and the cold air passed around me on its journey. I couldn't stand up and I couldn't kneel down. I was stuck in this halfway position and the only thing I could do for respite was to lean over the crossbar shackle and rest some of the weight from my body on my chest. This was painful as my ribs were cracked but I had no other option. The position was very exhausting and my body seemed to lose all of its new found strength that I had received from eating. They are wearing me down for something else, probably more interrogation, I mused.

Pig Eye kept me in this position for several hours. Occasionally he would peek through the sliding window to observe me. I grew weaker and more exhausted as time passed by. My mind became confused once more and I became desperate. I wondered what they were going to do to me next and I was frightened. My entire body was racked with pain and I was cold, dead cold like a corpse. The cold sank through me until I was thoroughly cold soaked, as cold as I would be in the arctic winter, but here I was in the tropics literally freezing my ass off. I guess it's all relative, I rationalized, in one of my saner moments.

When Pig Eye came he was all business. He released me from my shackled position, and led me to the interrogation room. He stopped at the doorway, spoke in Vietnamese and then signalled for me to enter. I limped in and walked towards the stool and a table behind which sat Rabbit and to his left the Pro.

I stood as erect as I could before them but this was a painful endeavor. "Bow," said Rabbit. I bowed painfully, as best I could, and was told to sit down on the stool.

"Moo lig gun you must obey the regulations of the camp. You must answer the questions of the camp authority," Rabbit said. "Do you understand?" "Yes," I replied weakly and frightened. "You must know that since your capture the American people have made large demonstration against the war; in your capital city of Washington, more than 100,000 of them protested against Johnson's war. You can see for yourself in your own U.S. magazine." He held up a copy of a U.S. magazine. "When were you shot down?" asked Pro. "Sunday, 20 March" I answered. "Where?" "South of Vinh." "And your target, tell me your target?" "A bridge, on a road over some water," I answered. "Show me on the map," he said, as he produced a large Vietnamese aerial map of that general area. I looked at it and could find the estuary and the road but they didn't cross. "About here." I said. "Your maps are different from ours. On our map the road crosses the water shown. We thought a bridge was there and that was to be my target. I never got there, I never saw it. I was shot down here." I showed him the spot where I thought I had ejected.

The Pro was a chain smoker and the smell from his cigarettes awakened my own strong desire to smoke. I had been a chain smoker myself, two and a half packs a day on shootdown. Pro noticed my anguish. "Do you smoke?" "Yes," I replied. "Here," he handed me a half full pack of Vietnamese cigarettes and a box of small wooden matches, "have one." I lit it eagerly and began puffing away in contentment, the smoke seemed to revive my spirits and calm my anguish.

"Do you drink tea or coffee?" said Rabbit. "Coffee when I have the choice." I replied. He spoke to Pig Eye who left and soon returned with a hot container of thick black Vietnamese coffee heavily laced with sugar. Rabbit poured out a cup and placed it before me. "Drink, it will make you warm," he said. I sipped the coffee and smoked the cigarette until I had almost finished it down to a tiny stub which burned my fingers. I squashed out its final glowing embers on the small ash tray and waited for something else to happen.

Mickey Mouse came in carrying something under his arm that looked like a rectangular piece of aluminum. He sat between Rabbit and Pro and spoke something in Vietnamese. Rabbit leaned forward and asked, "What is your squadron number?" I sat mute as he repeated the question. The Pro said, "We know you fly the Skyhawk, we know who you are and where you come from. We know all about you and your compatriots." Then he held up the piece of metal and turned it until I could read VA-36 *USS ENTERPRISE.* It's from my own plane, I thought.

Pro said, "Why did you not fly with Alcorn on the attack against the power plant near Haiphong?" "I was busy doing something else," I answered. He reached down and held up a pilot's knee board with the run down of the strike against the Hai Duong Bridge and a pilot's map of the entire attack from launch to recovery. "Do you know this?" he asked. "Yes," I replied, "it's the plan for the *ENTERPRISE* Hai Duong Bridge attack and the downed pilot's knee board. Is he alive?"

"He is well in another camp with many other American criminal pilots," responded Rabbit. Bill Shankel from VA-94 was the only pilot we lost on that strike, so now I knew that he was alive and that three of us from *ENTERPRISE* were POW's.

"Why does your squadron come to the *ENTERPRISE* from the East Coast of the United States when the air wing of the *ENTERPRISE* comes from the West Coast?" Asked Pro. "They needed us because we have much experience," I lied.

The sugary hot coffee had cleared my muddled mind. I need medical attention badly. If I can make these monkeys think that I am valuable and will cooperate with them, they'll probably see that I get to a hospital. I decided I would play them along and crank up a big bullshit story. If nothing else it may help me stall for time to recover my senses a bit, I rationalized.

Taking the offensive I said, "You know all about me. I was the one who planned both of those attacks in December. I did not fly in the first attack on the power plant because I was planning the second one on the Hai Duong Bridge. I was on *ENTERPRISE* because I was the expert from the East Coast in offensive attack tactics." In survival school they said if you lie make sure your story is plausible. If they catch you lying you'll really pay the penalty. Remember that if you are a POW, you probably are much smarter and better educated than your captors. Use your brain but be careful, and don't underestimate any interrogators. I saw their glances and nods of approval as they swallowed the bait.

"Moo lig gun you can yet be a good man. You can help the camp authority by your good attitude. You must prepare for us some documents. You must tell to us how the Americans make their attacks," said Mickey Mouse.

"I will try but I am wounded. I must go to the hospital soon. I am a very sick man and I am very tired. Your guard did not let me sleep today and now I feel very bad. If you do not let me return to my room and rest I am going to fall from this stool at your feet. When I am better I will try to answer your questions." I did not have to feign fatigue or injury; I was really exhausted and I was hurting over my entire body.

They spoke in Vietnamese and Mickey Mouse said, "You may return your room," and waved me out with his hand. I rose slowly, bowed as graciously as possible for a subservient American pilot and followed Pig Eye back to my cell. Once inside I rested on the bunk before I saw that soup, bread and tea were waiting. Pig Eye left and I started to eat immediately.

The meal was the same as I had eaten previously and I downed everything with relish. The food warmed me and I felt more comfortable now. I relieved my bladder and washed the infectious areas on both wrists and then rinsed off the excess urine smell with the remaining tea. There were many tea leaves in the bottom of the pot so I patted them gently in the pussy infections, hoping that the tanic acid from the tea leaves would be of some medicinal value.

I sat on the bunk and looked out the window. The sky was covered by a low overcast, the wind was blowing and the temperature must have been in the mid-forties (fahrenheit) at the highest.

The guard returned for my empty dish and once again refilled my tea pot. I stood and bowed as instructed when he entered, and also again as he was leaving to shut me up for the night. I remembered that when I was at survival school in Brunswick, Maine in March of 1965, just about a year previous, one of the aggressor instructors in the POW compound said to me, "If you are ever a POW make sure you do everything in your power to stay on the good side of the guards that are in charge of your food and living conditions. Don't get them angry and remember to do as much as you can to help them get their household jobs done; like eating and washing, without causing any unnecessary delays to them." I put this advice to immediate practice and I found it to be of great value through-out my captivity. The guard was pleased at my new found subservient bowing act and he even smiled at me as he departed.

The effects of the warm soup and bread wore off quickly and I became very cold as the icy wind blasted its way through the cell. As darkness suddenly began to arrive, I managed to urinate once more. I washed off all the tea leaves I had placed on the worst spots with the hot stream of urine. I poured tea from my container over the cleansed area as I tried to rid myself of the urine smell. It was a superficial effort and it didn't work. I still smelled to high heaven.

I crawled between the reed mats on the bunk and tried to keep myself out of the wind, as much as possible. It was more or less a vain effort. The room was pitch black before the tiny ancient light bulb came on over my cell door. I was exhausted from the day's activities and my physical condition was such that I felt I was more dead than alive. "Lord, I hurt all over, I don't know how long I can last, please watch over my family and my country and have mercy on me," I prayed before I fell off to sleep.

Mickey Mouse was shaking my right arm and shoulder. "Get up, get up you go to hospital now," he said. I didn't know where I was at first, I was still in my dreams and confused at this sudden intrusion. "What?, What?", I mumbled as I slowly staggered to my feet. He led the way and I followed, painfully bending to get under the crossbar shackle. Outside my cell door in the center of the darkened hallway was a stretcher. "Lie down here," Mickey Mouse ordered as he pointed to the stretcher. I got down on it with some difficulty. Someone covered me completely from head to toe with a blanket and I was hoisted up and jostled down the hall and put into some type of vehicle. With the canvas from the stretcher under me, and a large blanket over me, my body became warm and comfortable for the first time.The vehicle got under way and we were out of the jail area and on a main street within a few seconds. I could hear the honking of other vehicles and the ringing of bicycle bells as well as the murmurs of human voices. We must be downtown on a crowded street, I thought. I tried to make a mental picture of what turns we took but soon gave up and just relaxed and enjoyed the warmth of my surroundings. We started and stopped frequently and moved slowly when we were in fact moving. I heard a noise that I identified as an old fashioned trolley car. It was an old familiar noise I had not heard since my early childhood back in Lawrence, Massachusetts when we had a trolley car system. In fact, one of my uncles was a trolley car operator. During my trip the same noise passed us many times so I felt we were still on a main thoroughfare.

I don't think we went more than a mile or two when the vehicle pulled in off the street and came to rest in a relatively quiet area. We must be at the hospital, I thought.

The cab doors slammed shut and the rear doors were opened. I was lifted out and carried for some ways, still covered by the blanket so that I couldn't see or be seen. Finally I was placed down on a floor. The blanket was removed and I could see that I was in a long hallway of an old building.

A man completely dressed in white came up to me, peered over and scrutinized me carefully, then looked at Mickey Mouse, who was standing alongside of me and said, in perfect English with an American accent, "What are you trying to do, kill this man?"

He looked at me and said, "I am the head doctor of this hospital. I want you to know that your country is bombing my country. You are killing and wounding many of our innocent people. You are causing us death and destruction and I don't approve of that. But I don't approve of what they have done to you either." Turning to Mickey Mouse he said, "There is no need of this, I am going to make a full written report of this case to the General Staff in the morning and I don't care which of you I hurt by this action. We have too much to do with our own casualties without this unnecessary burden caused by your barbarity."

"What's wrong with your arms?" He asked as he looked at me. "What caused this?" "Ropes," I replied. "Ropes! Ropes did this?" he exclaimed. "Yes," I said. "Ropes that were tied tight and were then soaked with gasoline poured over my hands."

"How long were you like this in ropes?" "I don't know," I said. "How long have you been in Hanoi?" "I don't know." "How long has he been here in Hanoi?" he said angrily to Mickey Mouse. "Some days," said Mickey Mouse. "Why was he not brought to me immediately? You know the regulations, why do you not obey them?" Mickey Mouse was silent. Turning to me he said, "Don't be afraid of them." He snarled out with contempt, "They will not hurt you anymore."

Pa Ma
Phong Tho
Hok'ou
Hoang
Pa Kha
Lao Cai
Bac Quan
Muong Te
Muong Boum
Mt. Fan Si Pan
Sinh Ho
Chapa
Binh Lu
10308
Pho Lu
Vinh Tuy
Red
Bao Ha
Lo
Muong Nhie
Ou Tay
Lai Chau
Than Uyen
Van Ban
Luc An Chau
5295
Muong Khoa
4
2
T O N K
Hatsa
5922
Luan Chau
Quynh Nhai
Nhan Nghia
Chay
Yen Bai
Muong Hun Xieng Hung
Muong Muon
9787
NORT
Ou
Nghia Lo
Muong Hua
Khe Long
Thuan Chau
Phu Tho
Mt. Chien Pau
6043
Dien Bien Phu
Son La
Ban Cang
Ma
Ta Khoa
Hung Hoa
Sop Nao
Mai Son
Van Yen
Yen Chau
Muong Hiep
Muong Hung
4508
Muong Loi
Black
Muong La
Muong Et
Moc Chau
Muong Sai
Muong Ngoi
Muong Peu
Xieng Kho
Suoi Rut
Nam Bac
Het
Muong Liet
Sop Hao
VI
Seng
Muong Lat
Beng
Ou
Ban Se
Muong Son
6
Samneua
Hoi Xuan
Muong Ham
Mt. Loi
7405
6821
Muong Soi
Pak Seng
Muong Xi
Suong
Phaphay
Muong Peun
Chu
Lang Chanh
Muong Hiem
Hua Muong
Pak Pong
Sam Teu
Luang Prabang
Ban Nin Lan
Khan
6
Muong Khao
Sam Thong
Bai Thu
Xieng Ngeun
L
Tranninh
7346
Mt. San
Ban Ban
Ke Ban
N
Muong Soui
Plain of
Nong Pet
Nong Het
Qui Chau
7
Nam Tiat
Jars
Khang Khai
Muong Sen
3560
Xieng La
Ban Nam Pit
Plateau
Xieng Khouang
7
Cua Rao
Phu
Ngum
A
8894
Ca
Khe Bo
Muong Kassy
Nam Keng
Ban Thieng
13
Pak Lane
Mt. Bia
Tha Thom
Con Cuong
9242
Do Luon
Ban Diaye
n
2677
A
Lik
Muong Huong
3461
Muong Cham
5961
Ban Hin Heup
Borikhane
Ban Hin Lech Fai
Vu L
Tourakom
Muong Cao
Keo Neua Pass
13
Ban Keun
Ban Kouei
Pak Sane
Pakkading
Ban Hat Kieng
Ban Thouei
Bung Kan
Soppone
Nape
554
Ban Tha Ngone
Ban Rai
Kham Keut
1371
Mekong
Theun
Ban Sot
Lak S
Ngum
Vientiane
551
13
Phon Phisai
Na Kang
Ban Na Pach
2500
Phon Tiou
Nong Khai

Cao Bang

n Binh

Phuc Hoa

T'aip'ing

Nanh

Suhsü

Ch'ungtso

Tat'ang

Luw

Lungching

Ngan Son

Dong Khe

003 +

That Khe

(4)

P'inghsiang

Tungmenhsü

Hsiaotung

Ch'inpei

Ch'ir

oa

Bac Can

Na Sam

Ningming

Haiyüan

Shangssu

ho Chu

Munan Pass

Dong Dang

Nach'in

N

Pho Binh Gia

Lang Son

Loc Binh

Fangch'eng

Hsiyan

20

Thai Nguyen

Van Linh

(4)

3825

Tunghsing

Chiangp'ing

Luu Xa

Dinh Lap

+

Mong Cai

Nha Nam

Binh Lieu

Hai Coi

Mui Ngoc

Peihai C

Tam Dao

Bac Giang

Tien Yen

Dam Ha

Lo Chuc San I.

Vinh Yen

Luc Nam

Van Hoa

Phuc

3428

Cai Bau

Ching Lan Xan I.

Weicho

Yen

Bac Ninh

Dong Trieu

Quang Yen

Cam Pha

Hsiehya

Hanoi

Hai Duong

Hon Gai

Cu Xu Island

ong

Ke Sat

Haiphong

15

Lai Tao I.

Binh

Ninh Giang

Kien An

Cat Ba

(Apowan)

Hung Yen

Do Son

Phu Ly

Thuy Anh

13

G U L F   O F

Nam Dinh

Thai Binh

1

Lac Quan

Red River Delta

19

Bach Long Vy I.

(Nightingale)

h Binh

Van Ly

a

Phat Diem

Hau Loc

25

25

Hait'

Trung

Thanh Hoa

19

T O N K I N

Ch'angchiang

Sam Son

38

1

Tinh Gia

22

25

(Peili) Ch'angkan

Giam

Me Island

33

Paso

Bien Son I.

14

38

Tungfa

Phu Duc

(Kanen) Kanch'eng

17

Phu Dien

33

Lingt'ou

Cua Lo

Mat Island

Yingkohai

Loc Chau

Ben Thuy

10

Linh Cam

31

Huangliu

ng

1

Ha Tinh

Ya

Cam Xuyen

40

(Y

Huong Khe

Cape Ron

82

Duc

843

+

Ky Anh

55

36

Tuyen Hoa

Ron

35

"Do you know what day it is?" "No," I answered. "Do you remember much?" "No, just some things," I said. "When were you shot down?" "Sunday, 20 March," I answered. "Where?" "South of Vinh." "How long before you came to Hanoi?" "I don't know." "Did they beat you?" "Yes, some of them did but I don't remember it all."

He bent over, flashed a light and looked at my eye pupils, then he put his stethoscope on my arm, and chest and listened. "You are a very sick man. I must feed you before we can even take x-rays of your shoulder and chest. It is late in the night. It is Friday night, the date is April 1st. Can you get up? Can you walk?" he asked. "Yes," I replied and painfully got to my feet. "Come with me," he said and led me into a large room, flicked on the room lights and walked towards an operating table which was the only thing in the room besides a group of over hanging lights that hung from the ceiling over it. A nurse entered and put a sheet over the table and told me to lie down on it.

"I have many students here and they will watch as I try to make you more comfortable. But first I will have to feed you for you are very, very weak."

I shivered as I lay on the table. They hung a bottle filled with clear liquid and inserted a needle into my left foot. I watched the bubbles of air as they slowly rose in the bottle and then I dozed in a stupor half asleep and half awake.

It seemed like a long while before the bottle was emptied. It was replaced with a second and the process continued. I was cold but managed to lie still and caught cat naps until the feeding was finished.

He removed the needle from my foot and took x-rays with a large portable machine that was rolled into the room. When the x-ray procedure was finished, the plates were taken away for development. He stood over me and spoke softly. "In the morning you will be permitted to bathe. They will give you soap, and you are to clean out the infection from both of your wrists. Take all the time you need to do a good job. A medic will paint the area with disinfectant and cover it completely with sulfa powder and then he will bandage both forearms; you are to keep these areas absolutely dry. The medic will clean the wounds and change the bandages each day. The infection is very bad so you must cooperate and keep the area clean and dry. Do you understand all I have said?" "Yes," I replied.

"Do you sleep well?" he queried. "No." "Are you cold?" "Yes." "How many blankets do you have?" "None," I answered. "None? What do you cover yourself with?" "The reed mat from the other bunk. I sleep on a reed mat and I put the other one over me."

He turned to Mickey Mouse who was standing next to the wall observing all that had been going on and said angrily: "When he returns you get him two blankets. Do you understand? Two blankets!" and he shook his head in disgust.

The x-rays were returned and he and an associate studied them and spoke quietly in Vietnamese. A group of medical students came into the room and stood watching them and watching me.

"I am going to put you to sleep for a little while. You have very bad and complicated injuries. It is very late and we cannot do much at this time, but at least you will be more comfortable." He said something in Vietnamese and a nurse handed him a syringe. "When I inject this into your arm I want you to count slowly backwards from ten to zero," he said. He inserted the needle. "Ten, nine, eight, seven, six, five . . .," and I fell into a deep sleep.

I don't know what he did but I felt the pain in the midst of my dreams and then the next thing I heard was snap, snap, "Wake up, wake up," and he was snapping his fingers in my face. I blinked and awoke. He said, "You will feel much better now. There is still very much work to be done for you. In addition to all of this I think you are a very sick man. When did you have your last complete physical for flying?" "A year ago," I said. "We are scheduled for it on our birthday. I would have had mine on the 27th of March but I was captured then." "That's unfortunate," he said, "I think if you could have had your physical, you would not be here now. They would not have let you fly. We do not have the facilities to do an extensive physical here. We will do what we can to heal your wounds. When you are released, make sure that they check everything. I feel there is something else wrong with you."

"They will take you back now. Sit up and we will help you get on the stretcher." "Thank you doctor, you have been very kind to me. Thank you, thank you," I said.

Once on the stretcher the blanket was placed over me from head to toe. I was tired and fell asleep as soon as they had me back in the vehicle.

I awoke lying on the stretcher in the hallway in front of my cell. The guard opened the door and Mickey Mouse ordered me to "get up and return your cell." I arose and walked in feeling physically much better than when I had left it for the hospital.

The guard put two blankets on the bunk. I bowed politely to Mickey Mouse and the guard and said, "Thank you." They left and bolted the door.

For the first time since I was captured I felt physically strong. I reviewed everything that had happened to me at the hospital. I'll have to be careful about the infections on my arms, keep them clean and dry. I wondered about the wisdom of my urination cleansing process, take tea and pee. I was thirsty so I drank a cup of cold tea and then went to my bunk and covered myself comfortably with the two blankets. My mind was clear for the first time. Remember the date, it is now Saturday, the 2nd of April. I wondered where all the days had gone to between the 20th of March and the 1st of April and what else happened to me on the way to Hanoi?

I thought of my family, my wife and children, my mother and father, my brothers. I'll make it, I vowed. I'll make it through somehow, no matter what happens or no matter whatever else they do to me. Lord, thank you for putting me into the hands of that Vietnamese doctor. My mind now clear and responsive, I prayed fervently this prayer of thanks. "Our Father, Who art in Heaven, hallowed be Thy name, Thy kingdom come, Thy will be done . . ." and when I finished I fell into a deep restful sleep.

EASTER DINNER

When morning came, I awoke to the ringing of a distant tocsin whose reverberations were carried by the wind as it summoned its Vietnamese victims to their required rising on a new people's work day. Though I could feel the cold air on my head and nose, I was quite comfortable snuggled between the folds of my two blankets. The wooden planks and reed mat covering which served as my mattress were becoming more acceptable as I adjusted quickly to the primitive life style.

I began the day with a prayer of thanksgiving for the Lord's protection I had received during the night. From this day onward my daily ritual would be permeated with prayer, from crisis to crisis, from wake up reveille until turn in taps. I had my senses now so I placed myself squarely in the hands of the Lord. "Thy will be done, oh Lord, but please help me in my miseries to become a better man, a better Christian, and on my liberation, a better father and husband, and a better American." This petition was the main spring of my resistance from that day onward, during my entire incarceration. Above all else I wanted not only to survive the ordeal, but also to grow intellectually and morally from the miseries and suffering I would have to endure.

I stayed under the blankets and thought of home, my wife Louise and my six sons whom I had left in Jacksonville, Florida, in the fall of 1965. I knew this burden would be heavy for her. But she was strong and had the necessary moral character to meet the challenge. I didn't doubt for one second that she would survive this experience, as I would, and that one day with God's blessing we would be united again as man and wife. It will be harder on the boys, I thought. They were young and the loss of their father would be a bitter experience for them to endure. I was confident that Louise would be able to sustain them.

The thoughts of my family saddened me. I resolved then and there that I would not succumb to self inflicted sadness by lamenting about my wife and children. The Lord will watch over them as He will watch over me. What more can I ask? Keep the faith, look forward to tomorrow and freedom and never, never, never give up, I resolved.

The guard's heavy footsteps interrupted my reflections. He opened the cell door and motioned for me to follow him after he had shown by sign language that I was to empty my portable toilet facility, an old five gallon can with a loose cover. This honey bucket cleansing routine would be a daily ritual for me for many years.

I walked through the hallway following the guard who had turned left after leaving my cell. In a few short steps we turned right and went into a small courtyard. He turned left, walked to the end of the yard and went up a couple of steps to a closed door. After unlocking it, he led me into a wash room area adjoining three solid stone Vietnamese privies. It was a three holer, I hadn't seen anything like this since I vacationed with my Uncle Jack Cayer's family when they lived in a Boston and Maine railroad house in North Wilmington, Massachusetts, in the early thirties.

I emptied the bucket and rinsed it out with cold water from a badly leaking tap. It still stank to high heaven after it was cleaned. My captor brought me a square bar of old fashioned brown soap and a ragged but clean wash cloth and told me in poor but understandable English to "washie, washie."

He left and locked the door. I immediately went to the door and through a small crack was able to see him leave the courtyard. I was curious and the coast seemed clear so I searched the privy area and the wash area, but I could find no signs that indicated any Americans had been in them.

I saw a large wash bucket in the shower. The showers were all broken so I filled the tub with cold water. As it was filling I soaked my wrists in the water which, though unheated, felt warmer to me than the chilly winter air. I soaped up the wash cloth and gently cleaned up the infected areas on both wrists. It took a long time before I was satisfied that I had cleansed them as well as I would be able to. I couldn't believe how deep the ropes had cut into my flesh. Just to look at the infections was enough to nauseate me. I sure hope this stuff isn't gangrene, I thought. It was the foulest infection I had ever seen or smelled for that matter.

My whole body was filthy so I sat in the tub and cleaned every inch. I noticed when the dirt was removed that I was covered with small cuts and many blue colored bruises. I looked as if I had received a severe beating, and I guess that I had somewhere along the line on my trip north to Hanoi.

When I had finished cleaning my entire body, I washed my skivvy shorts and torn skivvy shirt. I couldn't believe the dirt I got out of them. After thoroughly rinsing out the soap, I put on my shorts and swung the shirt to get rid of more of the water that was still in it.

The guard came back to get me and in a few seconds I could hear him unlocking the door. He entered, and as we returned to my cell I struggled to carry the soap, wash cloth, skivvy shirt and honey bucket.

I was clean but cold. The icy wind was still blowing. Once in my cell I covered myself with a blanket and sat on the bunk. The guard stayed at the door obviously waiting for someone. In a few minutes a tall Vietnamese dressed in a white smock entered carrying an assortment of medical paraphernalia in a canvas bag that was attached to a strap slung over his left shoulder. He made his way to the bunk bending under the crossbar and motioned for me to keep sitting. I held out my arms and he carefully inspected each one while carrying on a soft conversation with the guard. I had the impression that he was talking about my physical condition, specifically the infections.

His inspection completed, he gently painted each infected area with merthiolate by dabbing it on a soaked piece of cotton. When this was completed, he poured what appeared to be sulfa powder on the areas and then wrapped them in a heavy layer of cotton batting. He then wrapped the cotton with a wide gauze bandage and secured both tight with strips of plaster. I must admit it was a professional job. I said, "Thank you," stood up and bowed to him and the guard as they left. My mind was somewhat relieved now that my arms had been treated. I vowed to myself that I would do everything in my power to keep the infected areas clean and dry.

Feeling more chipper, I decided to make a close search of the cell. I saw some scratchings on the black painted steel cell door. The only name that I could recognize was Ron Storz. I thought about the POW names I had discovered so far and reviewed them for my memory: Risner, Stockdale, Denton, Shumaker, Alvarez, Alcorn, Shankel and my-self. I wondered how many more POWs there were in Hanoi, and I promised myself that I would remember each name that I came across. I learned nothing else as I continued my search for clues of other American POWs. I wondered where they were kept; certainly not around here or else I'd have seen or heard them.

They brought me more green soup, bread and tea. I say they, because this time when the guard opened the door two Vietnamese women were carrying the food and drink. They put it in the cell and looked at me curiously, like I was an animal on display at the zoo. When they left I made a beeline for the food. I had already learned that food was more important than clothing for the body when it was cold. My lessons on the importance of food and proper diet were beginning to sink in, but I would have a much better appreciation on this aspect of living in the coming months. For now I was determined to eat everything I could, no matter how bad it tasted.

I was resting comfortably during the noon siesta when I suddenly started to have stomach cramps. At first I blamed the green soup and then I realized to the best of my recollection, I had not had a bowel movement since I was shot down. I made my way to the portable toilet facility and with great difficulty and pain, I finally managed to rid myself of the block-age causing the cramps. I made a mental note that I would be alert for any signs indicating the need for a bowel movement and respond to it im-mediately. I saw the importance of attending to the normal body functions as a prerequisite for survival in these primitive circumstances.

I rested well for the remainder of the nap time snuggled beneath the blankets which kept me comfortably warm. With my wounds attended to, my body washed clean, and my stomach filled, I felt as if things were improving.

Things suddenly turned for the worse when Pig Eye unlatched my cell door. I got up, bowed and watched him unfasten the crossbar shackles. He motioned for me to place my arms in them, then he closed the crossbar over my arms, and once again I was firmly locked in place bent over, half standing. It was a position that would fatigue me quickly.

These little bastards play rough, I thought. First it's the carrot, then it's the stick. They must be softening me up for more interrogation. My chest began to hurt as I rested it on the bar taking some of the weight from my bent back. He kept me in this position for about four hours until night had fallen.

Pig Eye came back carrying soup, tea and bread. He released me from the shackles, but instead of allowing me to eat he took me to the interrogation room.

I entered and bowed to the somber faces of Rabbit, Mickey Mouse and the Pro sitting behind the table. When directed I took my seat on the stool and awaited their questions. I was cold, tired, and I must admit frightened of what was coming. I said a mental prayer and asked the Lord to help me, guide me and protect me.

Rabbit began, "How are you today?" "I'm better." "You have received the human treatment from the Vietnamese people. We give you medicine and food. Since today you must obey all the regulations of this camp and you will enjoy the human treatment from Vietnamese people."

The chain smoking Pro had already lit a Vietnamese cigarette, and after his initial drag he cut off Rabbit's conversation and said, "Tell me how you make your air attacks against us?"

"It's very complicated," I said. "It's a function of run in altitude, drop altitude, dive angle and gyro computer sight setting. I don't think you would understand it unless you have had aviation experience," I replied.

"I work long with the Vietnamese people's air forces and I understand about such things," Pro said. Mentally I said to myself, well I'm at the crossroads; I have either got to lie like hell and get away with it or else clam up and not say another word. I'll feed him some technical bullshit that isn't true and see how much he swallows. If it looks good I'll just string him along for as long as I can get away with it.

"The attack depends on the run in altitude. I come in at a certain altitude. I will release my bombs at half that altitude. If I run in at 28,000 feet I will drop the bombs at 14,000 feet. My dive speed will be the same as my run in speed generally 500 knots. My dive angle must be between 30 degrees and 80 degrees and I must hold it steady with the center of the bomb sight on the target. The gyro computer compensates the sight setting, and a light comes on which tells me to pull out of the dive and the bombs drop automatically at the right point of the pull out. Normally the pull out must be between 6 and 8 g's. Do you understand all this?" I asked. "Ah yes," he replied, "it is very similar to the manner of our own air force." Bullshit, I thought, you dumb bastard, if you swallowed that one I can get you to swallow anything.

My mind went back to Brunswick, Maine, and the Navy's survival and escape training school that I attended in March of 1965. One of the instructors, a talented young black man, once said to me in an academic situation, "Commander Mulligan, if you are ever a POW use your head; remember you are better educated, have more experience and are much smarter than your captors will be. So be careful about what you try to do, but always try to outsmart them."

I had made the big choice. From now on I would smile and string them along as best I could. I'd milk them for all the humane treatment that I could get and build my physical strength back up to par. I decided to go along with the bullshit as long as I knew it was working. I'd retreat back to a hard line as soon as I had to pay a price that was unacceptable.

The three of them were pleased by my military information "give away." They looked at one another approvingly and spoke in Vietnamese.

Rabbit offered me one of the Pro's cigarettes, which I accepted. I lit up and he spoke softly, "We would like you to write for us some of your impressions. Write about your childhood and tell to us something about your country the United States. Can you do this?"

I sat back and feigned deep thought. Then I replied, "Yes, I suppose I can do that for you. It would not really violate the spirit of the Code of Conduct which I am bound to live by."

I continued, "You know I am in poor health and your doctor said I would go back to the hospital. I am tired because your guard keeps me bent over in the shackles for a long time. I can only write for you in my room so that when I am tired I can rest."

"We understand," Mickey Mouse said. "My guard will permit you to rest, and he will bring to you the pen and paper for you to write for us. I myself will talk with you of our needs. Now you may return to your room. Tomorrow I will give to you the pen and paper, and you will write for us about your country."

"Yes," I replied. They all stood. I rose and bowed as graciously as I could. Pig Eye led me to my cell then bolted and locked the door.

It was dark and the small light dimly illuminated the cell. I picked up the bread and bowl of soup and noticed that the rats had already been feasting on the bread in my absence. I broke off the piece where they were eating and ate the remainder of it gently dunking it into the green soup.

I was barely finished when I heard a moan from the next cell. The man began crying out in French. "Pourquoi! Pourquoi! Je ne sais pas! Je ne sais pas!"

Why? Why? I don't know! I don't know! My high school French only permitted me to understand these laments. I could not comprehend what else he was saying but I was sure he was old and I was sure he was French.

He seemed to be taking his imprisonment very badly for he moaned and groaned through most of the night. I didn't know it then, but I'm sure now that he was being kept on his back in leg shackles. This form of restraint seems to be harder to cope with the older you are. I'm sure he was at the end of his resistance as a result of this treatment.

It was Saturday night the 2nd of April. The wind was still blowing and winter was apparent by the cold temperature. I still only had my skivvies and worn socks for clothing. I wrapped myself completely in a blanket and sat on the bunk until I got tired. I said my evening prayers, asked for protection and guidance and fell sound asleep securely wrapped in the folds of the two blankets. I could hear the old man moaning in French, "Pourquoi? Pourquoi?" and I prayed for him, whoever he was, because although unknown to each other, we were allies against a common foe.

When I awoke on Sunday morning I immediately knew that I had slept late. The weather was still cold and the sky still covered with a dirty gray overcast. The damp air gave me chills as I used my toilet facility. I guess they don't ring the wake up bell on Sunday, I thought.

I wrapped myself in my blankets and sat in the corner of the bunk to try to keep out of the icy blasts as much as possible. I mentally attended Mass back on the *ENTERPRISE* with my friend Father Gallagher, devoting about an hour in prayer and meditation to this effort. I was rewarded with the peace of mind and solace of soul that came to me. In Hanoi, alone and lonely, I found it much easier to reach into the inner depths of my heart and soul and talk to God. My situation made me realize my utter dependency on the will of the Lord. Fatalistically I gave myself to Him much more easily there in Hanoi than I ever did before. It's amazing what a little personal suffering will do to a man. Like most 20th century male Americans I felt quite self sufficient. But suddenly there I was wrapped in my own insignificance and totally dependent. I wasn't using my religion as a cop out for my problems. It was rather that my present state was forcing me to see into myself and understand the realities of life. I was beginning to reflect and sort out my priorities. No matter what the outcome, I would be a different man, (and a better one I hoped) as a result of this experience.

The guard came to open the door, and the two women brought me my mid-morning meal. The menu was exactly the same. Eating two meals a day was a new experience for me. On *ENTERPRISE* we had twenty-four hour, round-the-clock feeding. This was some come down. Weak green soup, bread and tea, not much but I said grace as fervently as if it were a feast.

The old man in the next cell had a visitor. She sounded like his wife consoling him. They spoke in French but I was not proficient enough to be able to understand any of it. He kept on moaning and moaning and he started to get on my nerves. It was hard for me to have compassion about someone I didn't know and whom I couldn't understand. Why couldn't he be another American POW, I selfishly thought, finishing all of my chow.

Pig Eye came in later and ushered me off to an interrogation with Rabbit. It was just a bullshit session and I had the impression Rabbit was just filling in squares by talking with me. He was bright and seemed quite friendly and why shouldn't he be, for to the Vietnamese I looked like I was going to be a most cooperative captive. He wanted to know about the United States, its history, geography and culture. I was flippant as I discussed them in obscure generalities. This bastard thinks he is setting me up, I mused, as we played mental games, each giving the other nothing of any worth. After the lengthy but mild interrogation, Rabbit told me to stay on the stool while he went to get Pig Eye to return me to my cell. He made the mistake of leaving his large stack of notes in his folder on the desk. I could hear his footsteps going down the hall so I quickly rifled through the pages.

I saw all kinds of statements on various subjects written by Americans. One paper had a list of names that I glanced at. There must have been fifty or more of them. There were other papers neatly typewritten that purported to be statements of confessions of crimes similar to the ones shown to me during my first interrogation. They were so similar in length and typewritten format on the clean white paper, that I thought they must have been mass produced by one man. I was sure that everyone of them was phony, for when I quickly read a few they didn't sound authentic. The sound of footsteps interrupted me and I hastily closed the folder, put it in its place on the desk, and resumed my erect position on the stool.

Rabbit came in with Pig Eye. He gave me a pencil and paper and told me to take it to my room and write some of the history of the United States for him. I stood at attention and bowed politely, which pleased him and Pig Eye immensely.

Back in the cell I found my cold soup and bread molested by the ever present rats. I ate what was left of the bread, cursing the rats for their boldness as they popped in and out of my cell, through a small hole in the wall that was apparently there as a drain for any excess water on the floor. The tea kept me warm, and I was thankful for it, but wished it was black coffee instead.

I forced myself to mentally perform a medical examination of my body. I was in much better shape than when I had come to, lying on the floor in a pool of blood. I had received medical attention, was eating regularly, had two blankets and was clean. My left arm was still hanging uselessly, though nowhere near as painful as it had been. My ribs hurt badly and I walked with a distinct limp from my hip injury. My kidneys and bowels were functioning better each day. My arms were bandaged and healing. I was making progress but I had a long way to go before I would be physically normal. My mental attitude was improving as I adjusted more and more to my captivity. I have a lot to be thankful for, I thought, but I sure wish I could shave and brush my teeth. The heavy stubble from a two week beard was itchy and annoyed me.

I resolved to improve my body condition by doing whatever mild exercise I could and started by walking. I forced myself to hobble around the cell for a few minutes, but I had to stop as I soon was exhausted from this effort. I've got to keep moving. I'll have to do a little more each day until I'm back to normal, I thought. I reflected on the events of the day, said my prayers and fell into bed between the covers tired, yet contented considering my circumstances.

In the ensuing days I settled down into the monotonous routine of being a prisoner. My daily schedule didn't vary much. I arose about seven, performed the usual body functions, sat on the bunk under the blanket, and mentally commiserated with the Lord, and then reflected on my own circumstances until the guard came to take me for my daily bath. I looked forward to the time out of my cell and the guard obliged me by letting me wash for an hour before he returned. I moved slowly because of my injuries, and even though I was improving physically I never allowed the Vietnamese to learn about it. I maintained the same pace in everything I did to make them unaware of my slowly improving condition.

The food was always exactly the same and I ate everything they gave me. Each afternoon after siesta I had a quiz. First Mickey Mouse, then Pro. Rabbit seemed to disappear. I wrote pure bullshit info about the history and geography for Mickey Mouse on Monday and Tuesday. Wednesday the Pro wanted me to write about the attack and defense phases of air strikes. I took it slow on this one and conned him into believing it would take me at least a week to accomplish. He bit the bait and I settled down to writing a completely fictitious narrative on this subject. I was very careful to make sure that all the details seemed very logical. I described everything so clearly that I felt I could almost believe this fiction myself. I knew that my story wouldn't fool a professional military aviator but I felt that it would last a long time before its falsehood would be detected.

Mickey Mouse quizzed me briefly in the afternoons, and I assured him I was hard at work on the air strike paper for Pro, but that because of my poor physical condition I needed lots of time. He swallowed this line readily because the guard kept checking to see that I was writing in my cell and would report back to him.

Late Friday night, April 8th, I was put on a stretcher, covered by a blanket and whisked to the hospital. The English-speaking doctor took one look at me and said, "Don't you have any more clothes than this?" "No," I replied. He turned to Mickey Mouse and said, "Tomorrow you get him some clothes, do you understand?" Mickey Mouse replied with a weak, "Yes."

"Your arm is still very bad. We will take more x-rays and then try to make you more comfortable." He removed the bandages from my wrists and inspected my arms to see how they were healing. He was satisfied with their progress, but cautioned me about keeping the infected areas clean and dry and then said, "Your wrists will be healed in a month."

After the x-rays had been taken and read, he put me to sleep again and performed some more work on my left shoulder and arm. I was groggy when I came to, but remembered to thank him for his kindness before I was taken from the operating room on a stretcher and once again covered by a blanket.

Exhausted from my hospital trip, I managed to sleep completely through the remainder of the night, and awoke only when I heard the guard at my cell door coming to take me to bathe. Mickey Mouse was with him and gave me some Vietnamese prison garb which included two pairs of plain khaki shorts, two blue T-shirts, one full length khaki pant pajama suit with matching khaki blouse which buttoned down the center, and another blue pajama suit. The blue blouse had two pockets which made it unique and one of its kind for American POWs. On both sets of pajama suits was stenciled TU-31. I appreciated getting the clothing for it was still windy, cold and wintery.

The Frenchman left sometime Saturday morning when I was bathing. To the best of my knowledge all the other cells were empty, and once again I was alone.

I had half finished my mid-morning soup when I realized that it was Holy Saturday. Lent was over, Easter would come the following morning, and I had almost forgotten about the major events of Holy Week, which had somehow been displaced by the rigors of my new circumstances. I finished my meal and meditated on the events of Good Friday, Holy Saturday and Easter Sunday and marveled at the strength of the Lord, the God-man who had endured the harshest of physical suffering to redeem mankind.

Though I was eating everything that I received, I was hungry. Compared to my normal American diet I was on short rations. I thought about the fast and abstinence regulations of Catholicism and for the first time in my life I saw the meaning in them. A little deprivation of food and drink and self mortification would help improve my self discipline.

I prayed that I could offer the suffering I was undergoing as atonement for those actions of my life that I would have done differently if given another opportunity. I thought about the sense of loss that I was suffering as a human who has lost his freedom, and I wondered how much worse would be the pain of loss suffered by a soul lost for eternity. I thought about my wife and children and I longed to be with them. I was sad and almost on the verge of self pity. Lord, I am lonesome for human company but there is none to be found. I vowed to arise at sunrise and conduct my own Easter sunrise service.

When I awoke it was the false dawn of morning's arrival that first greeted me. Then the sun rose into a clear blue sky and the fullness of Easter was upon me. I prayed the Mass as fervently as I could and thanked the Lord for the blessings He showered upon me.

At mid-morning Mickey Mouse accompanied the key guard as he brought me my morning meal. When I bowed, he greeted me all smiles. "Today is your day of celebration, you know, He who gets up, so I have had my cooker prepare for you the oisseau." My prior French studies told me oisseau meant bird, so I was expecting a big piece of chicken or turkey to pop up from under the covered dish that the guard carried in addition to the soup and bread. Mickey Mouse lifted the cover and said, "Le oisseau." I couldn't believe my eyes. It wasn't a chicken breast or turkey leg, it was a full grown sparrow! A genuine sparrow! I thanked Mickey Mouse, bowed as he left, said grace, prayed that my main course wasn't English, and promptly ate every bit of meat on him. Easter I found was different in North Vietnam.

During my interrogations I noticed that the Vietnamese quiz masters had the same time schedule and followed the same pattern. Mickey Mouse and Pro left their notes on the table when the quiz was finished and then went to find the key guard so that I could be returned to my cell. I took advantage of this lapse and rifled through their notes as best I could. Most were concerned with propaganda statements of one type or another. In addition there was some biographical and military info which I scanned and considered mostly bullshit. I hit upon the idea of stealing some of these documents randomly just to screw up their efforts. Each opportunity I had I managed to steal some more notes, hide them under my long pajama coat and under my shorts. When I got back to the cell I would tear them into small scraps and soak them in tea in my cup and then make them into small paper balls which I would sink in my portable toilet. I was pleased with my efforts.

One day I heard someone whistling American songs during the siesta. I couldn't find out where the music was coming from and it frustrated me. Each day at bath I looked all over for signs of the American, but I couldn't see any. I was just resting during siesta time when I heard someone speak softly. "Yank in cell #1, what's your name?" He repeated this query several times before it dawned on me that I was his objective. I answered out the window, "I'm Commander Jim Mulligan from the *ENTERPRISE,*" hoping that he would hear me. He said, "I'm Jim Stockdale, CAG-16 from *ORISKANY.*" I remembered that the *ORISKANY* had lost its Carrier Air Wing Commander shortly before I arrived in the combat zone, but I didn't know his name.

He asked me my physical condition and I filled him in. "What have they got you writing?" he asked. I replied, "I'm doing some phony military bullshit just to keep them off my back." "Be very careful and remember everything for they will make you do it again and then compare both copies," Stockdale advised.

Lord, I hadn't thought about that possibility and it frightened me. How dumb can I get, I thought. "What about you?" I asked. He filled me in on his physical condition, which was very bad, and said, "I'm writing to try and get these guys to stop torturing our guys for political statements. They are talking about a trial for some of the senior POWs and they are getting this bullshit to bolster their case. I'm trying to stop them."

The siesta tocsin rang out signifying the end of nap time. "See you tomorrow and God bless," he called out as he ended our dialogue.

I reviewed the bullshit military paper and took detailed notes so that I could duplicate my effort if required. When the notes were compiled on one sheet of paper I hid it in between the boards of the bunk. I did such a good job of hiding the notes that *I* had a hard time finding them.

Friday night they took me to the hospital for more X-rays. When they were developed I saw two Vietnamese doctors reading them. They got into a heated discussion about what they saw, and were obviously in strong disagreement as to what to do. Nothing happened and I was returned to my cell.

At the next siesta talk session I told Stockdale about these events and he informed me that "The Vietnamese are about 25 years behind in bone work." He elaborated about how they had worsened his bad leg by their inept surgery.

On Saturday night I had a long quiz with the Pro over my military paper. He swallowed everything, hook, line and sinker as I rationalized and explained away all of his questions. He was jubilant. This dumb bastard really thinks this paper is his thesis for a Ph.D in attack aviation, I thought, smoking each additional cigarette he passed me as my reward. It was late when he had the guard return me to my cell.

Sunday dawned bright and clear. The temperature warmed up considerably. The wind gently brushed the leaves on a large tree across the street from the high wall outside my window. I saw some small birds flittering by in pairs. It was mating time. Spring had arrived.

I had finished my green soup and was resting on my bunk day dreaming and waiting for Jim Stockdale to initiate our daily conversation. We had exchanged information but I found myself having a difficult time retaining what he was telling me, because I couldn't relate to anything in Hanoi except my immediate surroundings. My physical condition was slowly improving but I was still in bad shape. I could hold my empty tin drinking cup in my left hand but I couldn't lift it, not even one inch. I wondered if I would ever regain the use of my left arm or if I would be crippled for life. My rib and the entire left side of my body still hurt. I decided that my injuries must have been caused when I ejected from that violent spin my plane was in, and by the wild flailing my body went through as the chute was opening. Don't bitch; you're damn lucky to be alive, I thought. My mind kept wandering through the recent events in no apparent order or direction.

Suddenly I heard loud rumbling explosions and felt the earth tremor. Boom! Boom! Boom!, echoed the blasts from an anti-aircraft gun emplacement. It was joined immediately by a concert of followers from every direction. "It's a raid on Hanoi! Hurrah they finally lifted the damn restrictions on bombing Hanoi — go get 'em Yanks," I cheered. The roar of jets passing overhead drowned out everything else. Then the small arms fire started from all around. Outside my window a guard was shooting skyward. The planes were retiring on the deck at maximum speed to stay out of the SAM perimeter. It was over in a few minutes. The entire area of the camp was bedlam with Vietnamese running and yelling hysterically at the top of their lungs. I prayed for the safety of the attacking American pilots. My morale rose one thousand percent. Lord, it's a great day. I thought, this damn war is finally going to get off top dead center now that the restrictions on bombing Hanoi are lifted. I etched the date in my mind, April 17, 1966, first raid on Hanoi.

Stockdale didn't call that day because the Vietnamese were up and running around in nervous apprehension.

That night I had a very late quiz by Rabbit, Cat from the general staff and a man obviously his superior that I had never seen before, and never saw again. My morale was sky high and, though I bowed, I sat ten feet tall on the stool before them. Rabbit railed at me, "The American air pirates have bombed our beloved Hanoi. They kill many women, children and old folks. They destroy our hospital, churches and pagodas but we will punish them. You will be made to pay for your crimes against the Vietnamese people, all of you. You will be tried as war criminals. You will receive the wrath of the Vietnamese people as well as that from all the peace and justice loving people in the world. You are all criminals. You air pirates. You are not Prisoners of War, do you understand? You have no rights here."

"Batshit!" I said as I lost my temper. "According to the Geneva Convention which North Vietnam has signed, I am a Prisioner of War. Anytime you want to start a war crime trial you can begin with me. But first I demand an international lawyer of my choice and enough time to prepare my defense. I am not afraid of your threats of a trial."

Cat interrupted and said, "You must be polite or I will have you punished." The other man spoke in Vietnamese and Rabbit resumed, "Do you think the United States will continue to bomb Hanoi?" "Yes, I am sure they will." "Why?" "Because your country has not responded to the peace initiatives from President Johnson, and because Easter Sunday has passed."

"I do not understand about Easter Sunday," said Rabbit. "You don't because you don't understand America. In our country each year the Congressmen and Senators go back to their home districts and states for a spring vacation. They have found out what their followers are thinking and are now back in Washington. Johnson has talked to them and one week after Easter we have bombed Hanoi. We will continue to bomb Hanoi you can be sure of that," I concluded.

Rabbit spoke in Vietnamese and then said, "I promise you that things will be very bad for the captured American criminals if the United States continues to bomb our beloved Hanoi. You may return to your room." I stood up and felt ten feet tall but bowed in compliance with previous instructions. I was getting braver, but not brave enough to risk the consequences of not bowing.

Soon after reveille on Monday morning, Pig Eye came and took me to a quiz with Mickey Mouse. He wanted me to rewrite completely the bullshit military papers I had done for the Pro. "It will take me some days to do for it is long and complicated," I told Mickey Mouse. He sent me back to the cell and Pig Eye brought me more paper and another pen to write with. Stockdale was right. Thank God he warned me and I had been able to keep an exact set of notes. Each day I wrote another section of the bullshit paper. I could almost reconstruct it paragraph for paragraph, sentence for sentence and word for word, and I was sure that the Vietnamese would swallow the whole line of falsehoods once they had compared my copy to the original I gave to Pro.

The weather was warmer each day. After my morning bath I would hang my clothes on the line and bask in the sun for ten or fifteen minutes before I returned to my cell. I enjoyed these few moments of relative freedom in the yard, and the sunshine seemed to help rejuvenate my aching body.

Each day during siesta, Stockdale and I would have a brief conversation. I wondered what he looked like. We spoke of home and our families. He was very concerned about his leg which was badly mangled and causing him great difficulty.

Wednesday night I had a late quiz with Mickey Mouse. I noticed his notes seemed more extensive than usual. When he left to get the key guard to return me to my cell, I rifled through the papers on the desk and stole about ten sheets from the center of the stack. I also stole a few matches from a box on the desk.

Once back in my cell, I folded the papers and put them under my "honey bucket". I'll destroy them in the morning when it's light enough to see what I'm doing, I thought. What a mistake that was!

Shortly after the morning tocsin clanged out its message, Pig Eye came into my cell and he was mad as hell. He started rifling though my papers. He didn't find what he was looking for and he searched everywhere except under the "honey bucket". Finally he left in a huff. I immediately retrieved the stolen papers. They were all numbered and had Vietnamese writing in the margins. I didn't even try to read them as I was in a hurry to burn them. I had three matches hid in the draw string of my shorts. The first two wouldn't light. The third caught and I burned each sheet dropping the ash remnants into the honey bucket. When I was finished I crumbled everything into pure ashes and then washed the black tell tale clues from my hands with tea. The smoke from the burning paper blew out the window. I dried my hands and started finishing up my bullshit paper. In minutes Mickey Mouse returned with Pig Eye. I played dumb and denied all of his accusations about taking his papers. They both searched me and the entire room, even looking under the bucket, but found nothing. Finally they left. I decided I'd better stop stealing their papers. I was afraid of the consequences if I was caught.

On Friday noon the medic changed my wrist bandages and shaved my entire chest. He showed I would receive major surgery by indicating that a cut would be made from my shoulder across my chest. I told Stockdale about their plans and he advised me against letting them perform the operation if I could stop it. "They'll butcher you like they did me," he said.

I resolved to fight against the operation. After dark that night Mickey Mouse and the medic came to take me to the hospital. I fussed and fumed and refused to go saying that if forced, I would make trouble in the hospital. Mickey Mouse left for a few minutes, then returned and said, "Pack your things, you are moving to another camp." I put all of my gear into the blankets. They blindfolded me and put me into a vehicle and we began our journey. I was apprehensive about the unknown but thankful I was not going to be operated on. Stockdale's advice was the best guidance I could have gotten, I determined many years later.

THE ZOO

The ride to the new camp took about twenty minutes at a snail's pace. I could hear our progress being hampered by other vehicles; bicycles, carts, trolleys and hordes of people, all of which sounded as if they were in the middle of the street. I tried to keep track of our turns but gave up after the numerous twistings completely baffled me.

The jeep came to a halt. I could hear a guard query our driver. A gate noisily swung open and in we drove, coming to a halt in a very short distance.

Still blindfolded, I was taken from the jeep, led up a walkway and three stairs and placed in a cell where my blindfold was removed. I blinked as my eyes adjusted to the light from a bulb which was hanging through a small opening high on the front wall, close to the ceiling. I had never seen the three Vietnamese who were in the cell with me. One had a gun and obviously was a guard on patrol and making his appointed rounds. One had a set of keys. He seemed efficient and obviously knew what was going on. He gave me a mosquito net and indicated that I should sleep in the left bunk. The third man was a Vietnamese lieutenant. He had a sardonic sneer on his effeminate face and from the moment I saw him I considered him "bad news". Later on I found out that the POWs had named him "J.C.", in honor of his supreme position over us in that camp. Much later he would be known as "Dum Dum" to the POWs.

They slammed the cell door shut and locked it. I looked around at a room about 14 feet by 8 feet which had no windows and one door with heavy louvered shutters firmly fixed in place so that I couldn't see outside. There were just two small openings high on the forward and back walls to allow some air to enter.

With the cell door shut it was stifling hot and I could not feel any air entering or leaving. The cell was mosquito infested. I erected my protective net with some difficulty and took a safe position under it, away from the numerous Asian predators who were hungry for my blood. Since childhood I had learned that mosquitoes were attracted to me, so I was not surprised at the onslaught against the net. I couldn't believe the noise that their buzzing made. This must be a great place for malaria, I thought.

I tossed and turned in my new surroundings as the heat and lack of fresh air brought more discomfort with each passing hour. I couldn't wait for dawn to arrive. When it did I was greeted by a small ray of sunshine which entered through the two small openings at the top of the front wall, and which for a few brief minutes, illuminated a portion of the ceiling before moving slightly to the right and then out of the cell completely. I was left in total semi-darkness for the rest of the day, except for those brief moments when the cell door opened to bring me food and drink. It was a totally depressing atmosphere, and I was lonesome and depressed. I begged the Lord to give me the faith and strength to survive. I was having the first inklings of life in solitary confinement and I didn't relish the prospects of surviving in such an atmosphere and environment. I had a premonition that things were going to get worse. And they did.

Physically I was still in bad shape. I resolved I would do my best to help improve my condition. I've got to keep moving to survive, I thought, as I began a daily walking program. I paced the cell like a caged animal as I tried to walk myself into better shape. I found myself alternating my direction of turn at each end of the room, to help me keep my mental and physical balance. I counted each complete lap, computing I had traveled twenty-five feet. My mental gymnastics told me twelve laps equalled one hundred yards and that fifty laps was not quite one quarter of a mile. I set my initial aim at walking fifty laps between rests. It was a difficult struggle because I was still limping badly from my hip and leg injuries. I urged myself on in spite of the pain and exhaustion. I gradually worked this walking program into a daily routine and increased my goals as my physical condition slowly improved.

My left shoulder was shattered and broken at the socket and hence my left arm was almost totally useless. At first I could barely hold my empty cup. Each day I would try to raise my arm in a set of very light exercises, moving it in any direction and any amount that I could accomplish. My daily progress was infinitesimal, yet I knew I was slowly making progress so I continued my efforts for my remaining years in Hanoi. I was finding out that the human body is a magnificent self-healer.

I conducted a full scale war against the mosquitoes. By day's end I would have cleaned most of them out but at night they would replenish their numbers, and on the following day I would once again resume my battle. It was a never ending war that persisted throughout the entire year.

I had achieved my first and lasting inner solace from prayer, and as a result I began each day and ended it talking to the Lord. The silence was so oppressive that I began talking in a low level to myself in these conversations. I verbalized my frustrations by saying, "Lord, I've got to get out of here. You've got to get me out of here Lord." I made this plea so many times that it became instinctive and part of my personality to such an extent that even now, after years of freedom, in sudden moments of frustration or quickly awakening from sleep, I find myself repeating these same phrases.

Two days had passed, and I hadn't seen or heard a thing other than the key guard bringing me my food. The tropic heat was oppressive. I wasn't hungry but I forced myself to eat all the soup greens and bread provided to me twice daily. On the third day, in mid-morning, the key guard came to my cell and took me out to bathe.

The sun was high in the clear blue tropic sky dotted by a few wisps of feathery cirrus. The air rustled gently through the trees. My eyes strained in the sudden burst of sunlight. I quickly scanned the area, saw seven buildings arranged in a square around something that looked like an old swimming pool. This place didn't resemble any POW compound that I had ever seen or imagined.

The guard led me to a small shed between my building and an adjacent one, opened the door to a washing area and then locked me inside. The area was illuminated by an old-fashioned light bulb which hung on the wall. The metal connector at the base of the bulb was missing. Two wires were connected directly to the base of the filament. It was a primitive jury rig if I ever saw one, but it worked.

I was filthy. I stood under the dilapidated shower head and rinsed off under the cold running water. The brown soap was strong on my skin and lathered poorly. Nevertheless, I used it to the best of my ability and got clean, being careful not to get any of it in my eyes.

I was enjoying the effects of the cold water running down my back when suddenly I happened to look at a wooden roof beam that stretched before me. Written in some type of red crayon were the words, "Smile, Ur on Candid Camera!"

This silent message made my whole day and my spirits lifted, for I knew that I wasn't alone, and that some Yanks must be nearby. I finished my bath, washed my clothes and waited a long while before the guard came to unlock the door and return me to my cell.

In mid-afternoon I was taken to a quiz. The key guard told me to put on my long blue pajama suit which was the formal attire I wore at all interrogations. When he led me out of the cell and onto a small porch, a very short rifle guard slammed a live round into the breech. He then jabbed me in the back with the bayonet attached to the gun and pointed in the direction he wanted me to go, grunting out directions in Vietnamese which I didn't understand.

I limped and hobbled along as best I could, my left arm dangling uselessly at my side. He would gently prod me with the bayonet as he sought to get me to move faster. I ignored these urgings and went at my own pace in spite of his anger. I hope the little bastard doesn't accidentally shoot me in the back, I thought. I felt this procedure was completely unnecessary and downright dangerous for prisoner safety. In my condition, I couldn't present a threat to him or anyone.

I limped past the pool and went to a building at the northern end of the compound. The guard halted me at a door, went inside and sounded off in a loud military cadence, as he snapped to attention. He motioned me in and I faced J.C., who was sitting behind a plain table wearing a contemptible smile.

I stood at attention before him. "Boo down, boo down. You are impolite," he yelled at me. I bowed under the strain from my aching ribs and faked that it hurt worse than it actually did. He motioned for me to sit and I settled on the childlike stool at the foot of the table.

He lectured me on the importance of obeying the regulations of the camp and doing all that was demanded by the authorities of the camp. I sat mute, listening to his sing-song lecture given in poor but understandable English. My absolute silence provoked him to unrestrained anger, and he grew more excited and disturbed by the minute.

From the first moment I had set eyes on J.C. I took him to be a weak man. Now I tested my assessment and just glared and said nothing. He became furious and his voice reached a higher and higher pitch as he rambled on about the regulations of the camp. Finally he shrieked, "You are impolite. You have bad attitude. I will punish you." "I am not afraid of you," I replied coldly. "You can't hurt me any more than I am hurt right now. You can't punish me any more than I am being punished. Your own Vietnamese doctor at your hospital told me not to be afraid of the camp army men. I have not broken any regulations or done anything wrong, and I am not afraid anymore." He sat and glowered at me. Finally he called the guard who was waiting outside. "Return your room," he yelled at me. I stood, half bowed in faked pain and limped back towards my cell. I heard the guard slam the live round into the breech as he trailed behind me.

Once back in my cell I mentally congratulated myself on my performance. I've got that Gook buffaloed, I thought. I'm going to hang in tough from here on out and see what happens.

I was sitting on my bunk eating when I heard someone tapping to me from the adjacent room. He must have moved in while I was at quiz with J.C. His tapping didn't make sense and I gave up in complete frustration trying to make sense out of his raps. I remembered that Jim Stockdale mentioned that the POWs had developed their own code. I couldn't recall anything else on this matter, though I mentally racked my brain seeking an answer. Someone whistled, "Mary had a little lamb" during the siesta and I heard some Yanks passing info to one another. I couldn't make any sense out of what they were saying because I as yet did not know the names of the buildings, guards or even the POWs. They were using POW name initials to identify who was doing what and this completely baffled me. "e.g., H.J. quiz Rabbit", meant Harry Jenkins went to an interrogation with the Vietnamese the POWs had named Rabbit.

During a lapse in their conversation I yelled out the door. "I'm Commander Jim Mulligan." I didn't get a reply and became very frustrated. Finally in desperation I yelled, "You Yanks don't have a hair on your ass if you won't talk to me."

A clear calm voice replied, "Ok Commander Mulligan, keep your shirt on, we know you're there but we have more important information to pass while it's still clear to talk." It was the nicest put-down I ever got. I buttoned my lip, and mentally kicked myself for putting their communication operation in jeopardy by my indiscretion and lack of self discipline.

I was exceptionally good at Morse Code so I went to the wall and began sending A, B, C, over and over to the man next to me. I used a rap from my knuckle for a dot and a thump from the heal of my good right hand for a dash. I sent the letters A, B and C, over and over. Finally the man rapped excitedly and started to communicate with me in Morse Code. His proficiency was poor but improved greatly as we conversed slowly in this manner.

His name was John Fredericks and he was a Marine. After I gave him my name and rank he tapped to me and that afternoon passed to me the new and faster POW tap code. It was a twenty-five letter code where the letter K was omitted and the letter C was used to replace K. (Keep would be sent ceep). The box code went like this:

	1	2	3	4	5	1-1 = A	1-2 = B	1-3 = C
1	A	B	C	D	E	2-1 = F	2-2 = G	etc.
2	F	G	H	I	J	3-1 = L	3-2 = M	etc.
3	L	M	N	O	P	4-1 = Q	etc.	etc.
4	Q	R	S	T	U	5-1 = V	etc.	
5	V	W	X	Y	Z			

John told me in Morse Code to practice the new code mentally so that we could communicate more rapidly the next day. "You must learn to think in the POW code. It's important for our survival," he said before he closed off with a "good night, God bless," the traditional POW night sign-off message.

Deep in my guts I felt that it was very important that I master this new method of communicating completely. I sat for hours under the net and sent myself mental messages, tapping them out completely on the side of the bunk. I focused completely on my task and rapidly gained in proficiency. "Lord I'm so lonesome, I've got to be able to really converse with John in POW tap code by the time morning arrives," I said.

I drilled myself without let up. It was like learning the multiplication tables from the good nuns at St. Patrick's School in Lawrence, Mass., my hometown when I was a kid. I stayed awake most of the night engaged in arduous practice as I firmly implanted the new code in my mind. I wanted to be able to communicate with John Fredericks the first thing in the morning. God, was I lonesome for human companionship. The eerie silence of complete solitude was an oppressive load that bore down on me mentally like a ton of bricks. I hated each second of it, but now I had a way out. I only needed to master the POW code, and I would have the ability to join the social structure again. This thought gave me sufficient motivation to continue my practice for many hours that night.

I must have been asleep for only an hour or two when the morning wake-up gong summoned the camp to life.

John Fredericks was up like a shot and immediately tapped the "shave and a haircut — two bits," call-up sign which was the standard POW manner of initiating wall-to-wall communication. I replied with the usual two quick taps which signaled that I was ready for communication and that it was safe to communicate. John sent me a series of taps. I copied "RUOC" and didn't understand it. I sent a series of taps for a repeat and again I copied, "RUOC" from John. Damn, I thought, I must have done something wrong, this doesn't make any sense at all. John must have read my mind, for he sent slowly and clearly this message, "Are you all right?" The light dawned and I now understood that "RUOC" meant, "Are you ok?" the POWs used phonetic spelling and abbreviations for everything. I sighed a sigh of relief and tapped back, "Yes, how r u?", very pleased at my new-found ability. I had mastered the code, and I was in the system. My loneliness left me as we exchanged information during most of the day.

John filled me in on the camp. It was named the Zoo, and was a few miles from the center of Hanoi, not too far from the downtown Hanoi Hilton. He thought there were close to sixty POWs in the Zoo at this time. Cdr. Denton had been the SRO (senior ranking officer) but he had disappeared weeks ago. Col. Risner and Cdr. Stockdale were not in camp and had not been seen for a number of months. I told him Stockdale was back at the Hilton and Risner was there somewhere other than where they kept me in New Guy Village. John said, "Denton's orders were don't give the gooks anything and hang tough." I was pleased at Denton's hard line approach to resistance. He and I had served in Air Wing Seven on *USS INDEPENDENCE* in the early sixties, and though I did not know him well, he had impressed me with his leadership and flying ability. On carrier deployments, you get to size up your fellow aviators quickly even though they are in other squadrons. After a few months on *INDEPENDENCE* I classified Jerry Denton as an okay guy. I said a prayer for his well-being and hoped the gooks weren't being too rough on him.

Fredericks continued to fill me in. The camp was rectangular with a high wall along the perimeter. I was in room six of the Barn situated on the southwest side of the camp. The building alongside, and north was called the Garage. The northern camp area comprised the Gate House, offices, and quiz rooms used by the Vietnamese interrogators. The Gooks lived outside of the rectangular area but normally hung around the camp offices during their off-duty waking hours. Directly opposite the Garage and the Barn, on the other side of a real swimming pool, was the Auditorium, some quiz rooms and the Pool Hall. At the southern end of the swimming pool was the Office and the Pig Sty. Next to the Pig Sty and behind the Pool Hall, running parallel to it, was a structure named the Stable.

The POWs were well organized and had communications verbally between buildings during the siesta. They had established a guard following clearance procedure, and one side of the camp would verbally communicate between buildings when the guards were at the other side of the camp, as they made their usual rounds.

In a couple of days, Fredericks was moved out and I had no one living on either side of me, so I was incommunicado, lonesome and depressed.

The Vietnamese gave us three cigarettes a day. One in the morning after bath, one in the afternoon following siesta and one in the evening just prior to the "turn in" bell. I was a two-and-a-half pack a day smoker on shoot down, so these three cigarettes were the highlight of my day. I savored each drag as if it were nectar and smoked each cigarette down to a nub where I burned my fingers getting the last possible puff out of each one.

Though I had soap and bathed daily, I did not have a toothbrush or tooth paste. I asked J.C. for these necessities when he was inspecting my cell but he refused to supply them saying, "You have a bad attitude and are crime-in-all of wah." My teeth felt like they had hair on them. I rinsed my mouth with tea and constantly tried to massage my gums and teeth with my forefinger but this did little to relieve the discomfort that I was feeling.

J.C. quizzed me daily and for the most part I remained mute except when I demanded to be treated as a POW according to the Geneva Accords. We remained at an impasse over my quiz conduct, and complete lack of cooperation in conversation. By the day, J.C. became more furious and ended each quiz in an absolute rage threatening me with severe punishment. For my part, I hobbled pitifully to and from quiz at a snail's pace, twisted and bent in pain from my injuries. I was healing and making progress physically but the Vietnamese were unaware of the change, because I always faked my physical condition to be worse than it actually was. For my part, I was infuriated by the guard slamming home a live round in the chamber and then sticking his rifle in my back each time I went to and from a quiz. I resolved to make an issue of this procedure at the first opportunity.

On my return from quiz in late April, I found that someone had moved into room five. I initiated communication on the wall and made contact with Dick Bolstad and Bob Lilly, two Air Force POWs who were shot down and captured on the same day in November 1965. Bolstad informed me that I was the senior ranking officer (SRO) in the Barn and requested my instructions for resistance. I followed Denton's lead and told Bolstad to pass along this policy: "Resist and don't give the Vietnamese a damn thing at quiz, no write, no tape."

On May 2nd, after siesta, the key guard took me to a propaganda library located in the end cell of the Garage nearest the Barn. The room had many Vietnamese publications written in English. I was instructed in pantomime by the non-English speaking guard to read the magazines. As soon as he locked the door and left the hallway, I heard a POW contact call-up come from the adjacent cell. I gave a two rap reply and awaited the message. It said, "Hi X.O. It's Re (Ray) Alcorn, u look ok." I was stunned to hear from the man who had been my number four man in my flight division back in VA-36. What a break! I tapped furiously as I filled him in on his family, the Squadron and my own condition since his shoot down in December of 1965. Though we couldn't see each other, our emotions ran high through our knuckles as we exchanged every bit of info we could think of. The guard left me unattended for an hour or more, so we were able to fully exchange info without being interrupted or caught communicating. On return to my cell I was elated at having had contact with Ray Alcorn. Now that I knew he was alive and well, my mind was relieved of a great burden. I resolved to get his name out to the world and his family at the first opportunity.

Dick Bolstad had a wealth of information. He brought me up to date on the POWs and the various camps. He passed me the names of known POWs and I became a memory bank from that time on till my release, when I had over four-hundred-fifty POW names stored in my mind. The POW memory bank was a passion for me. I mentally went through my POW name list at least three times each day; first on wake-up, then at siesta, and finally just as I turned in for my night's sleep. I never missed a chance to pick up a new name, and I never deviated from my mental gymnastic exercise each day as I maintained or added to my list.

From the very first, the Vietnamese attempted to exploit the POW issue to their own advantage. They did everything possible to keep the number and names secret except for those instances of public exploitation of a small number of relatively senior POWs. In their attempt to divide and conquer us, they kept most prisoners in small groups of four or less, and tried to isolate these groups one from the other. A small group of seniors, who led the resistance effort, were kept in solitary confinement for years, as were a small group of junior ranking POWs, who were classified as trouble-makers and potential resistance leaders.

The Vietnamese went through a massive effort to hide POW identity and prevent POW communication networks from being developed.

There was much confusion in the American Armed Forces on the status of military air men shot down over North Vietnam. Men who were not seen to eject were thought dead, when they actually were alive and captured. Others seen on the ground supposedly safe and uninjured never showed up alive as POWs in Hanoi. In 1965 men were classified KIA (killed in action) and funeral services were held in their memory, when they were actually alive and in the hands of the North Vietnamese.

In late 1965 and early 1966, the POW classification issue became so confused that the United States settled on a uniform policy of classifying all downed aviators in North Vietnam as MIA, (missing in action).

The Vietnamese efforts to hide the identity of many POWs only clouded the issue. To add further confusion, the North Vietnamese published photos taken from American I.D. cards and claimed these men as captives, when in reality they were known to be dead.

The importance of the POW name memory bank became more of a necessity as the years went by and the number of POWs increased. I dedicated myself to this effort and thought that it was the most important thing I could accomplish. My effort was not unrewarded, for the mental exercise I went through daily helped sharpen my mind and improve my memory, as well as helped me pass the time more profitably during my forty-two months of solitary confinement.

In late April and early May, the number of raids on targets in Hanoi increased. I could hear heavy tracked vehicles being moved after each raid, and was convinced the North Vietnamese had SAM (surface air missile) sites around the immediate area of the Zoo. The guards dug one man shelters in the courtyard, surrounding the pool and took refuge in them during raids. They all shot wildly at American planes passing overhead on their retirement from the attack. The air raid warning system was so poorly developed in May of 1966, that the first inkling of a raid came from the explosions of the first bombs as they hit the ground. Often the attack was over before the air raid warning alarm was sounded. The frequency of the raids raised my morale. My captors were getting more jittery by the day as American air power kept pounding targets in their capital. The attacks seemed to come at exactly the same time each day, in mid-afternoon just as siesta was about to end. I was apprehensive about this consistency of attack time and hoped that it wasn't just a bad habit that some strike planner had gotten into.

The Vietnamese moved a new rapid firing gun somewhere close to the high wall behind the Barn. It sounded deadly as it resounded with a sharp bang at attacking aircraft. I didn't know what type it was, but it sounded different and deadlier than any other anti-aircraft gun I had heard being fired.

After three consecutive daily raids, the gun itself must have become a target for attacking aircraft. A cluster of bombs was dropped close behind the Barn where I thought the new gun was situated. The gun which was firing at a rapid rate, suddenly was silenced by the bombs dropped on it. The concussion shock wave was so close to me that I saw a ripple go completely up and down the wall like a wave on the ocean.

Ceiling plaster fell, and for a few moments I thought the ceiling and walls would all come crashing in. The guards were shouting excitedly at the nearness of the attack, and were so confused that they didn't fire at the attacking planes making their low level departure over the camp. That gun was silenced and I never heard it fire again from that position.

The raids infuriated the Vietnamese and they turned their wrath on the POWs. J.C. was almost hysterical at the daily quizzes he held. Again and again he threatened me with a war crimes trial. The Vietnamese held Hanoi sacred, and could not believe that the Americans would bomb within the confines of the city. The raids were having a bad effect on the morale of the Vietnamese officers and guards. Every one of them was tense and jumpy.

More prisoners kept arriving as the tempo of the raids increased. The Zoo was filling up to capacity so the Vietnamese began moving POWs from the Zoo to the Briar Patch, a camp located thirty-five miles Northwest of Hanoi. Ray Alcorn, one of my squadron mates was one of the first to go. For some unknown reason, the Vietnamese never sent any of the senior officers to the Briar Patch, preferring to fill it with junior ranks.

The guards were becoming ugly and began to physically abuse the POWs. Usually the key guard would forget to lock a cell door and somehow the rifle guards would find this out, and after dark enter the cell and beat up on the occupants. This type of incident had happened in the Pig Sty and Office. I decided on a policy for the occupants of the Barn to follow if they tried the same tactic on my men. My order was simple. If a POW heard the guards enter an adjoining cell at night and they started to physically abuse the occupant, the POW would shout "Bao Cao" at the top of his lungs and the remaining Barn POWs would join in.

Two days after I passed this order, I heard the guards enter Bolstad and Lilly's cell after dark. From the scuffling noises, I determined that the guards were working them over, so I immediately pounded my cell door and shouted "Bao Cao" repeatedly as loud as I could. This action caught the guards by surprise and they rushed to my cell door but it was locked and they couldn't get at me. The officers and all the guards in the camp came running to investigate the commotion. My policy had worked. The offending guards stopped beating up Bolstad and Lilly. I noticed that my voice was the lone participant in this action for none of the other POWs in the Barn joined in as I had directed. I was disappointed at their lack of involvement and assumed they were all afraid of what the gooks would do to them in retaliation. I was frightened and shaking nervously in anticipation of severe punishment for my actions. I said a quick prayer, asked for the Lord's protection, and said to myself, "What the hell, there are certain times when you just have to put your ass on the line and stick up for your rights and the rights of your men." This was one of those times. The cell door was opened by the key guard and he told me to dress in preparation for quiz.

The guards were obviously angry at me for spoiling their fun. A mean little rifle guard that we called "Toothpick", slammed a round into the chamber of his rifle and then prodded me angrily with his bayonet as he ushered me to a quiz room located at the end of the walkway, next to the Auditorium.

I entered the room, bowed, and when told took a seat on the stool in front of J.C. and the camp commander we called the Fox. I had never met Fox, though I knew who he was. J.C. railed at me for causing a disturbance and violating the regulations of the camp, and continued on for sometime with threats of severe punishment and trial if I did not change my bad attitude.

He translated each English sentence into Vietnamese in an effort to convince me that Fox did not understand English. I didn't know what kind of game they were playing, but I figured I'd go along and gave no evidence that I knew Fox was the Camp Commander and spoke English.

J.C. asked why I caused so much trouble for the camp. Deep inside I was frightened, so my trembling vocal reply was more realistic than the act I intended to put on. "I did not want to cause trouble to the camp authorities," I replied, "but I knew that the guards were not to punish the American POWs unless directed by the camp officers. As an American senior officer I knew that the Vietnamese soldiers often would exceed the authority given them by the camp commander. I said 'Bao Cao' loudly because I wanted the camp commander to be aware of the situation." I told them of the letter the Vietnamese doctor had written to the general staff on my behalf, and indicated if an American was seriously injured by the guards, that the responsibility would be placed on the camp commander. "I wanted the camp commander to know of this incident." I said as I bowed my head in fear, "I would like the opportunity to speak to the camp commander and explain to him myself."

J.C. translated everything for Fox who kept pretending his ignorance of English. After J.C.'s translation Fox gave me a verbal tongue lashing in Vietnamese as he alternately raised and lowered his voice in anger and contempt. J.C. translated everything as I sat, a pitiful sight of a physically broken and frightened man.

Then to my astonishment they didn't do a damn thing to me except send me back to my cell. The whole episode took about an hour. Back in the cell I tapped to Bolstad. "I ok, bullshit quiz with J.C. and Fox. How r u?" Bolstead replied, "TXFT help" (thanks for the help); "We're bruised but ok. GBU, (God bless you); GN (Good nite)."

I was exhausted from the strain of the night's proceedings. I rested on my bunk and gave thanks to the Lord for his guidance and protection. I reviewed the events that had occurred, and made a mental note that I would use similar tactics in the future if needed. I felt that the guards didn't want the officers to know about their extra curricular activities and that just the threats of a loud "Bao Cao" should be enough to scare them off and stop unauthorized physical abuse of the POWs. I felt good because of the small victory I had won over my captors. My victories were few and far between in this hellish environment. I relished whatever small successes I did have.

In mid-May each day, I could hear a small reciprocal-engine light plane fly back and forth over and around the camp. I couldn't see outside of my cell so I had no idea what it looked like or what it was doing. The day after my night quiz with J.C. and Fox, while I was outside hanging my clothes to dry on the bamboo fence, I saw the light plane fly overhead. It was an old fashioned bi-winged plane and it was obviously used to teach Vietnamese student pilots how to land a fast jet aircraft. The plane made a fast, shallow angle landing approach to an air strip that must have been in a field behind the Barn. They must be getting ready to transition to MIGS, I thought as I watched the plane go through its approach. I spent hours dreaming how I might escape and fly out of Hanoi if I could only get to where that plane was kept.

That afternoon, when I had finished eating my soup greens and bread the guard let me out of my cell to pick up my clothes which had dried in the hot summer sun. I had gathered everything, when suddenly from in back of the Pool Hall I heard a loud rifle shot. There was lots of shouting in Vietnamese and I could see guards and officers running helter skelter behind the Pool Hall. I could only speculate that someone had been shot and I prayed that it wasn't an American POW. I had been concerned that the Vietnamese guards always slammed live rounds into their rifle chamber when they took us to quiz. I felt sure that this unnecessary procedure would cause one of us to accidentally get shot, and I resolved to make an issue of it at my next quiz.

As luck would have it, my opportunity came the following afternoon when I was led off to another quiz. Toothpick was his usual ugly self as he slammed the round home and pushed me in the back with his bayonet. I hobbled and limped along at my own pace which only served to irritate Toothpick. He stopped in front of the quiz room, sounded off with more military bearing than I had seen him use before or knew that he was capable of, then he stood at rigid attention in the doorway as I limped towards the ever beckoning foot stool. To my surprise J.C. was missing. In his place sat Rabbit, my nemesis from earlier quizzes in room 18 back at the Hilton. Next to him sat an older man, heavy set, with bad teeth, dressed in Vietnamese army khaki, and wearing the rank insignia of general officer. I bowed and waited.

"How are you today Moo lig gun?" Rabbit asked. "I am in poor health as you can see," I replied. "My wounds are slow to heal and I am very angry that the Vietnamese officers in charge of the captured Americans permit their soldiers to risk our lives by allowing them to put live rounds of ammunition in their guns, which are held at our backs when they take us to interrogation. It is very dangerous and unnecessary, and soon there will be an accident and they will kill one of us. Only yesterday, as I was getting my clothes from the wash area, I heard a gun shot and saw many Vietnamese officers and guards run to the area. Did you kill an American yesterday over there?" I pointed in the direction of the Pool Hall.

The General didn't speak English and wanted to know what I was so upset about. Rabbit gave an abbreviated version of my concerns in Vietnamese. "Is he a general officer?" I asked. "Yes," said Rabbit. "Then tell him everything for he should know about these things."

"You lie," said Rabbit. "My guard does not endanger the lives of the American criminals." I was angry and pointed at Toothpick. "He has a live round in his chamber right now. Make him open his rifle and you will see for yourself," I said. Rabbit spoke to the General and I pointed to Toothpick and I pantomimed that he should open his chamber. Rabbit was embarrassed and furious. The General understood my effort, and said something in Vietnamese to Toothpick. He hit the bolt and a live round flew out and landed on the floor. "See, it is as I said. There is no need for this. I am wounded and cannot cause you harm. If you keep this up, your guards will kill someone. Maybe they did just that yesterday when I heard the gun go off, " I said, "bang" and pointed to the Pool Hall area with my forefinger. The General seemed to grasp what I had been saying, and he spoke in Vietnamese. Rabbit answered him with a long reply. I guessed that he was voicing my full complaints for he pointed at me, at Toothpick and at the Pool Hall area. When Rabbit was finished the General offered me a cigarette which I readily accepted. He said a few words in Vietnamese which Rabbit relayed. "He thanks you for bringing this to his attention. He wants to know if you have other concerns?"

I told Rabbit about the guards going into cells after dark, and physically abusing the POWs and explained my role when the men in the next cell were beaten by the guards. Rabbit was caught in the middle and had to translate my concerns. When he was finished the General spoke and Rabbit translated. "Only the Vietnamese officers can punish the captured American air pirates. If you obey the regulations of the camp you will receive the human treatment and will not be punished." The General pointed to the door, said a few words and Rabbit left and went next door to Fox's office. He returned shortly and said. "The Camp Commander has been informed of your concerns. Since today the guards will not put the live rounds at your back and they will not punish you without permission of the camp authorities. Do you understand?" "Yes," I replied. "Please thank the General for me." Rabbit complied and the quiz proceeded on.

The General began to speak slowly and in a low voice. Rabbit translated as he went on in words like this:

The North Vietnamese were going to conduct a progress to education program for all captured U.S. airmen. They knew that the program wouldn't be accepted by many, and they had decided that the Americans would fall into three categories.

In the first category would be a small group of men who will see the error of their ways and come to understand the position of the North Vietnamese. They would receive lenient and human treatment. They would receive good food, have time to bask in the sun and exercise. They would have a fine living area, play games, write and receive mail and might even be released and sent home to their loved ones. He said the Vietnamese knew there wouldn't be many in this group, however, there would be some.

In the second category, there would be the vast majority of the captured Americans. They would listen to the progress for education program but because of their background, they would be unable to accept the benefits of this education to social responsibility. However, the Vietnamese understood their position and would treat them humanely and ultimately release them at the end of the war.

Then there would be a third group. They were the die-hards. They would refuse to listen to the progress to education program. They would lead the others to resist this program. They would not listen. They would be obdurate. This group would be isolated from the others. They would not receive the lenient and human treatment. They would receive poor food. They would be kept in small dark rooms, alone and in shackles, and when the war was over, they would not be released. They would die in Vietnam. There would only be a small group of these die-hards but there would be some.

"It is all up to you. Only you decide which group you will join. Do you understand?" Rabbit asked. I nodded affirmatively and said, "Yes." "Soon the program will begin over the radio of the camp. You must pay attention to what we tell you over the radio. You must study, you must learn, you must think of your own situation. Do you understand?" "Yes," I replied weakly.

Having explained his mission the General smiled and, through Rabbit, asked me if I would like some coffee. I said, "Yes, thank you, but I cannot accept it for myself while the other Americans do not have any." Rabbit translated this and replied to me. "In that case all of you will get coffee tonight from him as his gift." "Thank You," I said.

The General nodded and Rabbit said, "You may return to your room but remember it is up to you to make your own choice. The treatment you receive from us only depends on you." I stood, bowed and left quietly. Toothpick didn't put a live round in the chamber and didn't even prod me with his bayonet. I had won another small victory. That night we all received coffee.

A TOOTHBRUSH

Each of my days, more or less, settled down to a normal routine. I arose at the sound of the tocsin, said my morning prayers, reviewed the POW name list, and attended to my personal bodily necessities. I performed as much light exercise as possible, and began walking laps around the room to improve my physical stamina. The key guard was active, giving out the tea and morning cigarette during this time, so tap communications were kept to a minimum until after the morning bath period was completed. Each day at bath, I washed in cold water, both myself and some clothing, being careful to remove all traces of soap from the clothes. I found out early that the Vietnamese brown soap was irritating to the skin and caused severe rashes if not rinsed completely from the clothes. Whenever I was out of my cell heading for the bath or emptying my personal toilet facility, I cased the entire camp area for signs of other POWs, and for possible methods of escape. Although the physical possibility of escape was remote, because of my poor physical condition and geographic location, I nevertheless constantly plotted methods of escape.

John Helig, a newcomer, ended up in room seven on one side of me. Dick Boltstad and Bob Lilly, the old timers, were on the other in cell five. Helig's tap comm ability was not up to speed and he, like all recent shoot downs, was very depressed. I forced him to stay on the wall and communicate because I felt he would be moved to the Briar Patch. At first he was reluctant to stay on the wall for long periods communicating, but as his comm ability improved he became more active and not so depressed. For diversion he and I challenged Bolstad and Lilly to a game that I made up, which went like this. On the first day each team would have to think of girls' names that began with A; on the second day girls' names that began with B, etc. Nicknames and abbreviations were not allowed. This contest kept us busy for many hours as we vied to come up with legitimate names. We exchanged the total each day with Bolstad and Lilly and kept a running score. As I recall it, Helig and I were the final winners having come up with two more names than our opponents did in the three and a half week contest. I had never given it any thought before so I was surprised at the number of girls' names that we managed to come up with. It was a pleasant diversion to an otherwise boring life in solitude.

John left camp one night and I assumed he went to the Briar Patch. His place was immediately taken by a human dynamo type of POW, Air Force Major Dave Hatcher. Dave was shot down on 30 May and he had all the latest news from the war front, the U.S., sports, stock market, etc. He caught me up on all the current events, and I eagerly passed the info on to Bolstad and Lilly, who in turn gave it to the rest of the POWs in the Barn.

With the advent of the "make your choice" program in late May, the Vietnamese eased up on their rough treatment of the POWs at the Zoo. Each day we would be bombarded with propaganda blaring at us from the camp radio. Each cell had a squawk box, and the Vietnamese required that we sit on our bunks and pay attention to the latest lecture in our progress to education program. We American air pirates were supposed to confess our crimes, repent and cross over to the side of the peace and justice loving people of North Vietnam. We would, of course, prove our sincerity by our deeds, and then we would enjoy the human and lenient treatment that our captors would shower upon us.

Each day after the lecture, J.C. would come to my cell and demand that I make my choice. I feigned that I couldn't understand the sound track or said the speaker's English was too poor for me to understand. In all instances, I politely refused to do anything. My policy as the SRO in the Barn was not to do anything. It was based on Denton's original order of, "no write!, no tape!"

A junior Vietnamese officer who we called "Spot", because of the burn scars on his neck and face, was studying English. He was one of the poorest English speakers at the Zoo but managed to make one of the tapes for the "make your choice" program. When this particular tape was played it was of such poor quality and content that I couldn't make any sense at all out of it. When the lecture was over, Spot came to my cell and asked if I understood his presentation. He was overjoyed when I told him that he spoke better English than the other officers and that I understood him best of all. He was elated at my lies so I bullshitted him along. Afterwards every time he made a tape, he would come to my cell after it was played and I would tell him how good it was. I couldn't believe his naivete.

In May, Fox started to separate the buildings in the camp by combination brick and woven bamboo walls. He was determined to stop all POW communications. Solid wooden doors replaced the heavy wooden French louvered doors in every building. The POWs' ability to track the guards and clear the areas for interbuilding communication was drastically reduced. By mid-June most of the work was completed and camp communications were at an all time low for us. The Barn lost communications with the Office and the Garage and we were isolated from the rest of the camp. Similar conditions prevailed between the other buildings. Just as it looked like the Vietnamese had stopped comm they would transfer a POW from one building to another, and this would immediately update all the news in camp that both buildings had acquired. The idea that their inter-building transfers were self-defeating to their communication control program, was an idea too complicated for the Vietnamese to fathom. All of Fox's efforts were going for naught. He had slowed down the POW comm network but he had not stopped it.

Dave Hatcher was a very alert and aggressive POW. If the Vietnamese left him in the quiz room alone for a few minutes, he would immediately sabotage the camp radio and tape recorder. Hatcher seemed to live a charmed life. For some reason he was always in a position to see fellow POWs and once in his view he would be able to identify them by name the next time he saw them.

In June, he reported to me that he saw Risner in leg irons living in the Gate House and that Stockdale was back in the Garage. A day later he reported Denton was living in the Pool Hall. We had the seniors back with us but we couldn't establish comm with them. Each building SRO ran his own show as the Vietnamese kept on pushing their "make your choice" program. The Barn men followed my orders and refused to do anything. J.C. became very angry at our unified acton and threatened me with severe punishment for my bad attitude.

One morning I was taken early to a quiz with J.C. He had several sheets of paper with thirty-six military questions imprinted on them. He gave me a pen and told me to answer the questions. I read them all. Some things I knew and some things were foreign to me. I never picked up the pen and just sat on the stool beside the desk. J.C. had his guard periodically report on my progress which was absolutely nothing. He kept me on the stool all day, through the morning meal, and through siesta before finally sending me back to my cell at dusk. I was tired from spending all day on the stool, but happy that my refusal to write had prevailed. My soup greens were cold, but the bread was tasty and nourishing as I savored each bite.

The air raids around Hanoi were exhilarating and raised my morale. Sometime in late June, a mid-afternoon major strike against a refinery and oil storage facility, was particularly effective. During the raid, I peeked through a small opening in the solid door that I had made with a nail I'd found in the yard while hanging clothes. With patience and perseverance, I had managed to work through an area that had been eaten by some wood boring bug. The hole was at my eye level when I stood on tip toe. It was high and out of view of the Vietnamese in the camp, all of whom were much shorter than I. My viewing area covered across the swimming pool to the Pool Hall and Auditorium. I was looking into this area when the explosions of the first bombs started a massive oil fire which hurled flames and smoke skyward thousands of feet. I was elated by the success of our attacking aircraft and immediately tapped my discovery to my POW neighbors. The news spread like wild fire through the Barn, and most men had a chance to see the fireworks by standing on the shoulders of their cellmates and peeking out the small air opening in each cell, high on the wall next to the ceiling. The attack was over in minutes but the fire and smoke raged. The Vietnamese guards were humiliated and moaned and groaned as the fires continued. About an hour after the raid, a series of tremendous explosions rocked the area. They were either caused by delay time bombs or else by massive secondary explosions caused by the oil and gas fumes. The fire took on new vigor and the smoke rose to an altitude of about thirty thousand feet before spreading out like a black umbrella, covering the azure blue sky.

This was the most spectacular display of destruction that I had ever witnessed. The Vietnamese in the camp were so embarrassed that they delivered the soup and bread to the cell doors, opening them partially so that the food could be slid into the cell without the POWs being able to see the destructive fire. The fires raged all night and glowed in the darkness. At first light I could still see the smoke rising. During the night there had been a large movement of POWs in vehicles and I awoke to find Bolstad and Lilly gone.

The camp radio announced that many planes had been destroyed in the raid and many American air pirates were captured. On the morning of 30 June, they played the Voice of Vietnam featuring Hanoi Hannah, and an interview with a captured Air Force Pilot. I prayed fervently for his well being, for I knew that the Vietnamese would vent their frustrations from this raid fully upon him. I added the name Murphy Neal Jones to my memory bank of known POWs and kept praying for him for I understood the torments they must have put him through to get him on the tape so fast.

The frustrated camp authorities began making a hard sell on the "make your choice" program. At quiz J.C. lost complete control as he screamed at me with threats of a war crimes trial. The refinery raid incensed him more than the failure of their program. After one taped program he came to my cell, took me outside and made me go down three steps and stand facing him while he lectured to me looking down at me from the top step. This was his method of intimidation, but it had no effect, and as usual, I ignored his rantings.

I was making progress with my physical exercise program but I was still in bad shape. I walked with a pronounced limp and my left arm was only a little better. My rib cage was healing but hurt when I coughed. I ate all the food they gave me, but I was losing weight rapidly. The heat was intense, and the lack of ventilation in my cell caused me to sweat profusely. My teeth were filthy. I hadn't cleaned them with a brush since the morning I was shot down. The sores on my wrists had healed leaving only some small thin scars to remind me of the pain I went through with the ropes and gasoline. I was in good spirits mentally and tried to be an effective SRO for the men in the Barn under my jurisdiction. We were all holding to a hard line and no one, to my knowledge, had written or taped anything.

Prayer played an important part in my everyday routine. Each Sunday, during siesta, I would thump the wall hard and cry out "Attention in the Barn." We would have an individual prayer service closed with a collective Lord's Prayer which we each said aloud. We ended the service by making the Pledge of Allegiance.

This group effort was the high point of each week for me. We were never interrupted by the Vietnamese guards, and I doubt if they were even aware of our action, for Sundays were stand down days for them and their security measures were at their weakest then.

Though I had good communications using the tap code, the heavy burden of loneliness assumed greater and greater proportions. I longed for human companionship as I became more and more withdrawn and introverted. I was suffering a mental pain that I never even knew existed. I constantly found my mind wandering completely in fantasic flights of fantasy about escape possibilities. I daydreamed about home and family, and slowly started to relive all the events of my past life in reverse sequence to when they happened.

I thought about my squadron mates aboard *ENTERPRISE* and wondered if they had all gotten home safely to their loved ones. In particular I wondered about the well-being of my wingman Ken Brust who had flown almost all of his combat flights on my wing. He was such a loyal and competent wingman that the other junior officers called him X.O. junior in jest, for he was always with me, like a first-born son following in the footsteps of his father. I knew my capture would be especially hard for Ken to accept, and I prayed for his physical and mental safety.

July 1st was my wife Louise's birthday, and I was sad calling to mind those times, when due to the hustle and bustle of my career, I had failed to remember it. I promised myself that in the future I would be more considerate of those important days like anniversaries and birthdays, which meant so much to her. I hadn't meant to be negligent about those little remembrances which make living so pleasant. It was just that I hadn't gotten my priorities straight, as I rushed headlong through life pursuing a successful military career. I vowed to reform; I would take time to stop and smell the flowers before life completely passed me by. Unknown to me, I was receiving the first hidden benefits from a life of solitary confinement, where for the first time in my life, I had little more to do but sit and reflect, and weigh all the actions of my past life. This is a time for personal growth, I thought. I prayed that the Lord would help me come out of the experience a better man than when I arrived. Don't ever let me forget the lessons learned in this place Lord, never, never, never!

The 4th of July was my mother's birthday, but that American holiday had no significance at the Zoo where the daily routine continued on as normal. The Vietnamese conducted a room inspection, and an officer I had never seen before or since came in and looked me over. I bowed as he entered, and stood politely at attention wondering all the while if something special was going on. He checked the room and my clothes very carefully. "Where is your toothbrush?" he asked. "I don't have one," I replied. "When did you last brush your teeth?" he continued. "On March 20th, the day I was captured." "Why did they not give you a toothbrush?" "Because the officer of this camp says I have a bad attitude and that I cannot receive the human and lenient treatment from the Vietnamese people." "You will receive your toothbrush now." He spoke to the key guard in Vietnamese, and in moments the guard delivered a toothbrush and a blue tube of toothpaste with the Vietnamese name Bac Ha inscribed on it. Also written in English on the tube were the words, "Much Bubble, Nice Taste." I thanked the officer, and bowed politely as he left, then spent the entire day brushing each tooth over and over again in an attempt to clean my filthy mouth. The Bac Ha toothpaste had a peculiar soapy taste, that in a free competitive market would have caused it to be a flop, but there in Hanoi it had no competition and was infinitely better than nothing at all.

I was concerned about the condition of my teeth as they had always been more or less of a problem for me. Because of a bad overbite, I had to have my front teeth replaced with a permanent bridge to enable me to meet the Navy's flight physical requirements.

I recalled an incident concerning my teeth that took place on *USS INDEPENDENCE* in November 1962, as that ship was on alert standby waiting for the Cuban missile crisis to wind down. I had been attached to one of the *INDEPENDENCE's* attack squadrons for two years and had befriended a Dental Officer from ship's company whose name was Joe Williams. We ate at the same table in the wardroom and often shared a drink together when on liberty. Due to a family crisis, Joe suddenly decided to leave the Navy after sixteen years of active duty. He was due out just before Christmas of 1962. One day at dinner Joe said, "I'd like to replace your bridge and all of your fillings with some special stuff that I'm working with." It was a generous offer but I was reluctant to go through that ordeal. Nevertheless, over my mild objections, he persisted in offering his services to do this work. Finally I agreed, and for a three week period he worked on my teeth, replaced every filling and installed a new bridge. When the job was completed, I thanked him. He spoke these words to me as I sat in his dental chair. "Jim you never know what's going to happen to you in the Navy. Who knows, you might find yourself a prisoner in a foreign country for a long period where there isn't any dental care. If this ever happens, you'll be damn glad I did this job for you." His words then were just a verbal aside, but as I sat recalling them in Hanoi, they took on the meaning of a self-fulfilling prophecy. I said a lot of prayers and thanks for Joe Williams' foresight and generosity over the years that I was a POW.

There was an ominous threat in the air at the Zoo on 6 July 1966. The guards performed the daily routine much faster. Something definitely was up and I wondered what it was. We ate the afternoon meal early and when the dishes were removed, I was told to dress for quiz. I put on my long khaki quiz suit and waited. Soon Spot arrived. He was excited. He and the key guard Smiley hurried me off to quiz. This was strange because usually the rifle guard took me to quiz while the key guard went about his appointed chores. The fact that Spot came with us made me all the more apprehensive. We had a saying, "Beware of smiling Gooks," and that afternoon Spot was smiling from ear to ear.

It was a beautiful day. The tropic sun was shining brightly. My eyes strained to adjust to the abnormal amount of sunlight. My windowless cell was always in semi-darkness, even at high noon, so the transition to instantaneous brightness caused severe eye strain. Spot and Smiley led me to the quiz room next to the Auditorium. I noticed that the window was closed tightly and was covered by a piece of dark blue cloth. The doorway was blocked by a large piece of the same type of cloth. Spot stood me against the outside wall and went into the room. In a few minutes he spoke in Vietnamese and Smiley pushed me into the room. It was pitch black and I couldn't see a thing. Spot took me by the arm and led me to the stool and had me sit. My eyes had not yet adjusted to the darkness and I still couldn't make out anything. As I sat Spot pushed my head forward and down. Someone lit a cigarette lighter close to the floor in front of me. When I looked down at its flame the flash bulbs went off and I knew that I had been tricked into some type of propaganda photo.

The room lights came on and I could see a group of Vietnamese, two photographers with cameras, Fox, the camp commander, J.C., Rabbit, Spot and Smiley. Fox spoke and the cameramen nodded approval. They took some more pictures and then returned me to my cell. On the way back, I saw a truck heavily camouflaged with tree limbs drive into the courtyard and park in front of the Garage. I knew something big was brewing but I had no idea what it was.

Late in the afternoon every man in the Barn was told to dress in his formal quiz long sleeve suit. The men left blindfolded two by two and were placed in trucks which filled the driveway around the courtyard. It wasn't a camp move because the POWs didn't take their sleeping mats, mosquito nets or blankets. Soon I was the only one left in the Barn. I waited for my turn, but nothing happened. An older Vietnamese officer came to my cell, pointed at my broken shoulder and said, "No you, no you." He told me in sign language to take off my formal quiz suit for I wasn't going anywhere. In a gesture of sympathy, he gave me two of his own personal cigarettes, lighted one and then left me smoking and wondering just what in hell was going on.

It was a lonesome wait for me as the hours passed slowly by. Long after the turn in tocsin clanged its signal, I heard the trucks return. The guards were excited as they hurried the POWs back into their cells. I tapped to cell five, "RUOC?" He replied, "Yes, they marched us through the streets of Hanoi and a mob beat us up. We are battered and bruised but are ok. God bless, good night."

I lay on my bunk and thought about the night's activities. Those little bastards are playing rough. I wonder if they are going to go through with their war crimes trial. Later on I found out that the only POWs that didn't go on the Hanoi March were those who were still seriously injured.

They released single photos of me and Dave Hatcher which received worldwide dissemination along with phony statements condemning the war, which they attributed to us. Back in the States, my wife and children finally found out that I was still alive.

In the days that immediately followed the Hanoi March, the Vietnamese stepped up their "make your choice" program. They began a physical torture program by taking POWs from the Zoo back to Heart Break Hotel at the Hanoi Hilton (Hoa Lo prison). There they would torture them until they got the propaganda statements they wanted, and then the POW would be returned to the Zoo and the sequence repeated by another POW. It was a vicious program.

At the Zoo I received daily quizzes by J.C., Rabbit or Spot. They demanded that I make my choice and write a confession of crimes statement like the one they tortured me to sign on my initial arrival in Hanoi. I was scared, but I refused to do anything.

My physical condition took a severe turn for the worse when I contacted dysentery. I had lost a great amount of weight even though I ate every bit of food they gave me.

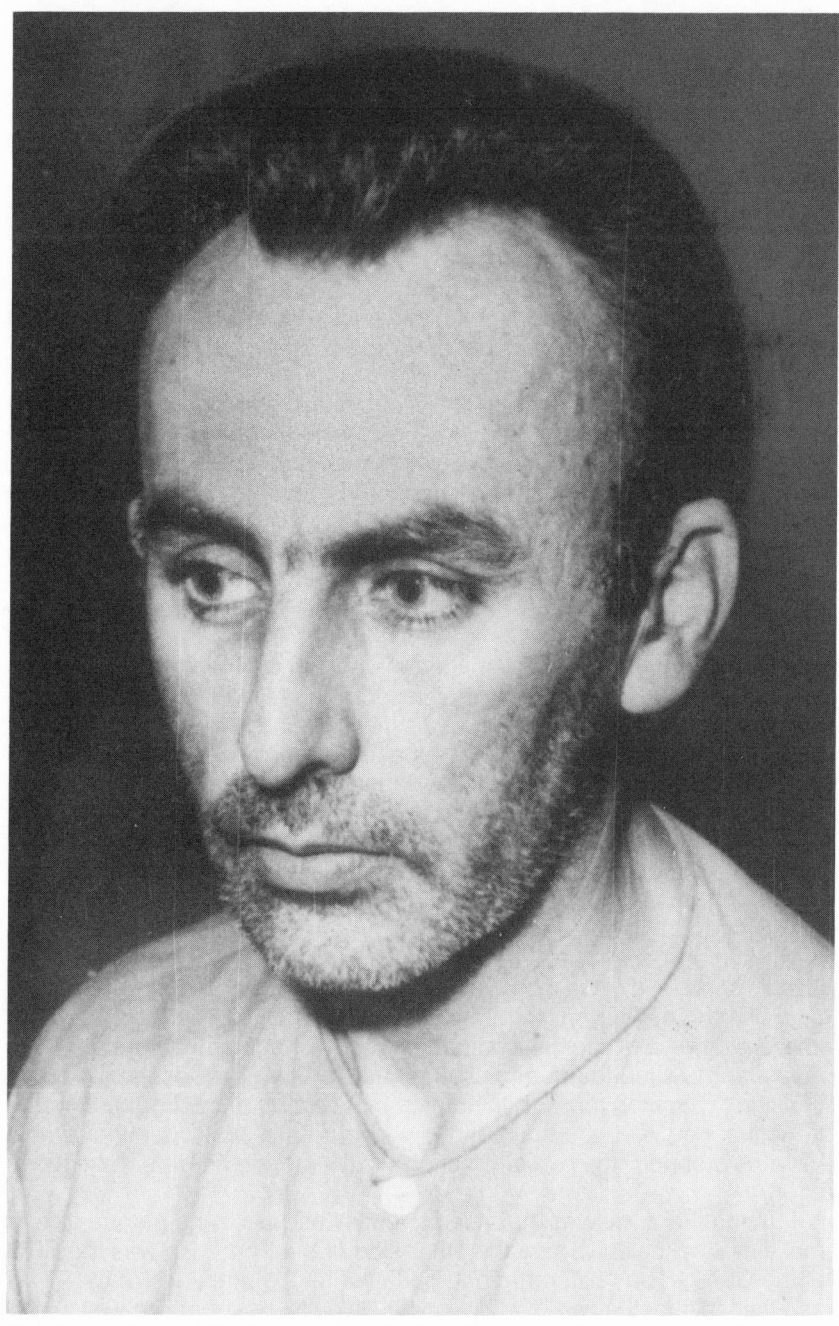

Wire photo released by Hanoi July 7, 1966 — First proof Captain Jim Mulligan was alive! Photo delivered to Louise Mulligan at the home of her in-laws in Ipswich, Mass. by Mr. Ray Maynard of the Lawrence Eagle-Tribune.

Early in July the Vietnamese stopped giving us bread with our soup and replaced it with a plateful of rice. It wasn't long before I was infested with rice worms. I constantly had diarrhea and my personal convenience bucket bubbled with small live vermin after each bowel movement. It was always terribly hot in my semi-dark cell and I perspired constantly. We didn't have any salt in our diet so the more I sweated the more dehydrated I became. I kept up my mild exercise program which mostly consisted of pacing back and forth the length of the cell. I felt like a caged animal. My world was closing in on me as I became more frustrated. The lack of daylight in my cell caused me to become more and more depressed. My eyes were strained in this environment and I began to have severe headaches. Headaches were something I had never really experienced before I was a POW.

The Vietnamese constantly had communication purges, so I had to be careful that I was not caught tapping on the wall. They considered POW communication efforts a major crime and severly punished offenders. As a result I was constantly under the great psychological pressure of the fear of getting caught at comm, yet I couldn't reduce my communication effort because of my responsibilities as SRO and because in solitary, comm was essential to the preservation of my sanity. Added to these contentions was the major Vietnamese "make your choice" program, and their threats to try me as a war criminal.

Life, to say the least, was very unpleasant for me at the Zoo in the summer of 1966. I had never developed any feelings for or against the Vietnamese as a people, because I simply had no knowledge of them or their culture. In summer of 1966, I started to build up a personal hatred for the Vietnamese that grew worse during the remaining years I spent as a POW, and which I am ashamed to say, still persists down deep in the recesses of my heart and mind.

In mid-July, they moved me from the Barn to the Garage. The Zoo was in a turmoil as J.C. lost control of his master program to move the POWs around and stop comm. For three days, the Americans were being shifted back and forth from building to building. By the time J.C. was finished, every building was fully up to speed on all the POW news, and also the news from the new shoot downs. Just when they had our inter building camp comm stopped this move negated every anti-comm measure they had taken against us. The North Vietnamese in the camp constantly amazed me with their inept moves to stop our comm. It was a trend that persisted the entire time I was in Hanoi. Just when they would have us stopped, they would make a POW move and defeat their own effort.

In the Garage I was surprised to find two Thais living on one side of me. Jim Stockdale lived on the other side of the Thais. He was the SRO of the Garage, but his comm had been cut by the presence of the Thais and the fact that the two POWs who had lived in the room I now occupied had refused to learn the tap code. I had become aware of this obstacle when as SRO of the Barn, I had comm with the POWs in room one of the Garage via a note drop in the common shower area which we had established. Stockdale had been here at the Zoo for six or seven weeks living in the Garage, but he was not able to make contact with anyone else in the camp. The men living next to the Thais were not capable of tap code communications so my effort to contact Stockdale stopped dead at their room.

Not understanding our capability to cover a long distance on common back walls they didn't see the urgency of learning to tap, and as a result they frustrated my attempts to hook up with Stockdale. I was furious when I learned of this obstacle which I considered needless and unnecessary, but because our link to the Garage from the Barn was very slow, there was little I could do to alter the situation.

At noon siesta, when I saw the Thais leave and go outside, I went to the back wall, thumped out the call up "shave and a hair cut two bits", and thumped out my last name "Mulligan". I put my ear on the wall and kept my eye on the door watching for a suspicious guard. In seconds I could hear the soft thump, "Stockdale", in reply.

Stockdale filled me in on the events that transpired at the Hilton since my departure. He confirmed that Risner had been removed from the Zoo, and most probably returned to the Hilton. I told him Denton was in the Pool Hall but that inter-building and complete camp comm had been cut, and that building SROs were running the resistance movement at the Zoo.

Our thumping comm had to carry through about twenty feet on our common back wall. It was much slower and more fatiguing than ordinary tapping, but because of the distance between us we had no other choice. I had much info to pass to Stockdale in order to bring him up to speed at the Zoo. He didn't know the names or locations of the buildings, or the names of the guards, and the names of the Vietnamese officers and their position in the camp. In addition to this info, I wanted to pass him the POW memory bank that I had acquired. The number was over one hundred and growing rapidly because of the increased tempo in the U.S. bombing effort over major target areas of Hanoi and Hai Phong. I was mentally wondering how long it would take me to get all of this info to Stockdale, when suddenly the Vietnamese solved my problem.

J.C. quizzed me on the "make your choice" program. I remained adamant in my refusal. Much to my surprise, he said, "You may think about this in your cell and I will have my guard bring you pen and paper on which you can make your choice."

I returned to my cell and shortly Smiley brought me pen, ink and some writing paper. I knew that J.C. would have Smiley count the sheets of paper so I couldn't use any of it to write notes on to pass to Stockdale. However I did have extra sheets of toilet paper which I had collected and hoarded when in the Barn because of my daily problem with diarrhea. I told Stockdale I would send him the info about the camp on notes which I would hide in the commom shower washroom that each of us used daily.

My first effort was very successful and went off without a hitch. I drew up a complete map of the Zoo, labeled it with all names of buildings,

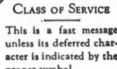

CLASS OF SERVICE
This is a fast message
unless its deferred char-
acter is indicated by the
proper symbol.

W. P. MARSHALL
CHAIRMAN OF THE BOARD

WESTERN UNION
TELEGRAM
®

R. W. McFALL
PRESIDENT   4

SYMBOLS
DL=Day Letter
NL=Night Letter
LT=International
Letter Telegram

1966 JUL 20 PM 4

The filing time shown in the date line on domestic telegrams is LOCAL TIME at point of origin. Time of receipt is LOCAL TIME at point of destination

```
.===BB055 SSC046
B SGB091 GOVT PD=TDG PWS WASHINGTON DC 20 249 EDT=
=MRS LOUISE KOLCE MULLIGAN REPORT DELIVERY=
CARE JOHN MULLIGAN 50 LAKE ST HAVERHILL MASS=
=THE SECRETARY OF DEFENSE HAS DETERMINED THAT THE BEST
INTEREST OF THE PERSONNEL MISSING IN ACTION IN VIETNAM
WILL BE SERVED IF THOSE PERSONNEL WHO WE HAVE REASON TO
BELIEVE TO BE PRISONERS OF NORTH VIETNAM ARE SO LISTED.
ACCORDINGLY YOUR HUSBAND CDR JAMES ALFRED MULLIGAN JR
04324/1310 USN IS NOW LISTED AS CAPTURED INSTEAD OF MISSING
IN ACTION. THIS DETERMINATION DOES NOT INDICATE THAT THE
NAVY DEPARTMENT HAS RECEIVED   ANY ADDITI NAL INFORMATION
```

WU1201 (R2-65)   THE COMPANY WILL APPRECIATE SUGGESTIONS FROM ITS PATRONS CONCERNING ITS SERVICE

CLASS OF SERVICE
This is a fast message
unless its deferred char-
acter is indicated by the
proper symbol.

W. P. MARSHALL
CHAIRMAN OF THE BOARD

WESTERN UNION
TELEGRAM
®

R. W. McFALL
PRESIDENT

SYMBOLS
DL.=Day Letter
NL=Night Letter
ational
Telegram

The filing time shown in the date line on domestic telegrams is LOCAL TIME at point of origin. Time of receipt is LOCAL TIM (19) .stination

```
OVER THAT GIVEN YOU PREVIOUSLY. BE ASSURED THAT IF ANY
ADDITIONAL INFORMATION IS RECEIVED I WILL COMMUNICATE IT
TO YOU IMMEDIATELY. WE REGRET THE CONTINUED REFUSAL OF
NORTH VIETNAM TO COMPLY WITH THE PROVISIONS OF THE
GENEVA CONVENTION AND TO FURNISH THE NAMES OF THE
PRISONERS BEING HELD=
VICE ADMIRA B J SEMMES JR CHIEF OF NAVAL PERSONNEL BUPERS=
```

WU1201 (R2-65)   THE COMPANY WILL APPRECIATE SUGGESTIONS FROM ITS PATRONS CONCERNING ITS SERVICE guards, officers and their descriptions. I hid it high on a beam in the shower and Stockdale retrieved it the next day without being caught.

J.C. and Smiley kept checking me daily to see if I was writing. Each day Smiley would urge me to write and showed his displeasure at my refusal when I shook a firm no to his request. He pantomimed that I would be beaten and put in irons. This gave me a clue that they were getting ready to physically torture me to make my choice.

I spent two days writing in alphabetical order the name, rank and shoot down date of my POW memory bank list. I had one hundred and five names written on one piece of toilet paper. It was completed just at the end of siesta, and I was smug in my self congratulations when suddenly I got one helluva scare. The Vietnamese pulled a room inspection that afternoon. Luckily for me they started in cell one and Jim Lamar who was in cell two was able to see what they were up to, he tapped me a quick warning of what was coming. I had no place to hide the note so I folded it in a flat square to rip up and stick in my toilet bucket but Smiley was too fast for me. He came quickly and unlocked my cell. I stuck the note under the ball of my right foot. I had my Vietnamese rubber tire sandals on when I stood and bowed as he entered. He motioned for me to stand against the wall while he searched my bedding and folded clothing. Spot and J.C. entered with two other guards and the room was completely shaken down. They checked my shorts and short sleeve shirt, including the area of my crotch and arm pits. I never moved and they never checked between the ball of the foot and sandal. It was pure luck that I wasn't caught. When they left I breathed a sigh of relief and said a quick prayer of thanks to the Lord. I passed the note in the shower the next morning and Stockdale retrieved it the same day.

I reviewed my note procedure and realized that I had been too confident and very careless. I could have been in serious trouble if that list had been discovered. Also, I would have compromised our memory bank system as well as our comm system. I decided from that time onward that I would be extra careful and train myself to think and act like a master criminal before I attempted to put something over on my captors.

Gradually I was coming to realize that time was always in the POWs' favor. Except in very rare instances, nothing was so important that it couldn't be put off until tomorrow or a safer time.

The "make your choice" program was coming to a head. J.C. punished me by not allowing me to have my daily ration of three cigarettes because of my bad attitude. For several days they fed me only before noon. When the late afternoon meal came they would keep my food up next to cell one. J.C. must have thought he could starve me into submission.

The key guards didn't like to deprive me of food, so they gave me an extra large plate of rice in the morning on their own. On the fourth night of this starvation program they brought me my cold soup and rice after the turn-in tocsin had rung. I ate a couple of spoonfuls of rice and then in disgust and anger dumped the remaining rice and cold soup into my toilet bucket. The guard was very upset but there was nothing for him to do except take the empty plate and bowl and lock me in for the night.

He must have felt sorry for me because before he left he gave me a cigarette and light. I sat on the edge of the wooden bunk and savored each drag. The sudden effects of the smoke had made me feel light headed and helped to reduce the hunger pains which I was just becoming aware of. I didn't know it then but that was the last cigarette I ever smoked or ever hope to smoke.

THE HUNGER AND THIRST ORDEAL!

I had bathed and washed my clothes and was back in the cell, sweltering in the intense heat wave that was settling over Hanoi. Smiley came and unlocked the door and told me to dress as I would if going to a quiz. To my surprise, instead of leading me off to quiz, he made me wrap up all the gear I had in my sleeping mat and then led me off heading in the direction of the quiz rooms. The move was so sudden I didn't have an opportunity to alert anyone that I was being shifted from the Garage. Stockdale will find out soon enough when I don't respond to his comm call up after the siesta begins, I thought silently as I hobbled along behind Smiley.

He took me to the Auditorium and I had a premonition that this was bad news. Some info had filtered back from the Hanoi Hilton concerning bad treatment in the Auditorium. The message flashed through my mind, "Be careful in the Auditorium, they keep the poison in the water jug." Dave Hatcher had gotten this and passed it to me many weeks earlier. My pulse increased in anticipation of what was to come.

Smiley opened the cell door to a room that was absolutely filthy. The floor was covered with rolls of dust and dirt. Cob webs hung everywhere and were strung in all directions. I entered into a cloud of mosquitoes that had taken flight after being disturbed by the oncoming light, the opening of the door and possibly by the smell of an incoming human victim.

On the left wall there was a barred window covered so completely by a thickly woven reed shield that it allowed almost no daylight to enter. A wooden pallet, to be used as a bed, was flat on the floor next to the right wall. Just behind it, close to the far wall, was an uncovered portable toilet bucket, ninety percent filled and crawling with hundreds of maggot-like worms. Next to it, turned upside down resting on the floor, was a half rusted out cover.

Smiley had me put my gear on the pallet. As I completed this task and stood erect, he suddenly turned on me in anger. He gave me a blow to the chest and shoved me hard against the wall. I doubled over in pain and began to cough and couldn't stop coughing. Each cough increased the pain and tears came to my eyes. My mind was slowed, and I couldn't figure out what this was all about. Smiley had no stomach to cause me any more pain. Though crippled, I had always tried to expedite my wash routine so that I would not be a hindrance to him in the accomplishment of his daily chores as the POW turnkey. He was aware of my effort and had shown some sympathy towards my poor physical condition.

He recognized my plight, and made no further physical effort against me. Instead he watched as, doubled over, I continued my coughing fit. I was hurting bad and he knew it. As I looked at him I felt he had regret for his actions which were the cause of my misery. Nevertheless, he reprimanded me in Vietnamese, pointing his finger and using tones that obviously were meant to display his displeasure.

He pointed to the pallet, slammed the door and left. The room went pitch black and I couldn't see a thing.

My coughing fit under control, I slid down exhausted on the pallet, resting my head on the reed sleeping mat which contained my gear. The mosquitoes buzzed around my head and began to attack but I paid them no heed, and I lay suffering on the wooden pallet. They were only an annoyance, though they were feeding on me voraciously.

Suddenly the light flashed on, the door was unlocked and in walked J.C. followed by Smiley. "Moo lig gun you have violate the regulations of the camp. You resist us. You do not make your choice. You are obdurate and refuse to confess your crimes and to see the error of your ways. You are a bad man. You will not receive the human and lenient treatment from the peace and justice loving Vietnamese people. I punish you and you must stay here in this place to think things over so that you may see things more clearly."

He pointed to my water jug. Smiley picked it up and followed J.C. out of the cell, then returned with a filthy looking water jug and set it down near the door. He turned, left, closed and locked the door. The cell went back into absolute darkness.

"So that's it," I said softly to myself. "The little bastards are tired of playing games, and now they are going after me for real." I have to think. I've got to get my composure and decide on my own method of attack. I've got to resist them even if it kills me. I'm half dead now so it won't really make any difference. I've got to take a stand for my rights as a human being. Even if no one else will ever know or even care, I know and I care. This is a moral question and I know what my moral obligations are, and I'll die for them right here in this filthy infested cell if I have to. Damn these Communist bastards. They are all the same. They have no respect for the rights of the individual. Ultimately that's what this damn war is all about, even if the world press calls it a war of national liberation. In the end, it's nothing more than a war of national enslavement, but I won't be a part of it. I'll die first, and at least I'll have my own self respect. It would have been a helluva lot easier if the damn ejection seat had never worked. But it did, and I'm here, and I'll see it all the way through to the end. These thoughts were running through my mind as I sought to assess my new predicament.

I brought myself up short and back to the immediate world of reality as I now found it. "I've got to get myself squared away in this filthy black cell as best I can and then I'll develop my resistance plan," I half mumbled to myself.

By sense of feel I unrolled the mat. I felt my mosquito net and my drinking cup, toothpaste, brush and soap and the socks I had on when captured which somehow I had managed to keep along with my torn American skivvies. My blanket and a full set of clothes were out in the sun airing and drying from the earlier morning wash. I wondered if I'd see them again.

I was wearing everything else I owned; shorts, blue T-shirt, full dress blue long pajama suit, top and bottom and my rubber tire sandals which the POWs had named "Ho Chi Minhs" in honor of that dogged Communist leader.

Though my eyes had fully adapted to the darkness and although it was almost high noon, I could not really make out the outline of the walls. A little light entered under the door but the opening was so small that it only affected a small area close to the door. If nothing else this made the rest of the cell seem darker.

The first thing I seized upon as a necessary objective was to relieve my bladder and bowels. I removed my long sleeve quiz suit and made my way in the general direction of the honey bucket. With great difficulty I managed to find it, position myself and after some degree of difficulty accomplished both objectives. When completed, I eased on the rusted out top as best I could and slid the bucket as far into the corner away from my sleeping pallet as possible. Just the thought of the crawling maggots was enough to send shivers down my spine.

I made my way back to the pallet, and felt for the net. Fortunately, I had a long piece of twine tied at each corner so I was able, with great difficulty over a long period of time, to tie the net to the bars over the window in a makeshift jury rig that went back to the far corners of the pallet. This enabled me to erect the net, in a half-assed fashion, raised fully on one side of the pallet sloping down to the floor on the far edge. It was the best I could do with what I had. I took refuge under the sloping net and reclined in exhaustion to think over my situation.

It was past noon already and I hadn't been fed. I hadn't eaten a meal for more than twenty-four hours, and then not too much. My stomach gnawed with hunger but my personal anger at the Vietnamese was so intense that I ignored my stomach's calling. "Screw you Gooks, I don't need your food. I won't eat anything. I'll just fast like Ghandi did and lie here to conserve my strength. Besides if I don't eat anything, I won't have to use that maggot infested bucket." I saw this as a bigger threat than hunger as I rationalized aloud to myself.

It was intensely hot in the cell. A tropical heat wave had fully set in after gradually building up for days. I resolved to reduce my movements to an absolute minimum and I alternately sat and lay under the raised part of the net. I thought about the message concerning the poison in the water and resolved that I wouldn't take one sip out of the filty water jug that they had left in place of my own. "Maybe they drugged the water," I conjectured.

My strategy for resistance was established in my mind. Eat nothing, drink nothing, do nothing. Just think and resist and pray for strength and guidance. "Lord, I'm in your hands completely! Thy will be done."

I was uncomfortable as I stayed under the net. It was stifling hot, it was very dark, and it was depressing. I alternated my position from time to time. First I'd lie flat on my back fully stretched out, then I would pull my knees up and put my heels close to my buttocks, finally I would sit up and lean my chest against my knees and wrap my arms around my legs to maintain my balance and take some of the effort out of sitting up without a back rest.

A smiling guard brought me rice and a bowl of soup late in the afternoon. The light came on and I saw him set the food down next to the filthy water jug. I remained under the net protected from the numerous mosquitoes that were buzzing around as a result of his disturbance. The guard went out and returned with my blanket and the rest of the clothing which I had washed that morning. He threw them in a ball next to my net, closed the door and locked it. Once again the cell was plunged into complete darkness.

I leaned out from under the net, groped for the blanket and clothes, and finally was able to retrieve them. I folded the blanket as best I could, rolled it into a pillow and placed the other clothes on top of it as a pillow case. I was more comfortable than before, and I laid back and dozed off, ignoring the food that sat in the darkness at the end of the room.

I awoke when the light came on. The smiling guard came in to retrieve my empty dishes. He was surprised and upset to see that they were untouched. I kept still under the net and ignored him completely. In seconds he had gathered up the soup bowl and plate of rice and left muttering incoherently in Vietnamese. Just before the cell was plunged back into darkness I noticed that he had left the dirty water jug in the same position that it was originally in. The jug puzzled me. It seemed like a threat.

I knew I could withstand the hunger but thirst was something else. I can't touch it, I thought as my mind sought to solve the riddle of the poison in the water. I prayed for strength and relaxed completely flat on my back in a directed effort to fully conserve strength and energy. Then I really concentrated and thought out as completely and rationally as I could the defensive posture I had decided upon. How long could I last without eating? Probably ten to twelve days if I really kept myself prone or just sitting most of the time. How long could I go without water? Maybe five or six days, but I would have to be careful about losing control of my mental faculties. What effect would this have on my overall physical condition? Not much because my weight was already down to one hundred pounds or less. What could the Gooks do? Not much because physically I was still so bad off that any major effort to physically abuse me would either kill me or send me back to the hospital. I thought they would not know what to do at first, and wouldn't risk hurting me more. "If I get through the first three days I've got them licked," besides I had let every Vietnamese Officer know about the letter their doctor wrote to the General Staff concerning my condition when I first went to the Hanoi hospital. I had a gut feeling that this letter had raised hell with Mickey Mouse and the others involved, and that they would be wary of doing anything drastic. "I have just got to have the guts to see it all the way through to the end. If I lose I'll die, or they'll get what they want, but I can at least say I did my best and put my own ass on the line for what I believed in."

So that was it. The decision was final. I raised my heart in prayer and asked the Lord to sustain me in my effort against my enemies. I offered up my suffering for those human failures of my past life, and I turned myself over to Him. "You've got it Lord. You suffered alone for your beliefs so you know what I am about to go through here in the darkness and heat, all alone. Please Lord, help me!"

I tossed and turned all night under the slanted mosquito net covering me. My hunger pains suddenly vanished completely just when I thought I couldn't stand them any more. I felt relieved for I had read somewhere that after thirty-six hours of fasting you were over the hump as far as hunger pains were concerned, I was sure this time frame would differ from individual to individual, but I felt that as far as I was concerned I had conquered the hunger pains and from here on out they would be one less element I would have to be concerned about. I was correct in this assessment.

The thirst was something else. Though for the most part I was prone on my back I occasionally sat erect with my hands and forearms wrapped around my legs for balance. I had sweated profusely the first few hours. The cell was a veritable hot box. It felt like a closed-in attic at noon in the middle of summer. I called on every bit of self control, and tried to relax completely and breathe slowly and deeply, so that I would not cause myself to suffer any further anxiety from the oven-like heat. I thought about the British Colonel in the movie, "Bridge Over The River Kwai" who was buried up to his neck in sand and kept in the sun by the Japanese as they tried to break him down. I recalled how his men cheered when he held on and the Japanese finally gave in and returned him to them. Win or lose, there won't be any cheers for me, I thought. No American knows where I'm at or what's happening to me or what I'm doing. But that doesn't make any difference, I know and the Lord knows and that's all that really counts. It gets down to a simple question of personal integrity and moral character. Do I have the moral character to see this thing through? Do I have the personal integrity to suffer for what I believe is right? I answered an unqualified yes to both of these queries. I thought more about the story of the "Bridge Over The River Kwai" and it seemed to make my own condition easier for me to accept. I resolved to fight to the end. My mind wandered and I tossed and turned as I slept, while the hours dragged by.

The ringing of the morning wake-up gong jolted me from my reverie. I had a sudden strong urge to urinate, so I dragged myself out from under the net and made my way by feeling along the wall towards the bucket I knew was in the far corner. I groped in complete darkness and finally found it, removed the rusted cover and strained terribly for relief. I managed to finally produce several drops of fluid and felt relieved. I must have been almost completely dehydrated. I placed the cover back on the stinking can and finally got it to fall into place, and then I worked my way back to the net and pallet and resumed my supine position.

It was still hot and I felt dirtier than ever, having crawled through the dirty floor and cob webs to use the maggot infested bucket. The cell was pitch black so I relaxed in complete oblivion to my surroundings, and went through my morning prayer ritual. Then I followed this effort by repeating all the names in my memory bank, and reviewing all the information I had on the POWs and the camps that I knew about. I was meticulous in my review. I had long ago decided that the maintenance of my mental faculties could be a major problem that would result from long term solitary confinement if I did not do anything to counteract the utter loneliness that I constantly felt. Drill repetition improved my retentive powers and helped me develop my powers of concentration. I was slowly teaching myself to memorize all meaningful data accurately and rapidly. Putting things in some form of order helped me speed the memory process, so I developed time frames and alphabetical listings which I used as a frame of reference to fix the data firmly into place. Once I had some fact or name in place and mentally referenced, I kept the info current by constant repetition in my daily reviews. I was learning to use my mind more efficiently and effectively than I had previously. My very survival depended on it.

The smiling guard interrupted my mental gymnastic exercise when he turned on the light and brought me some soup and rice, which he left on the floor near the cell door far out of my reach. He looked at me, pantomimed that I should eat and left. The light went out and I was plunged back into darkness.

I noticed he had not replaced the feared dirty water jug, and that convinced me more than ever that they wanted me to drink whatever was in it. I had no hunger pains so the food presented no threat to my resistance plan. My mouth was dry but the fear of poison in that water jug easily overcame my thirst. I stayed on my pallet, reclined and offered up my sacrifice to the Lord as a means of obtaining increased faith. "Lord grant me increased faith, give me everlasting hope and teach me perfect love so that I may one day return to the free world a better man than when I came here." I prayed, talking to myself audibly, as I raised my thoughts to a higher world. It must have been late mid-morning. I could see some light at the base of the crack under the door. The daylight made a small outline of the blocked up window clear enough so that I knew what it was and where it was situated. The rest of the cell was in total darkness.

"This must be the Vietnamese hot box and dark room," I reminisced thinking about the escape and survival training I had received at the POW school in Brunswick, Maine. I remembered when I was there one of the "enemy" guards had put me in a small coffin-like box they had half buried in the ground. Though I was cold I fell asleep for several hours. Someone goofed and they forgot I was closed up in the box. They finally missed me from the group I was assigned to and initiated a frantic search. I awoke from my sleep to peer up at a guard standing above the raised lid and shouting, "Here he is, here he is. You ok Commander? Get up out of there." "I'm ok," I replied, "I'm just a little cold." He took me to an interrogation room where he let me warm up and thaw out. One of the camp officers came in, gave me a cup of coffee and apologized for keeping me so long in the closed coffin. "That's ok," I replied, "I know the course ends in two more days. It was good training. Besides I know you won't let anyone go too far in this academic situation."

The Vietnamese didn't have the same restraints that existed in the Brunswick School but they probably didn't want to kill someone they had kept alive for so long. I kept calm, and maintained absolute control, resisting to the absolute limit of my endurance. I'll aim for seven full days. If I don't eat or drink anything for a week, they will know I'm serious and they just may quit trying to get me to write.

I was determined I would not "make my choice", that I would not write my "confessions of crimes" and that I would not write a biographical history which was the latest demand they had laid on me.

It was quiet. From outside the window I heard a guard sound off like they did when they delivered a POW to quiz. I heard some mumblings which I couldn't make out. Then I heard a clear "slap" and an irate Yank say loudly, "You sonofabitch, what the hell did you do that for?" "You are impolite," a Vietnamese whose voice I didn't recognize heatedly replied.

As hard as I tried I could not make out what they were saying. Once in a while I heard a clear "no", so I figured the Gooks were still pushing all their propaganda programs on the POWs. I fervently prayed for the safety and well being of all the POWs. We had a common bond for we all tried to live by the Code of Conduct. I felt close to the many men I had been in comm with even though I had never actually met them or seen them for that matter. I wondered about Fredericks, Stockdale and Dave Hatcher, Helig, Lamar, Bolstad, Lilly and the others. Mostly I wondered about Alcorn and Denton, the only two men I'd know if I saw them. Lord, I sure hope I get a cellmate one of these days. Wouldn't it be great if he was either Alcorn or Denton! Not much chance of him being Alcorn, for "Baby Ray" had left the Zoo and was probably at the Briar Patch. I lapsed into sleep once again and the time wasted by.

After the siesta wake up had been sounded on the tocsin, the smiling guard returned to get my dishes. He saw they had not been touched and had a puzzled look on his face as he left. I stayed under the net motionless and ignored him completely. A few hours later he returned with more soup and rice and put them down next to the insidious dirty water jug. He left and the cell returned to complete blackness. Even the dim light that seeped through the covered window was gone. I couldn't see a thing, but I was not afraid or even mentally depressed. I was mentally alert and responding to their challenge. My mouth was as dry as a cotton ball and my lips were cracked. I had the urge to urinate badly so I made my way blindly to the bucket but was unable to produce any output. I went back to the net and reclined on the pallet. Even though I had not actually relieved myself, I felt better. The urge went away and I decided to ignore any similar physical sensations. I'm dry, my kidneys are just getting confused from the lack of fluid, it's all mental, I calculated.

The guard came to remove the dishes but left them in the same position when he saw that the food was untouched. I maintained my resistance posture, stayed under the net and languished the hours away mentally reminiscing about home and family. I wondered where Louise and the boys were living. I had left them in Jacksonville, Florida but figured they would have moved from there by now. The heat and humidity of that city's climate had not been too appealing and the boys did not have roots there as we arrived in that area only in February of 1965.

Virginia Beach! I hoped she had moved back there to that lovely climate and its beautiful beaches. Louise and the boys and I had spent our happiest years there. Often we spent the entire weekend on the Navy beach at Dam Neck. The boys loved the water and the waves and surf fishing. Now they were into surfing so that would make Virginia Beach even more attractive. Louise will move back to Virginia Beach! She and the boys had many friends there so it would make life easier for them. Yes, Virginia Beach would be where I'd find her whenever I left this God forgotten place. I daydreamed for hours of the wonderful times we had. I yearned for the comforts of my wife and the love of my children, as the hours passed by. Three full days had gone by since I had eaten anything, and more than two days had gone by since I last had anything to drink. I spent a restless night dreaming, reminiscing and mentally wandering in all directions except during those brief moments when I was either engaged in prayerful reflection or else going through my memory bank drill procedures.

The long night over, I awoke to the clanging of the primitive Oriental alarm clock. It was my third day in the Auditorium, and the heat was more intense than ever. I said my morning prayers and went through my usual mental drills. I was feeling strange. I was much weaker physically as my mind flittered from one fantasy to another in uncontrolled hop scotch like jumps as I thought of home, escape, my family, my friends. My body and mind were beginning to revolt in earnest at my total fast and complete abstinence from water. The darkness of the room closed in on me completely as I alternately sat and lie down under the womb-like protection of my mosquito net. It was damnably hot and I was completely miserable in my surroundings, yet I remained resolute and steadfast in my resistance effort. No eat, no drink, no write. The hours dragged by as I rested in a stupor waiting for something to happen. I wondered if the Vietnamese were aware of my actions. Will they let me go all the way? Can I hold out until I'm past the point where it won't make any difference? Lord, give me the strength and the guts to see this thing through to the end, one way or another. No one else knows Lord, but you and I know, and that's all that's necessary. You suffered for your beliefs, and I must suffer for mine. Right is right if no one's right: wrong is wrong if everyone's wrong. In my action am I right or wrong, Lord?

The light flashed on and the door flew open. I must be losing control for I didn't even hear the guard undoing the latch bar or opening the lock. He looked at the food and looked at me but made no sign one way or another as he scooped up the bowl and plate and left bolting the door behind him. The lights went out and I retreated mentally to the safety of my self-constructed womb. I thought about what was different at this latest entry. Finally it came. He didn't smile, he just looked, like he was puzzled and not sure of what was going on. Damned inscrutable Orientals, they're hard to figure. They don't think like Westerners. But he was serious and he was worried. Maybe he's afraid he'll be the fall guy for the officers if something happens to me. He's in the middle. He loses no matter what happens to me. They blame him if I win, they blame him if I die. Poor little Gook guard, he's a loser no matter what.

He was back in an hour with soup and rice but I ignored him as before and stayed under the net, protected. In the short time the light was on I could see that I had a rash of spots blossoming on the back of my hands and lower forearms. I tingled and my skin itched. I felt dirty and crawly and my opened pores stunk. Lord, I'd like a bath. At that time the most important thing in the world to me would have been buckets of cool clear water cascading down over my head and body.

Late in the afternoon he checked my food and left it there as he had the day before. I passed a miserable night romping from one nightmare to another until morning came and the tocsin rang again.

Four days gone by. I was much weaker. My throat was sandpaper dry. My lips parched and cracked. My tongue thick and numb. My body cried for water yet the fear of what was in that dirty jug overcame my thirst. I resisted the drive of thirst by a stronger drive of fear. How much longer could I last before crazed thirst would overcome all.

It would be soon. Maybe I can go two more days, but I'm losing my sanity now. Maybe I'll be insane in two days. Maybe I should quit now, no one will ever know. It would be so easy! But I can't, I can't. I must hold on. Oh Lord, how in hell did I get into this mess. It's that damn war that nobody wants to win. It's been a lousy war right from the start. It was the best kept secret in the country, especially the six months before the national election. They crucified Goldwater as a war monger and elected LBJ as a responsible leader. Hell, even I believed him and voted for him, then I found out it was a sham. "Cool Vietnam talk until after the election", he told the military, and they did. Now that he's safely in, LBJ is twisting the Communist arms like he twisted arms when he was the Senate Majority Leader. But arm twisting won't work on the Communists, and by the time he finds this out he'll have lost his hat and ass in Vietnam. Barry had the right idea, blow Hanoi off the map. The only thing those Communists bastards understand is force.

But even that action wouldn't change the war from its "no win" atmosphere. I recalled the Newsweek Vietnam Correspondent Francois Sully's talk with me back in my room on the ENTERPRISE earlier in the year when my squadron hosted him as he covered the carrier air war for Newsweek. "Jim, the U.S. is losing this war and the only way you can win it is to march North of the 17th parallel and occupy North Vietnam, but the U.S. won't do this because China might come in as it did in Korea. The jungle is killing the U.S. like it killed the French and on top of this Vietnam is more a political upheaval than a military venture. In the south, "Charlie" controls most of the land except for the bigger cities. You yourself have led your planes on bombing raids in the south from Cape Cameau to the DMZ line at the 17th parallel so you know what I say is true."

Sully was right, the war was a mess. I recalled the Special Forces Sergeant who had spent his R&R visiting his Navy brother on the ENTERPRISE early in February 1966. A professional soldier in his mid to late thirties, he told me that on the ground, the Special Forces were taking a helluva beating because the VC were using women, kids, and old folks as well as their regular forces. The whole damn countryside was booby trapped, and the U.S. was suffering high casualties. They would suffer many more as the number of green troops were brought into the area. On top of this, the South Vietnamese army didn't show much professionalism. They were in the field from Monday through Friday and then took the weekend off. Without their U.S. advisors, they were almost worthless and for the most part had little stomach for the war. They expected the U.S. to do the brunt of the fighting, and take the majority of the losses. Besides, most of the ground forces and their leaders didn't share any enthusiasm for the Air Force General Ky who was the latest in a long list of U.S. installed and supported South Vietnam leaders. "No matter how you cut it, the whole damn war is a fiasco from start to finish and doesn't make any sense at all to the men in the field," he concluded.

"And don't forget Symington," I mused as my mind wandered back to ENTERPRISE and the reflections of the war I had personally gained or had been exposed to. Senator Stu Symington was not stupid. Early in 1966 he toured South Vietnam and was going back to Washington to report his findings to LBJ. He stayed on ENTERPRISE and I was scheduled, with some other Commanders, to have dinner with him but an unexpected change in the flight schedule prevented me from returning in time to attend the dinner. I liked Senator Symington and was upset that I missed the dinner. I asked CDR Dodge McFall what transpired and he replied, "Symington says he's going back to tell LBJ that the war will last at least five more years and maybe even longer than that." "You know that's about the way it looks to me," I replied. "The whole damn thing is turning into a can of worms."

The light came on in my cell and the door opened. My reverie was interrupted and I returned from my world of fantasy about the war back into the ugly world of reality under the mosquito net in the Auditorium. My skin felt funny. I looked at my hands and forearms and they were covered with hundreds of little yellow dotted pimples. My mind wouldn't focus properly and the guard left with my food dishes and turned off the light before I had fully realized where I was or what was going on. It was pitch black again and I returned to my world of mental existence, half awake, half asleep, half dreaming and nearly half dead.

I tried to go through my POW list, but I couldn't concentrate. My mind was like a runaway film strip flashing senselessly in a blur on the screen. "Hold on, don't quit," I was fast approaching the end of my resistance plan. I could hardly remember why I was here or what I was resisting.

Time meant nothing, only events. Lights on, open the door, bring in food, leave, lights off. Twice a day. The rest nothing. Just blackness and fear and anger and frustration all rolled into one big ball, which was me. And I wasn't even sure of who I was.

Later that day he came again and left almost unnoticed as I fell deeper into my stupor. Sleep, precious sleep. It didn't hurt so much when I was asleep. My mind seemed to enjoy my dreams while asleep more than it did my flights from reality when I was awake. It was a topsy-turvy world and each minute it got further and further beyond my control. I was getting to the ragged edge, and I wondered how much further I could go before I couldn't stand it any longer.

Day slid into night and I couldn't tell the difference. My ears were ringing an eerie melody that shut off all the usual noises of human activity that emanated in the camp outside my cell. The night was long and restless, but body weakness was an overpowering fatigue which overcame mental activity and lulled me into uneasy sleep. Sometimes I awoke with a start and lay there flat on my back wondering for moments where I was or what was happening. Then my mind would slowly react, and it would all come back, and I would leave my dream and join the agony of my reality and then I'd fall asleep again and almost hallucinate half way between my physical and mental nocturnal world.

The night passed on and my level of response had become so low that I missed entirely the morning wake-up gong, or the usual noises that permeated the camp after it had been rung.

I didn't see the light or hear the door. I awoke flat on my back looking up into two blurry Vietnamese faces hovering over me and speaking to me in Vietnamese. One was the smiling key guard, the other frocked in a long white coat was the camp medic.

They helped me to my feet and I stood unsteadily. The medic examined my eyes and looked at the hundreds of little red pimples with yellow tips that covered my entire body. The food from the previous late afternoon meal was in the corner next to the filthy looking water jug which contained the poison. The smiling key guard left the cell and returned with my own water jug filled with hot tea. He poured some into my cup and handed it to me.

It was day five and I was now at the end of my rope. I took a swig and let it roll around my sandpaper parched mouth before it trickled down my throat and wound its way through to my stomach. I followed its progress as each part of my tormented body cried for liquid. I grew weak and light headed, almost to a faint, so I slid down and sat on the pallet still grasping the cup of tea. My body tingled from head to toe as I slowly drank more tea. I finished the cup and asked for more and repeated the process from my sitting position.

My body seemed to come completely alive. I had the sensation of being able to feel every organ and every inch of flesh, that, lumped together, was me. The tea seemed to touch my finger tips as it flowed through my body. It was as if each of my cells was responding and crying out for liquid and somehow knew it was coming, yet couldn't wait. I tingled through my entire body as if I was receiving a mild continuous electric shock. I was coming alive again, my mind was clearing and I became afraid. I had lost the battle. I only held out five days and now they would bend me good and get what they wanted.

The medic left and the key guard had me put on my long pajamas and led me off to a quiz in the corner interrogation room just across from where I had been kept in the Auditorium.

I entered to find Rabbit and Spot seated behind the desk. I bowed and on command sat down on the small stool in front of them. "How is your health?" Rabbit asked. "It is bad," I replied. "I get no protein or fresh fruit so I think I have scurvy. My skin is covered with infections from the bad conditions in the place you keep me. I have not washed for six days. I am probably going to die if conditions do not change soon. You must tell that to the camp commander."

We will give you soup with meat broth and bananas, will you eat them?" said Rabbit. "Yes," I replied meekly. "Good, then return to your cell, eat the food we provide you and then I will permit my guard to take you to wash. When you are done you will be moved to another cell in the camp."

I sat on the stool waiting for him to demand that I "make my choice" and write my confessions of crimes and a biography. They looked at me but didn't speak.

Finally I asked, "May I return to my cell now? I feel sick." Rabbit replied, "Yes." I stood shakily and bowed, said, "Thank you," and left, guided by the smiling guard who led me back to my cell.

He closed the door but left the light on so I sat on the pallet and drank more tea. Then it dawned on me. I had won! I had beaten them! I had not written and they hadn't even asked me at the quiz. I was emotionally drained and in my Pyrrhic victory I sobbed uncontrolledly and thanked the Lord for standing by me during my hours of need. I drank more tea and with each sip I felt better, and my mind cleared as reality completely replaced the mental fantasy that had over powered me those past few days.

The guard brought me a bowl of meat gravy rice soup and a banana. I ate everything, savoring each spoonful and bite. It felt great to be alive. With the light on in the cell, the heavy oppressive burden of total darkness was removed. I felt it was more the darkness than anything else which pushed me into the claustrophobic mental fantasy of the past five days. With the light on, I could relate to my immediate surroundings and this brought me back to a mental stability, which had been lacking during my resistance effort.

It was high noon when the smiling guard took me to bathe in the Pool Hall bathing area. I stripped completely and stood in the hot tropic sun naked as a jay bird pouring bucket after bucket of clear cool water over my head and body.

Physically, I looked a mess. My entire body was covered with those ugly pimples. I guessed they were the result of no liquid for five days. I rubbed the primitive brown soap over my entire body in a weak lather and scrubbed and scrubbed and scrubbed. I washed my clothes and left them on the bamboo reed fence to dry. The sun felt good on my skin as I sopped up its warm rays for almost an hour before the guard returned to get me.

Once back in the cell he threw me a small Vietnamese hand broom, told me in sign language to roll up my net, mat and remaining clothes in preparation for my move to another cell. He closed the door, left the light on and was gone for about fifteen minutes.

I cleaned the cell as best I could, sweeping the dirt into the corner next to the honey bucket still filled with crawling maggots. I managed to clean off all of the cob webs as high as I could reach and killed as many mosquitoes and spiders that came within my reach. I was congratulating myself on the clean condition of the cell when the guard returned, told me to pick up my gear and led me off to a cell located at the far end of a building named the Stable. It was mid-afternoon of 13 August 1966 and my ordeal in the Auditorium was finished. He let me into my cell then closed and locked the door. I sat on the nearest wooden bunk and prayerfully thanked the Lord for my deliverance.

ISOLATED IN THE STABLE

The Stable cell was spacious. It had two bunks and four windows, three of which were covered by French louvered shutters which were nailed closed. The fourth was covered on the lower half only by a bamboo reed mat. I could pull myself up on the window ledge, and by grasping the vertical iron bars which prevented my escape, look out over the top of the bamboo cover. From this vantage point I could plainly see the back upper half of the adjacent Pool Hall as well as the walkway in front of the Pig Sty; however, this maneuver was risky. Up in the window I was exposed to the view of the meandering guards on their rounds as well as any other Vietnamese personnel in the immediate area. After my first careful glimpse I was extremely cautious before mounting the ledge to scan the surrounding area. There'll be hell to pay if they catch me up here, I thought.

Compared to the size, darkness, filth and heat of the Auditorium cell I had just vacated, my new Stable quarters was a palatial penthouse apartment. It was comparatively light and airy breezes flowed unimpeded through the window openings. I set my gear on the southernmost bunk and reclined, happy to be free of the rigors of my fast from food and water.

My spirits were high. I had won a major skirmish, and felt I could regain my health and resistance posture. I tapped on the wall abutting the next large cell but got no response. It's empty, I thought. Then I thumped as hard as I could on the back wall, and there was no response. I was still cut off from the other POWs. I regained control by rationalizing that it was too soon for me to expect a communications contact. I relaxed and enjoyed my new environment. It was the largest, cleanest, brightest and airiest cell that I had been in since I had arrived in Hanoi. Things are looking up for me. I've got to rebuild my strength and figure a way that I can get out of this place.

The smiling guard brought me my dried clothes, and then more rice and gravy soup, a pot of tea and another banana. I devoured everything slowly with great relish. When I was done I thoroughly brushed my teeth with the Bac Ha toothpaste, (much bubble, nice taste). It had been six days since my last brushing. I took it slow, scrubbing each tooth individually with precision and care. When I was finished my mouth felt clean for the first time in almost a week.

I consumed a sufficient amount of tea and finally I knew my liquid starved body had reached its saturation point when my kidneys signaled. The hot urine burned as it oozed from my dried penis in dark orange droplets. Once my kidneys were working again they functioned better each time, and it was only a couple of days before my urinations were back to normal.

My bowel movements were a different story. I had been eating four full days before my bowels began to indicate that they would move. I couldn't believe it. I was actually completely constipated. I spent half of my fifth day in the Stable sitting on the five gallon can which was my personal toilet facility. But nothing happened. I was suffering great abdominal and rectal pains. Finally with one massive effort I managed to pass a rock-like stool which seemed to be the main cause of my problem. The effort had taken a great deal of strength out of me and I flopped on my bunk half exhausted, yet relieved that I had released some of the blockage. I drank as much as I could and continued my efforts. Finally by that evening I had freed myself of the obstructions and I resumed having normal bowel movements.

As a POW I had recognized the importance of bladder and bowel control. I responded to every signal immediately in an effort to assist my body to maintain itself in the best possible working condition. In my primitive environment I had to force myself to analyze even basic body functions in relation to my personal survival. Thus I found that drinking a cup of water as soon as I awoke in the morning served both as a laxative and as a diuretic, and enabled me to function more regularly than I otherwise would.

I bathed daily at noon under the healing rays of the hot tropic sun. Try as I might I could not establish communications with anyone in my building, or the Pool Hall, or Pig Sty. To the best of my knowledge, I was the only one living in the Stable for the first two weeks I was there. At the start of the third week they moved someone into the last cell at the extreme north end of the building. I got a chance look at the POW when I picked up my food one day. He was a black American, so I assumed it was Fred Cherry, a badly wounded POW whom I had never seen or been in contact with.

My spirits were high in spite of my isolation. Daily my strength grew. I devoured every bit of food they gave me. My exercise and walking program was back in full swing. I kept my mind alert by reviewing my own personal POW history and the memory POW name bank. For diversion I spent days establishing a family investment fund for my children. This was a challenge to me and I refined my concept into a family mutual fund and a family savings and loan fund. I plotted my escape by the hours and developed a plan which would allow me to get to the roof of the Stable and outside of the camp's enclosed area. I needed another POW to accomplish the task, since my left shoulder would not give me enough support to climb the only entrance to the roof: a fence and a porch roof support pillar.

The bombing raids continued on Hanoi and my spirits remained high. One night a solo low-level flying aircraft flew directly overhead. It dropped a single bomb which exploded a few hundred feet behind the Stable in a rice paddy next to the brick yard that was outside my window. The flash from the explosion lit up the cell and plaster fell from the ceiling and walls. The raid alarm sounded after the bomb had gone off and the plane had left. I wondered what his target was. Guessing the target must have had a significant radar return for the pilot to be able to drop, I surmised it was probably a SAM site.

I had no quizzes and the days dragged on. I settled down to the monotonous living routine, known only to those who have experienced solitary confinement. Each day was the same: get up, pray, memory bank, eat, wash, eat, memory bank, pray, sleep through another night. My mind never stopped a second for all of my waking moments. I was lonesome and found myself talking out loud, answering my own mental questions.

Good fortune struck when I discovered I could loosen one of the laths on the heavy louvered French blinds covering the east window. After an hour of working I finally pried it loose. Using it as a lever I was able to separate the adjacent laths far enough apart so that I had a good view of the area behind the Stable. Much to my surprise most of the area encompassed a Vietnamese brick storage area. There were at least fifty piles of red bricks stacked five feet high in neat rectangles. One stack was separated from the other by a distance of six to eight feet. There was a low, heavily vine-covered fence about fifteen feet from the edge of the Stable running parallel to the east side of the camp. A small moat, covered with green algae, lay between the fence and a pathway made by the touring outside guards as they made their rounds along the perimeter of the camp. The walkway was also used by guards going to and from an outside observation post located south of the camp. As near as I could tell this post was continually manned and the changing of the guard took place approximately every four hours. Each carried his own rifle slung over his back in addition to a Chinese burp gun carried in his hands. These armed defenses seemed formidable to me as I prodded them mentally for any overt sign of weakness.

I was careful to clear the area completely before I opened up my viewing spot. Whenever I heard the guards coming I would retreat from my vantage point to a place of safety sitting on my bunk away from their view. It became a cat and mouse game I enjoyed playing.

There was little activity in the brickyard except for some small children who played there on weekends. One lad who looked to be about three years old was the concern of the others. Often times I heard him scream in terror at the approach of attacking aircraft. His ears were so attuned to the jets that his scream was the first warning that an air attack was imminent. I felt sorry for him for I could understand the fright and anguish that he was going through. He had been crying in this manner for the past few months and, though I was aware of him, I had not actually seen him prior to my stay in the Stable. He was playing one day and I happened to have a good view of him as I peeked out from my observation spot. An attack came and he ran screaming home towards safety.

One Sunday a group of his peers, only a little bigger and older than he, installed him in a firing position from a simulated anti-aircraft position on a brick pile. Then each took a turn at climbing another brick pile, simulating an aircraft wing by outstretched arms and then jumping towards the newest defender of Vietnam. He fired his gun in mock cowboy versus Indian style, and each mock attacker flopped over dead from his accurate shots. They played this game with him for an hour and convinced him of his invulnerability to attacking planes. He quickly gained confidence and shot them down one by one in childish glee. When the game was over they congratulated him with affectionate pats and he strutted off with them, a victor over his previous fear. It was a memorable sight. I noticed that never again did I hear the frightened scream of that little boy.

At the end of August I suddenly had an acute attack of diarrhea and began passing many black and white worms in my stool. I ate all of my food but I was noticeably weaker and more fatigued. I spent much of each day simply reclining on my bunk. The guard noticed my plight and a medic checked my bucket but no medicine was administered.

On Sunday afternoon the 4th of September, I saw a Vietnamese man enter the brickyard. I could tell from the way he was sneaking about that he was up to no good. He left after inspecting the piles of bricks and soon returned with three Vietnamese women each of whom had two large wicker baskets attached to a carrying pole slung over a shoulder. He removed the top layer of each pile of bricks and the women toted them out of the yard to whatever destination he had previously determined. The process took several hours. The Vietnamese man was very nervous and kept scanning the entire area to insure that the operation was unobserved. Except for me, I guess it was. I sat at the shutter and watched the whole show. It was a panorama of human greed. The people were stealing the people's bricks from the people's brickyard. I wonder what Uncle Ho would think of this? He's probably stealing much bigger things from his people than bricks, like maybe their own individuality, I thought.

The Vietmanese women were free like the freedom that the beast of burden enjoys. Those women worked like pack animals under the harassment and haranguing of their male overlord. Back in the U.S. we put our women on a pedestal so that they can help bring out the best that's in each of us males. What a contrast there. There everyone's equal but some are more equal than others. Shades of ANIMAL FARM and equal rights.

Late that night I was awakened from a deep sleep by the cries of an American who was located in one of the end rooms of the Pig Sty. "I'm dying, I'm dying, my God I'm bleeding to death," he cried out. He repeated his cries, and I asked him for his name, but got no reply. He moaned and groaned in agony.

I couldn't help him or even know what was wrong, so I jumped up in my front window and yelled,"Bao Cao," (Bow Cow) repeatedly at the top of my lungs in the direction of the camp's duty offices. I heard the responding guards and officers as they rushed helter skelter in my direction. I got down out of the window and stood by my door. The guard came to my door and said, "Bao Cao Mun," (Mun was my Vietnamese name). I said, "No Bao Cao Mun; Bao Cao," and then pointed to the Pig Sty. At that moment the Yank cried out again. The guards rushed to his room. I don't know what happened but the ambulance came and they took him away on a stretcher. I never knew who he was or where he went or if he even survived. I had done my best by alerting the Vietnamese. Now I could only offer a silent prayer for his well being.

The next day I watched the people's labor force come to move out all of the remaining bricks from the yard. Eight ox cars, each pulled by two oxen, came into the area under the yells and curses of their drivers and the other men and women that made up the labor force. The carts were mounted on truck axles and large rubber tires giving testimony to the Vietnamese's inability to properly maintain mechanized motor vehicles. I couldn't believe my eyes. A tenth-century ox cart with twentieth-century rubber tire wheels. "Only in Vietnam," I said to myself as I shook my head in disbelief.

They unhitched the oxen and let them graze while each pile of bricks was methodically loaded into a cart until it wouldn't hold any more. It was heavy work but the Vietnamese women seemed to share more of this burden than their men counterparts.

At the siesta, they reclined on the grass and partook of tea and rice provided by a cook who had set up her outdoor kitchen almost like a chuck wagon. When the meal was completed the leader of the group stood and gave a long speech in Vietnamese to his workers, who were sitting more or less in rapt attention. They gave nods of approval at the appropriate times and seemed generally to be in agreement with him. When he was finished they all rolled over and slept in the open sun until the end of siesta was signaled by the camp's tocsin.

The carts were fully loaded when they hitched up the first two oxen. It was a massive struggle of human effort to position the carts and harness up the beasts, but they managed amidst the cursing and yelling emanating from unorganized mob decision.

When the first wagon was ready to go, the driver slapped his long bamboo whip on the oxen and a group of workers pushed the cart from behind in an effort to get it moving. The oxen resisted all movement stubbornly, but finally after much beating, shouting, and pushing they started to get under way. The cart lurched forward and picked up speed. Unfortunately the route of egress was particularly rough at one spot. This didn't seem to bother the Vietnamese as they drove the oxen through the rough spot. The sudden bumpiness caused the load to shift which broke the wooden yokes and brought the oxen to their knees and the broken cart to a stop. It was a helluva mess. The oxen were flat on their bellies, legs outstretched, unable to move because of the weight of the broken cart. Wildly excited Vietnamese ran in all directions. Everyone was shouting. No one was in charge. It was an uncontrolled committee action at its wildest, and I couldn't believe what was going on before my eyes. Finally they unloaded the wagon, unhitched the oxen, pushed back the emptied cart and got the oxen back on their feet. The entire evolution must have taken almost three quarters of an hour.

To my amazement they repeated the same scenario with the second cart. When they finally got their second misadventure squared away they started on their third. If I hadn't seen it myself I wouldn't have believed it could happen. The third ox cart went through the exact maneuver as its two predecessors, with exactly the same results. When the debris was finally cleared, an old Vietmanese man went to the bumpy area, pointed out the obstacle and then walked through a smoother section whereby the carts could leave the area without shifting the load of bricks with such disastrous results. One by one they all retraced his steps and came to an agreement that this was the way to take the carts. The five remaining carts were hitched up and moved out of the area without incident. Three rickety ox carts were brought in to replace the three carts that had been broken. Everyone pitched in and loaded them as quickly as possible. The job was finally completed and the carts moved out just as sunset was occurring.

For me it had been a pleasant day of observation. Just to see human beings at work was a relief from the boredom of solitary confinement. I had witnessed the people's power at work in its rawest version. These damn North Vietnamese are barely out of the trees, I thought as I recollected their primitive efforts in the brickyard. They are rushing ahead to full progress like leaping head first from the tenth to the eleventh century. My God, who the hell are we fighting and what are we fighting for? A picture is worth a thousand words, and the pictorial epic of the broken ox cart scenario contributed greatly to my knowledge of the Vietnamese. I was a novice on Asia and the Asian when I was captured. Orientals truly were inscrutable to me. When I thought over the day's events, I had a hard time convincing myself that what I had seen happen was real.

Life in the Stable grew more monotonous. I was still unable to communicate with anyone. The Vietnamese were playing a waiting game with me. I had no quizzes, no threats, no visits, nothing at all. My dysentery grew worse by the day. I managed to eat all of my food, but got little sustenance from it. I grew weaker and spent more and more time on the bucket. The Vietnamese were aware of my condition, but did nothing to alleviate it. The medic came and in broken English said that my bad attitude was responsible for my poor physical condition. On Friday night J.C. looked in at me and said, "You must think about your condition, and when you see the error of your ways my medic will make you well." He slammed the small peek-in door shut and left as quickly and as quietly as he came.

On Monday, 12 September, I was taken to a quiz with Spot. The medic examined me with Spot looking on. When finished he spoke in Vietnamese. Spot spoke to me in English. Pointing to the medic, he said, "My medic says you are sick because you have not thought properly about making your choice," "Bullshit," I said in disgust. Spot continued, "Since today I move you to another cell so that you may think about your decadent ways. When you have thought enough about your situation I will talk to you again to see if you have gained the proper attitude."

He sent me to my cell where the guard had me wrap up my belongings in preparation for the move. I had barely completed the job when the guard came and moved me to a cell in a building called the Gate House. The cell was hot and dark, a bad omen of things to come, I thought.

The door was barely closed when I heard the familiar "shave and a haircut two bits" call up sign from the other wall. I was elated. I had not communicated with anyone since I had left the Garage over five weeks before. "Rap, rap," I answered. "Al Brunstrom," he tapped. "Jim Mulligan," I replied. It felt good to be back in the system again even if my living conditions were worse. Nothing's as bad as being alone, absolutely alone.

MAKE YOUR CHOICE

Al Brunstrom told me the Gate House was being used by the North Vietnamese to keep Americans who were being physically forced to "make their choice," write confessions, and biographies. The POWs were kept handcuffed, but with typical American ingenuity, they had discovered a way of opening the cuffs with small nails which they had hid in each cell of the Gate House. I was not cuffed and kept expecting them to be put on, but the Vietnamese spared me that extra ordeal. Late in the afternoon, I heard Brunstrom receive a terrible beating from a group of guards and then he was taken away.

Brunstrom's place was taken by John Borling. He was next in line in their torture program. During the next few days, John was subjected to numerous quizzes followed by severe beatings. My cell door was flimsy with numerous cracks and small openings which allowed me to see most of the camp quadrangle area as well as observe POWs close to me go to quiz, bathe, or get their food. I could see Borling slowly wilting from the constant onslaught of physical abuse. Anguish seized me as I watched the results of their unnecessary inhuman abuse.

I sweltered in the hot room and my dysentery got worse by the day. I put my personal convenience bucket next to the door and sat on it by the hour observing all of the goings on in the camp. Each day during siesta time, the camp jeep would arrive with new POWs. Most of them seemed to be injured one way or another. Most had limbs in casts, walked with limps or crutches and were bandaged. They were led to either the Office or Pig Sty and kept there. From all that I could see, the POWs in general were in very poor physical shape. This was more the result of the poor diet and miserable conditions than anything else. I was convinced however, that the constant physical and psychological pressures from the North Vietnamese "make your choice" program was also a major contributor to our overall condition. Most men had been, were in the process of, or soon would be, physically tortured. As a result, we were a haggard and down trodden lot, and looked the role to any discerning eye.

The Vietnamese had once again fragmented the POW camp communications network. They had completed the brick and bamboo fences which now separated one building from another. The resistance movement was restricted to each building, and each had its own policy. I didn't know who the SRO in the camp was. Jim Stockdale was in the end room of the Garage, but was cut off from the rest of the camp. I had heard Jerry Denton was in the Pool Hall, but that was back in June. Robby Risner was out of the picture, kept somewhere back in Hoa Lo prison in downtown Hanoi. We had no acknowledged leader, yet to a man, everything I witnessed during my stay in the Gate House, pointed to a strong resistance movement. From what I could see, the Vietnamese were not getting anything for nothing from their captured Yanks. They beat the hell out of John Borling every day in an effort to get him to cooperate. I tapped to John constantly and watched him go to quiz or go out for food. I remembered Robby Risner's instruction passed to me months ago by Jim Stockdale in the Hanoi Hilton after I was first captured: "Resist to the limits of your ability but don't take a permanent physical or mental injury opposing their efforts to get mere propaganda statements."

Borling was beaten badly again and tapped to me that he didn't know how much longer he could hold out. When he came out to get his food, I saw his pitiful condition and when he was back in his cell I tapped to him and said, "John, don't get hurt anymore. You're in bad shape. I know Robbie Risner's policy is to resist, but not take a permanent injury. Get out of it as cheap as you can, God bless." John capitulated that afternoon and they moved him out.

I was completely heartbroken at what was happening to the POWs. My physical condition had progressively worsened. The dysentery was still the culprit. If I took a swallow of water or ate, it passed almost directly through my body. I was weak, exhausted, depressed and as sick as I'd ever been in my life. As a last resort I stopped eating. Lying on my floor pallet I was ready to die.

On Sunday, the medic came with J.C. and brought me a fist full of little brown pills. There were sixteen. J.C. said, "Moo lig gun, take all one time." I responded slowly. He screamed, repeating the same instructions. Gulping water, I swallowed them all. They then brought me a bowl of rice soup and a banana and told me to eat. I did. Much to my surprise, I was able to hold everything, and my dysentery ended. I gained strength from the food and felt much better. I was still weak, but I felt I was on the way to recovery. Unfortunately, I was wrong.

Early Monday morning I had a quiz with Spot. He asked me what my thoughts were and I flunked the quiz when I said, "They are the same as before." I didn't like Spot and the feeling was mutual. "You move to another cell," he said, "but you have no light." The guard had me pack my belongings and I was moved to cell three in the Pool Hall. I was glad to be out of the Gate House, but wondered what was in store for me.

A CHRISTMAS LETTER HOME

The Pool Hall was filled. Jerry Denton was in cell one in solitary and was the building SRO. Dave Hatcher, my old tap mate from earlier days in the Barn, was in cell two next to me. I was elated to be able to communicate with Hatcher. He and I had become fast friends during our many hours of communicating back in June.

I filled Hatcher in on my exploits since we parted company. He brought me up to speed quickly on what was going on in the Pool Hall in particular, and in the camp in general. The North Vietnamese were going full speed ahead with their "make your choice" program proceeding methodically building by building and cell by cell. Everyone in the Pool Hall had already been through this ordeal. Some men had been taken downtown to the Hanoi Hilton to receive their working over. Others had been processed in the Gate House. The Vietnamese had stepped up their efforts. They wanted everyone to "make their choice," and write the other propaganda statements they desired. The torture was, for most, fast and brutal. The whole process now took only a day or two before most POWs caved in from the intense physical abuse.

The Pool Hall had good internal comm but was isolated from the remainder of the buildings in the camp. Cell three was nine feet long, eleven feet wide, had two bunks and, except for the solid door, had no other openings except for two small air vents high on the front wall. It was relatively dark in the cell and the sun's rays never managed to find a way to enter. The removal of the small electric light meant that at day's end I was left in complete darkness. Night comes fast in the tropics and I could barely finish my late afternoon meal of rice and seaweed soup before I was engulfed in darkness.

My worm and dysentery problem returned bringing both mental and physical anguish. Completely depressed, I took to my bunk and couldn't even maintain good communications with Dave Hatcher. The guards and turn key harassed me daily. They were like a pack of dogs chasing a wounded animal. I was under my net away from the ever present onslaught of Vietnamese mosquitoes. I never did get accustomed to them. In Vietnam the mosquito problem never improved. They attacked year round, and though more numerous in the summer, they were more vicious during winter.

Jerry Denton ran a good show. He continually put out resistance policy and established an intelligence-gathering information bank whereby each cell had a definite area of responsibility. This info ranged from clocking guard movements to recording the amount of vehicle traffic we could hear. The Pool Hall definitely was a hard liner building, and all of its occupants were *Tigers*. Jerry was an inspirational leader. He never gave any quarter to the Vietnamese and he never asked any POW to endure any physical abuse which he himself had not already endured. He went first, heading the line of resistance and paid the full penalty for his dedication to the moral principles he believed in and lived by. Living up to the Code of Conduct was a moral obligation for him. Jerry constantly lived up to the letter of the law as he understood it. While this caused him to receive excessively harsh and inhumane treatment, he nevertheless gained the complete respect of those junior officer POWs in his charge. Like him they were tigers of resistance.

The Vietnamese knew Jerry Denton was the real obstacle to all of their propaganda programs. In the early days of the POW years, namely from 1965 through 1970 when the going was roughest, Denton was the unquestioned POW leader. He more than any other senior, gave purpose and direction to the resistance movement. Though he authored the policy of passing the lead to the next in command for any senior officer who was under too much pressure to be an effective leader, he never availed himself of this legitimate outlet. Jerry Denton played the role of leader every day of his POW incarceration. His was the strongest voice of resistance when torture was rampant and others in command had been broken and had assumed docile resistance profiles, not causing the

North Vietnamese any apparent problems. He was at his absolute best when the treatment was at its absolute worst. He more than any other was truly the POWs' POW.

In October of 1966 the Vietnamese began to torture Denton on a trumped up charge that they had caught him communicating. He was put in leg irons which were progressively tightened by a rope pulley system until the irons were cutting deep into his ankles. He was kept in this rig for days. The pain was terrible, but he continued to communicate and lead the resistance. The North Vietnamese just wanted him to capitulate and turn himself over to them, but as usual they were doomed to disappointment. Denton was in such bad shape that even the Vietnamese key guard we called Happy felt sorry for him. Happy would bring Jerry his food and then come to my cell. On numerous occasions I saw Happy with tears in his eyes in obvious compassion for Denton. Finally they gave up on Jerry Denton and suddenly moved him from the Pool Hall back to the Gate House.

I was in very bad shape. The rice and seaweed soup went right through me, barely slowing down on its passage. The nights grew cool in late October and early November. I was left in complete darkness from sundown till sunrise. The North Vietnamese felt that by depriving me of the electric light they were punishing me. In a way I guess they were because I was not only sick but mentally depressed from my surroundings and the harassment. After dark the guards would bang on my door to disturb me. On several occasions they had the key guard enter and make me stand with my arms upraised against the wall while they verbally taunted me in Vietnamese. If I hadn't been so sick they would have been more effective and I would have been more frightened. But as things were their efforts were only petty inconveniences.

I had one major problem. At night I had the urge to urinate many times. The colder it got, the worse this problem became. I put my bucket next to a crack in the cell door where I could find it, remove the lid and perform my bladder relief maneuver in the dark. Mostly I hit the bucket but sometimes I missed. I was up ten or more times a night and my sleep was never restful. I thought about my dilemma and sought to isolate the cause. Finally it came to me. No salt! The Vietnamese considered salt a flavoring for our food, so to punish us they deprived us of any salt. Rice and seaweed soup were little more than water. I decided that I was literally pissing away whatever meager benefits I received from the inadequate diet.

With Jerry gone I was the SRO (Senior Ranking Officer) in the Pool Hall. I continued his policies of resistance as well as the intelligence gathering tasks assigned to various cells: frequency, times and nearness of air raids, vehicular traffic, movement of all air defense gun emplacements in the immediate area, frequency and scope of POW quizzes, etc.

Dave Hatcher moved into cell one and then was soon moved out of the Pool Hall. Cell two was empty but four had two POWs, Quincy Collins and A.J. Meyers, both of whom had bad leg injuries and walked with cane and crutch. Directly behind my rear wall was cell eight. Its occupants were Jerry Coffee and Larry Spencer. Spencer was the rear seat man of an F4 lost from *ENTERPRISE* some weeks before I was bagged. His pilot, Jim Ruffin, was observed in a chute after ejection by Spencer but had never been seen by any POWs. On the day they were shot down, Spencer's radar gear was malfunctioning. Ruffin, the pilot, was under the control of an air defense destroyer controller. Somehow the destroyer put Ruffin's F4 thirty miles inland over North Vietnam flying a combat air patrol defense station over a deck of clouds. A second destroyer radar detected the error and Ruffin was vectored out of North Vietnam. Unfortunately, the F4 was hit by a surface to air missile (SAM-2) before reaching the coastline. Back on *ENTERPRISE* we knew only we'd lost an F4 under odd circumstances. The fate of its crewmen was completely unknown. When I got this story from Spencer I filed it with other essential POW info that I wanted to get back to the U.S. if ever given the chance.

Jerry Coffee tapped to me to keep my morale up. Each cell had two occupants except for myself and Bob Purcell. We were still kept in solitary. Bob Purcell was a young tiger who had been a thorn in the side of the North Vietnamese ever since his capture. I kept hoping he would get a cellmate. The Vietnamese were still shuffling POWs from building to building so this was a definite possibility.

Jerry Coffee was the first POW shot down in 1966. He was an A5 driver and was bagged on a photo recon flight soon after he arrived in the combat zone. He and I had many acquaintances who were serving in the heavy attack wing and squadrons on the east coast. The wing home was in Sanford, Florida and I was familiar with the base. We had much in common. We were also both practicing Roman Catholics and our wives and children were our main concern.

Jerry Coffee reminded me that October was a month that Catholics dedicated to Mary the Mother of Jesus. Each October the Rosary was said in unison by devout Marian followers. From the day he first mentioned it to me in October of 1966, the Rosary became a part of my daily prayer ritual. More than anything else it seemed to help me bear the pain of loss and permitted me to cope with the many contentions that mentally and physically oppressed me.

Coffee knew I was lonesome, and he established a building clearance procedure during the siesta hour. When all was clear, he would make a horse collar out of his blanket, like the hole in a big doughnut. Then he'd put it on the wall and talk directly through the wall to me. I had a drinking cup on the wall exactly opposite to him. With my ear on the cup, and my eye on the cell door for self protection, I could hear every word he said and still be safe. I rapped twice at the end of each sentence if I understood him. When he asked questions, I answered yes with two raps and no with one. A series of raps sent by me meant that he had to repeat his last sentence. The system worked very well and my morale was raised to new heights. I kept praying that cell two would soon be occupied so that I could set up clearance and be able to talk to Jerry as he was talking to me.

November 9th was my brother John's birthday. John was three years younger than I and though we weren't close in grammar and high school we had become more devoted since his return from duty in Korea with the U.S. Air Force in late 1952. He had visited with us for extended periods while we were stationed in Pensacola, Florida, Virginia Beach, Virginia and Washington, D.C. My kids loved their Uncle Miggs, (his nickname since childhood). To them he seemed more like a big brother than an uncle. He was thirty-seven on 9 November 1966, married, with three children. He taught in the Grammar School system of Haverhill, Massachusetts. He loved kids and he loved teaching. Some years earlier we had come to a mutual agreement. If something tragic happened to either of us, the survivor would assume the responsibility of looking after the other's wife and children. When I thought of him now I was relieved. I knew he would already have put his end of our mutual agreement into effect. I was reminiscing about John that day, remembering all the many little details of personal interaction between us over the years, most of which had slipped into the back of my mind. It was pleasant to think about him. It raised my spirits and made the time pass more easily. Solitude, I found, allowed me to delve deep, recalling and reconstructing much of the pleasant past which I had not bothered to think about during the hustle and bustle of a military career and personal family concerns.

The past became an obsession with me and I became a slave to it. I didn't know it then but absolute solitude would eventually force me to completely relive my life year by year, month by month, day by day until I would reach back into my earliest infancy and recall things that happened to me somewhere between the age of one and two.

Suddenly my reverie was interrupted. The key guard, Happy, came and told me to dress for quiz. I hadn't been quizzed since I last saw Spot. That was over six weeks earlier when I was moved to the Pool Hall. I was apprehensive and edgy. I wondered aloud if they were going to start up the "make your choice" program again. I urinated nervously. Then I dressed in my long blue pajamas, the upper half of which had, in addition to the six buttons down the middle, two full pockets. I always wore the blue pajama suit to quiz because it was distinctive and the only one of its kind that I had seen.

All the other POWs had been issued long khaki-colored pajamas. These were later replaced with a dull red and gray vertical striped outfit I called the clown suit. In late 1966 clown suits were becoming the general issue to newly downed POWs. I had long ago been identified as the POW in the light blue suit and this enabled other POWs to easily keep track of my movements when I was taken from my cell to quiz. Besides, I had acquired the habit of putting my hands in my blouse pockets when I sat at quiz. For some reason this annoyed the Vietnamese quiz masters. They didn't know what to do about it and I derived a small bit of personal satisfaction in the game of one upmanship with them. I bowed graciously but kept both hands in my pockets more in a manner of defiance than acquiescence. It was a very minor victory for me, but I gloried in accomplishing it and repeated my performance at every opportunity.

It was a clear sunny cloudless day as I walked to the quiz room adjacent to the Auditorium. On entering I bowed graciously to a Vietnamese officer that I had never seen before. He was a man in his early fifties, larger than most of the Vietnamese I had been exposed to, and he spoke fluent English with a deep French accent. "Take your seat Commander if you please," he politely spoke, surprising me by referring to my Navy rank. I sat on the usual stool and scrutinized his features carefully. He had a distinctive lump high on his left forehead, and wore the typical Vietnamese officer's khaki long uniform with no visible rank. I took him to be a man of some importance, because he wore an exquisite pair of high priced leather shoes. Their illuminating shine gave testimony to the exceptional care which he obviously gave them.

"I am new to the army and this camp," he spoke slowly and distinctly. "Only a short time ago I answered the call of our beloved president Ho Chi Minh to serve in the Army of Vietnam and oppose the war of U.S. aggression. I have only come from the university some days ago, and now I am here at this camp to talk with you and come to understand you."

Though his voice was mild and cultured and his manner overtly friendly I was doubly alerted mentally to this "nice guy" approach. It was a definite change from the usual quiz. Be careful, don't trust him, I thought.

He offered me a Vietnamese cigarette which I declined politely. "How is your health?" he continued. "Do you really want to know?" I answered. "Of course, I must know your health so that I can make my report on the conditions of this camp," he continued. "Then let me show you and you can see for yourself," I said. I arose, unbuttoned the blue coat, then removed it, and stood bare from the waist up. When he looked at me, I saw his eyes did not quite believe my pallid frail frame. My chest showed every bone. My shoulders and arms were sparrow-like thin. I could put my thumb and forefinger of my right hand over the biceps of my left arm and almost complete the circle. My left wrist showed every bone going to my forearm and there was no flesh covering them, only white mottled aging wrinkled skin. "Now you have seen for yourself; I'm in bad health, and so are the others," I said. "Do you eat all your food?" He asked as I buttoned the coat and sat back down on the stool. "Yes," I replied. "I eat all the soup and the rice they give me." "Then why are you so thin?" he queried. "Because we get no salt," I responded. "You get no salt, no salt at all?" he questioned dubiously. "Why do you get no salt, and what does this have to do with your condition?" "The Vietnamese who run this camp say that salt is flavoring," I replied. "Because the Americans have shown a bad attitude they cannot receive the lenient and humane treatment from the Vietnamese people so we cannot receive salt. You see, they do not understand that salt is much more than flavoring. It is a necessity for the body to retain water. We eat seaweed soup and rice. This food is mostly water so without salt we get thin. The cold weather causes us to make water many times each night in our buckets. In the United States the doctors put our wives who are going to bear a child on a salt free diet so that they will pass much liquid and not gain much weight. That diet is good for that purpose but here a no salt diet is breaking down our bodies. Do you understand all that I have said to you?" I concluded. "Yes, and from today you shall all receive salt with your meal," he answered. "Thank you very much," I replied politely. "It will help us to live through the cold Hanoi winter." "You can return to your room now. I will see you again soon," he concluded.

I stood up, bowed with my hands at my side, turned and left. There was no guard waiting to accompany me so I walked slowly to my cell. I was almost there when Happy the key guard spotted me. He came running and joined me in the remainder of my journey. He looked puzzled and I deduced that the man with the French accent and the lump must really be a new guy to send me back to my cell alone, unaccompanied by a key or roving patrol guard.

Once in my cell I tapped the results of my quiz to the men in the building. When the food came later that morning there was a big plate of unwashed, unrefined salt sitting next to the rice plate. I scooped up a handful and munched on it like an appetizer. It was the first salt I had in almost eight months of captivity. After one mouthful my body craved more, as if it had awakened to a drastic need long unmet. For some days, the salt was the most delicious edible thing that I could remember eating.

The salt made a big difference to me. Over a twelve hour period my nightly urination trips were reduced to one or two. I slept much better, and was in fact warmer, because I retained more body fluids. I was pleased with my successful effort, and I felt it was a giant step towards my own physical survival.

We named the new Vietnamese officer, "Lump." I went to a quiz with him the next day and thanked him for giving us the salt. He seemed pleased at my congeniality, and then began to tell me about the wonders of the Hanoi Symphonic Orchestra. He knew that I had been raised near Boston so he asked me about the Boston Symphonic Orchestra. I told him some fictitious tales about Arthur Fiedler and the Boston Pops Orchestra playing outside near the Charles River. I had to make up a story and embellish it for actually I had never personally attended a Boston Pops Concert and in reality had very little exposure to, or knowledge of the world of music. He said he played several musical instruments. I was careful to let him know that my musical expertise was restricted to listening and enjoying what I liked. I told him Tchaikovsky's Nut Cracker Suite was my favorite. This elated him. Suddenly he asked me if I liked bananas. I answered yes and he said, "Beginning today you will receive bananas for your health." Then he called for the guard and sent me back to my cell. I bowed, said, "Thank you," and returned to report the latest quiz to the Pool Hall members. That afternoon I got a banana with my soup and rice. The good guy treatment was on. Lump wasn't being friendly because he liked Americans. I wondered what he was up to but since my health was really poor, I figured I would milk him for everything that I could get before I turned him off.

I didn't have long to wait to find out what he was after. At quiz the next morning, Friday, 11 November, a day I had always known as Armistice Day, Lump played his trump card. After my bow and our mutual exchange of small talk, he said that he had a document that he wanted me to read over. It was a personal autobiographical sheet from birth till shootdown. I read it slowly and carefully, stalling for time, wondering how I could handle this overture. As I read it he said that the Vietnamese needed this information to process our release at the end of the war as well as to establish contact with the International Red Cross in order that we might receive mail and packages from home. I recognized this play as pure bullshit, but played along with him.

When I finished reading the form he asked if I could complete the document for him. I said that I could understand the necessity for the records. I was lying. I added that in the past the camp authorities had tortured me for a propaganda statement and also treated me inhumanely, because I refused to "make my choice." "I will not violate the Code of Conduct and I will not write my confessions of crimes or 'make my choice'. I will think about this document only if I am assured by you that I do not have to 'make my choice' or write a confession of crimes." Emotionally I was fatigued and asked if I could return to my cell to think about his request. He gave a friendly willing yes and called a guard to bring me back to the Pool Hall. I bowed and he said, "Good day Commander, you will get more bananas." He was the good guy and the bananas were the bait. They desperately wanted the biography sheet. I decided to think this one clearly through before doing anything one way or the other.

Back in my cell I sat and evaluated the entire situation. What would I get and what would I give to get it? I wanted to be able to write a letter home at Christmas. First, I didn't know if my family even knew I was alive. Second, the information concerning POWs was so sparse, and the intelligence reports on them so poor, that I felt our government had no idea of the identity and numbers of military aviators who had been captured and sent to Hanoi. Prior to my capture on 20 March 1966, *ENTERPRISE* had four POWs in Hanoi but was not aware any had survived and been captured. I had personal knowledge from my memory name bank that *ENTERPRISE* had seven men as POWs as of November 1966. I also had knowledge that Lt. Jim Ruffin, who had been shot down with Larry Spencer, had actually been seen in a functioning parachute by Spencer but had never been seen in any POW camp, and was probably not a survivor. As the senior POW from *ENTERPRISE* I felt it was my responsibility to pass this vital info one way or another as soon as possible to the Navy. A letter home at Christmas might permit me to send this and other information I considered vital to the POWs and the United States government's interest. I decided that I would fill out the biographical sheet giving authentic information like date and place of birth and schools attended until I was age 17 when I joined the Navy. From the time I entered the Navy I would construct an entirely fictitious naval career except I would acknowledge my role as Executive Officer of Attack Squadron 36 on *ENTERPRISE* at shootdown, a fact that I knew they had knowledge of. I spent Saturday and Sunday memorizing my fictitious Navy career and mentally writing a letter home which would contain the intelligence data I wanted to get out of Hanoi and back to the States.

On Monday I had a quiz with Lump, and he asked me if I could complete the biographical document. I said I could if he did not make any demands that I "make my choice" or write a "confession of crimes" statement. "This document will be sufficient; I have no need of the others," he replied. "Then I will do it for you," I said. He beamed approvingly, giving me a workable fountain pen and ink along with the biographical sheet. He said I could complete it in my cell. "How is your health? Do you enjoy the bananas?" "I am tired and weak but I eat my food and the extra bananas," I answered. "Do you get vitamins?" "No, never," I replied. "Since today you will get vitamins for your health. You may return to your cell now." He went to the doorway and called a guard. I stood, bowed and said, "Thank you," as I left.

Back in the cell I mused, "Bananas? Vitamins? This guy really thinks he has me on the hook. I'll fill out the false bio sheet, see if he buys it, then play it by ear." I went to work and filled out the form. I checked my memory against what I had conjured up until I was satisfied I had it all down pat. I knew that once I had committed myself, I would have to maintain absolute recall. I knew the Vietnamese would check me on it in the future. Lie but don't get caught they told me at survival school training in Brunswick, Maine. I remembered that lesson well and was sure that I could cover my tracks if they checked.

That day, in addition to my usual food, I received two bananas and twelve vitamin pills. The good treatment is on, I thought to myself, so I'd better be careful.

This new treatment failed to filter down to the guards. They had been harassing me for months, banging on my cell door. The rule of POW behavior required that we stand and bow if the guards opened the small peek-in door to check on us. The guards began playing games and kept popping my little door open just to see me stand up and bow. Finally I had enough, and I refused to acknowledge that the guard was there when he opened the peek-in door. They were rifle guards on patrol, and had no access to the cell, unless they could find the regular turn key to open it and let them in. My inaction infuriated one guard in particular. He was the tallest Vietnamese guard in camp. He had been hostile to every POW and possessed an ugly manner which prompted us to name him "Big Ugh". While he wasn't bright, he seemed to have an animal-like instinct which made him more dangerous and threatening than the other rifle guards.

When I had finished the false bio sheet in the afternoon he came with the hot drinking water bucket and opened my small door gesturing for me to give him my drinking container, an earthenware spouted pot which held almost a quart of liquid. Usually this task was performed by the water girls but they were nowhere to be seen and since the same scenario had been enacted before when the water girls were absent for some reason or another, I was not suspicious of Big Ugh. I arose and took the jug passing it to him through the small opening. He threw out the remainder of my morning water and handed the pot back to me gesturing that I should hold it while he filled it with steaming hot water from a large container. I did as he requested and was completely unprepared when he poured the steaming water over my hands after he had filled the pot. I managed not to drop the pot but my hands and wrists were red from the scalding water. Big Ugh laughed and I knew he had paid me back for refusing to bow when he played his games. My hands hurt like hell so I rubbed toothpaste on them to help ease the pain. I was angry at myself for being duped by Big Ugh and vowed I would get him in trouble with the camp authorities, one way or another.

The opportunity came the next day when Happy, the key guard, told me to dress for quiz. When I was ready to leave the cell, Big Ugh was on duty to escort me to the quiz room.

When we reached the quiz room, he sounded off in Vietnamese and then ushered me into the room where I faced Lump, who was sitting behind the desk. I walked to the stool in front of Lump, bowed and said, "Good morning sir." "Please sit down, Commander," he said in his best deep cultured French-accented English. "How are you today?" He beamed as he eyed the completed bio sheet that I clutched in my right hand. "Your guard has burned my hands with scalding water," I replied. I explained to him Big Ugh's actions of the previous afternoon. "What guard did this to you?" he asked when I had completed my complaint. "The big one outside the door who just brought me here." He called loudly in Vietnamese. Big Ugh came in, and stood nervously at attention as Lump spoke angrily in Vietnamese to him. I couldn't understand a word he said, but from his tone and expression I knew that Big Ugh was receiving a verbal tongue lashing. He dismissed him from the room with an angry wave of his hand and turned to me. "Some of our army men are cruel to you because they have lost members of their families killed by your air raids. The big guard's mother was killed by bombs and that is why he acts badly towards you. But I have told him in the future he must not do anything to the Americans that will bring on disgrace to the Vietnamese Army."

This sounded like a typical Vietnamese story used to cover loss of face for some action they were ashamed of. Versions of the same story were often used by Vietnamese camp officials in later years to explain away their barbaric treatment towards us. I was sure of only one thing from this quiz episode: Big Ugh probably wouldn't bother me too much as long as I was getting the good guy treatment.

Lump asked to see the biographical sheet and was openly pleased that I had filled it out completely. He asked me about my boyhood in Massachusetts and asked if I would describe the geography of New England. I gave him a verbal picture of the area. He seemed pleased that our relationship had reached a level where he could get ready answers from me. I was not fooled at all by his new tactic and felt I had the entire situation completely under control and could return to an absolute hard line any time I felt I couldn't go on with my plan.

He asked about my parents, wife and family. I gave him a description of them all, including ages and general information. Then I lowered my eyes and said the Christmas season was coming and I hoped I would receive some mail from my wife and be permitted by the camp authorities to write a Christmas letter home, to tell my family of my health and the "humane treatment I was receiving in Hanoi." While I initially started out play acting about my loneliness for them, by the time I had completed my verbal description of home and family and Christmas I was genuinely sad and tears came to my eyes. He showed open sympathy, and said that the authorities might grant my wish because of my good attitude. The quiz ended and he sent me back to my cell accompanied by Big Ugh. Big Ugh didn't give me any abuse or show any emotion and I assumed he was afraid of something Lump had said to him.

I was back in the cell. I had set the scene with Lump about Christmas mail. I prayed it would work out, and thought about the essential info I wanted to get out. My mind went back to the incident in survival school when the young black instructor took advantage of an academic situation to give me some of his own personal advice to follow if I was ever a POW. "Remember you are better educated and smarter than the personnel who are in charge of the POW camp. Use your brain and outsmart them and you'll do ok." I thought about plausible ways in which I could hide information I wanted to get out. It would have to fit in as part of my regular letter and not arouse any suspicion. My story had better be good or I'll fail completely, I thought, as I continued to work out the problem mentally. Nothing at all might come from my effort, I reasoned, but I must be ready in case it does. I'd get one chance and I'd better make it good. I tossed and turned and dreamed of writing a letter all night long. I knew what I wanted to say. I wanted to tell about solitary confinement, the number of POWs I knew were in Hanoi, the number of survivors from *ENTERPRISE* who were POWs, the fact that Jim Ruffin was not one of them and I wanted to make sure what I wrote would not be cut out by a Vietnamese censor so I planned to make the tone of the letter indicate that I was receiving the best treatment available from the North Vietnamese.

At noon on the sixteenth of November, Lump came to my cell, opened the peek-in door and told me I would be permitted to write a Christmas letter home. He gave me a pen, ink, three lined sheets of Vietnamese writing paper and said that this letter would be a rough copy and would have to be approved by the camp authorities before I could rewrite it in the smooth for mailing. He said that I must hurry and he would be back for it later in the afternoon. As soon as he left I tapped joyfully to Jerry Coffee, "Lump came and I am writing a letter home for Christmas. I don't have much time. See you later."

I sat on my bunk and printed the following letter as rapidly as possible:

From   James Alfred Mulligan
Address   Camp of detention of U.S. Pilots captured
                                    in the Democratic Republic of Vietnam
                                    c/o Hanoi Post Office, D.R.V.

To   Mrs. Louise M. Mulligan
                                5446 Floral Ave.
                                Jacksonville, Florida U.S.A. 32211
Please Forward

                                              16 November 1966
My darling wife and children,
My captors are allowing me to write a letter home. BIG DEAL! I hope that
it arrives before Christmas. You all know my feelings, how I like things
and what I expect you to do. This separation is difficult but it will end and
we will resume our lives together once again. I won't discuss much about
life here. I am a prisoner and if I had a deck of cards I could play that
famous game of solitaire. When you write to the Roadrunners tell them
I'm ok. Let's get the bad news over with. Physically I have some problems that will need attention when I get released. My left arm, shoulder
and left side of my chest will need some work and my left hip is still sore
but should be all right with a little attention. I was quite sick for a few
months and lost a lot of weight. I have been getting lots of vitamin pills,
bananas and oranges for my health at meals. In addition to meat and
vegetable I get piles of whole grain rice, plenty of warm soup, and a pot of
water, and now estimate my weight at 150 pounds or what it was on the
day I enlisted in 1944 when Uncle Mark and Aunt Ginny drove me to
Boston. Give them my love. My blood pressure is down and I will need a
good physical to determine the final effects of my high speed ejection. I
will be ok but it looks like my flying career has come to a screaming halt a
bit sooner than I had anticipated. The care in food, shelter and medicine
that the Vietnamese have given me is better than I had expected. The
climate is hot and damp like Jax, only worse. I will of course be glad to be
repatriated. On being captured I was given medical treatment, fed and
taken to a camp. Of course I miss all of you, and you are in my thoughts
and prayers at all times. Each day I feature one of you in my prayers.
Sunday is Mom's day, Monday, number one son, right on down till number six on Saturday. Though my days are filled with boredom I still
manage to keep my sense of humor in the hope of better days ahead.
Life is very much like the religious retreat I made a few years back only it
is much more quiet here and I have more time for thinking and meditating. Give my best to Father Gallagher. You know, he is some athlete, he
got six hits out of seven at bats, scored all six runs and beat my softball
team 6-0 and all against my best pitcher. Oh, tell him I found his altar boy
Paul Daly to have a good backhand but he was rough in missing his
forehand shots and needs a lot of work to smooth them out. I do feel with
practice and a good tennis coach, he can go a long way professionally. I
trust that you will have a reputable insurance man help you decide on the
flight coverage in my insurances. Since I am over 40 years old, rates
should change and much of it might be cancelled temporarily at least.
You have power of attorney and legal documents so you should be able
to accomplish everything. You may change, cancel or take out any allot-
ment of my pay that you may desire. If you run into any serious trouble,

From   James Alfred Mulligan
Address Camp of detention of U.S. Pilots captured
in the Democratic Republic of Vietnam
c/o Hanoi Post Office, D.R.V.

To   Mrs. Louise M. Mulligan
5446 Floral Ave.
Jacksonville, Florida U.S.A.
Please Forward   32211

16 November 1966

My darling wife and children
My captors are allowing me to write a letter home. Big
Deal! I hope that it arrives before Christmas. You all know
my feelings, how I like things and what I expect you to
do. This separation is difficult but it will end and we
will resume our lives together once again. I won't
discuss much about life here. I am a prisoner and if
I had a deck of cards I could play that famous game
of solitaire. When you write to the Roadrunners tell them
Im ok. Lets get the bad news over with. Physically I
have some problems that will need attention when I get
released. My left arm, shoulder and left side of my chest
will need some work and my left hip is still sore but should
be all right with a little attention. I was quite sick for
a few months and lost a lot of weight. I have been
getting lots of vitamin pills, bananas and oranges for my
health. At meals, in addition to meat and vegetable I get,
piles of whole grain rice, plenty of warm soup, and a pot of
water, and now estimat—

Mrs. Louise M. Mulligan
5446 Floral Ave.
Jacksonville, Florida USA
32211
Please Forward:
905 Kempfer Dr.
Virginia Beach, Va 23454

legally, don't hesitate to use Red Rafferty, of Norfolk, immediately. I have confidence in his ability and integrity. When you start writing to colleges in addition to your present list, get info from Univ. of Tampa, Univ. of Omaha, SMU, Univ. of Maryland, Univ. of Mass. and Magill in Canada but don't get set on anything until I get home. I assume all the boys are doing their best in school and also are helping mom out as much as possible during this difficult time. Just keep doing what you think I would want you to do and things will work out fine. Above all keep busy with sports and scouts, etc. And have lots of family fun but don't neglect your school work. As for you my beloved wife, once again you must bear the harsh burden of life's cross alone. Keep your faith and spirits, my darling, our love can do nothing but grow stronger. Remember me in your prayers but have no regrets. I will phone Jax as soon as I am released and if you have moved I'll track you down from there. So leave word with the phone company in Jax. You should have all of my personal effects so check my little green address book for names you don't have in your file. I would like you to have this letter printed or mimeographed and sent out to our friends as you see fit. Give my best wishes to my folks, all our relatives and friends and ask them to remember me and all the men out here in their prayers. I would like it fine if during the coming Christmas season each one of them would raise his glass just once for me and I hope that I will be able to join them as soon as possible and reciprocate. You and the children try to have an extra special Christmas this year; filled with the joys of living and remembering that the seed of hope grows with faith. Thank the good Lord for sparing my life and join me in prayer to the Prince of Peace, that lasting peace will soon be restored to this war-torn world and that we will joyfully be reunited once again. In the meantime, keep your spirits up, have faith in the future and live your days one by one as joyfully as you can. I love you all and miss you all very much and though I am a prisoner, I remain as always, ever with you in my thoughts and prayers, and remembering in my heart, that they also serve, who sit at home alone and wait. God be with you, happy and joyous Christmas. Be very careful; and take good care of yourselves. Love one another. Your devoted husband and father, Jim
(instructions)
1.   address to: James Alfred Mulligan
                           Camp of detention of U.S. Pilots captured
                           in the Democratic Republic of Vietnam
                           c/o Hanoi Post Office, D.R.V.
2.   Letter must be sent by regular or air mail.
3.   Each envelope may contain letters, cards or photos
      not exceeding 20 grams (total weight) including envelope.
4.   Only one envelope of 20 grams maximum weight per month.
      In the envelope may be letters from wife, children, folks, etc.
      I covered the solitary confinement with the comment about playing solitaire. Also I had made a religious retreat at the Jesuit retreat house in Pass Christian, Mississippi back in 1957 where I had to live alone and follow the silence rule of the retreat and I knew Louise would pick this up.

From the monthly increase in additions to my POW memory bank of names I carefully estimated that when the letter got home for Christmas there would be 150 American POWs in Hanoi. On my release I learned the actual number was 149. I wrote POW by using the first letters in three consecutive words in three consecutive descriptive phrases . . . *Piles of whole* grain rice, *plenty of warm* soup, and a *pot of water* . . . everyone in my family knew that when I joined the Navy I had to eat bananas and drink lots of water to make the 120-pound weight required to pass the physical. Uncle Mark and Aunt Ginny were Admiral and Mrs. Clarence A. Hill, one of my former Commanding Officers for whom I had the highest admiration and respect. I knew that if "Mark" Hill saw that letter the information in it would be unravelled and get to the right places.

I knew that Father Gallagher would be able to figure out that I had found six POWs from *ENTERPRISE* from the bullshit story about a softball game that never occurred. Paul Daly was in the same squadron with Jim Ruffin and Larry Spencer. Since Spencer was a back seat radar operator in the F4, I highlighted him by referring to him as a good back hand and Ruffin by saying he was *rough in missing* his forehand. Ruffin, the pilot, was the F4 front seat man who was missing and who never did show up in any camp.

The Vietnamese had often threatened the safety of my wife and children by action from American anti-war activists who would carry out Hanoi's orders. I was concerned about this possibility so I referred Louise, if she ran into any serious trouble (by which I meant threats or actions against her or the children) to a close friend, Dick Rafferty, who was a special agent in the F.B.I. and was last stationed in Norfolk.

The rest of the letter had no intelligence info and was written with my feelings and concerns for my family. I said some things about treatment being better than I expected just to get the Vietnamese to send out the letter. I had a gut feeling that they wouldn't catch on to my efforts and that they would be happy to send out info that gave them a good image.

I finished the letter. It was printed so that the North Vietnamese couldn't copy and falsely use my handwriting in other propaganda statements. After reading it through once carefully, I was satisfied with my attempt. The afternoon tocsin then rang and in minutes Lump was at my cell door to get the letter. I was fatigued; the entire effort was a rush job. Emotionally keyed up, I prayed they would buy it.

I tapped to Coffee and told him what I was trying to get out so that he could pass it to the others. I ate my afternoon meal and the cell was engulfed in complete darkness right after sundown. My night was long. My sleep was disturbed by nervous apprehension from the day's events. I reminisced about my family and the letter and the coming Christmas season. I was saddened and lonesome. This was my second consecutive Christmas away from home and loved ones. I wondered when I'd spend Christmas with Louise and all the boys again. If I had known then that it would be in 1973, I might have given up and just quit and died there on the spot. However, the unknown future allows rays of hope to exist in circumstances, which when viewed in retrospect, would seem to warrant little more than utter despair. My POW days in Hanoi were a reflection of this, days of despair overcome by rays of everlasting hope.

Two days after I had written the rough draft copy of my letter home, Lump came to my cell with it, more paper and a sheet of instructions with info I would send to Louise on the format and procedures that she was to use when she wrote to me in Hanoi. I felt that this was an indication of some breakthrough on the mail situation and that I would probably be getting letters at Christmas or soon afterwards. However, I was doomed to disappointment on this hope for a long time to come.

The Vietnamese had not touched one word of my letter and I was overjoyed. I copied it completely in the smooth and after rereading it, I underlined lightly the words, ROUGH IN MISSING to highlight my info on Jim Ruffin. Lump collected the letter, writing materials and instruction sheet and seemed pleased at the entire event. This occurred just as it was getting dark so he found my cell slipping into night's blackness as he opened the peek-in the door. "Why do you have no light?" he asked. "Because one of the officers of the camp said that I had a bad attitude and must live in darkness," I replied. Before going to sleep, I thanked the Lord and recited a fervent Rosary for my family and myself. I was lonesome for Louise and the boys. I ached with nostalgia. "Lord when will it end, when will it end," I sobbed, as I dropped off into a deep sleep.

The key guard, Happy, put in a new light early in the morning and let me have an extra half hour bathing at noon. The sun was high, the sky blue and clear of clouds and the temperature balmy. I sopped up some rays after my bath and clothes washing chores were completed. The warm sunshine seemed to invigorate my emaciated body, and I longed for freedom as I observed a few small sparrows flittering to and from a hidden nesting place located somewhere in the eaves of the Pool Hall.

Not even a sparrow falls without His hand, I thought as I gave thanks for the benefits I was enjoying. I was slowly learning that the real meaning of life is food for the starving man, water for the parched thirsting man and human companionship for the solitary confined man, and that these were hardships that could be borne more easily with complete faith in the Lord and hope in the future.

"Lord grant me increased faith, everlasting hope and teach me perfect love. Please send me home to my family and country a better man than when I came here. Thy Will be done. Amen," I prayed.

The air raid alarm sounded and I saw bursts of flak high to the southwest. Two SA-2 missiles roared from their hiding places a little north and I watched them heading into the combat sky. Then Happy rushed into the wash area and hurried me back to my cell.

That night, Hanoi Hannah, speaking on the Voice of Vietnam, claimed that an intruding American air pirate had been justly punished by the missiles of the Vietnam People's Air Force when it was downed eight miles south of Hanoi. She didn't claim that a pilot was captured, so I prayed that the story was false, but deep in my heart I felt that we might have lost another Yank over Hanoi. The air war was getting rougher and more and more POWs had been arriving all that summer and fall.

"I wonder when in hell LBJ is going to use the B-52's, crank up a blockade and really hit these guys where it hurts? When that happens, I'll be going home soon. The only thing these little bastards will ever understand is brute force," I mused. The night tocsin rang and I went to sleep in a lighted cell, angry and frustrated about the war and more lonely than ever.

TALKING THROUGH THE WALL!

Sunday was a minimum work day for the Vietnamese guards and camp personnel. We Americans took advantage of this reduction in the normal working routine by engaging in maximum communications effort within, and where possible, between buildings. A few shifts were made in the past week and each Pool Hall cell was occupied. Jerry Coffee had established an elaborate clearance procedure in order that I might be able to talk through the wall using a rolled up blanket resembling a horse collar. This method was very effective provided the area was well cleared of guards. Coffee had been talking to me regularly through the wall using this technique. I put my drinking cup on the spot on the wall directly opposite to him and I could hear him clearly and distinctly.

I had not spoken directly to an American since I conversed with Jim Stockdale in New Guy Village back in the Hanoi Hilton the previous April. Consequently I was elated at the prospect of being able to talk to Jerry Coffee in relative safety. Jerry was a warm, personable and sensitive young man. He was concerned about my loneliness and my morale and did everything in his power to cheer me up with his daily conversations. I couldn't quite believe I was going to be able to actually talk in safety. On my first attempt my voice cracked with emotion and tears filled my eyes. I gulped a couple of times, dried my eyes with the heel of my right hand and got back into the horse collar to try again. The system worked well and in minutes I was bubbling over, bending Jerry's ear about my POW life since capture. I filled him in on my wife and family and what I wanted to do after the war. I must have been on the wall for an hour or more when I suddenly received a danger thump from Quincy Collins and A.J. Myers, who were living next to me. I was safely sitting back on my bunk when a pimply faced snooping guard slowly opened my peek-in door. On spotting him I arose, bowed and returned to my position on the bunk. The siesta wake-up tocsin rang and ended our conversation. In minutes the food and water would be delivered throughout the camp and it would no longer be safe to communicate by voice. I said a quick verbal, "Goodbye, God Bless," to Jerry Coffee. "Talk to you tomorrow," he replied as he signed off with his, "Goodbye, God Bless."

Back on my bunk, I said a quick prayer of thanksgiving for Jerry Coffee and all the guys in the Pool Hall, who had set up and maintained the clearance procedures which allowed me to regain control of my spirits. Solitary confinement, I was discovering, was a most depressing state to live in. Absolute loneliness nagged at my intellect. It confused and frustrated my will. Under this duress I constantly found my mind flying off in flights of fantasy. I'm sure that many of my awake dreaming hours were more irrational than rational. In the abject loneliness that I endured, time itself became a mass of confusion where minutes stretched into hours, hours into days, days into weeks, and weeks into months. I was existing in a dreamland half dead, half alive, in a never, never land where the hopes for tomorrow were the only bulwark against the frustrations of today. More and more I turned inward, becoming a complete introvert.

My mind kept hopscotching from one idea to another. I built a new house mentally, then I furnished it, and finally landscaped it. When that was completed I returned to running a family investment fund. For hours, days on end, I relived my life. I was slowly moving backwards in time as I mentally exhausted myself, retreating backwards reliving first my Navy career and married family life. The pieces of my previous existence began falling together. I developed a serious guilt complex from all of my previous failures as a husband, father, Christian and American. I wanted to be able to live my life over again, to be able to undo the many human failures I had acquired over the years. I wanted to make amends, make my life more meaningful when my stint in that earthen purgatory ended. Hanoi is a cleansing place for my soul, I thought over and over again. It's a second chance, *if* I survive. I vowed daily to the Lord that I'd do better; that I'd grow spiritually from the suffering I was undergoing.

I noticed as my physical condition worsened that my will to resist and spiritual stamina increased. They could only do so much to my body once it reached a critical point, where any further deterioration would end in death. I felt I was almost at this juncture physically. I was literally starving to death from poor diet and almost dying from utter loneliness, yet felt I was the conqueror, first over myself and my failings, second over the North Vietnamese. Individually I held them in contempt. Collectively I maintained an inward compassion for a people, I now knew, had never tasted true freedom and most certainly never would. I hated Communism for what it did to the human spirit, but I prayed for the people in this Communist country. What a helluva existence they've doomed themselves to live in, I thought. Like a colony of ants, millions united as one working for the advancement of the Motherland — bullshit! What bullshit! How naive and sad. Doomed to mediocrity by having no freedom they have no heights to conquer. Just millions united as one. A million ants, one just like the other. Where the hell did their humanity go to? I surmised that when North Vietnam replaced a Divine cause with a human goal, it had doomed itself to oblivion forever, or at least until it got out from the yoke of Communism.

As I lay on the concrete bed my mind wandered aimlessly on Marxism. I thought about what it was and where it was going. Communism is nothing more than a religion of society. It has a human origin and a human end. It has no soul, no spirit, no infinite cause to explain life and its meaning. How shallow it stands compared to the religious depth of the individual human soul that each human being subconsciously longs to understand. Who am I? Why am I here? Who made me? Where did life start? Where will it end? Everlasting, infinite, universal?

Shut up individual human beings! Forget those questions. In their place Communism will fill your belly, give you a bowl of rice and a purple shirt. Millions united as one, all alike, look alike. The benevolent Communist state will protect you all and give you all your worldly possessions. But the price you pay is your own humanity. Poor little North Vietnamese. Poor little Communist bastards. "Our Father who art in Heaven. . . . help them see the light."

Monday morning I heard strange noises, squeaks and squeals, unrecognizable noises that didn't make sense. A sudden tap call-up on the wall from Jerry Coffee came to me. "At bath we saw a bunch of skinny turkeys in the yard. Looks like meat for Thanksgiving or Christmas," was Jerry's message.

Thanksgiving was coming and I had almost completely forgotten about it. On *ENTERPRISE* on our way to Vietnam last year I had eaten a Thanksgiving dinner that was fit for a king. The Navy always feeds its personnel well, but on major holidays at sea, the cooks pull out all stops. The thought of food made my mouth water. God was I hungry. I longed for meat and fresh vegetables. I started thinking more and more about all those things that I enjoyed eating in my daily diet as a free American. The contrast between that diet and my rice, sea weed soup and pot of hot water in Hanoi was almost unbelievable and my emaciated body showed its effects. Since capture my hair and beard had grown gray. My skin was wrinkled, pale and mottled, like that found hanging loose on an old man in his eighties. Though I could run in place indefinitely barefoot and without getting winded, physically I was weak and had little strength. Daily I ran and ran and ran in place, toughening up my feet, building up my capability to keep moving if the chance of escape ever came. I literally ran the frustrations of solitary confinement into submission. Though in fact starving, I had long ago stopped thinking about food. It was a memory from my past which when activated brought pain. I would not be able to keep food out of my thoughts completely, however. At night in my dreams I would return to a life filled with chocolate, peanut butter, hot dogs, hamburgers and steak. One dream about steak was so vivid that I mashed my teeth into my tongue. I awoke with a bleeding mouth.

The days dragged by all too slowly. One day Lump quizzed me briefly about my health and asked if the bananas and vitamins were making me feel better. I replied, "Yes". Then he told me the Vietnamese would show the captured Americans their human and lenient treatment by serving turkey on the occasion of the American holidays of Thanksgiving and Christmas. When I left to return to my cell I could see a flock of strange looking birds on the other side of the swimming pool. They were the worst looking turkeys I had ever seen. I was sure that the only reason Lump had me for quiz was to insure that I actually saw the turkeys.

Big Ugh was the roving guard that night. When he opened my peek-in door I stood and bowed then sat back on my bunk. He looked but didn't hassle me and left. A few seconds later I heard a loud slap coming from the direction of cell four. Then another slap resounded and everything became quiet again.

A few minutes later Quincy Collins tapped softly to me. "Big Ugh came to the door and motioned me to come close to him. When I did he suddenly reached in and slapped me in the face. I turned the other cheek and he slapped me again. I turned my other cheek and he looked at me confused. He didn't know what to do so he closed the door and left. GBU." (God Bless You).

Quincy was still badly injured and walked with a limp. Big Ugh had met his match from the actions of a very good Christian American.

The day before Thanksgiving, the Vietnamese held a surprise room inspection and personal search. As usual they made me stand facing forward against the wall with my arms raised as high over my head as I could get them. One guard checked me and another checked the cell and my gear. My broken left shoulder and shattered shoulder socket prohibited me from raising my left arm any higher than head high. This seemed to infuriate the little obnoxious guard known as "Toothpick". He demanded by signs and in Vietnamese that I raise my left arm to a fully extended position. When I couldn't he became angry and physically pulled on the arm. The pain shot through my body. I lost complete control, turned suddenly on him and bellowed, "Bao Cao (Bow Cow), Bao Cao, Bao Cao," at the top of my lungs. Bao Cao were the words we were told to say when we were in extremes and we wanted to speak to a Vietnamese English-speaking officer.

Toothpick and his companion were completely taken by surprise. Happy the Key Guard came running followed by Smiley who was the senior enlisted guard in the camp. "Mun, no Bao Cao, Mun, no Bao Cao," pleaded Happy as he tried to keep me from screaming any more. I quieted down and by sign language told Happy and Smiley what Tooth-pick was doing to me. They held a small conference and kept looking to see if any of the Vietnamese officers had heard me and were coming. When none came and they were assured I would remain quiet, they upbraided Toothpick for his actions. He was unhappy about the turn of events, but there was little he could do about it. For my part I had learned another basic lesson as a POW. The guards would get away with as much as the POW would let them, but didn't want the officers to be aware of their actions. I filed this lesson in my mental bag of important informa-tion for survival. Just the threat of a loud Bao Cao is enough to scare the guards off from their planned shenanigans, I thought.

On Thanksgiving, Toothpick was a roving guard. When I came out for my food he pointed to a plate holding the smallest piece of turkey, a sliver of curled carrot peel and a tiny piece of greenery I had never seen before. He had gotten even in his own little way for the embarrassment I had caused him. I returned to my cell with the plate, a bowl of real cabbage soup and a pot of tea. After saying Thanksgiving grace I ate the vegetables, meat and cabbage soup, savoring every mouthful. I hadn't realized that cabbage soup could taste so good. I chewed the turkey bones and sucked out what marrow was in them. For the occasion my hot water pot was filled with hot tea. Later the Vietnamese came with a half a cup of sweet thick coffee. I sipped it, drop by drop, trying to make it last as long as possible. I was thankful for what little I had. Compared to our daily diet, our meal that day was a banquet. It opened up old memories, of Thanksgiving at home with Louise and the boys. That night after my prayers I sobbed myself to sleep. I ached with the pain of loss for my wife, family, home and country. I was at the edge of despair. "Get me out of here, Lord. Get me out of here," then finally sleep came, only a sleep permeated with dreams of home, family, country and friends. My night was very restless and I awoke fatigued and down in the dumps. Loneliness, I was convinced, was the most bitter pill of life that I would ever swallow. I still think so, even to this day.

From Thanksgiving until mid-December things came to a complete standstill in the Pool Hall. No one in the entire building had been to quiz in weeks. We were effectively cut off from the other buildings in the camp and had not even one iota of an idea of what was going on.

We kept up our daily building communications and intelligence reporting. The clearance procedures allowed me to talk through the wall to Jerry Coffee at each noon siesta. I regained control of my vocal chords and was very pleased at having the opportunity to be able to communicate directly and almost normally with another American.

I had two men who were in bad shape under my jurisdiction as senior ranking officer. LCDR. Jack Fellowes, had lost the complete use of his hands as a result of rope torture he received shortly after capture. He could not do anything for himself, eat, wash or take care of his personal needs. Fortunately his cellmate Ron Bliss was an understanding man. He literally kept Jack Fellowes alive for months. Air Force Captain Norland Daughtry, though one of the earliest POWs, still suffered great pains and agony from an open wound near his elbow. He received little medical attention from the Vietnamese and I was worried about him.

Fortunately for me, both men were tigers, and had cellmates who could assist them. They also kept me informed of their conditions. As senior ranking officer there was little I could do for them, except keep apprised of their condition. It was another responsibility of command that in reality was beyond my power to control. However, at quiz I kept getting my oar in by demanding better medical attention for our wounded Americans. Since my capture, at each quiz I made it a point to demand that the Vietnamese treat me and the other captured Americans according to the Geneva Accords regarding Prisoners of War which Hanoi had ratified and signed.

My efforts, except in rare instances, came to naught. The North Vietnamese had decided long ago that captured Americans were not Prisoners of War. "You have no rights. You are criminals of war, captured American air pirates," was the standard retort I received from J.C., Mickey Mouse and Spot. I nevertheless persisted in my efforts, because I was convinced I had a moral obligation as well as a moral right to demand humane treatment as a POW. My demands caused the Vietnamese to decide early in the game that I was obdurate and had a bad attitude, which meant for the most part I was merely uncooperative. I was in fact the ugly American at quiz. I had not yet learned to control my tongue and temper, and this indiscreet behavior would cause me much unnecessary pain and anguish before my captivity was terminated. I was under a handicap in that I did not understand the ways of Orientals and made no effort to remedy that deficiency. As time moved on I learned to assume a more stoic role, uncharacteristic to a twentieth century attack jet pilot.

The cell walls seemed to be moving in on me more and more each day. For the most part the weather was overcast, damp, and quite chilly. The daylight hours grew shorter, the nights, longer and lonelier. I longed for warm sunshine and blue skies. I hadn't seen a sunrise or sunset for nine months. I missed seeing the moon as it moved from a fiery red ball on an ocean's horizon to a silvery sliver barely visible to the naked eye. I began to associate freedom with people and open spaces, sunrises and sunsets, moon passings and skies filled with thousands of twinkling stars. Swallowed up by the four walls of a windowless cell, I longed for them and yearned to be free to enjoy them all again, and on top of this, Christmas was coming. Christmas, the season of joy, of love, of family, of the Christ Child born to set all men free. I must prepare myself spiritually for His coming, I thought as I mapped out my brief Advent devotions of more prayers and more meditation. I could only offer up my own suffering, physical and emotional. Keep the faith, believe, ask and you shall receive. What could I ask for? That this yoke of loneliness and captivity be lifted? No, never! Ask the Father only for the grace to bear this burden, for the strength to accept it all and survive to return a better man. Ask for forgiveness from the infinite source of love. Thy will be done? Oh Lord, let me accept, accept, accept!

CHRISTMAS 1966

A few days before Christmas, Lump had me brought to quiz. He was overly pleasant and in a very talkative mood as he discussed the plans that the North Vietnamese were making for us to celebrate the coming feast. There would be turkey and a full meal that day. The Vietnamese would decorate a Christmas room; it would be the very room I was being quizzed in. "Where should the tree be placed?" he asked. "In the far corner," I pointed as I wondered what a Vietnamese Christmas tree would look like. Then came Lump's curve ball. "We permit you on the occasion of Christmas to send a message over the radio to your family." They want a tape, I thought. My mind flashed back to the first and only tape I made, forced on me by the torment of the gas-soaked ropes. I shuttered as I recalled the torturer, Pig Eye, cutting the pus-covered ropes soaked in blood and torn skin. Never again, never again! I'll die before I make any tapes for them. "I can't do that," I said quietly to Lump. I was nervous. I imagined I was going to be physically tortured. My heartbeat quickened. The palms of my hands grew moist. A cold sweat of fear overcame me. "Why cannot you do this?" Lump asked. "Some of your compatriots have already sent the Christmas message to their families. They will be played over the voice of Vietnam and you yourself will hear them over the radio of the camp." "I am sad for my family at Christmas. I do not wish to share with others over the radio the privacy of my family life," I replied. "If you send a message over the radio the authorities of the camp may give to you a letter from your family on the occasion of Christmas," Lump added. I'm being blackmailed. They are trying to buy me with the promise of a letter from Louise. More than anything else I wanted to hear from Louise and the boys. Just the thought of them put a knot in my stomach. "No, I am too sad about my family. I cannot send a message over the radio." Lump was disturbed at my lack of cooperation. "Return to your cell," he directed gruffly. The honeymoon is over between Lump and me, I concluded as I arose, bowed, and silently limped back to my cell. On the way back I saw the flock of turkeys. They were the skinniest birds I'd ever seen. No letter for me this Christmas; Lump will see to that.

That night I had my first hearty laugh in Vietnam. One of the POWs who had taped a message home really pulled one over the North Vietnamese. In a sing song voice he distorted the pronunciation of his first name. He said Eedwood for Edward and Ahalan for Alan, and described how he longed for his favorite food dish, cabbage soup! When he concluded in sing song that the whole event was one "BFD (that's big fine dinner in Americanese," he said), it completely broke me up. The North Vietnamese had been outwitted. Hanoi Hannah's voice of Vietnam program sent this bogus message to the entire world. It gave audible testimony to just how naive the North Vietnamese really were. I laughed till the tears were in my eyes. I had lost so many skirmishes I was overjoyed at hearing someone who had completely turned the tables.

I bathed late the next morning, close to the morning meal and siesta time. When the food was distributed, Happy, the Pool Hall key guard, told me in sign language to be sure to listen to the American on the voice of Vietnam. The program was a replay of the previous night's and it made me laugh even harder. "If they will swallow this bull and play it over the voice of Vietnam, then they probably swallowed my entire letter and sent it home intact to Louise," I mused. My spirits were raised at this turn of events.

Christmas Eve, long after dark, I was taken to quiz in a room that was completely decorated with tree, ornaments and a nativity set. Fox, the camp commander, sat beside Lump who conducted the interview and did all the talking. I sat stoically on the stool and refused politely his offer of a cigarette. They wanted to show the captured American air pirates the lenient and humane treatment that the Vietnamese had always extended to their captives, Lump said, as he proceeded through a long harangue about the victorious history of the Vietnamese people as they conquered valiantly first one invader and then another. Though bored stiff by his inept effort at propaganda, I remained attentive hoping against hope that I would receive a letter from home. When he finished his speech he closed by wishing me joy on the occasion of Christmas. "Will I get a letter from my wife?" I asked. "If your wife writes, the camp authorities will give you the letter," he answered. I said a mental bullshit, bowed and sadly made my way back to my cell. Maybe next year I'll get a letter, was my only thought.

Late that night I composed a Christmas greeting which I passed by tap code to the eighteen men living in the Pool Hall. My message simply said, "Remember at Christmas as we celebrate the rebirth of Christ, that upon our release, we also will be born again into a free world, better men than when we came here. God Bless! Happy Christmas!"

It was the longest and loneliest night of the year for me. I soaked myself in self pity; I yearned to be with my wife and family. I longed to be able to go to Mass and Communion and to be able to partake of those holy graces on this most Holy Day. I longed for the Christian fellowship and open friendship that were always so visible at Christmas.

But there in Hanoi I had nothing. A barren cell with four blank walls hemming me in constantly, physically and mentally. I conjectured that my barren cell was my own poor nativity stable.

Just as the birth of Christ brought hope to a waiting world, so did His rebirth bring hope to me in Hanoi. "It is a holy time and I must pray for the grace to enable me to endure this sacrifice that has forced itself upon me. I must keep my faith in God, my country and my family and I must never, never, never give up. I must learn to suffer and accept and survive. Above all else I must survive and emerge a better man than when I came here."

That Christmas night set the tone of the moral resistance posture I would follow during all of my remaining days in captivity. Christmas of 1966 was my own rebirth. I reviewed the events of the past nine months since I had arrived in Hanoi, reliving step by step and day by day each item of my existence. I was convinced I would have to survive on my own efforts. That I would be kept in solitary confinement seemed a foregone conclusion. I would have absolutely nothing but myself and the Lord, and in the end it would be His show.

I felt that during the past nine months of living in solitary confinement, I had become a completely private man. I had grown to like the reflection allowed by silence and could see some of the benefits of monastic life, though I would not voluntarily impose it on myself if given the choice. I could sense that I was changing inwardly; the hardship of POW life was toughening my moral fiber. I was rearranging my priorities of life into a simplistic pattern where I would strive for order, discipline and moderation in my everyday living.

Order: everything in its proper place in priority; the order of things and events according to their relevant importance; render to Caesar the things that are Caesar's but to God the things that are God's . . . and God comes *first! Discipline:* the ability to make myself do those things which are right and avoid doing those things which I know are wrong. Discipline means self-discipline. It means sacrifice for a cause. It means paying the price for what you believe in, even though no one else knows or even cares that you pay the price. Discipline means living to a self imposed standard which says right is right if no one is right, and wrong is wrong if everyone is wrong. *And Moderation!* Enjoy God's benefits in all of their abundance but enjoy them in moderation! Once you have been starved, moderation becomes a more meaningful objective! These would be my new rules of living: order, discipline, moderation; where God comes first!

Religion became more personal and less humanistic to me. I no longer confused my spiritual and divine goals with social and human objectives. Carried to its ultimate conclusion, religion became a one-on-one encounter; hence to me it was more personal and less communal or social. One man, one God, one soul, one life, one judgment, one reward or one punishment. I concluded this type of religion would prevail if there was only one man in existence. The idea of collective social worship became a convenience that in no way enhanced my religious encounter with God.

This concept was new to me. From then on, a religious ceremony would be nothing more than an assist, and not really intrinsically linked up with my beliefs and commitment. I could maintain my religious encounter in complete solitude and without the trappings of worldly ceremony. I wanted to attend Mass, but with this option removed by solitary confinement my own person and daily living became my Mass. I experienced solace from the knowledge that my captives could deprive me of everything except my faith. I was next to the bottomless pit of despair, but the Lord sustained me and I offered what sacrifice I could in thanksgiving for my new found state of mind. My soul was being purged and my knowledge of this made the loneliness of Christmas more bearable, and Christmas itself even more meaningful. I prayed for my country, family and friends and fell asleep finally with these greetings on my lips as dawn's first light crept in through a small opening under my cell door. "Merry Christmas Louise, Merry Christmas James, Kevin, Terrance, Mark, Sean and Neil; Merry Christmas Mom and Dad, Ken and Miggs my brothers. Merry Christmas friends. Merry Christmas America. Thanks Lord for sustaining me. Merry Christmas! Merry Christmas!"

It was late when I was awakened by Happy the key guard, as he unbolted my cell door to let me out to empty my personal convenience bucket. The air was crisp and the sky absolutely clear. I limped to the dumping area next to the Pig Sty. I took longer than usual to accomplish this daily task. I knew that since it was a holiday I wouldn't get the usual outside time to bathe and wash my clothes. Happy had kept me till the last so he wasn't in any hurry and didn't rush me in his usual manner. Once my bucket was cleansed and rinsed, I returned as slowly as possible to my cell, sucking in the cool fresh air, drinking in the sky and sunshine, trying to capture as many additional seconds of outside time as possible. I hated my four wall cell. I hated its dank smell, its shadows and semi-darkness which hung threateningly over me at all times. Happy seemed to sense my frustration and was unperturbed at my slowness. For a second I thought I saw a glimpse of compassion come over his face. Then mindful of his other chores he finally chided me: "Queekly, queekly, Mun," and he rushed me into my cell slamming the door.

I had a piece of turkey for dinner and some carrot shavings. The soup was comprised of clear noodles laced with meat broth. I mixed my rice in the soup and made a heavy mush. The meal wouldn't win any prizes for appearance but in comparison to our daily menu it was a feast fit for a king. I ate the carrot shavings, turkey and soup in that order taking lots of time to enjoy each mouthful. When finished, I licked my plate and bowl clean and sucked on the turkey bone for dessert. The water girls delivered steaming thick sugary coffee, filling my cup to the brim. I sipped it for more than an hour. The abundance of warm food and the sugared coffee seemed to make me come alive. I felt better than I had since before my capture. I finally realized that the daily diet which I had grown accustomed to was barely sufficient to keep me alive. I inspected my body closely and estimated that I couldn't possibly weigh more than one hundred pounds. I looked like pictures I had seen of Jewish prisoners, kept in German concentration camps. It was horrible and frightening as the full realization of my own physical state finally dawned on me. The diet, the dysentery and the worms had been taking their toll on my body for nine months. If the American people could see me now they would get so angry we would win the war in a month, I thought.

In mid-afternoon, Happy opened my cell and told me to dress. I thought I was going for a quiz but instead I was taken to the main hall of the Auditorium. The Vietnamese had rigged up the room into a series of pens using heavy ropes over which they hung blankets. It was the damndest sight I'd ever seen. They put POWs from each cell into a blanket pen so that we could see a propaganda movie but not be able to see one another and communicate. I was one of the last to arrive and got a glimpse of American heads in some of the pens before Happy made me bend over and keep out of sight. I entered the room and made my way over and under ropes to my appointed place.

As I approached the spot reserved for me, Big Ugh stuck his foot out and gave me a shove which knocked me down and sent me sprawling into my pen. I got myself up into a sitting position just in time to see

Quincy Collins and A.J. Meyers enter, hobbling with canes. Someone pulled Quincy's cane and he flopped into his pen out of sight. A.J. followed him in.

I didn't pay much attention to the movie because I wanted to see if I could communicate with some other POWs. Big Ugh had a different idea and he kept me under his constant surveillance, pushing my head down whenever he thought I might be able to see another POW. The entire movie episode was weird. Right in the middle of the show the air raid alarm went off as a U.S. low level reconnaissance aircraft flew directly over the camp. I was ushered back to my cell by Happy. On the way I passed J.C. who said indignantly, "The American air pirates bomb us on Christmas when we give you the human treatment." "Bullshit," I replied, "The U.S. just took pictures of the camp to make sure we are here and say Merry Christmas to us." "Return your cell, you are bad man," screamed J.C. who obviously was frightened by the recce and the implications of my retort.

Back in the cell Jerry Coffee tapped to me that Bob Purcell had gotten a roommate whose name was Bunny Tally. Bunny had been a spotter for the Baltimore Colt football games and had worked as a lifeguard at Manhattan Beach in California. "That's all the info Purcell tapped to me. He's too busy talking to his roommate to tap any more today," said Coffee.

I was elated at this news. Everyone in the Pool Hall now had a roommate except me, and because of my rank I didn't expect to get one. It had been a good Christmas after all. I thanked the Lord for the blessings he gave us that day and crawled under my blanket as the cool night air settled in. "Maybe next year Lord, maybe next year I'll be home with my loved ones at Christmas. But with Your grace and protection I'll survive somehow no matter how long it takes. Good night my Louise, good night my boys, good night my parents, relatives and friends. God bless you all and Merry Christmas 1966."

YEAR'S END

The week after Christmas the Pool Hall POWs were undisturbed from their daily prisoner routine. The Vietnamese ceased all interrogations during this period. Each day was a repeat of the preceding; arise, empty the honey buckets, bathe and wash clothes, eat the mid-morning meal, communicate during the siesta period, eat the afternoon meal, bring in the clothes and retire when the tocsin rang at about 8 p.m.

Jerry Coffee and I conversed daily through the wall using the horse collar technique to muffle the sound of our voices. The POWs living on either side of me provided excellent and safe clearance so there was no way that I could be caught unexpectedly by a snooping guard. Communication in any form was considered a mortal sin by the Vietnamese. If I was caught I would be punished severely. The risk of this happening, with the clearance procedures we had established, was almost nil. I enjoyed each sentence of conversation with Jerry as the lull in the interrogation program left me still extremely lonely. I could hardly wait for the noon siesta when I would be able to talk again. Coffee's communications effort was a boon to my sanity. More than anything else his pleasant voice brought me some form of mental stability. Yet in a way this effort only whetted my appetite for more social intercourse.

Aristotle said, "Man is a social animal". My solitary confinement in Hanoi proved him to be more right each day.

On New Year's Eve I tapped a "Good night, God bless, happy New Year," to my adjacent neighbors, then I went to sleep, rolled up in my blanket, wearing every bit of clothing I possessed. A cold front had brought winter's chill. I was chilled to the marrow and shook like a rattling bag of bones covered by a loose shroud. At midnight a celebrating guard fired off a small string of firecrackers and managed to revive me from slumber long enough that I mumbled to myself, "Happy New Year; maybe 1967 will be the year I go home. Damn, I sure hope so." I then fell back to sleep and my dreams of a better life in the better days that lay behind me.

1967

LONELINESS AND MEMORIES

The weather stayed cold. It wasn't the freezing temperatures of the temperate zone but in a way the coldness of life in Hanoi made me feel as cold as I ever felt before. The dampness settled in as the wind constantly blew in solid low overhanging clouds. I don't think the flight ceiling was ever more than five hundred feet. It was a dreary life. One seemed to complement the other and the net result was even more misery than usual. Tempers grew short between cellmates. Guards were testy and more miserable than usual and they sought to inflict more abuse on the POWs than was normally the case.

Some men began coughing and soon were sick. Most only gave themselves a cat lick wash when allowed to bathe. Freshly washed clothes wouldn't dry. The dampness seemed to stick to everything and irritate everyone. I was miserable. Though I had not had a cigarette in over six months I developed a deep hacking cough which was only relieved when I would hack up a slug of greenish phlegm from the depths of my lungs. The cough was much more than an irritant, it actually hurt like hell. When a coughing fit finally saw its way to completion, I would flop exhausted and hurting on my bunk and hope that the incident wouldn't be repeated too soon. For some days I remained in this condition. I hurt so badly when I coughed that it became a mental obsession with me. I'd force myself to supress an oncoming cough only to finally give in to an uncontrolled fit of coughing which eventually completely disabled me. Soon I hurt all over from head to toe especially in the area of my chest and cracked ribs. In a week I had decided that I'd probably die from this condition and was about to accept this particular fate, when suddenly my condition improved and in a day I was cured. The human body is a marvelous self healer, I thought to myself, and I thanked God for seeing me through this latest ordeal.

In mid-January, suddenly the men of the Pool Hall were whisked off to quiz one by one, with a Vietnamese officer whom none of them had ever seen before. "He speaks excellent English, almost like a Yank. He is trying to get information concerning the air power available to the East Coast units of the Navy and Air Force. Sounds like he thinks that things are going to break out in Cuba once again." This was the info passed to me after several men of the Pool Hall were quizzed by this newcomer to our camp. "Don't give him anything but pure bullshit and overplay our hand on what we will do to Cuba with planes if they decide to make such a dangerous move," I instructed the remainder of the Pool Hall men.

It was late at night, long after I had turned in at the sound of the go-to-bed tocsin, when I was rudely awakened by Smiley. He opened my cell door, ordered me to dress and ushered me off to a late night quiz. I knew where I was going, what I was going to be quizzed on, but had no idea who my quiz master would be. I was confident, relaxed and calm for I knew I had the winning cards on my side. I made my way to the quiz room next to Fox, the camp commander's office and stopped at the entrance while Smiley barked his military arrival to the unknown man inside. I heard a Vietnamese reply and was ushered into the quiz room. As I made my way forward to a position in front of the quiz master's desk I could hardly believe my eyes. It was the Pro, the Vietnamese I had exploited with my fake military air tactical information last April. I bowed and stood silently at attention. "It's you, it's you!" he said angrily, and I knew that my fiction of last April had been discovered. He was sufficiently excited and disturbed in his uncontrolled greeting that I was sure I had caused him great embarrassment by my detailed fictitious paper. "I shouldn't waste my time on you. You are a bad man. You lied to me before and you will lie again," he shouted. "You're damn right," I said sarcastically. "I won't tell you a thing." "How many planes does the U.S. have on the East Coast?" he asked. "You're wasting your time trying to find out if the U.S. will respond to a Cuban threat on the East Coast. Let me tell you to forget it. You're crazy if you think Castro will make any move to take the heat off you in Hanoi. The East Coast Navy Air can blow him away in minutes so don't get your hopes up. You aren't going to get any help from Castro no matter how much solidarity is exchanged between Communist Hanoi and Communist Havana." "You are arrogant, return to your cell and suffer. When the war ends you will remain in Hanoi. You will die here!" "Bullshit! That's nothing but pure bullshit," I replied as I bowed, turned and left him more abruptly than when I entered.

That's one mad Gook, I thought as I walked back to my cell. I must have caused him to lose a great amount of face with last April's paper. I chuckled to myself feeling good for having won one small victory over my captors.

Back in my cell I was wide awake from the chilling cold and my late night quiz with the Pro. My mind reflected on my flying career in the Navy. Cuba itself was all too familiar to me. From early training flights from carriers off Guantanamo Bay in the late forties, I managed to find myself off the shores of Cuba both in the Bay of Pigs episode and the Cuban Missile Crisis. As a professional Naval Aviator I had served all my sea duty assignments in East Coast squadrons based on East Coast carriers. The Carribbean, the Atlantic and Mediterranean Sea were as familiar as the shores of the East Coast itself. I had experienced a wide variety of flying assignments both in attack carrier squadrons and as a flight instructor in Pensacola, Florida. Later, in the replacement air wing training squadron at NAS, Oceana, Virginia, I trained pilots returning to sea-going flying duty from shore duty assignments or from the training command. Consequently, I knew most of the middle and senior ranking officers who were running the East Coast jet squadrons, air wings and attack carriers. They were an elite group of dedicated professionals who liked their work. I was pleased to number myself among them. Over the years I could identify easily those aviators who were forging ahead to become the leaders of their profession. Early on I trained myself to identify those young "tigers" who were natural leaders and superb aviators. If you weren't good you wouldn't survive the normal rigors of peace time carrier flying and even then you needed a certain amount of luck or you might find yourself just another fatal aviation statistic. I had lost many an acquaintance over some personal pilot error or by a freak aircraft accident caused by a material failure. Design deficiencies and just human maintenance or installation errors, by one of the hundreds in the manufacturing or support tail, were always threats to a pilot's safety. The bottom line of the attack carrier is the pilot who day in and day out depends on the professionalism of the mechanics, catapult and arresting gear crews and the numerous other support personnel who insure that his aircraft and equipment function properly. To me, the carrier was the epitome of teamwork and I was proud to be a prominent part of that team.

From my early youth the challenge of naval aviation had fascinated me. I loved airplanes for as long as I could remember. My first flight was in a Ford tri-motor in the early thirties. It was piloted by Clarence Chamberlain, who for $5.00 a ride would take passengers up for a fifteen minute flight over Lawrence, Massachusetts and the surrounding area. I was the apple of my paternal grandmother's eye and I coached her into paying for my first sky excursion. The experience opened up a whole new world for me and from that day on aviation would be my career.

With World War II in full swing I joined the Naval Aviation V-5 program on 6 February 1944 while I was still in high school. When the war ended I was on active duty in San Diego awaiting assignment to Pre-Flight School. Peace time saw the Naval Flight Training Program dragged out, with one phase after another being added. My perseverance prevailed and I finally received my commission and wings at Pensacola, Florida in mid-August of 1947.

I did my first sea tour in Attack Squadron Seventy-Five flying Grumman TBM Torpedo Bombers and later Douglas AD Sky Raiders. My contract as a reserve officer expired in November 1949 and much to my sorrow I was released to inactive duty. During 1949 the Navy was suffering massive cutbacks during the Louis Johnson era and consequently there was little opportunity to augment into the regulars.

Louise and I had been married in the base chapel at NAS, Quonset Point, Rhode Island in October, 1948. She liked our Navy life and friends as much as I did and was just as disappointed as I was when we were forced to return to civilian life.

Once a civilian, I returned to Lawrence, Mass. and enrolled at Merrimack College in order to obtain my college degree. I immediately drove to NAS, Squantum, Mass. and joined a reserve fighter squadron flying Chance Vought F4U Corsairs. I flew two Sundays a month with the reserves and managed to get a two week stint of active duty when school finished in June. I was in summer school when Korea broke out so I immediately volunteered for active duty by telegram. The Navy took me back on 8 August 1950, the day after I finished my summer school exams. I was ordered to report to COMNAVAIRLANT, Norfolk, Virginia for further assignment. I reported in Norfolk at 8 a.m. on a Monday and was immediately assigned to Composite Squadron Twelve at Quonset Point, R.I. and flown there by noon of the same day. In VC-12 I flew the single engine Douglas airborne early warning aircraft and became familiar with the electronic aspects of airborne early warning and anti-submarine warfare tactics. I made numerous short term deployments and a nine-month Med cruise aboard the U.S.S. CORAL SEA. VC-12 had been a good administrative and flying experience. I had responsibilities in personnel and administration and managed to accomplish an extensive amount of all-weather and night flying from the U.S.S. CORAL SEA. Under Admiral Dan Gallery's direction, the composite squadron detachments assigned to CORAL SEA did pioneer work in night and all-weather CCAs (controlled carrier approach). This was a challenge I especially enjoyed for I knew that the Navy had to develop the attack carrier into a night and all-weather platform, or else carrier aviation would have to go out of business. In August of 1952, unable to apply for augmentation into the regular Navy, I returned to civilian life.

Once again I resumed my college career. I enjoyed my college years at Merrimack and attended class full time days while working nights and weekends. One weekend each month I flew with a Reserve Fighter Squadron out of the air station at South Weymouth. We flew F4U Corsairs and then transitioned to Grumman F9F-6 jet fighters. I still had the flying bug bad and my weekend flying with the Reserves served as a safety valve for the rigorous academic and work schedule I maintained. I enjoyed flying and the close relationship provided by the other Reserve Officers who, for the most part, were well established in their civilian careers. They flew because they liked the challenge. I was fortunate to gain a wealth of flying experience from many of these officers who were seasoned combat veterans from carrier squadrons in the Pacific during World War II.

My family life, though hectic because of my academic and work schedule, was very enjoyable. Louise was busy being a mother and housewife as she produced a bevy of sons. James came in October 1950, Kevin in October 1951, Terrance in January 1953 and Mark Brendan arrived in May 1955 in time for graduation. We were blessed with healthy children and our marriage grew stronger under the impact of the mutual sacrifices we made which enabled me to gain my college education. I graduated in June 1955 and was Valedictorian of my class.

That summer and fall I made my living by ferrying aircraft from South Weymouth to the Navy storage facility in Litchfield Park, Arizona and by taking my two weeks' active duty cruise with a reserve squadron.

I applied for recall to active duty in the Navy and was assigned to flight instructor duty in Pensacola, Fla., reporting in January 1965. There I taught formation flying, instruments and night navigation and acquired over fourteen hundred hours of accident free time during my three-year tour. In May of 1958 while I was serving as the Operation's Officer for the Instructors Basic Training Group, I was augmented into the regular Navy. I had achieved my goal and I now knew that the Navy would be my career for good.

In January 1959 we were transferred to NAS Oceana, Va. I served in the Replacement Air Group Squadron as an instrument and tactics instructor. I flew the Grumman Cougar, Lockheed Starfire, and Douglas Skyhawk jets until the fall of 1960 when I was assigned to serve as Operations Officer for VA-72, a light attack A4 Skyhawk squadron that was deployed to the Med on the *U.S.S. INDEPENDENCE*. The Commanding Officer of VA-72 was Commander C.A. "Mark" Hill, a superior performing officer who was rushing forward at flank speed to flag rank. We became close friends. He served as an inspiration by his professional performance both as an aggressive aviator and as a polished naval officer. During my twenty-six month tour in VA-72 I completed three Med cruises: the Bay of Pigs affair, the Cuban Missile Crisis and many other short deployments in the Atlantic flying from the deck of the *U.S.S. INDEPENDENCE*.

At home, Louise had been busy adding to our family of boys. Sean came in Pensacola, in 1957, and Neil David in April 1962 while I was in VA-72. She had her hands full raising six sons while I flitted off on one deployment after another. We were a very close family and were never separated for any reason except when I was on board a carrier. We spent most of our free time swimming and fishing at the beaches near us. The boys were well disciplined and were rapidly growing into manhood. I was exceptionally pleased with Louise's role as wife and mother. Our marriage bond grew stronger by the year. I considered myself very blessed and fortunate to have married such a wonderful person. Our marriage was a mutual commitment that both of us endeavored to fulfill completely. We placed it and our children ahead of all other competing social obligations.

My next shore duty assignment was an eighteen-month tour in Washington, D.C. as the Chief of Naval Operations Standardization Officer for Jet Fighters and Attack Aircraft. This shore duty was topped off with a five and a half month hitch at the Armed Forces Staff College, Norfolk, Va., and then I was assigned as Executive Officer of VA-36 home based at Cecil Field, Florida or on board the *U.S.S. SARATOGA*. I completed an abbreviated replacement pilot training syllabus and joined the squadron in the Med on *SARATOGA* in early May 1965. Back in the States the squadron was transferred to *U.S.S. ENTERPRISE* in September and we deployed for Vietnam in October traversing the Atlantic, rounding The Cape of Good Hope and proceeding eastward across the Indian Ocean until we finally arrived at our destination in the South China Sea on Yankee Station.

I flew combat from early December until I was shot down on 20 March 1966 when my active flying career ended. I had accumulated almost five thousand hours of flight time. I had enjoyed the Navy since the day I first took the oath which swore me in. If given the opportunity to live my life over I would choose to follow the exact same course I chose the first time around.

The Navy was more than a career for me. It was a way of life. I lived and worked in a man's world facing the challenges and hardship that dedicated warriors of all generations have faced. I was raised by my parents and taught in the Catholic school system to be a true democrat spelled with a small d. I believe in the inalienable rights of man as guaranteed by the Constitution of the United States. I believe in equal opportunity for each human being to grow and develop to the limit of his own capabilities without restraint by color, creed or nationality. The Navy afforded such opportunity to its members and that is why it had such an added appeal to me.

I found Navy men to be men of ability and integrity. If you didn't measure up to the standard of Navy expectations as an enlisted man or officer you were soon found out, identified, labeled and shunted aside. I had learned early in my naval career that men of all grades and ranks were labeled by their service reputation. The Navy is small enough in size that If you wanted to take the trouble to check out a man's service reputation, it could be done with relative ease.

The Navy was always considered a conservative elite service, where operational experience was the single most important factor for advancement up the ladder to command positions. In order to succeed to command, you flew the hours, manned the ships, paid the price of family separations, survived the obstacles in the way, and above all stayed combat ready. This was the way the Navy would win wars after years of standdown with nothing but training exercises during peace time. If you stayed currently operationally qualified for war, the Navy would always have a place for you. You would remain, when all others more technically specialized or educated would go. That was my career objective, to stay in active flying billets as much as possible. When the balloon goes up, be ready to go. The true test was combat readiness in active hostilities. All else was secondary.

During my entire naval career I looked for those who would fit this mold, those senior to me, those of my own vintage and those junior. They would be the guys you would go to combat with. They would all fight to win and in the final analysis they would overcome all obstacles and win. That's the only reason the military exists — to *win* wars!

In the East Coast Air Navy, I had detected a subtle change to this operationally qualified philosophy. I first noticed it during my short tour of shore duty in Washington. The Department of Defense under Robert McNamara and his band of whiz kids were unfolding a new military philosophy based on cost effectiveness and procurement efficiency. The ultimate bottom line was the transfer of combat decisions from the battlefront to the Pentagon command center. Command and control was the name of the game, whereby the political hierarchy of Washington would make the day-to-day decisions in the combat area. This move required that military career advancement to higher rank be based on academic and technical qualification. The easiest way to accomplish this was to institute a youth movement, and jump over most of those officers approaching Flag Rank selection who had, over the years, paid the price to develop their own operational expertise. Thus, in the early and mid-sixties the Navy was deprived of some of its best combat readiness leadership, when the most experienced group of aviation Captains were suddenly skipped over for Flag Rank. I didn't like the implications of this sudden shift. I certainly wasn't against advanced education or technical expertise, but I felt that command assignments should be based more on operational qualification than any other factor. My own operational experience had long ago taught me that the academic solution to an operational problem often would not work. Successful innovation to solve on-the-spot operational problems depended more on the depth of experience of those in command than anything else. Wars were fought and won by successful innovations on the battlefront, and nowhere else, least of all in the Washington political arena.

I worried about our military decisions in Vietnam. Washington was running the air war completely. Target assignments came in from Washington daily on a printout supported by a multi-billion dollar world-wide communication system. The President or Secretary of Defense could talk directly to the on scene commanders. The whole damn system was the epitome of perfection. The marvel of twentieth century electronic capability gave complete command and control to the highest political echelons in the nation. In spite of this, I felt from my on-the-scene view of air combat, that the Vietnam air war was falling flat on its ass, and that the entire Vietnam commitment was a can of worms. The restrictions imposed by Washington on the conduct of the air war were unrealistic. I recalled the Russian trawler Guidfrion, on station trailing the *ENTER-PRISE* and seeing Russian ships loaded with hundreds of trucks pass close by on their way to a safe unloading in Hai Phong. One of my missions as an attack division leader was to try to locate these same trucks at night as they headed South through the mountains, forests, and dirt roads so that we could destroy them before they delivered their supplies to the occupying North Vietnamese firmly entrenched in South Vietnam, Laos and Cambodia. I felt that a night *visual* road recce was an impossible task. It was a gross misuse of our air power capability and just plain stupid.

It was 1967. January was half over. I had a sickening premonition that the Vietnam war was stuck on top dead center. My gut feeling told me that I'd be a POW for a helluva long time, unless things changed, and I couldn't believe they would. LBJ's twisting Ho Cho Minh's arm like he used to twist arms in the Senate, but it won't work, I thought. His bombing pauses and target restrictions had conditioned Hanoi, nullifying the effect of battle shock. Only the B-52's, a blockade and possibly an invasion of North Vietnam would make a lasting impression on Hanoi. Everything else left time on Uncle Ho's side. Lord maybe a Cuban threat might wake them all up back in Washington. God I hope something happens to turn this can of worms around!

I was angry and frustrated. It was hard to maintain my own morale because I felt Vietnam was a no win situation. I finally fell asleep, embittered and lonely, filled with self-pity for myself and my family and the military establishment. When it's all over they'll blame the military, I thought. I vividly recalled the Secretary of Defense wearing khaki shorts and holding a pointer as he briefed the American people over TV on the surgical bombing of North Vietnam's bridges in August 1965 and a Life magazine cover of him launching an A6 from the deck of the *USS INDE-PENDENCE.* He looked so clean and efficient it was frightening. Lord, save me from these specialized technicians who have no idea that war at its best, is a dirty game. Lord, save me from the politicians who have the nerve to engage me in war but who don't have the guts to let me win it. And Lord, give me the strength to resist to the end if necessary. But please Lord, don't let this bitter experience warp my sense of values, or destroy my belief in those democratic principles which I have enjoyed and fought in good conscience to preserve.

I awoke mentally exhausted and depressed. The cold dreary weather, joined with my cold weary existence, left me numb and mentally incoherent. I seemed to be at the edge of despair and yearned for something to happen. But everything had stopped; no quizzes, no pressure, no nothing; just the dreadful repetitive prisoner routine of daily living. Solitary confinement was closing everything in. My only respite was the daily comm session with Jerry Coffee. I was trying to keep my sanity and asked the Lord to make something happen. Anything at all to return my humanity to its normal state. I was a caged animal, the lost soul in limbo, more dead than alive, more irrational, more irritated, more puzzled, perplexed and mentally confused than I had ever been before. "I'm almost a basket case Lord," I prattled to myself. "If you don't do something to change things soon, I'll be a valid case for the funny farm."

I knew that I was mentally thrashing myself. I tried to regain some balance to my disturbed mental condition. Deep down I knew what I believed in, and I knew the personal sacrifices I would have to continue to make on behalf of those beliefs if I was going to maintain my own self respect. Nevertheless, it was hard not to become bitter. I lulled myself into a mental state of stoic acceptance, telling myself that my condition was merely due to the "breaks of naval air". "In life you win some and you lose some," I rationalized. "I guess Hanoi is just one of my bigger losses."

I had emptied my bucket and was sitting in the middle of my wooden bunk wrapped in my blanket and daydreaming. I had reviewed my memory bank of POW names and had completed my formal prayers, which were a prominent part of my daily ritual. Once these tasks were completed, and oftentimes repeated, I only had mental projects or past memories to occupy my mind. I was slowly running out of mental stimulation and prayed for something to happen, anything at all, which would change my routine and lift me out of my deep depression. A couple of hours passed by and I figured Happy the key guard was leaving me so that I would be the last one to bathe. He skipped my cell and went from cell two to cell four where he led its occupants to the bathing area.

I was startled to hear him quickly return. He unlocked my cell and came in. He signaled that I was to dress for a quiz. "Queekly, queekly, Mun," he admonished. I relieved my bladder, as was my custom, before going to any quiz. You never knew how long you'd be gone or what they were up to, and this practice had on more than one occasion paid off. I discovered that a strong urge to urinate impeded my mental faculties at quiz. Besides, each quiz brought a tremor of fear which often resulted in a nervous urge to urinate. Let's face it, I thought, these quizzes just scare the piss out of me.

I put on my formal blue pajama suit and followed Happy to the main quiz room. He barked his arrival in military fashion and I was ushered into the room. Lump was smiling, sitting behind the desk. Sitting in front of him was an older looking gray haired POW dressed in formal khaki pajamas. The POW turned to look at me. I instantly recognized him as Commander Jerry Denton, formerly of VA-75 and the *USS INDEPEN-DENCE*. I hadn't seen him since I left the *INDEPENDENCE* in December of 1962, over four years previously. He was emaciated, a shell of his former self. His neck tendons were strung taut. His face was pallid; his eyes were sunken. He had a week's growth of beard and looked twenty years older than his actual age. His eyes lit up and he burst into a full fledged smile as he recognized me. "Hi Jerry, I'm Jim Mulligan," I said as I reached over and extended him my hand.

"You know each other?" Lump said questioningly, in a faked make believe manner, for he damn well knew beforehand that we were long time acquaintances. "Yes, we served together on the East Coast on board *INDEPENDENCE* some years ago," I replied. "Good," he replied matter-of-factly. "Denton, how many aircraft do you have on the *INDE-PENDENCE?*" he asked quickly. Jerry sat mute and didn't reply. Lump ignored Jerry's silent rebuttal and turned to me. "How many aircraft does the *ENTERPRISE* have, Mun," he asked as he addressed me in my Vietnamese assigned name. "Normally about one hundred and fifty or so," I replied flippantly, as I almost doubled the capacity of *ENTER-PRISE*. Lump mildly rebuked Jerry. "Denton, you see the good attitude Mun shows by answering my question. You must learn yourself to be more cooperative. Since today the camp authority permits you to live together, you must not talk loudly and must obey the regulations of the camp," he went on.

Thanks Lord, thanks! I was choked up with emotion as I gave this mental prayer of thanksgiving for the sudden improvement in my condition. I looked at Denton and I could see the tears in his eyes. It was one of those rare emotional moments in life when two people recognize just how much they need each other.

I was overcome with pity for Denton as I recognized the terrible physical and mental condition he was in. I knew he had been captured in

July of 1965, about nine months before I was shot down, and I quickly compared his condition to my own. I was in bad shape. I concluded quickly that Denton must be a helluva lot worse than I was. That poor man, what have they done to him these past eighteen months, I wondered silently to myself.

Lump was running off at the mouth, but I didn't pay attention to a word he said. I couldn't take my eyes off Denton. God it was good just to see another American. Suddenly the full realization of the inhumaneness of the North Vietnamese hit me. Look at what they have done to Jerry Denton in a year and a half. My God it's unbelievable! My compassion for Denton rose to a new high. I mentally assessed his condition. Then I looked at Lump and he melted into a mental picture of all the North Vietnamese who had ever abused me. I hated them all. Every damn one of them. These little Gook bastards are nothing but animals, I thought. Look what they've done to Jerry Denton. I can't believe this has really happened. I'd never felt this way before in my life. One and at the same time I was filled with love and compassion for Denton and with hate and contempt for Lump and all the North Vietnamese he represented. The hate was etched deep in my heart, where even today it festers and gnaws at me when I recollect the conditions of those days.

"You may return to your cell with your friend," Lump said. I stood and bowed, said "Thank you" and headed out of the room. Denton completed a similar ritual and followed me out. Happy, the guard, was smiling as he led us back to cell three in the Pool Hall. He seemed to be genuinely pleased that Jerry and I would be cellmates. "Thanks Lord, thanks for giving me a roommate," I prayed over and over again as we trekked silently to our destination. I felt that the weight of the world had been lifted from my shoulders. It was the 23rd of January 1967, and the best day I'd ever have in Hanoi, save one. That would come much later on 12 February 1973, the day I was repatriated.

THE THREE DAY HONEYMOON

Jerry put his rolled up sleeping mat containing his blanket and what little clothing he had on the empty bunk. Happy, the key guard, indicated we would bathe soon, as he closed the cell door and went off to get the occupants of cell four who were still at the open air bath.

Jerry and I gazed at each other with tears in our eyes. We rushed towards each other and exchanged a triumphant handshake. We hugged each other and pounded each other affectionately on the back. "God, I'm glad to see you," I said. "I've been asking for a roommate since early last summer. Each time I asked to live with you or my former wingman Ray Alcorn. Ray was moved to the Briar Patch in May and I knew I had no chance of living with him. I've been so lonesome that the past couple of weeks I thought I was losing my mind. You've been solo for eighteen months, twice as long as I have. I don't know how you kept your sanity?" "Jim, I prayed a lot and it helps more than anything else," he replied. "Watch for the guard and I'll pass the word to Coffee that you are with me," I said as I went to the wall and tapped rapidly the following message, "J.D. Mv in W Me — Gog wash soon, CU after chow. GBU." (Jerry Denton moved in with me. Going to wash soon. See you after chow. God Bless you.)

I came off the wall and heard Quincy Collins and A.J. Myers limping back to cell four. Happy locked them in and then let us out to go to bathe. It was later than usual and the sun was beginning to rapidly burn off the low overcast.

I looked at Denton as he stripped off his long pajama suit and got down to bare skin. He looked physically frightening. I could see every bone in his chest and upper shoulders. He immediately began inspecting a small lump high on his chest and seemed very concerned about it. "I hope this thing isn't malignant," he said matter of factly.

"Jerry, you look like one of those starving Jews in the German concentration camps," I said as I undressed completely. He eyed me closely and replied, "Jim, I might look bad, but I don't look as bad as you do. You must weigh about ninety pounds. When you were first shot down I saw you last April in the yard at New Guy Village hanging out your clothes and you looked twice as big then as you do now. Are you eating everything they give you?"

"Hell yes! I eat everything but I've had the shits since last summer. Every once in a while I pass a bucketful of worms. Last month I got rid of a tape worm that was over three feet long. It scared the hell out of me. At first I thought that I had passed some of my intestines. Finally, I realized what it was. The Gooks even gave me extra bananas and some vitamin pills for a while but it didn't seem to make much difference."

We took turns using the hand bucket to dump water over our bodies and then soaped down as much as possible. "How about washing the middle of my back," said Jerry. "I haven't been able to reach it and feel clean since I was shot down."

I soaped his face cloth and scrubbed his back as hard as I could and then he returned the favor and cleaned mine. We finished bathing, washed our clothes and waited in the sunshine for Happy to come and return us to our cell. Happy chose to be generous with our outside time. He put the food out before coming for us. We picked up our chow on the way into the cell and were soon locked in as Happy went about his feeding routine.

Jerry said grace aloud. We gave thanks to the Lord for our new-found condition. It felt much better eating with someone else. The usually bad seaweed soup and rice tasted like it was a banquet meal. With human companionship, I became a human being again. My deep depression and acute frustration vanished immediately.

We were so excited that we babbled unceasingly at each other, alternating stories concerning the events of our shootdown, captivity, treatment and torture. I spoke to Coffee for only a few minutes and gave him just enough info to let him know Jerry was fine, and that we were catching up on Navy and family news.

For two solid days and nights, Jerry and I talked each other's ears off. We exchanged our own personal and family histories from boyhood right up to the present time. Our voices often cracked with emotion as we spoke of parents, family and friends. I could see a tremendous sadness in Jerry's eyes as he spoke of Jane and his children, and I developed a deep empathy for him. Instinctively I knew that he was a good man, a man possessed of an incredible faith in his God, his country and his family. He was as devout in his beliefs as he was loyal to commitments which these beliefs engendered. As I looked at him I knew that he was a living martyr who was dying for a cause. I understood the horrors of his eighteen-month captivity and marveled at his resistance posture. I could see that he was but a shadow of his former self. The agony of solitary confinement and physical abuse had left visible scars on him physically and mentally. In spite of his emaciated outward condition, I sensed he had an inner strength which would enable him to prevail over his tormentors until freedom was achieved. In only three and a half days, Jerry and I became the closest of friends. I knew that no matter what outcome our incarceration would bring that this friendship would last as long as we lived.

Our honeymoon ended as suddenly as it began. We had finished our late afternoon meal of rice and seaweed soup and were waiting for Happy, the turn key, to gather up our dishes. It was Thursday. The sun had already set and darkness quickly covered the camp. Happy gathered our dishes and then returned and replaced our portable toilet facility with one that was completely rusted out and falling apart. Jerry and I objected, but to no avail. Happy gruffly completed his switch and left with our almost new personal bucket. Jerry shook his head sadly. "It's another move Jim, I guess we won't be living together after tonight." I refused to believe him. "No Jerry, they wouldn't do that to us so soon," I said, half believing myself, yet half in doubt.

We sat and talked nervously when suddenly Happy opened our cell door and told Jerry to get dressed into his formal pajama suit and wrap up his gear. Happy left and Jerry sadly got dressed and packed up his gear. I tapped quickly to Coffee. "J.D. mvg," (Jerry Denton Moving.)

We sat sadly and said our goodbyes, hoping against hope that this move was not a reality. The door opened. Smiley, the senior enlisted guard, motioned to Jerry to leave. We shook hands with tears in our eyes. "God Bless, Jim," said Jerry as he left. "God Bless, Jerry," I answered. The door slammed shut and the locking bolt hammered home. I sat on my bunk and the tears ran down my cheeks. I was alone for only a minute and already I was desperately lonesome.

Sometime later, Coffee tapped quickly, "Big MV in camp," (big move in camp). I responded with a "Roger, Roger," tapped quickly.

I was under my net and half asleep when my cell door suddenly opened and Smiley told me to dress and get ready to move. When he closed the door, I tapped to Coffee that I was moving and closed with a GBU (God bless you).

Smiley returned and led me to the main room in the Auditorium. Toothpick, and a pimply faced guard tried to handcuff me with French mechanical cuffs behind my back. My left arm could not be put in this position. I was in great pain as they pursued their endeavor. With tears in my eyes I gave an audible "Bao Cao." Smiley popped in and saw what was happening. He immediately took charge and put my arms in front of my body and handcuffed them. The cuffs were uncomfortably tight but caused nowhere near the pain that Toothpick had been inflicting with his effort to put me in rear cuffs.

After some minutes waiting, I was blindfolded and put into a vehicle. I couldn't see a thing and had no idea if any other POWs were in the vehicle with me. We lurched off and soon were meandering through the streets of Hanoi. I could hear the noises from other vehicles: bicycles, trolley cars and the voices of people in the streets or on the sidewalks. After about fifteen minutes of slow traveling the vehicle pulled over and I was ushered out. They removed my blindfold and I saw that I was next to a high brick wall on a sidewalk adjacent to a street. I was led through a door and into a courtyard, lighted enough that I could see that it was surrounded on all sides by brick buildings. I followed my leader and entered through two large green wooden doors into a passage way that was lined with cells on each side. I saw the solid gray doors and was surprised to see that each cell was separated from its neighbors by a three foot passage. These cells were actually isolated from each other on the sides. It was another Vietnamese attempt to stop tap code communication between cells. I was put into a cell that had two double bunks. The room itself was only about eight feet wide and nine feet deep. Opposite the door was a high window, barred and covered with a wire mesh screen. Outside the window I could see the lighted upper portion of an eighteen-foot high brick wall, topped with broken glass from bottles stuck into the concrete and covered with live electric wires. I was back in the Hanoi Hilton, in a section that I never knew existed. This new area was called Little Vegas. I was in cell six of the Desert Inn. The other sections were named Thunderbird, Riviera, Golden Nugget and Star Dust. Between the Desert Inn and Thunderbird was a small isolated area with three tiny cells that we named "The Mint", for its obvious security.

I unrolled my sleeping mat, placed it on the right side lower bunk, erected my mosquito net, then wrapped myself in my blanket and went to sleep. I was tired, lonesome and frightened of what was to come.

The uncertainty of the future, caused by a change of environment, always presented a threat. In such instances, fear of the unknown always ran rampart for some time until an adjustment to the new circumstances was accomplished. This took time. Sometimes days, sometimes weeks; in every instance it was a difficulty to be overcome. As a prisoner I soon learned to hate any change in my routine or circumstances.

On Friday morning I gained comm with the next cell by thumping out the tap code with my fist in a series of loud thumps that carried through the air space separating our cells. This was a tedious and slow process. Because we had no clearance procedures, this form of communications was most risky. I thumped to Jim Lamar and he passed info that Dave Hatcher had acquired a large number of names of men in the camp. Hatcher was able to get up in his window and view POWs moving through the courtyard. Fortunately he was able to identify almost all of the POWs he saw. I had some idea who was in the camp from Hatcher's reports. Most of the seniors had been moved into this camp along with a group of younger POWs who were considered troublemakers.

The daily POW routine was not in operation in Little Vegas. I didn't get to bathe for almost a week. I was busy thumping code early Saturday afternoon when a Vietnamese rifle guard came to my cell, peeked in and caught me cold. I injured my right wrist as I abruptly finished thumping. In minutes the guard came with an officer I had never seen before. Later on I learned the POWs had named him "Bug". Bug harangued me viciously about my communications. "I punish you, Mun," he screamed, and then had the key guard put me in leg stocks. They left in a huff and I found myself lying flat on my back with my ankles locked by iron restraints.

The weather was cold and I had on my long pajama suit to help keep myself warm. Since I could only move from a lying position to a sitting one, I was soon chilled and started to shake uncontrollably. I pulled my blanket and net over my body as best I could, but I was unable to get warm. I stayed in this condition for many hours, until long after the "go to bed" tocsin rang. Periodically a roving patrol guard would peek in at me. I was shivering visibly and I'm sure he noticed it and reported back to the Bug.

My cell door suddenly opened and a strange guard removed me from the leg stocks and took me to a quiz with Bug. Bug was a short fat little Vietnamese, whose black-eyed pupils crossed and zig zagged around the room as he berated me in passable English. "You communicate, Mun and I punish you for violating the regulations of the camp. You must write to the camp authority and apologize for your acts." I said nothing and stared at him without blinking. It was an eyeball to eyeball showdown. Finally his eyes blinked and then lowered and he looked away from me.

It was so cold that our breaths vaporized and were visible. He had on his full uniform and a heavy khaki top coat that seemed to reach his ankles. In spite of this dress he was shivering. I stood stoically before him, and with sheer stubbornness I outwardly showed all disdain for the cold. He lost all control, yelled, "Stand in corner, I punish you," and pointed to where I was to receive my punishment. I ambled to the corner and took my appointed position. Bug left in a huff. He was literally freezing his ass off. The guard sat at the desk, lit a vile smelling Vietnamese cigarette and watched me. I stood in this position for about an hour before Bug returned. "It is very cold, 4 degrees, very cold for Hanoi," he said on entering. He sat at the desk and motioned me to come and stand before him. "We permit you return your room. I tell you this, you must not communicate or I punish you and you die here. Do you understand?" "Yes I understand lieutenant," I replied, referring to his one bar rank. "Go! Go!", he shouted and pointed to the door. I bowed and left, relieved that I had not had to face the threat of writing an apology for my act of communicating.

Back in my cell I wrapped myself in everything I owned, made a sleeping bag from my woolen blanket and went to bed. I made a hat out of my undershorts to cover my head, and wrapped the blanket around my head so that only my nose stuck out. Lord it was cold. I mentally calculated the temperature at about 38°F. It was the coldest temperature I encountered in Hanoi during my entire imprisonment. I said my prayers and thanked the Lord for getting me out of the stocks so easily. I shivered and shook all over for most of the night. I was so cold-soaked that sleep came only in brief increments.

Finally dawn arrived, and soon after, the clanging of the camp tocsin. I arose and paced the floor vigorously, wrapped in my blanket in an attempt to keep warm. With the top of the blanket made into a hood I must have resembled a medieval monk pacing back and forth reciting his daily prayers. I assumed the role and recited the rosary as I paced the floor alternating my turns at each end so that I wouldn't become groggy and lose my balance.

My days were boring. I could not communicate because of my injured right wrist. My left arm was still almost useless. I could eavesdrop and hear other POWs thumping to one another, so I was able to stay on top of the information they were passing.

On the night of February 2nd, I was awakened from my sleep and was suddenly moved into cell three in the Mint. Jerry Denton tapped to me from cell one. We were almost back together.

The Mint cells were very small. About 8½ feet long and 3½ feet wide. I could barely walk between the edge of my bunk and the side of the wall. The iron-barred window, covered with a layer of wire mesh, was as wide as the cell. I could see the high brick wall, electric wires and broken glass barrier on its top. To the left I could see most of the guard tower which was located directly opposite from Jerry Denton's cell.

I jury rigged my net and crawled into my makeshift sleeping bag, wearing every bit of clothing I owned. The wind blew fiercely through the cell and my sleep was intermittent and disturbed. There was a lot of POW movement that night, and the next day I learned that 26 men had moved in from the Briar Patch.

Denton and I were seemingly cut off from the rest of the POWs' communication network by our location in the isolated Mint. I could clear the entire front area of the Mint, including the entrance door, by lying on my stomach and peeking out under the door. This clearance allowed Jerry to talk out the window and down the alleyway to the men in the nearest room of the Desert Inn. Thus, on our first day in the Mint, we regained complete communications with the rest of the camp.

Since moving to Vegas from the Zoo, I had only been allowed to bathe twice in over a week. The daily routine to dispense food and water was in a state of chaos. The rice and soup were completely cold by the time I was allowed to pick it up from the food table, and our drinking water was not delivered on schedule. The daily routine was completely out of control.

Bug came to my cell with pen and paper and told me to write the circumstances of my shootdown and capture for the camp commander. I wrote my name, rank and serial number and added that I was captured south of Vinh on 20 March 1966. I then wrote a complete discussion of the camp routine and aired all of my complaints even suggesting that the camp commander bring in some of the camp personnel from the Zoo to help get the routine squared away. In an hour the key guard picked up my letter and pen and delivered it to the proper authority.

The next morning I received soap, toothpaste, toilet paper, and was allowed to bathe. After washing myself and my clothes I was allowed to stay in the bath area for some fresh air and exercise. When I was returning to my cell, I saw J.C. and some of the Zoo personnel working with the Vegas key guards on food and water distribution. My letter of complaint had produced the results I desired. From that day on our daily routine ran like clockwork.

VEGAS — LIFE IN THE MINT

I had my first attitude quiz at Little Vegas with Bug and a sleazy small Vietnamese officer we later named the Flea. They both were in a jovial mood as they discussed the glorious victories of the North Vietnamese air defense forces. I could see Bug was pulling my chain. I ignored his flaunting overtures of Vietnamese military victory.

"We in this camp want to know more of you," he said. "Tell us about yourself and your capture." "I'm Commander James A. Mulligan, United States Navy, serial number 504324 and I was captured 20 March 1966," I replied tartly. "You have no rank here. You are criminal of war. You have no rights. You have only what we give you," he bellowed. "That's bullshit," I replied. "According to the Geneva Convention which North Vietnam signed, I am a Prisoner of War."

Bug rambled on about the war and its inevitable outcome. I chose to sit stoically and ignored him with obvious contempt. This effort on my part caused him to fly into a rage and he verbalized all forms of intimidations and punishment if I did not see the error of my ways and change my bad attitude. "You are a bad man and that is why we have kept you in this bad camp in a very small room by yourself," he said calmly as he regained his composure. I lowered my eyes and gazed at the floor forlornly, hoping that this reaction would indicate that I was subdued and repentant. I'd better not piss off this Gook any more, he's a mean little bastard, I thought to myself as I continued with my act.

Flea spoke up in a low voice. "Do you know of our Tet?" he asked. "Not really," I replied. "It's some kind of holiday but that's all I know."

Flea spoke about the Tet and the Lunar New Year and its tradition in Vietnam for some time. He concluded, "You will receive special food and be permitted to meet with the camp commander tomorrow. We will make for you the sticky rice cakes that we call the Bang Chung." I came alive at the thought of special food. Seeing my favorable reaction, Flea asked if I enjoyed being outside in the fresh air. "Yes," I answered, "I like it but I have not been permitted outside except to bathe." "Ah, then today I permit you to go outside for some fresh air." He called the guard and turned to me saying, "Go, bask in the sun, Mun." I bowed politely and the guard led me to bath area five where he locked me in and left me outside for an hour. The sky was completely covered by a low black overcast. It was cold and damp. The wind was blowing, the temperature was in the forties and I froze my ass off. "Bask in the sun," I said over and over to myself. I found subtle humor in Flea's final statement. By the time I returned to my cell I was chilled to the bone but content that I had been permitted to be outside of my small cell for such a long time.

Each cell was oppressive to me. Every time I left a cell for quiz I secretly hoped it would be my last one and that I would soon be on the road to freedom. This feeling stayed with me the entire time I was in Vietnam.

The next evening I could hear lots of activity in the building. The guards were hustling here and there on errands connected with the upcoming Tet festivities. I thumped a good night, God bless to Jerry Denton in cell one through the walls of empty cell two. It was windy and the cold February air whistled over the prison wall into my cell through the large barred window. The draft brought discomfort and I rolled myself in my blanket wearing everything I owned to keep warm. I made my hat out of a pair of shorts and covered my exposed head. Within the confines of my covering, I paid my last respects to the Lord on that day and promptly fell sound asleep.

I awoke from a deep sleep slowly and confused when I felt someone pushing me on the shoulder. It was the key guard trying to wake me. I stirred and opened my eyes to see him motioning me to dress for quiz. I rolled out of my blanket, lifted the net, removed my makeshift sleeping hat and slowly got to my feet. Except for my Ho Chi Minh rubber tire sandals, I was fully dressed and ready to go. He led me to the main quiz room, located between the Stardust and the Desert Inn. The room was fully decorated with ribbons, cutouts, a bunch of propaganda war pictures and two beautiful miniature Cherry and Orange trees in full blossom.

I bowed politely to the three Vietnamese officers sitting behind the table. Immediately I recognized Rabbit and Flea, but the third man was a stranger to me. Rabbit acted as translator.

"The authority of the camp wishes you a happy Tet. He wants to know if you have been allowed to wash daily?" "Yes," I replied. "Have you soap, and toothpaste and toilet paper?" "Yes," I replied again. The older Vietnamese spoke again and Rabbit continued. "The camp commander thanks you for your letter concerning the operation of this camp. He says that his guards are new and that they were unsure of their duties for a little while. Your letter caused him to review the procedures of the camp and make changes. Do you have any more suggestions?" "No," I replied. "The routine is satisfactory now. We get to bathe and our food and water are served hot." "Do you eat all your food?" asked Rabbit. "Yes, everything." "Are you hungry or do you have enough to eat?" "I eat everything but I am hungry most of the time. Your rice and green soup are much different from my diet at home." "It is all we have," Rabbit answered. Rabbit offered me cigarettes and tea. I declined the cigarette but took the tea which was quite warm and served in a tiny tea cup. They showed me a book of Vietnamese art paintings, which I skimmed over quickly. I wasn't interested in Asian art culture or holidays. I was hungry and my eyes were riveted on a dozen or so Vietnamese candies set next to a square object wrapped in banana leaves. I surmised that the green square was the sticky rice called Bang Chung.

Rabbit bantered on, repeating the chit chat spoken by the camp commander. Flea smiled constantly but remained silent. He looked half in the bag to me and obviously had been enjoying something much stronger than the tea they served me. I must admit the camp commander made a super attempt at being hospitable. Rabbit refilled my empty tea cup each time I drank. I ate some candy and sugared peanuts they offered as the conversation continued. "Do you have a family?" asked Rabbit as he repeated the camp commander's question. "Yes, a wife and six sons," I replied. "When the war is over you will be with them again," translated Rabbit. "Yes and I hope it is soon," I answered.

"Has the camp commander a family?" I asked Rabbit. He translated and later replied. "Yes he has a large family but he is from the south and he has not seen them in ten years and like you, he hopes the war will soon be over so he can return to his family. Do you know that the Saigon puppets do not even let him exchange letters with his wife and children all these years?" Rabbit said angrily. "C'est la guerre," I replied. "Do you speak French?" Rabbit asked. "No it's just a phrase I learned in school."

The camp commander indicated that my Tet quiz was at an end. "It is late and you are the last American to visit with the camp authority. Here is your Bang Chung, take it and all the candy that is left to your room." I took the dozen or so small candies and put them in my blue quiz suit pocket. "Will you eat the sticky rice cake tonight?" Rabbit asked. "Yes," I replied. "I'll eat all of it." He translated this to the camp commander who replied in Vietnamese. "Eat it all; he will send you another one in the morning." I stood, bowed politely and said, "Tell the camp commander thank you and happy Tet."

Rabbit spoke and his boss smiled, then replied in Vietnamese something that really took me by surprise. Rabbit translated, "You and I are military men. I do my job and you do yours. I hope you will be with your family before too much longer. This war is a hardship on us all. Good luck to you." I couldn't really believe it. A North Vietnamese officer who obviously had some compassion. I left in a state of amazement and returned to my cell where I ate every piece of candy and the entire sticky rice cake. I went to sleep and never again saw the officer who was called the camp commander.

The next morning the guard brought me another sticky rice cake and some hot coffee. We had rice and a clear noodle soup for the main meal. It was a big improvement over our daily repast.

Some days after Tet, I heard the Vietnamese bring a POW and put him in cell two. I cleared the entry way to the Mint by looking under the bottom of my door. No Vietnamese were present, so I quickly tapped the POW callup, "shave and a hair cut." I got two fast raps in reply. I sent "Jim Mulligan, over," and he replied excitedly with a fast series of dots then "Mike Cronin." Mike Cronin was a young Navy Lieutenant I had been with in survival school in Brunswick, Maine. I wondered if he was the same man. The Vietnamese guards came and prevented further communication. I saw him leave by peeking under the door. In a few minutes the guards returned with a POW dressed like Mike Cronin. When they locked him in his cell and left I tried to communicate. I got no answer and was completely frustrated by this turn of events.

Later, I thumped to Jerry Denton the events on Cronin. Jerry replied that probably they threatened Cronin about comm with us and he was lying low for fear of torture.

We kept trying for over a week to tap to cell two but had no luck. As a last resort during the siesta Jerry and I talked to each other under our doors. Finally the man in cell two spoke up. He wasn't Mike Cronin, and he didn't know how to tap comm, so he couldn't answer us on the wall. That solved the Cronin mystery, but I still wondered if Mike Cronin was the young tiger I knew in Brunswick. Years later I found out he was the same man.

Julian Jayroe was the man in cell two. He was moved out a few days after Jerry and I contacted him.

The Vietnamese were on a massive torture program for military information from new shootdowns. I could hear the screams of pain from men who were being terribly tortured. It was ominous and frightening. The more the U.S. bombed the worse the torture got.

Little Vegas was equipped with a squawk box in each cell. The Vietnamese continued their propaganda efforts by playing us the Voice of Vietnam, starring Hanoi Hannah, every evening and repeated the following noon. It was frustrating to hear that Vietnamese bitch pushing propaganda at us and the world.

In mid-February, the camp radio suddenly featured one of the POWs reading Harrison Salisbury's columns, written while he was in Hanoi. Salisbury must have been in a different Hanoi than I was. While I never questioned his motives or intent for being in Hanoi I marveled at how much use the North Vietnamese managed to get out of him in support of their cause. I am constantly surprised at how easy the Communists are able to fool the intellectual elite of this country and the world. In my Hanoi, our POWs were being tortured, starved and dying from medical neglect, but my favorite American newspaper, which proclaims that it prints, "All the news that's fit to print," couldn't come up with a bit of news about the true condition of the American POWs. I was beside myself about Salisbury's columns. The only outlet I had to overcome the discouragement from them, was the fact that the POW reader managed to pronounce President Ho Chi Minh's name as President 'horseshit Minh'. This brought a small chuckle to my bundle of hurts.

The Mint was cut off from the Thunderbird and Desert Inn our immediate neighbors, and tap comm was impossible. At noon siesta time, after the passage of the roving guard, I would clear the Mint entry way by lying flat on my stomach and peeking under my door. Jerry Denton would clear the alleyway, and then he would talk out of his window and down the alley to the men in the Desert Inn closest to us. It was a good comm procedure and we were able to stay in communication with the rest of the camp, though we were physically isolated from them.

Hanoi was being bombed, regularly, but I noticed these raids occurred only if the weather was clear and visibility was unlimited. I could see United States planes diving on targets north of us as I looked out my window. Some of the targets were quite close. I could pick up the planes halfway down their dive and on pullout after the bomb drop. The sky was filled with ack ack and missiles but it didn't seem to slow down the attacking aircraft. With Hanoi being bombed the guards and officers became testy and ugly. Somehow they had acquired the feeling that Hanoi itself was a secured sanctuary. I kept telling myself that if enough pressure was put on Hanoi itself, the war would soon end. The North Vietnamese Communists could call for the country to sacrifice itself, but when the pressure was put on Hanoi, then they themselves weren't so eager. In early 1967, I concluded that the war would never end until Hanoi itself felt the full force of American bombing. This meant, to me, that sooner or later the B-52's would have to come with their awesome devastation. I prayed it would be sooner rather than later, and was somewhat disappointed that it had not already occurred. "It's a lousy war," I kept saying to myself, "and it will never end until these monkeys in Hanoi get to know what war is all about."

I monitored each raid as best I could and reported in detail to Denton all that I had observed.

My health was poor during my stay in the Mint. In addition to my emaciated condition, I suddenly found my feet and ankles were swelling for no apparent reason. My kidneys began to cause me an inordinate amount of pain and concern. I didn't know if I had a kidney infection or was just beginning to develop a problem with kidney stones. I took an excessive amount of time to pass a normal amount of water. Often my own count during one urination would go well over one hundred. This was twice the normal urine counts that other POWs experienced. I passed the same amount the others did but it took me twice as long.

My Mint cell was so narrow and small that I could do little exercise except pace three steps, turn and repeat my performance. In spite of my discomfort, frustration and inconveniences, I remained in relatively good spirits. I had good comm with Denton and he in turn had good comm with the Desert Inn. I had not been to quiz since the Tet. The Vietnamese were more concerned with newly captured POWs, and hence except for the solitary living conditions, abetted by the prowling guards seeking to stop comm, my own situation was bearable. I was, you might say, suspended in a state of limbo, merely existing from day to day. During this period of inactivity, I was sustained by prayer and by mental projects which I conceived to keep my mind active.

I had been adding to my POW name list daily, and since the bombing had increased in the highly defended Hanoi-Haiphong areas, we acquired new POWs at a rapid rate. Each day I added to the list and vowed I'd never forget a name if I stayed a POW for twenty years. By constant daily repetition I drilled myself to such a degree that remembering each name became a simple task. Little Vegas became filled to overflowing as new POWs moved in and then in turn were later moved to the Zoo.

The comm was so good that Commander Stockdale's resistance policy was delivered to the other camps by incoming prisoners from Little Vegas.

I had acquired over 170 names of downed aviators who were POWs by late March. On Monday, 20 March, 1967, I completed my first year as a POW. I had survived a year of Hell and hoped my second year would be better. I was doomed to disappointment on that hope. Unfortunately, things got progressively worse for me.

EASTER AND SPRING 1967

A few days before Easter, Rabbit had me at quiz. "Are you Catholic?" he asked. "Yes," I replied. "We have for you on the occasion of Easter, a Catholic Priest here in this room. Would you like to visit with him for a time?" "Yes," I answered. "I will put your name on the list of those who will see him." I returned to my cell and tapped the joyous news to Denton. He replied he had been to a quiz and had the same experience.

I had no idea when Easter would occur in 1967. I was not prepared when the following Sunday, after a raid or recce had occurred and the all clear sounded by the air raid alarm, I was taken to a quiz in the Riviera. I entered and bowed to a slight effeminate looking Vietnamese dressed in casual civilian clothes. Along side him sat a very old man dressed in the garb of a Catholic Priest. I recognized him as the so called Father Jean Baptiste Ho Ti Binh from pictures I had seen of him in the Vietnam

Courier, a Hanoi paper that the Vietnamese allowed us to read occasionally. The interpreter said, "We permit you to visit with your priest on the occasion of Easter. We give you the human treatment, even though the American air pirates attack our beloved Hanoi on this day of celebration."

I asked the old man how long he had been a priest and why he stayed in the North after 1954. He replied in Vietnamese which was quickly translated by the Vietnamese civilian. "He is a priest for almost fifty years and he stays in the North to serve his Catholic followers who chose to remain here." He asked about my wife and children and I told him of Louise and my six sons. "You will be with them soon when the war ends," he replied.

I knelt and said the Confiteor in Latin and he gave me general absolution and his blessing. As I left, he pressed a small medal into the palm of my hand. I thanked him for it and put it on a string I pulled from my blanket when I returned to my cell. I wore it around my neck for a few days. When the Vietnamese guard conducted a room search that week, he took the medal from me.

I celebrated my 41st birthday the day after Easter by engaging myself in an over abundance of self-pity. "If life begins at forty then I'm off to one helluva bad start," I told myself. I was excessively lonesome for my wife, children and parents, and promised myself I would try to make up these days of separation from them as best I could.

In early April, Jerry Denton had completed his talk comm out the window and down the alley to the Desert Inn. During this comm, I lay flat on my stomach looking under the door to keep the entry way clear of prowling guards. It was a safe procedure and we had not even come close to getting caught since we began using this method. When Jerry finished there was at least an hour left of the siesta; I wrapped myself in my blanket in preparation for a nap. I could hear the Desert Inn guys talking down the alleyway to either the Auditorium or the Stardust, but I could not make out what they were saying.

I was half asleep when I heard a commotion outside my cell window. In seconds a pimply faced guard jumped up and grabbed the bars, pulled himself up and looked in at me. He had heard the talk comm and thought it came from me. He dropped to the ground and in a minute he was at my cell door banging and indicating that I had been caught in comm. He left and returned in a few minutes with a Vietnamese officer named Rat. Rat screamed, "Mun, you communicated — I punish you." I tried to talk him out of it but it was a no go, and he promptly had the pimply faced guard put me in the leg stocks.

My feet and ankles were swollen and the stocks were small so I could do nothing but lie flat on my back or pull myself up into a sitting position. I couldn't turn my body an inch either way. My physical condition immediately deteriorated to a new low point. I was so restrained, that I could only sleep for very short periods. Every bone in my body ached and I felt like I was one hundred years old. The guard let me out of the stocks for a few minutes each morning so I could use my bucket. They brought me my food and water and I didn't get out of the stocks till the personal relief period the following day. I ate my rice and the greens, but hardly touched liquids at all. I was very uncomfortable and I didn't want to make things worse with a weak bladder problem.

I stayed in this condition for eight days, and each day I got worse. I was completely exhausted physically and mentally. My mind was like putty. I couldn't think; in fact, I was almost completely irrational.

A new guard came to let me out of stocks to use my bucket on the eighth day. He looked different from the other Vietnamese men I had seen. He looked at me with compassion as I struggled to get up and forced myself to move toward the bucket. He left and I went about completing my personal business. When I had finished, I sat on the edge of the bunk, let my legs dangle and awaited his early return. I was physically exhausted from the tight restraint I had been enduring. I could comm by thumping to Denton but there was little to say so we had kept it to a minimum. The guard left me out of stocks for well over an hour before he returned. On entering he looked at me curiously and by blessing himself and pointing to me, he asked in sign language if I was a Christian. I blessed myself and indicated I was a Christian. He looked out the doorway and into the entry way to see that no one could see him, then blessed himself and pointed to himself indicating he was a Vietnamese Christian. He brought me my hot water, let me stay out of the stocks and later came with my food. As I finished eating, another guard came and saw me out of the stocks. He returned with the guard who had secretly told me he was a Christian and I was put back into the stocks. The Christian guard pointed to my bucket and indicated he had let me out to take care of a personal emergency. The other guard seemed to accept this explanation and they left.

I stayed confined in the stocks a few more days when finally my body gave out completely. My bowels became uncontrolled and I had massive diarrhea and terrible cramps early in the evening. I cried "Bao Cao" and a roving guard returned with Rat. Rat looked at my pitiful condition and set me free saying, "You have been punished for communicating, and now I choose to remove you from the stocks. I will send you pills but you must promise not to communicate." "Yes, I understand," I replied, and crossing my fingers I said, "I won't communicate anymore." The guard returned with some large white pills, I immediately swallowed them, curled up in my blanket and slept contented until the morning toscin rang. I awoke refreshed and feeling better. I was still in terrible physical condition but the mental strain imposed by the close restaint of the stocks was gone.

The sun was out when they took me to bathe. I poured buckets of cold water over myself, scrubbed myself clean and then washed all of my clothes. I stood in the sun naked as a jay bird and let its rays dry me off. Even though the air was chilly, I felt I needed the Vitamin D from the sunshine. I tightened my skin and toughed it out till the guard came to return me to my cell.

I kept pacing back and forth in my cell. Three steps, then a turn, three steps, and another turn. There was little room between the edge of the bed and the outside wall of the cell, and I could barely walk without banging my shoulders into the wall. I kept moving, for I knew I had to somehow regain my strength.

John Fer, from the U.S. Air Force, moved into cell two between Jerry and me. He was captured in early February, '67 and brought with him a wealth of news from the outside world. We received a big boost in morale from him because he had an encyclopedic memory for details and events.

Later in April, the Vietnamese decided to show propaganda movies to the POWs. They rigged up the courtyard with a series of ropes which made rectangular squares. They took our blankets and draped them over the ropes so that they made pens in which they could put the POWs so that we could see the movie but not each other. It was a Rube Goldberg rig, right from the start. I saw the rope rig being put up when I came from my morning bath, but I couldn't figure out what it was supposed to be or to do. I got the answer that night after our late afternoon chow when the camp commander got on the camp radio and told us he was going to permit us to see some movies. His announcement came to us like this: "Ah low! Ah low! (Hello) American crimeinals. American crimeinals. This is the authority of the camp. This is the authority of the camp. Tonight the camp authority permits you to see the movies. There are some bad crimeinals who violate the regulations of the camp and I do not permit them to see the movies. The rest of you, make water, make stool, now, before you leave your rooms."

I heard the guards unlock the doors in Thunderbird and Desert Inn and begin taking the POWs out. Denton and I must have made the bad criminal list, we were not allowed to see the movie. I went to bed and could hear the sound track but I couldn't make out the dialogue.

About an hour after the movie started I heard a tremendous clap of thunder. Minutes later a torrential rain fell. The movie droned on through all the rain. After a good length of time, the sound track went dead and the camp commander came up on the camp radio. "American crimeinals, this is the camp authority. I permit you return your room."

They came back as they left, herded by the guards, but everyone was soaked completely and their blankets were wet. I laughed heartily to myself at this latest series of events. Even nature was against the North Vietnamese propaganda efforts. The Lord said, "Piss on you and your movies, camp commander," and He rained you out completely. I fell asleep more content than I had been for some time.

Our daily routine did not change for many weeks. It was get up, bathe, eat, comm during siesta, eat and sleep. We kept in good comm and managed not to get caught.

Out in the bath one day I heard voices in the courtyard. I peeked through a crack in the door. Four Yanks were hard at work digging a hole. The Yanks were gone when I came out of the bath and passed by their diggings. I could see water and wondered what was up. Flea was standing in the entry way into the building. "We dig wells so that we have much water for you to wash," he said as I bowed and then passed him by.

The wells were completed and round concrete cylinders were inserted in the holes to keep the sides from falling in. I noticed that, though we had received little rain, the water table was high. No chance to dig under the high outside wall to escape I thought. Clever guys those French jail builders.

Ho Chi Minh's birthday was a gala occasion and we got lots of propaganda about him. The spring bombing had gone on at an increased pace and Vegas was virtually filled. John Fer had moved and to my knowledge only Denton and I were in solitary along with Nels Tanner who was solo and being punished for a false story about Ben Casey and Superman which he made up to satisfy Gook requirements demanded of him. His hoax was actually published and the whole world knew that the North Vietnamese had had their chain pulled by Tanner. When the Vietnamese found out about it, they lowered the boom on him, and when done with him physically put him in solo in the Star Dust with the window completely covered by a woven bamboo mat. The cell was completely dark, hot and infested with mosquitoes. Tanner took it all in good stride.

On the night of the 21st of May, a guard came, told me to roll up my gear, then took me out to a quiz in the Riveria with the Flea. I was waiting outside the quiz room when another guard brought Jerry Denton in. We entered the room together and bowed to Flea. "The camp is very crowded with American prisoners. The camp commander permits you to live together. You must obey the regulations of the camp and not communicate. My guard will take you to your new room." "Thank you," I said and I bowed. Jerry followed suit and we went out, picked up our gear and tramped along after the guard who led us to Stardust five.

The cell was as small as the one I had left in the Mint only it had a double bunk. Jerry said, "I'll take the upper bunk, Jim, you'll never be able to climb up there with your bad arm." The cell was about 8 feet long and 4½ feet wide. It had a large window that was completely blocked off to the outside by a heavy woven bamboo mat. The mosquitoes were abundant and ferocious. We rigged our mosquito nets and climbed into our bunks keeping a running conversation going all the time. We filled each other in on what had happened to us since our last three days together back in the Zoo last January.

I went to sleep happy and contented. It was great to be living with another human being again. I thanked the Lord for His latest blessing and though it was intolerably hot, I fell into a deep restful sleep.

When I awoke the next morning and couldn't see because the room light was off and the window blocked tight, I knew our living conditions were deplorable. Jerry and I bitched about the window and decided that when the key guard brought us our water we would complain by saying Bao Cao. The guard arrived and hearing Bao Cao he went to the office and came back with the Flea.

"Our room is too hot, we need to have the cover taken off the window," Jerry demanded. Flea came in the room and concurred. "My guard will remove it," he said and left. In a few minutes the barrier was removed and the room was filled with sunlight and fresh air. We had a mock war and killed as many mosquitoes as we could see. Those that survived flew out the barred open window.

Life with Jerry Denton was fun. We washed each other's back at bath and managed to make the most of the primitive laundry soap to clean our clothes. Jerry was a very aggressive communicator. We managed to tap to other POWs in adjoining baths and exchange camp information. Normally when this occurred, I did the clearing and Jerry the tapping. He was as rapid as a Western Union key operator. We accomplished much comm in a short time.

In the Stardust, we communicated by flashing our hands under the door to the men opposite us. If the building was empty we could even whisper to them. Tapping on the back wall went all the way to cell eight which was next to the Auditorium and furthest from us. The day after we were in Stardust, we had a complete building communication network. Jerry was the senior ranking officer and I was next in line.

Summer's tropical heat set in and our captors gave us each a bamboo hand fan. I was so hot that mine was never out of my hand. I went to sleep fanning myself and often I awoke to find myself still fanning. It must have been an unconscious action caused by my continuous fanning during my awake hours.

I still had a major problem with worms and diarrhea and was quite disturbed and embarrassed at the stench I brought to the cell. Jerry saw my embarrassment and sought to mollify my concern. "Hell, Jim, forget it; we're lucky to be alive. All of Vietnam smells, not just this cell." I was most appreciative for his response to my unpleasant situation.

Each day at siesta we had a comm session with our neighbors. Jerry would end up talking out the window to cell six, while I would clear under the doorway to insure that no Vietnamese guard would enter the Stardust during the comm session.

Jerry was talking out the window with Hugh Flesher on 28 June. He had passed the news and was just making small talk so I yelled to him from my clearance spot on the floor, "Jerry get off the God damn wall! " I was in very bad physical condition and I didn't think I could survive if I were to be punished severely for comm again. "Wait Jim, I just got Red McDaniel on the line," Jerry replied. I didn't know Red McDaniel personally, but I recalled that he had flown AD Skyraiders for VA-65 with a friend of mine in the early sixties. McDaniel was an East Coast Naval aviator and he might have news. Jerry received personal news about his wife and kids from McDaniel. Finally Red asked if Jerry knew Commander Jim Mulligan from the *ENTERPRISE*. Jerry replied, "Hell yes, he's lying on the deck clearing under the door for me right now." Red said, "Tell Jim his wife is in Virginia Beach and knows he is a POW. Father Gallagher says they are all praying for him aboard the *ENTERPRISE*." I was elated when Jerry passed this info to me.

But the good news ended in a bad scene. Minutes later a guard heard Denton and jumped up and caught him cold comming out the window. It was siesta so we jumped into the bunk. In seconds the irate guard was at the cell door accusing Jerry. He left in a hurry and we both knew he would be back soon.

I was terrified. The Gooks had been on a comm purge and I feared the worst. Jerry looked at me and said, "Hell Jim, I'll tell them you were asleep and I was comming on my own out the window." "Thanks Jerry," I said in appreciation, but inwardly I feared that all was lost for me. They won't buy it I thought.

In a few minutes the key guard came, told Jerry to dress for quiz and took him away. When Jerry left another guard came and made me roll up all of Denton's gear. They took it away and once again I was alone.

I kept waiting for them to come for me but they never came. They must have believed Jerry's story, I thought. I lay awake long after the night tocsin rang and prayed for Jerry's well being. The 28th of June turned out to be a sad day for me but it was a much worse day for Jerry Denton; the Vietnamese punished him severely for his acts.

The 1st of July was my wife Louise's birthday; my mother's was on the 4th. Once again I was lonesome and depressed. Most of all I was worried about Jerry Denton. I had tap comm with the other cells but no one had seen Denton or Hugh Flesher, who had been moved out for the same reason. The air raids kept sounding but the war seemed thousands of years away from me. I seemed to be caught up in a sequence where time stood still and life meant nothing.

The Vietnamese increased their comm purge and stationed a guard in each building for most of the day. I waited hours for him to leave and then I would get a few minutes' comm in before he returned. It was a very nervous time for all of us. The pressure was on against any comm, and the Gooks meant business.

SUMMER IN STOCKS

Jerry returned late on July 8th. As I suspected, he had been tortured heavily. I thanked him for taking all the blame and keeping the Gooks off my back. "I'm just glad they bought my story, Jim," he replied.

The guards harassed us constantly about comm during the coming month. If they heard the least little noise coming from Stardust they immediately assumed Jerry was comming. He was the SRO and they knew it and would blame him for it.

We had to whisper to each other when we talked. Even then the guard sitting in the hallway would open our peek-in door and scream, "Keep silent!" Gradually our comm was greatly reduced until we no longer were able to keep in contact with the rest of the camp. New men were moved into Stardust cells 1, 7 and 8 and we could not even find out who they were. It was tense living, but living with Jerry was a helluva lot better than living alone.

On the night of 8 August, we could hear the guards raising a ruckus in the court yard. I was half asleep under my net when a guard came to my peek-in door. He was a little ugly Vietnamese we called Pimples. When I looked out from under my net, he motioned for me to come to the cell door. I did and bowed wondering what he wanted. He spit in my face. With a reflex reaction I launched a lunger which splashed him right in the eye. He was furious. "You son of a bitch," I said. "What's wrong, Jim?" Jerry asked. "Pimples got me up and spit in my face so I got him back right in the eye." "Jim, it's time to take a crap. They'll be here in minutes; the comm purge must be on good. Pimples didn't come here to do that; he was sent here." We both used the bucket and in a few minutes the Vietnamese known as Flea arrived. He put us in leg stocks. Jerry's irons were so rusted they had to hammer them in with a huge metal bar.

We only had a large rusted personal convenience bucket and it was just out of my reach at the end of the cell. I awoke and heard Jerry moaning. "Jim, I have to piss so bad I can't stand it," he said. I tried to reach the bucket but to no avail. He was in agony on the upper bunk above me. I struggled and could barely reach my drinking water jug. His was further away beyond mine. I looked at it, shrugged my shoulders, emptied the few drops of water remaining in it and then handed it up to Jerry. "Use this," I said, "it's the only thing I can reach. Besides I don't want to get wet down here." He used it and was out of his agony in a few minutes. "Thanks a lot, Jim," he said. "Jerry, that's the least I can do for a friend in need," I replied. "Besides I owed you a big favor."

They let us bathe the next morning. Getting Jerry out of his iron stocks was a difficult task for the guards. When we returned, they put us in stocks and they went through the same hammering routine to get Jerry's irons closed.

From that time on we bathed only once a week. Since I was in the lower bunk and my stocks were easy to manipulate, the guards had me do all the daily chores. Poor Jerry was locked in tighter than a drum from one week's bath to another.

Each morning I emptied our big bucket and cleaned it and a small bed pot at the latrine between the Mint and Thunderbird. I was let out of stocks to do this and walked a good distance there and back. I also was out of stocks twice more each day to fetch our food and water. As further punishment they took our mosquito nets and we were left at the mercy of the ravenous mosquitoes. I used the large bucket for my body functions each day when out of stocks. Jerry had to use the small white pot while he was still locked in leg stocks and this was a strenuous and difficult feat for him to accomplish. He had a great sense of humor and persevered quite well through this unpleasant ordeal. All told, each day I was out of stocks three times for a total period of about one hour. Jerry never got one minute of relief.

We talked constantly to each other throughout our ordeal. The guards would holler for us to "keep silent," but since we were in punishment, we paid them no heed.

During our twenty-five days in stocks we managed to completely cover the story of our lives. Jerry relived his boyhood in Mobile, Alabama, and I did mine in Lawrence, Massachusetts. We became very close and could name each other's friends and family and relate events that had been lived long ago in our past.

Jerry's career at the Naval Academy had been particularly harassing for him. As a Plebe he was in constant trouble with an upperclassman who literally ran him ragged. One day in late August, after being in stocks for almost three weeks, Jerry broke me up completely when he said, "Jim, if this place gets any worse it will be almost as bad as my Plebe year at the Academy." I laughed till my belly hurt and replied, "Jerry, I'll give you the same line Louise always gave me every time I bitched about something in the Navy; if you didn't have a sense of humor you shouldn't have joined."

There we were both half dead, in agony from restraint, yet laughing our guts off. A Gook guard came to the door to check on the commotion. He must have thought we were both crazy. He told us to keep silent but we kept on laughing.

Jerry had predicted that we would be released on the Vietnamese National Holiday on the 2nd of September. He was right as usual, and on that morning we were released from the leg stocks, weak, beaten down, but unbowed after our twenty-five day ordeal. To show us their concern for our welfare they gave us back our mosquito nets and had the old French doctor pay us a ten-second visit for appearance's sake.

The comm purge was still going strong and we were restricted to comm with the cells closest to us, and only then when the guard left the building, which was infrequent and only for a short time.

One day Bug came to our cell door and asked us if we wanted to go outside of the camp and do a little work so that we could get sunshine and fresh air. Suspecting him of the usual Vietnamese trickery for propaganda purposes, we rejected his offer by saying we were afraid of the wrath of the Vietnamese people and we wouldn't dare go out of the camp. Bug had no answer to our refusal because he had often threatened us with death from the wrath of the Vietnamese people. Later we learned that some Americans had been taken out of the camp and were filmed cleaning up the streets after a U.S. bombing.

On the 2nd of October, Jerry went out on a routine quiz. After he left they came and took away his gear. We didn't even have a chance to say goodbye.

I was alone again, but had comm with three other cells. The purge was on and it was a limited exchange. Once again I retreated inward and went back to the mental exercises and prayer routine which had sustained me in the past.

The air raid tempo increased dramatically, and I felt the U.S. was putting the heat on to get the war over with. On the afternoon of 18 October 1967, they took me to a quiz in the Auditorium. When I entered, I saw three Yanks sitting before the quiz master. They turned as I entered, I bowed and was told to sit next to them. "Today, I permit you to have roommates," the officer said. "Do you know each other?" I said no, and we introduced ourselves. The three were Commander Harry Jenkins, Lcdr. Bob Shumaker and Major Lou Makowski. After a few minutes of instructing us not to communicate and violate the regulations of the camp, we were dismissed and sent back to the Desert Inn room where they were living. The guard had rolled up my gear and brought it to the Auditorium so I didn't have to go back to the Stardust. I was gone before I was able to tell anyone in the Stardust I was moving.

I was in seventh heaven living with three Americans. They had a fixed daily routine of exercise, comm and conversation in that order. Everything was completely organized. The cell was immaculately clean, the bunks made in military fashion with all clothes stored as if ready for inspection.

For the first day or so I was completely overwhelmed by being with so many human beings. Each one had his own personality and was unique. Harry Jenkins, the oldest and senior, was a considerate but demanding leader. Bob Shumaker was the most clever POW I ever did meet. He had keen powers of observation and acute hearing to the point he could identify each room in the Desert Inn when its door was opened. Lou Makowski was a little guy with a good sense of humor and even temperament. Because of his size, the guards singled him out for harassment, but he easily withstood their threats and cruelties.

The guard sat in the hall and comm was tough, but with their determination, they came up with a unique solution to the problem. The barred window was covered with a heavy wire mesh. They managed to break a piece off about seven feet long. After straightening it out, they rolled it into a coil and hid it in a large crack in the concrete at the intersection of the wall and floor. Each morning, Lou Makowski would do his exercise directly in front of the peek-in-hole in the door to block off the view of an inspecting guard. Harry and Bob would unravel the wire. They put some water along the edge of the floor and far wall to lubricate it; then they would shove it through a small rat hole across the three feet of open space between the cells and into the adjoining cell via their rat hole. Each cell had rat holes to allow water or rats to escape from the cell. Harry would sit on the bucket and then by pushing and pulling the wire, he communicated using the tap code with both adjoining cells. I was flabbergasted, and marveled at their ingenuity. They had the guard fooled.

There was room to exercise and they were on a strenuous program to keep in good physical condition. I joined in as best I could.

Harry saved some rice and after the daily meals, we would sit quietly and watch two little mice scamper across the floor and eat what he put out for them. Harry knew a number of poems. He recited them and even taught Bob and Lou the entire poem titled, "The Cremation of Sam McGee." They entertained me by alternating the recital of each verse under Harry's encouraging direction.

I was relaxed for the first time since I was captured. The guards tried to harass us from the peek-in-door, but I instructed my cell mates to ignore them completely. They tried to get us to stand with our hands in the air up against the wall. I was furious at this and insisted no one obey the harassing guards. "Don't do a thing for them," I said. "If they want us against the wall they'll come with an officer and then we'll comply." After a couple of days of fruitless results, they finally left us alone.

The raids were coming fast and furious. The camp personnel were very edgy and the four of us kept seeing good signs that the war was ending with each bombing escalation. I was so optimistic, I was ready to pack and stand by to leave at any time.

A week passed and I was still getting used to being with three other men. I wondered about Jerry and where he was. We only had comm with our neighbors and didn't know what was going on beyond. The comm purge was still going as strong as ever.

The key guard came after the noon siesta and in turn took Jenkins, Shumaker and me individually outside in the yard where we had our picture taken. For some unknown reason they didn't bother with Lou Makowski.

I was the last to be taken from the room, so I knew from Harry who had gone first, what the trip was all about. I was taken to a middle age Vietnamese officer who had a camera and a chair positioned in place for a posed sitting picture. I bowed politely and said "Good afternoon, sir." He replied, "Please take your seat, Commander Mulligan, while I take some snapshots of you." I sat and he clicked off a couple of shots. "Thank you, Commander, you may go to your room now," he said. I bowed and departed in complete amazement. I didn't know this officer and had never even seen him before. The Vietnamese never acknowledged that we had any rank so his conversation was completely out of keeping with established policy. Something was going on, and I wondered what it was.

We had long since finished the late afternoon meal and were entertaining ourselves watching Harry's mice run around, getting the rice he saved for them, when our recreation was suddenly interrupted by a guard who opened our cell and told Jenkins, Shumaker and me to dress quickly, roll up our gear and move out. We said goodbye to each other and left, leaving Lou Makowski standing in the middle of the cell looking completely forlorn and sad.

They blindfolded me at the entrance to the courtyard and made me sit for a long time on my bedroll before coming to lead me away. I could hear men moving and the guards jibbering away in Vietnamese to one another. They put handcuffs on me and joined my arms in front of me. A guard helped me to my feet, then led me off with his hand on my shoulder. In a short time I was outside the camp. I could hear the vehicles and people from the street. They hoisted me into a vehicle and sat two guards on either side of me. I think two other POWs were in the same vehicle because I heard what seemed to be men hoisted aboard as I was.

The trip took only a very short time, probably ten minutes or less. We arrived at our destination and I was the last one to leave the vehicle. One guard led me while another followed on behind carrying my gear.The footing was uneven. I stumbled, but the guard was quick to save me from a fall. My blindfold was so large and effective that I couldn't see a thing. The lead guard opened a gate and led me in behind him. The guard carrying my gear tripped and bumped into me, knocking me forward into the lead guard. I heard a crash of broken pottery and rightly assumed that my personal water jug had been broken. I heard the lead guard open a door and was pushed and pulled into a cell. The lead guard took off the blindfold and removed the cuffs, threw my gear on the bamboo bed frame and slammed the solid wooden door shut. I looked at my cramped surroundings and went into a state of shock. I had a premonition that things had suddenly turned very bad for me. If anything, this initial feeling was a massive under-estimate.

ALCATRAZ — ELEVEN DIE-HARDS

I think that in each person's life as he passes blissfully through this world's vale of tears there comes a time when the fickle finger of fate rears its ugly head at him and he finds himself in a terribly uncontrollable situation which marks the lowest point of his existence. Here he comes face to face with the stark reality of complete despair. His own efforts, coupled with the odds of chance, often determine whether he survives this ordeal. He is at an absolute bottomless pit where he can either drown, physically or mentally dying, or else, like the Phoenix of old, he rises from those terrible ashes and climbs to new heights. I knew I was at that point late on the night of 25 October 1967. I realized fully that in this place I was like the *Master* in the Garden of Gethsemane, fully aware of the agonies that were yet to come.

The cell was ten feet long, a little more than four feet wide and had three solid walls and a solid door. Over the doorway was a barred opening completely covered by a heavy piece of iron sheet metal which had a series of holes about one quarter inch in diameter. Four feet in from the door the concrete cell floor raised about one foot leaving an area of six by four feet where they had put a bamboo bed frame on which I could put my reed mat. The bed frame was six feet long, a little more than three feet wide and about one and a half inches high.

It's hard to believe that they are going to keep me here in this cell, I thought as my mind flashed back to the "make your choice" program the Vietnamese came up with in May of 1966. "There will be those who oppose us and they will lead the others to oppose us. They are the

Die-Hards. They will not be many. They will live in small dark cells. They will get no sunshine or exercise. They will be put in the shackles, and have bad food and no medicine." "It's the camp for the Die-Hards. I wonder who else is here?" I mumbled to myself. Just then a soft POW call up came from the right wall. I tapped twice in reply. "Jim Stockdale," he tapped. "Jim Mulligan," I replied. "See you tomorrow," he answered. "GBU," for God Bless You. I closed him off with a fast series of "Roger, Roger, GBU."

It was quite late. I had my small drinking cup, tooth brush, tooth paste, a little piece of soap, my clothes, blanket, reed mat and mosquito net. My water jug was missing, broken by the guard just before I got to the cell. I saw a rusty personal convenience bucket in the left corner next to the solid gray door. Over the door was a small light which barely illuminated the cell. I rigged my net and made up my bed, got in, said my prayers and reviewed my POW name list. Lord I'm scared. I wonder what comes up next, I said mentally as I dropped off to sleep.

I was asleep for only a brief time, when suddenly I was awakened by a key guard opening my door. I looked up and saw the Vietnamese officer I knew as Rat. "Get up!" he yelled. I jumped out from under the net as fast as I could. My palms were sweaty and my heart beat rapidly with the fear of what was going to happen to me. I bowed, shivering in fear, like a house dog soaking wet on a cold winter day. "You are in the bad camp," said Rat. "Since tonight my guards will put you in the leg shackles as punishment for all your bad deeds." He motioned to a guard who came in with a set of black leg irons. Two U shaped irons were placed over my ankles with the opened eyes facing forward. He pushed a long iron bar through one eye over my ankle and then through the other eye continuing across to my left leg where he performed the same maneuver. Then he put a lock on the hole at the end of the bar and shut it tight. Rat closed the door and they left me standing there. I tried to walk but at first couldn't. Then I bent over and lifted the iron bar and was able to shuffle one foot at a time. I made it with difficulty to the bucket and took a nervous pee. Then I made my way backwards till I could sit on the bed and swing my feet up and under the net. It was a difficult feat for me at first but later as the months passed by I became proficient moving in traveling irons.

The Vietnamese guard was so retarded that he had put the irons on backwards. This meant that when I lay flat on my back the heavy leg iron rested on both my shin bones. It caused me a great deal of discomfort and I had difficulty sleeping. All in all it was a terrible night but only the first of a long series of hardships that would prevail in this God-forgotten place.

The morning tocsin rang but it was a long while before the key guard came, unlocked my door and removed the leg irons. He let me out to empty my bucket and I got my first glimpse of my surroundings. I was in the middle room of a small three-celled building. I walked past a longer building on my left which had ten identical doors just like the one I had come from, except these doors had a four or five inch opening under them, whereas the doors in my small building went to within one half an inch of the concrete floor.

I cleansed my bucket and went back to my cell. The compound was quiet as a morgue. I had no idea who or how many other POWs besides Stockdale and myself were there.

The guard let Stockdale out for the same routine. There was a crack on the mortar located on the upper hinge. I stood tiptoed and found I could get a clear view of six of the ten cells. I saw Jim Stockdale clearly for the first time since I was in the Gate House at the Zoo in September 1967. He still limped badly and had aged twenty years since then. He now looked like a man in his late sixties. His face was drawn taut and his body stooped like he had been carrying St. Christopher's burden of the world on his shoulders.

The guard locked him in and went to the other cells across from us. I tapped, "I saw you good. You're limping badly. Does your leg still hurt?" "Hell yes," he replied. "The Vietnamese doctors mangled me for good."

"I can see out," he tapped. "Let's see if we can find out who's in camp with us!" "Roger," I replied. "I have a well protected peephole that covers most of the yard and the bucket cleaning area. C U later," I said and closed off with a series of taps.

I didn't recognize the first man who came out. The second man to empty at the latrine was Harry Jenkins. The third man was unknown to me. Bob Shumaker was the fourth man out. I didn't recognize the 5th, 6th, 7th or 8th man. Jerry Denton was the last man out and he looked like he had been in severe punishment. His face was drawn, his eyes seemed recessed behind a heavy five o'clock shadow, and he was moving very slowly like he was both in physical pain and mental torture. God, Jerry, what have they done to you now! I thought, as I watched him return to his cell.

I told Stockdale about my three identifications and he added Sam Johnson and Howie Rutledge to the list. We had five out of the nine identified that first morning.

In a few days they moved me into cell 11 separating me from Stockdale by a guard hangout and equipment room in cell 12. In the other building they had Jerry Denton in cell 10 and a guard room in cell 9. Obviously they were attempting to cut off Denton, Stockdale and myself as much as possible from the others.

It took a couple of weeks before comm was established with the other building. Each day when I went to empty my bucket, Stockdale would lie on the floor and send tap code by flashing his hand next to the opening between the floor and the door. I would look at his door to see if his moving hand could be seen from outside in the courtyard. I looked at his door surreptitiously from all angles but I could never detect any movement or even see that he was lying on the floor trying to communicate.

Once we determined this was a safe comm method, he was able to establish good safe flash comm with Nels Tanner who was in cell 6. We learned that in addition to Tanner and the other five already identified that Ron Storz was in cell 5, George Coker in cell 7 and George McKnight in cell 8.

Storz, McKnight and Coker were junior in rank and considerably younger than the rest of us. Each was here for a specific reason. Storz had been a thorn in the side of the Vietnamese ever since his capture in April of 1965. McKnight and Coker had escaped from another camp but were caught within a day and were sentenced to confinement in this bad camp we later named ALCATRAZ.

This line-up for the ALCATRAZ ELEVEN then was as follows:

MAIN BUILDING

Cell 1 Cdr Howard Rutledge	U.S. Navy
Cell 2 Cdr Harry Jenkins	U.S. Navy
Cell 3 LtCol Sam Johnson	U.S. Air Force
Cell 4 Lcdr Bob Shumaker	U.S. Navy
Cell 5 Capt Ron Storz	U.S. Air Force
Cell 6 Lcdr Nels Tanner	U.S. Navy
Cell 7 Ltjg George Coker	U.S. Navy
Cell 8 Capt George McKnight	U.S. Air Force
Cell 9 Empty — Guard Shack	
Cell 10 Cdr Jerry Denton	U.S. Navy

SMALL ANNEX

Cell 11 Cdr Jim Mulligan	U.S. Navy
Cell 12 Empty — Guard Shack	
Cell 13 Cdr Jim Stockdale	U.S. Navy SRO

In the days immediately following our arrival at Alcatraz, Hanoi targets were heavily bombed by attacking U.S. aircraft. Some of the targets must have been very close to Alcatraz because the force of the exploding bombs blew concussion waves that hammered my cell door. The officers and guards hid out in a shelter in the courtyard. At these times I took the opportunity to look out as much as possible through a small opening high on the right side of the door. I could see the sky covered with flak and occasionally I saw planes in dives or in the process of dropping bombs. If I'm lucky, one of those bombs will land smack on top of me, I thought. The raids gave a large boost to my morale. I was surprised to see that I had absolutely no fear though the concussions were close enough that the pressure waves slammed against the door in my face like a blow from the heavens. Nevertheless, I stood by and waited for the dust to clear in order that I might see more of the action. I could see SAMs launching north of us as well as hear their banging liftoffs. It was a thrilling show to watch and I cheered the Yanks on as if I were rooting at a football game.

The raids were close enough that Rat came and instructed each of us to sit in the corner with our heads in our hands and covered by our blanket. I thought this attempt at survival was absurd but assumed the demanded position when the alarm sounded.

The guards would quickly check me and then when the shooting started they flew for the safety of their shelter. At this time I would then go to the door to see the action if possible. Fragments from exploding shells and bombs would shower the courtyard and after the "All clear" the guards would gleefully pick up the pieces they could find.

There must have been a juicy radar target near me. On several occasions I heard the swish of incoming U.S. missiles and their explosion very close by. The bombing at that time in Hanoi was as severe as it would ever get except for the massive B-52 raids in December 1972.

I felt this heavy pressure on Hanoi would help bring a quick settlement to the war. I hoped they were hitting Hai Phong just as hard and had also instituted a complete blockade. It was wishful thinking on my part but even so it gave me something to hang my hopes on. You gotta have faith, I kept telling myself.

My physical condition, which had been exceptionally poor, took a sudden turn for the worse about 10 November. My skin turned yellow and my eyes became blurry. I had severe pains under my left rib cage as well as in the kidney area. An intense fever consumed me and I just flopped on the uncomfortable bed and lay there like a dying animal. The Vietnamese ignored my condition but because of the peeking rifle guards were aware something was wrong with me.

Finally, Rat came unexpectedly and looked me over. He said something to the guard and they left, returning in a short time with the big medic I had last seen at the Zoo in January.

The medic looked into my eyes, felt under my left rib cage and I doubled over in pain. He took out fifteen large white pills and made me take them all. "You will get special food," Rat said. Beginning that day and for the next six weeks I received a gruel of rice and meat broth. I ate every bit of it and my strength returned as the pain gradually subsided.

I didn't have a water jug. All I received to drink was two cups of water daily. My enamel water cup was smaller than the regular cups; consequently I was always thirsty. I kept asking for a water jug but got nowhere. Finally they gave me one, two days before Christmas.

My POW name list was well over 200 names and I drilled myself three times a day. I arose at the tocsin, said my prayers and did my name bank. Then I just sat and fantasized until the guard came and took off the leg irons. I was in leg irons over sixteen hours each day. They didn't hurt but always caused me much mental anxiety and I never did get accustomed to them.

Using tap code, Jim Stockdale and I caught each other up on our lives since we last communicated in July 1966 at the Zoo. We exchanged information on our families and the mutual friends we had in the Navy. He would comm with Tanner from the other building during siesta and then would pass any info to me. After the afternoon meal I would tap to him a fictitious menu that we both could enjoy mentally that evening. I always made it an elaborate repast, finished off with a special dessert. Because of my under-nourished condition I found myself thinking more and more about food.

December came and the weather chilled. The cells were soaked cold and no matter what I did I could not get warm. It was colder inside the cell than outside. I always bathed first or second when the morning chill was still on. In spite of this I would stand stark naked and pour buckets of cold water from the cistern over my head. No matter how hard I tried to get clean, I never felt clean the entire time I was in Hanoi. They gave me a bar of old fashioned brown soap about every six weeks. It was harsh and wouldn't lather. I looked forward to the daily bath. It meant I'd be out of my oppressive cell for about fifteen minutes. Bucket cleaning time took five minutes or less. The only other time I was out of the cell was to pick up the food or dried clothing. This took a minute or so. Total time out then would be only a bit more than twenty minutes each day on the normal routine from Monday through Saturday. Sundays we were kept in except to empty our buckets and pick up our food.

It was Advent. I seriously began to prepare myself for the coming of Christmas. I increased my prayer and meditation time and asked for guidance and strength to see me through this latest ordeal.

For recreation I began mentally constructing a new house. The first item to come to mind was a huge food storeroom. I decided to fill it with all types of food before I commenced with the rest of the house. After many hours of careful preparation I mentally stocked it with sufficient food to last a year. I calculated the cost based on my last known food prices and decided I could purchase it all for $2500. It's the first thing I'll do when I get home, I thought.

The ready availability of food became an obsession with me. It still is. In Hanoi I learned firsthand that the cardinal drives of man are self preservation, thirst and hunger in that order.

I had a quiz with Rat the week before Christmas. He asked me what desires I had for Christmas and I replied, "A letter from my wife." He asked if I was a Christian and I replied, "Yes, I am a Roman Catholic." "We have Catholics in Hanoi," he ventured. "I know," I said. "Last Easter I visited with the priest Jean Baptiste Ho Ti Binh at the big camp in downtown Hanoi."

"Do you think you are in Hanoi," he asked. "Yes," I said, "I'm about right in the center of the city." "You are mistaken," he said. "You are many, many kilometers from Hanoi." Rat was an absolute liar but I didn't push the point. The quiz ended and I was sent back to the cell.

Lord, I hope I get a letter from home at Christmas. It's the only thing I ask for, Lord, so please do Your best for me. I prayed for a letter night and day from that time on.

Two days before Christmas Rat came to my cell with pen and paper and said, "Write letter home." He put on so many restrictions pertaining to length and content that I finally gave up in frustration and wrote the following letter which he accepted as meeting his requirements.

23 December 1967

My Darling Wife and Children,

Isn't it nice of them to allow me to write to you about my health on the occasion of Christmas.

Medical care is adequate and I receive extra food. I know you are all well. If you write you can only mention the health of you and the family. I pray for you all daily. God bless you all and say thanks to Father Ed. Say hi to my folks and everyone.

Your Husband and Father,
James A. Mulligan

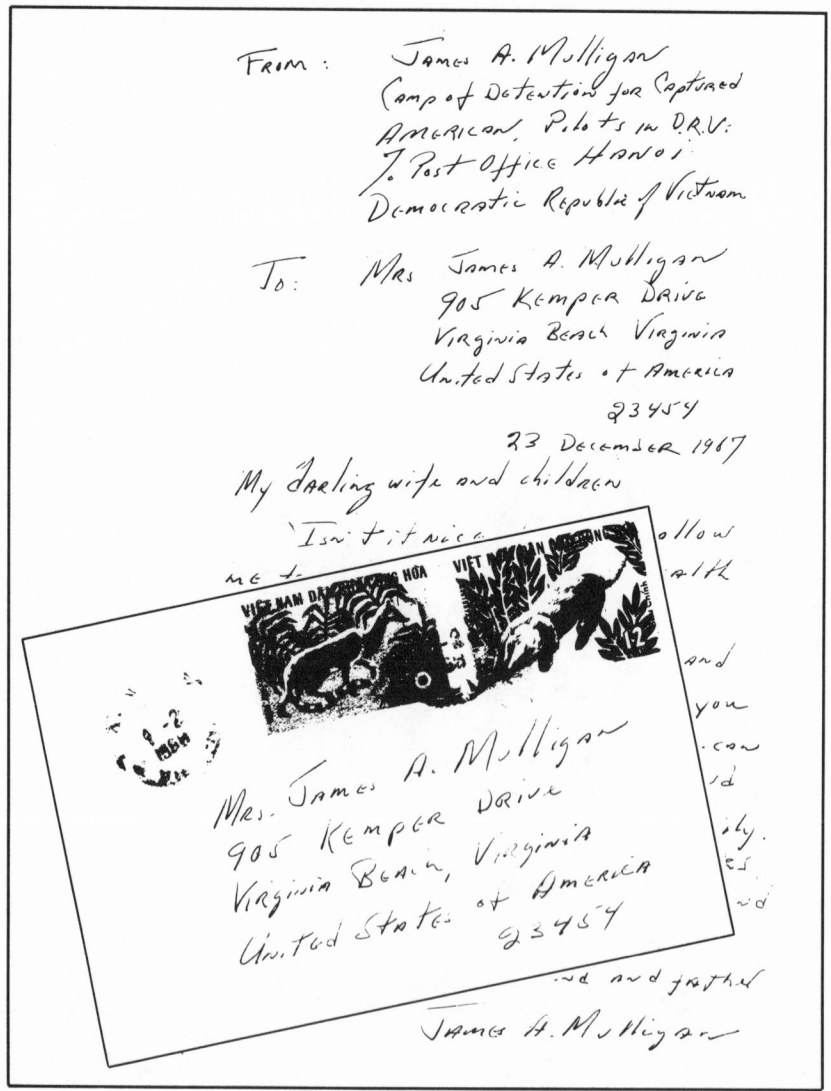

CHRISTMAS 1967

Late in the afternoon, after chow and before Christmas Eve, the guard locked me in leg irons. I sat on the edge of my bed hunched over with head in hands and uncomfortable from the weight and restrictions of the irons. This was my third Christmas away from home and my second in Hanoi. Because of my circumstances in Alcatraz it was one of the lowest points of my POW career. I couldn't do anything but reminisce about Christmas, my wife and children, my parents and brothers. I was overcome with self-pity and was on the verge of uncontrolled tears. I stayed in this condition for a couple of hours when suddenly the guard came and took off the irons, told me to dress for quiz and led me off to the quiz room.

On entering I bowed to Rat who sat stiffly in full uniform behind the desk. He motioned me to the stool and chitchatted about the Christian Holiday. "For tonight we remove you from the shackles," he said. He had some chess and checker boards and asked if I played them. "No," I replied, "not for many years." He offered me one but I refused. I kept hoping for a letter but none was forthcoming. At last he gave me a small bag of Vietnamese candies and bid me return to my cell. I stood at attention and bowed more in sadness than obedience to this humiliating Vietnamese regulation imposed upon me. I was about to turn and leave when Rat reached beneath a resting book and pulled out a large envelope. "The camp authority has for you on the occasion of your Christian Holiday some documents from your family," he said as he reached out the letter in my direction. "Thank you," I replied, struggling to hold back the tears which were swelling inside me. "Return your room," he ordered. I repeated my bow and hurried as rapidly as I could back to the confines of my cell. The escort rifle guard had to half run in an effort to keep up with me.

I saw that the long white envelope had already been opened and inspected by the Vietnamese. I recognized Louise's familiar bold sweeping handwriting on the address and noticed that she and the boys were living in Virginia Beach as I had learned the previous June from Red McDaniel. Inside the envelope were two pictures and two wonderful letters, one from Louise and one from my youngest brother John.

The picture of Louise was taken by a neighbor, Mary Metz, of Virginia Beach in her house at Christmas 1966. I was overwhelmed with joy at just being able to see a picture of my Louise. She looked wonderful, full of life, vivacious and beautiful as she sat at a table facing the camera with her beautiful smile and dashing eyes. My body ached to be with her, to hold her in my arms and never let her go.

The second picture was one with my six boys. It was over two years since I had seen them and they had grown almost beyond recognition.

Louise's letter was dated February of 1967. Fortunately and wisely she reviewed what had transpired with my family since my capture. Louise described her trip to "visit mutual friends" in Washington in sufficient detail that I knew she had received my Christmas 1966 letter and had gotten its contents to the proper Naval authorities. I was elated at finding this out and felt I had accomplished a major victory over my captors by getting much useful info on the POWs back to our leaders.

My brother John's letter brought me a huge amount of joy. He had a great sense of humor and always managed to write interesting and informative letters. My life in solitary confinement had forced me to close my thinking process to my own self and my immediate personal problems caused by such an existence. Receiving the letters brought me back into the real world and out of my own narrow shell of self-concern and self-pity.

Just reading Louise's and John's prose made my mind alert and started my rational processes functioning normally. They liberated me from a situation much worse than I had imagined I was existing in.

John looked with great favor on the sport of horse racing and described his latest efforts at developing a system for picking winners during the early spring racing season at Scarboro Downs in Maine. Most of the horses came to Scarboro from the sunny south where they had wintered after the previous fall's racing season. Since they hadn't been racing for some months there was little solid information to go on which he could use to separate the potential winners from the losers. He finally settled on a sure thing, which would permit him to become a big winner. "With no information to go on, I look for a happy horse and figure if he's happy up in the cold at Scarboro, then he'll probably run faster than his counterparts," John wrote. At the first four races of the evening John couldn't distinguish a happy horse from an unhappy horse. In the fifth race one horse pranced and bounded around with such a gusto gait that he looked to be an extremely happy horse. "I put $10 on the nose and he came in by six lengths at seven to one," John continued. "I laid off for the rest of the night when I couldn't find another happy horse. I followed this system for my next three visits to the track and the net result is that most of the happy horses I selected managed to come in out of the money. At this point in time I am down $110 and am looking for a new system to replace my happy horse selection," he concluded.

The letters made me come alive. I was elated. I read and re-read each line, each word, devouring the contents and taking off wildly into flights of fantasy. After awhile the shock of my good fortune wore off and I just sat on the edge of my bamboo frame bed and agonized in my loneliness. The tears swelled up, and slowly trickled down my cheek.

I thought about my Louise and our sons, my parents and my brothers and all my relatives. I was sick and emaciated, living like a caged animal and on the edge of dispair. I reached out and asked for God's grace to help sustain me in this time of torment. "I don't have anything left, Lord, but my faith in You. You gave me everything, all that I have is Yours. Please, Lord, give me the strength to see this ordeal through so that one day I may return to my home and loved ones." I fell asleep, mentally exhausted and dreamed sweet dreams of home.

Christmas Day was a holiday routine for the camp personnel, the only difference being that the noon meal was somewhat better than normal. I received a bowl of clear noodle soup and a plate of rice and a small piece of meat. The guard brought thick sweet Vietnamese coffee which I nursed drop by drop for an hour after I had eaten all of my food. The sugar gave me a surge of energy as it flowed into my blood. Oh, how I missed the creature comforts I had taken for granted for so many years. If I ever get out of this place I'll never take anything for granted again, I thought as I gave thanks for my meager material blessings.

At the siesta hour Stockdale and I exchanged news from our letters with each other and with the nine other POWs living in solitary across the courtyard in the larger building. Though the only ones I knew personally were Denton, Jenkins and Shumaker, I felt a strong tie of friendship with all. I had come to know them from the detailed information we passed to each other during our constant comm sessions. The "Alcatraz Eleven" was the greatest team I would ever be on. I admired the POWs in Alcatraz more than any other men I would ever know. Each man there was a dedicated American who paid a terrible price in physical and mental torture for what he believed in. I considered it a high honor and a special privilege to be one of them. Each day I prayed for the spiritual and physical welfare of each of them. I knew in my heart that if I lived to be a hundred, I would never be in such special company again.

It was dark. I had been sitting on the edge of my bed facing the door. My leg irons had been firmly attached late in the afternoon by a surly guard whose unpleasantness reminded me that my holiday was over. "I'm back in the irons again," I sang mentally to the tune of, "I'm Back in the Saddle Again." I'm beginning to get a perverse sense of humor, I thought as I made up some mental lyrics which were appropriate to my situation. I was in a sort of mental malaise, a situation I often found myself in, when suddenly my cell door rattled as the guard struggled to unlock it. In a few seconds Rat stepped in, pointed to my cup and half filled it with a green liquid. "Drink quickly and put on," he said as he pointed to my blue pajama quiz suit. I took a swallow and reeled from the strength of it. It's pure booze, I thought. Strong as grain alcohol. After the guard had removed my leg irons, I quickly dressed. I finished the booze and was warmed and stimulated by it. Rat pushed me out of the cell and into the courtyard. I was immediately blindfolded and led away. "Tonight you will see your pryst," I heard Rat say as I stumbled forward between two guards who were leading and shoving me along. He means priest, I thought. I'll bet I'm going to see the priest again. Visions of my meeting with Fr. Ho Ti Binh the previous Easter flashed through my mind.

I tried to keep track of my movement but was soon disoriented as the guards spun me around obviously to induce confusion as to my whereabouts. I hadn't gone more than one hundred yards when Rat stopped the entourage and removed my blindfold. I was on a sidewalk under a large tree in front of a large wooden framed building. My eyes adjusted quickly to the darkness as he led me across the street. I noticed streetcar rails on the street. A few passersby made an effort to get out of our way as we moved some yards on the opposite sidewalk. Then we came to a small grassy courtyard leading to a row of long low buildings.

"Quickly, quickly," Rat urged me. He led me to a large building and up a wide set of stairs. I looked at the low building and decided other POWs must be harbored there. We went into a hallway and he pushed me into a room on the right which had a couple of chairs and an old French pool table. "Sit here," he said and left me under guard.

There were people moving in the hallway. I turned my head and looked out a window which opened on the courtyard facing the building I believed held POWs. I saw nothing out there but that building with no windows, and solid doors with a peek-in opening in their center.

Other guards came into the room and began to play French pool. They left the door open and I was able to see the backs of people moving down the hallway by looking through the hinged area of the opened door.

Suddenly I recognized the movement of POWs. They were all dressed in the faded red striped clown suits that were issued as standard clothing beginning in the late summer of 1966. I wondered what was going on. A door slammed shut and all the traffic ceased in the hallway. I could hear the sonorous tone of a Vietnamese speaking. When he stopped, a group of Americans began singing Christmas carols, along with some of the more popular contemporary Christmas music of our day. I was appalled! I couldn't see what was going on, but I felt that what I heard was part of a large Vietnamese Christmas propaganda show.

The guards continued to play pool. I didn't understand the game but watched as they eliminated first one then another. The final winner asked me to play with him. I indicated I didn't know how and he showed me how to line up a shot to bounce a ball off the back towards a center hole. I took the tipless cue, and with more luck than skill, managed to kiss the lead ball off the backboard and into the center hole. The game was over and I had won on one shot. I immediately retired as the undefeated champ. While I had good form and looked like a pro to the Vietnamese guards, only I knew I couldn't duplicate that shot once in fifty tries.

The guards were in a happy mood and became quite friendly. One of them noticed my interest in the hallway so he took me into it and across into another room. This room was filled with Vietnamese war propaganda pictures, pamplets and magazines. I was reading the first one on the 1967 mid-east war when Rat entered and gruffly sent me back into my original stash point. There was an Israeli-Egyptian war in the Middle-East and I didn't even know about it, or for that matter who won, I mused. Rat departed and the American Christmas show came to an end.

There was noise in the hallway caused by the exodus from the propaganda show. I could see men with writing pads and cameras in the hall. Asian correspondents I thought.

One of them, an Asian, popped his head into the room I was in and on seeing me, came over. "Are you an American prisoner?" he asked. "Yes," I replied. "Do they treat you humanely?" "No," I answered. "They keep many of us in irons and in solitary confinement. We have little food. We are sick and starving." Just then Rat came in and went into a rage at the Asian correspondent. "Mun keep sil-lent!" he yelled at me. "You have no right, you have no right," he yelled at the correspondent as he pushed him out of the room and into the hallway slamming the door closed as he left.

In some minutes the building became quiet. Obviously everyone had left. Rat returned and led me out of the building across the lawn to a building which looked like a movie auditorium.

"You are going to the Catholic celebration of Christmas," he said. "Do not talk to anyone here," and he led me into the auditorium.

It was a large hall with a flat ceiling about twenty feet high. In front of the auditorium they had set up a fully decorated altar with all the appointments for a Christmas Mass. On the right of the altar was a large Nativity scene, similar to the ones we have in U.S. churches at Christmas. I could see Father Ho Ti Binh vesting himself for Mass with two altar boy assistants and the same interpreter he had when I had seen him the previous Easter in Little Vegas.

I noticed that on the back wall from a projection booth the Vietnamese guards had hidden cameras on station ready to film the affair.

There were twelve POWs in red striped clown suits, sitting four to a row in chairs located in front of me. None of them saw me come in.

Two POWs made their way to the crib scene and were ushered back to their seats by a Vietnamese officer who made an announcement that Mass would soon begin and we would be allowed to visit the Nativity scene after the Mass was finished.

I was sitting between Rat and Mickey Mouse in the last row of chairs. The POWs still didn't know I was there, so I feigned ignorance of the officers' announcement and spoke up loudly saying, "Do I understand you to say that we will be permitted to visit the crib scene when the Mass is finished?" I stood up as I directed this query. On hearing my voice all the POWs turned around to look at me. The officer replied, "Yes, we permit you to visit the crib after the Mass." "Thank you," I replied to him. I noticed a short black-haired American with large ears turn to his fellows and say, "That's Jim Mulligan," clearly enough that I could read his lips. Though I had never seen this man before, he met the description that Jerry Coffee had given of himself to me over a year ago. That must be Jerry Coffee, I thought. I didn't recognize any of the others.

As the Mass progressed all I could do was plan to pass a message about the whereabouts of the Alcatraz Gang. I'll do it at Communion time, I finally decided.

Rat and Mickey Mouse kept a very close surveillance over me in order to prevent me from communicating with any of the other POWs.

The Mass was the universal Latin ceremony I had known ever since early childhood. Ho Ti Binh began with, "Et Entroibo Ad Altare Dei," "I will go unto the altar of God." From that moment onward I remembered every response which I had learned as an altar boy at St. Patrick's Roman Catholic Church in Lawrence, Mass. I had not been to Mass since 19 March 1966, the day before I was shot down. I immersed myself fully in the liturgy and for a while I was completely free, at least mentally and spiritually, from my oppressive captors.

I heard the whirring of the camera's reel and I flew back into reality. Silently I raised a solid thumbs-up with my right hand as I knelt facing the altar. I slowly changed this outward sign to a two-fingered V for victory which I had come to know during World War II from the British Prime Minister, Winston Churchill. I hoped that someone watching the film would pick up my signals indicating that I was ok and would hold out till victory.

At Communion time I made my way quickly to the line so that I was in its center. I spoke slowly yet audibly almost as if I were saying a verbal prayer. "Eleven of us are kept one block north, in solitary and in irons, we're ok," I repeated this several times bowing my head as if in prayer to distract my Vietnamese captors.

I accepted Communion at the rail. The tears came to my eyes. It's Christmas night and my thoughts aren't on Christ but on myself. I prayed for His forgiveness, my family and the other POWs in captivity. I arose slowly and deliberately, and step by step, made my way fervently to my place. I looked into the eyes of the man I thought was Jerry Coffee as I passed before him. "Merry Christmas Jim Mulligan," he said softly and I recognized Jerry Coffee's clear voice, a memory of the past which had been such a solace to me when I lived in the Pool Hall back in the Zoo a year ago.

Rat led me alone to the crib after Mass. I paid my spiritual respects to the infant and then was led back to the auditorium entrance. The other POWs had left. I was alone again. The Vietnamese officer we called Bug came up to me and said, "Mun, you look like you are in poor health. How do you enjoy the treatment of the Vietnamese people in your new camp?" "It's lousy," I said, "just like all your camps — Merry Christmas," and I bowed a deep contemptuous bow. He snickered in delight, his bad eyeball flickering in an uncontrollable fashion. God, I hate that little bastard, I thought.

Rat moved me out quickly and we retraced our route. They put the blindfold on at the same place they had removed it. A couple of whirling turns for confusion and I was quickly led back to Alcatraz. The whole trip took only a couple of minutes.

I was back in the irons and in my cell before I realized what was going on. I retraced all the night's events in my mind in order to fully brief Stockdale on them in the morning. Then I fell off into a deep sleep. I was bushed and the slug of booze must have been enough to knock me out for good on that night.

The next day when I described my trip to Jim Stockdale, he informed me that I had been taken to the camp known as the Plantation. The men in Alcatraz now had a good idea of where we were being kept in Hanoi.

1968

MIRACLE OR COINCIDENCE

From early January till mid-April 1968 the weather in Hanoi was overcast and drizzly. The dreary overcast and dampness consumed the cells. Literally we froze our asses off. Each day the U.S. conducted heckler raids. Often the only thing we heard was a loud explosion from an incoming missile. On several occasions a Shrike missile whizzed directly overhead to a target very close by. The swish of the missiles and the fury of the explosion were music to my ears.

Rat quizzed me two or three times a week. No programs were going on. He just seemed to be working the good guy approach to propaganda. I made him angry by not showing proper respect in my bowing or my language. The Vietnamese officers and guards were getting more disturbed daily over the interdiction raids. "Wait till the weather gets good," I taunted them, "then you'll see U.S. air power for real." Rat would sneer and briskly dismiss me to my cell. It was plain to me that I was getting on his nerves.

On 1 April I was suddenly whisked into a quiz with Rat and a new English-speaking guard we named Marty Mouthful because of the large teeth he had.

After my obsequious bow, Rat told me to sit on the stool at the foot of his raised desk and chair. "Since today you have lost the war," he said. "Your President Johnson can no longer bomb our beloved Hanoi." He went on the explain Johnson's latest bombing restriction.

"The U.S. has no capability left and we will defeat you," he continued. I didn't know what to think. "You will hear on the broadcast of the camp radio tonight," he said.

After my return from quiz a deathly silence pervaded the camp. There wasn't a sign of a raid or interdiction the whole day. That night Hanoi Hannah read Johnson's proscription about bombing north of the 20th parallel. "Bullshit," I said. "At this rate he will probably stop bombing a week before the U.S. Presidential election. Damn politics!! Here we are sitting on our asses and our political leaders are more concerned about winning the election than winning the war, or at least ending it." I was extremely bitter about this prospect which, as I had feared, eventually came to pass.

From: James Alfred Mulligan
Camp of detention of U.S. Pilots captured in the
Democratic Republic of Vietnam
C/o Hanoi Post Office. D.R.V

To: Mrs. James A. Mulligan Jr
905 Kemper Drive
Virginia Beach, Virginia 23454
United States of America

13 MARCH 1158

My darling Louise and boys,

It is great I've able to write and let you know that I am well and to wish you all a very Happy Easter. Last Easter I saw a priest and had a nice visit. It was a big event to me, second only to this past Christmas.

On Christmas EVE I received a letter from you with your picture that Mary took and the picture of the boys that you took. You all look wonderful and I was so excited I stayed up all night rereading your letter and my brother Miss's letter and just looking at your pictures. It sure is good news to hear that all of you are well and that you are Living in Virginia Beach. I'm glad that the boys are doing so well, you know my feelings about the importance of school.

Christmas day was a big event here. I received candy and fruit and visited the camp office which was all decorated for the occasion. At dinner we had a special meal featuring turkey, & the usual dish. The Vietnamese were certainly kind to us and went to a lot of trouble to see that we had a nice day.

Christmas night was the gala event. I atte...
Mass and went to Communion and Comm...
with joy and elation. We recei...
and also the Tet which...
coming of...
good...

Air mail

Mrs. James A. Mulligan Jr.
905 Kemper Drive
Virginia Beach, Virginia 23407
United States of America

VIA AIR MAIL

The Alcatraz Eleven were slowly wasting away. Our diet was meager. Our living conditions intolerable. The solitary confinement and leg irons were mentally and physically depressing.

"We're going to start having mental problems if something doesn't change soon," I tapped to Stockdale. I began to regress more and more each day. I felt myself dwelling more and more on the past. I had an obsession to return to my childhood. Through college, back through high school, then grammar school I traveled seeking to recall each and every name I had ever been associated with. I had made my way back over a period of months until I arrived in time to the first incident that I could clearly recall in my life. I was only two years old and I remembered the incident where I learned the word cemetery. We were in the car and I asked, "What's that Grandma?" She replied, "An Indian cemetery." I repeated, "Indian cemetery, what is it for?" "Jim," she said to my Grandfather, "he can say cemetery and he's not two years old." It was the spring of 1928 and we were on our way to Salisbury Beach. I was almost two years old.

I'm regressing, by God I'm going back into the womb, I thought as I sat alone in complete solitude. Events that occurred forty years ago were as clear as if they had happened yesterday. The past, in fact, replaced the present and the near past. My wife and family faded into oblivion as I relived my childhood day by day, hour by hour, minute by minute.

The chronology of the past seemed to demand my every waking moment. It was my life flashing before me in slow motion, with pieces missing here and there which eventually would fall into place only after exhaustive recall of a time long since past. I slowly put together the major parts of the masterpiece known as my life. This obsession would remain with me during my entire stay in Alcatraz and day by day I would add another piece to the puzzle of my life that I had long ago forgotten.

I prayed I wouldn't lose my senses, that I'd somehow survive this terrible ordeal. One day while in prayerful meditation I clearly saw that what I was experiencing was merely old age and loneliness. All alone, I was the last leaf on the tree, holding on before winter's cold breath would suddenly snap me off and send me drifting into the hereafter with all the others I had ever known and who were gone before me. If I live to get out of this place I'll never have to go through old age again because I've already lived it, every agonizing minute of it, all alone by myself, the last leaf on the tree.

"Better watch out for mental problems," I tapped to Stockdale the senior officer in the camp. "I wouldn't be surprised to see some infantile regression take place." My suspicions were confirmed some weeks later when he reported a couple of men had lost their bladder control and simply wet the bed while sitting on it.

In early May, Rat had me brought to a quiz about nine in the morning. I entered and gave my usual bow. He ordered me to sit on the stool before him. Marty Mouthful and another new English-speaking guard sat next to him.

My eyes popped out when Marty lifted a paper that was covering a tape recorder which was hooked up to an extension and ready to go.

"How are you today?" Rat asked obsequiously, feigning an interest that was non-existent. "Lousy," I replied. "Your food is terrible and you treat us like animals. We're half dead."

"You have bad attitude, Mun; you and your compatriots must be punished for violating the regulations of the camp authorities. If you do not change your attitude when the war is over you will stay here."

"Bullshit," I replied angrily as I stared at the tape recorder. "When the war is over I'll be sitting at that damn desk and you'll be sitting on this damn stool," I shouted.

Rat was livid with rage. "You must be punished for you are impolite to Vietnamese army officer and Vietnamese army men," he shouted. "You must kneel in the corner on your knees till you see the error of your ways." He spoke sharply in Vietnamese. The two soldiers led me roughly into the corner and put me on my knees.

I was emaciated, a bag of bones covered with loose skin. I didn't have the physical strength of a wet noodle but mentally I was Superman. I'm kneeling so I'll pray, I thought. I began saying the Rosary carefully, deliberately and with as much ardent fervor as I had ever possessed. I was halfway through my second Rosary when I felt myself collapsing. The guards had been checking me every few minutes since my sentence began and they were obviously under orders to watch me closely.

I wilted, hung on, and finally prayed myself into unconsciousness. I didn't even remember hitting the floor. Suddenly I awoke, raised up between the arms of the two soldiers. I was facing Rat who began yelling, "For your insolence I punish you, do you hear, for your insolence I punish you."

"You can't hurt me. I'm almost dead now," I replied, spitting out each word slowly as if it was my last.

The guards rushed me too quickly to my cell and I passed out cold, half on the concrete floor and half on the bed. I came to sufficiently to pull myself up on the reed mat. Rat came rushing in with his medic. The medic took my pulse and looked in my eyes, said something in Vietnamese and left. Rat gave me a copy of the camp regulations and told me to memorize it. I lay still bleary eyed and bushed but feeling I had won out in my battle against the tape recorder. In the excitement of it all Rat never had a chance to get around to the tape recorder and making a tape. More than anything else I considered taping propaganda statements to be a mortal sin which I would avoid under any circumstance.

After being chilled to the bone since I arrived at Alcatraz the previous fall my environment seemed to change almost overnight. Living in a refrigerator became living in an oven.

The sun, which came out in mid-April, got oppressively hotter each day. My cell was situated in such a way that the sun beamed on my left wall all morning then moved across until it pointed directly at my wooden door. The door absorbed the heat and radiated it into my cell. Each day as the sun moved higher in the heavens and shone longer and more directly on my door, the temperature in the cell would attain a new high. By May twentieth, I felt I was living in an attic with no circulation. Each day I just lie on the cell floor and gasped for what little air that came in under the small opening beneath the door.

The iron plate that covered the small barred window over the door formed a reflector oven and drove the temperature higher and higher. We were in the midst of a terrible heat wave. It hadn't rained for weeks. My cell must have reached a temperature of 130 degrees or more. I had never been in such an oppressively hot environment, not even when I was in El Centro, California, and the desert temperature was a measured 120 degrees.

My appetite vanished and my mental powers collapsed like a stack of cards. In a week I couldn't think or concentrate. All I wanted was a drop in the temperature.

On the night of 26 May, my Mother and Dad's wedding anniversary, I finally reached the complete breaking point. I was lying flat on my bed exhausted and almost mentally deranged from the circumstances. I was at the point of no return. "Lord," I begged, "You've got to help me. I can't stand it any longer, Lord. Lord You've got to do something. Let me hear Your thunder, Lord, let me hear Your thunder."

I had barely uttered my last plea when across the heavens a loud crash of thunder rolled off into the night. In seconds it was followed by another and then another. "Lord make it rain, make it rain," I pleaded.

The stillness of the air was ruffled with a rising wind which rapidly increased in velocity as it and the thunder moved closer to my cell. In only a few minutes I heard the first patter of large raindrops which rapidly grew into a torrential tropical rain. The wind howled. The thunder cracked and roared across the heavens. The lightening flashed and the courtyard flooded with water. The wind blew the cold air into my cell. The water rose until it also entered and covered the floor exercise area. The temperature dropped forty or more degrees and my cell cooled off miraculously.

My senses returned. "Thank you, Lord, thank you, Lord," I said over and over again. "When I get out and tell this story someone will say, it was just coincidence, the mere arrival of a fast moving tropical cold front. But You and I know it was more than that. In my direst need I begged for Your help and You answered me. Thank you Lord."

I fell into a deep restful sleep and only awoke long after the morning tocsin had rung when the guard was at my door ready to remove my leg irons.

The weather stayed mild for some days but I knew that if my circumstances didn't change I would soon be subjected to the torrid heat again.

By the second week of June the heat had built up again and I knew I'd never make it through the summer at the rate I was deteriorating.

Because my cell was dark I suffered severe eye strain and often had double vision. I had difficulty focusing on anything with any degree of clarity when I went out to bathe, get my food or empty the bucket. I had massive headaches, something I had never previously experienced.

I assessed my situation as logically as I could. I need air, I decided as I looked at the flat piece of iron which covered the barred narrow window which was over my door. Things would be okay if I could only get them to remove the iron cover and let the air come in.

I didn't know how to get their attention so I decided to go on a hunger strike. Each day for four consecutive days I ate absolutely nothing. I would only get water and leave the food on the makeshift serving rack. The key guard thought I was crazy but he kept urging me in Vietnamese and sign language to eat. I constantly refused and just languished on my bed throughout the day.

On the 19th of June, an officer I hadn't seen since I was first captured came into the courtyard. I viewed him through my peephole as he inspected the area. Stockdale gave me a frantic call-up on the wall. I rapped twice and he sent me a hurried, *"That's the Cat."* I replied, "Roger, Roger."

The Cat was the name the POWs had given to the infamous Major Buy who headed up the North Vietnamese POW programs. He ran the propaganda effort and had supervised numerous torture sessions, especially on the senior officers. Stockdale and Denton knew him well from past experience.

The guard came and took me to quiz. I bowed to Rat, Slopehead the camp commander and Cat as I entered. Cat sat at the extreme left in the position of seniority according to their army customs.

Rat acted as a translator for Slopehead and Cat. Slopehead knew almost no English and Cat was up to his usual tricks, playing dumb until the right moment when he would suddenly strike in all his demented fury.

"Why do you not eat?" said Rat. "I am not well," I replied. Rat translated and the two Vietnamese nodded. "Where are you sick?" he continued. "Do you really want to know?" I replied. "Yes," he answered.

"Then look for yourself," I said as I quickly stood up, removed my long blue quiz jacket and stood there naked from the waist up. You could see every bone. The loose skin hung sickeningly before them.

"You are impolite," said Cat in perfect English. "Put on your clothes. I will punish you for your bad attitude."

"You can't punish me any more than you punish me now," I replied. "I am more dead than alive. You keep me in the leg irons and you do not give me fresh air and I am dying here. I am lonesome for my family. I get no mail. I do not care what you do any more. I am sick and I am dying. If you punish me I will fall on the ground like I did when he punished me," as I nodded in Rat's direction. "It is too hot and I need fresh air," I concluded.

My unrestrained outburst half caused by craze took Cat by surprise. He paused, looked at me, then asked about my family. "I miss my wife and six sons. On July 1st it is the birthday of my wife," I said, in English phraseology he would understand. "If you eat your food the camp authority may have for you a letter on the birthday of your wife," Cat replied.

"Will you try to eat for me your meal today?" "I am too hot," I answered. "I need fresh air but I will try to eat some of my meal for you today."

The three of them spoke in Vietnamese and Rat bid me to get out by saying, "Return your room." I arose slowly, bowed politely, said "Thank you," and left, moving as if I was more dead than alive.

I was back in my cell only a few minutes when the three of them were in the courtyard with a Vietnamese supply officer we called Piggy. They were in heavy discussion pointing at the doors to the cells and the roof of the building housing the nine other POWs.

Piggy came to my cell, opened the door, came in, and looked around. The room was intolerably hot. I bowed politely and wiped my brow as a sign of my discomfort. Suddenly he inadvertently placed his hand against the center of the door. He pulled it away immediately in a reflex response to its terrible heat. He looked at his hand and at the door. I knew what was going through his mind. "If you think the door is hot, you should touch the metal plate over the window," I explained pointlessly as he didn't understand any English. He looked quizzically at me so I pointed to the iron plate, then to the door to get him to see the problem. I pointed to the iron plate, wiped my brow, pointed to the door and his hand. In a flash he saw everything and rushed into the courtyard calling out in Vietnamese to the others.

They entered my cell. I bowed from the far end as politely as I could. Piggy explained the situation. Cat touched the door, looked at the iron plate over the window and sent Rat out after a guard. They left my door open and the sun streamed directly into the cell.

Rat returned with two guards and some primitive tools. They removed the upper bolts holding the iron plate but could not loosen the lower bolts. Finally, using a long iron bar as a lever, they were able to bend the plate down so that it was almost parallel to the ceiling. The light streamed in and so did the fresh air. My cell was illuminated and I could see clearly without any eye strain. I thanked them for removing the iron plate and when they brought me a plate of rice, some sea weed soup and a banana I ate everything, gratefully celebrating my improved circumstances.

That afternoon they opened the other windows on all the remaining cells. The next day they built a straw covered false roof to keep the heat down on the larger POW building and they built a straw overhang over my window which kept the rain out but allowed the fresh air in.

On 1 July, much to my surprise, I was called to a quiz with Rat and Slopehead. I bowed and took my seat on the stool. Rat spoke to me and said, "Since today on the occasion of the birthday of your wife the authority of the camp has for you a letter."

After some chitchat from Slopehead about obeying the regulations of the camp in the future, which Rat translated into English for him, I was dismissed. As I bowed for my exit Rat added, "Eat your food, Mun. Do not make any more trouble for me."

I returned to my cell grateful for the letter, read its contents and passed all the latest news to Stockdale and the rest of the camp. With my four-day fast I had gotten lucky and killed two birds with one stone. I got my cell opened up for air and got a letter from home. My prayers of thanksgiving were long and intense that night.

A LONG SUMMER AND FALL

It was a long, lonely hot summer. The days dawdled by, one by one. Each seemed more exasperating than its predecessor and the nights were longer still. I hadn't seen a sunrise or sunset or even the moon since my capture in March of 1966.

We had almost no news except the garbage from Hanoi Hannah on her nightly broadcast which was passed to us over the camp radio.

Martin Luther King and Bobby Kennedy had been killed and with the death of the Senator from New York I gave up hope that the war would soon come to an end.

The U.S. was bogged down. Johnson was caught in a trap where he wouldn't win yet couldn't lose the war. The biggest sap to my morale was the discontinuance of the bombing of Hanoi. Safe in the shelter of their capital city, the North Vietnamese could plot a delaying strategy without even having to climb into a bomb shelter. It was a pitiful time for us in Alcatraz and the solitary confinement and leg irons only caused us to become even more frustrated.

We heard the GOP had nominated Nixon and someone named Agnew that none of us had ever heard of. Humphrey's running mate Muskie shared a similar position with us.

I didn't have a quiz from the first of July until September was half over. Nothing, absolutely nothing was happening to us. We had been abandoned to our own selves in a limbo halfway between heaven and hell. Each day our physical and mental condition worsened.

Rat was gone. An excellent English-speaking officer that we knew as Slick and later as the Soft Soap Fairy was in administrative charge of the camp.

I went to quiz suddenly and found myself before Rabbit and Slick. I bowed, and from the stool answered their impersonal questions in a very low voice. My voice was gone, lost, no doubt, to the months of inactivity.

"Can't you talk?" asked Slick. "It's hard," I replied, "I haven't spoken to anyone for months."

Rabbit mentioned that I looked very pale. "I haven't been in the sun for two years," I replied. "We will soon permit you to take daily time in the sun and do your outside exercise," he said. They seemed to be checking my physical and mental condition more than anything else. At last they sent me back to my cell promising that the POWs would soon be able to exercise and bask in the sun.

A week later they built a bamboo reed mat fence around our wash area so that a man could bathe and not be seen from the exercise area. With this setup they could have two men in the courtyard at the same time and still prevent them from outwardly seeing one another. We generally got a ten minute bath and a ten minute period of exercise each day at Alcatraz from that day onward.

The ten minute daily outside time did wonders for my mental condition as well as for my physical appearance. I'm sure the vitamin D helped me a lot.

We dragged on through the fall, and winter weather arrived. Slick had the guards bolt up the iron plate over the windows once again. I was depressed at being shoved back into the damp darkness. I wouldn't eat for two days and finally when I told him my story he made arrangements for the iron plate to be bent down. I was pleased with this and immediately began eating.

In November, Denton and McKnight were falsely accused of comm and were separately sent into punishment in the quiz room. Things had been too quiet for too long and I felt another program to elicit propaganda from us was in the making. Mickey Mouse, our old nemesis from the Hanoi Hilton, showed up as the new camp commander and we all sensed we were in for trouble.

Mickey Mouse came into my cell with pen and paper and told me I was allowed to send only a six-line letter home for Christmas. I was incensed at his initial censorship and I finally scribbled one that he accepted for mailing. It said, "Happy Christmas to my wife and family, mother and father, sons and daughters, brothers and sisters. I am, well and only thinking of you all. All my love and have a nice holiday." Love Dad. It was dated 26 Nov. 1968.

I didn't have any daughters or sisters and along with that obvious inference I put a comma after "I am, well" to show someone back home that something was radically wrong with me. Mickey Mouse was pleased with this effort and I was permitted to put it in the smooth for mailing.

Christmas 1968 would be my fourth away from my family. I carefully worked up a long and fervent Advent preparation for the coming feast day celebrating Our Lord's birth. I had nothing to offer except my best efforts to become a more fervent and better Christian. They had taken everything and stripped me of all except my memories and my faith. I was truly a lost soul crying out from the wilderness of solitary confinement in Hanoi. I was numb from the abyss of nothingness. Prayer, comm with Stockdale or Storz, exercise, reflection, sleep, and more prayer was my routine. When I was outside for my daily ten minutes of fresh air I did eye exercises focusing near and far. I also managed to mentally say the Rosary, keeping tab of my Ave Marias by counting the barbs on the barb wire fence that stood over the wall as a barrier to my escape.

Escape was always on my mind. A million ways, a million times, but with never a realistic chance to succeed, no matter how hard I thought or how long I figured each way out.

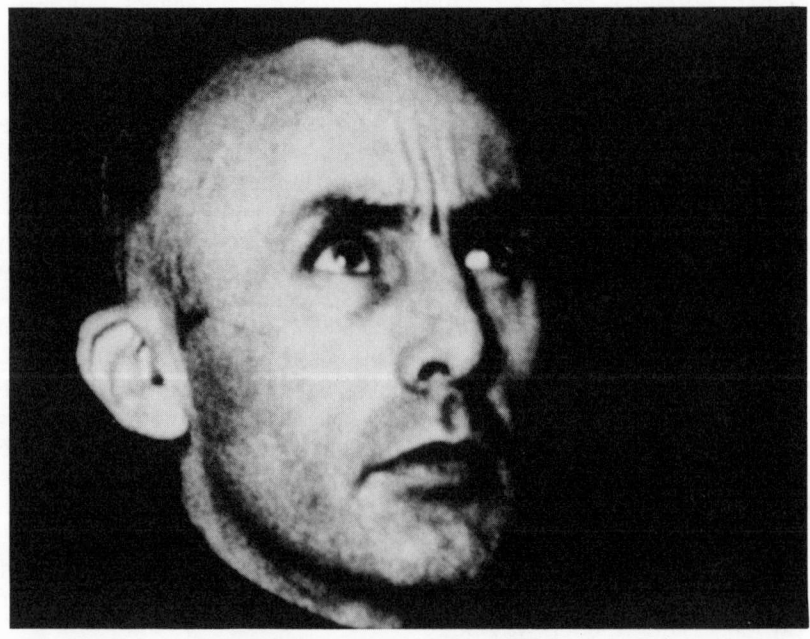

NGƯỜI GỬI (*Addressor*)

HỌ TÊN (Name in full): JAMES AffLed

SỐ LÍNH (Service number): 05

NƠI VÀ NGÀY SINH (Date & place LOWERAENCE, MAS

ĐỊA CHỈ (Address):

TRẠI GIAM P
NƯỚC VIỆT-
(Camp of
in the DEM

Happy Christmas to my wife and family, mother and father, sons and daughters, brothers and sisters. I am, well and only thinking of you all. All my love and have a nice holiday. Love Dad

NGÀY VIẾT (Dated) 26 Nov. 1968

James A. Mulligan

GỬI (*Addressee*)

HỌ TÊN (Name in ful
Mrs. Loui

ĐỊA CHỈ (Address):
905 Ke
Virginia B
United S

GHI CHÚ (N.B.):

1. Phải viết rõ và chỉ được viết trên những dòng kẻ sẵn (Write legibly and only on the lines).

2. Trong thư chỉ được nói về tình hình sức khỏe và tình hình gia đình (Write only about health and family).

3. Gia đình gửi đến cũng phải theo đúng mẫu, khuôn khổ và quy định này (Letters from families should also conform to this proforma).

Hanoi Cathedral Christmas 1968

In despair at my circumstance I retreated inwardly in frustration, but mentally I was angry enough to strengthen my resistance to it all and always climaxed each day with a Never, Never, Never give up Hope! Never! Never!

The food at Alcatraz was terrible. It was prepared at the Plantation, the display camp a block south that I had visited at Christmas 1967. To supplement our meager diet of rice, pumpkin or sea weed soup, the Vietnamese kitchen help would occasionally send over bananas. Most of this fruit was regularly pilfered away by the Alcatraz guards who were so unconcerned about our diet that they often stole the few pieces of pork rind and fat that the cooks put in the soup to give it a hint of flavor.

The guard-to-prisoner ratio at Alcatraz was always maintained at least at a one-to-one ratio which indicates the priority they put on the "Alcatraz Eleven."

By Christmas of 1968 our physical condition had deteriorated badly and I'm sure our individual mental conditions were at the same low level.

Utter frustration and despair would best describe my mental attitude. My POW memory name bank had increased from additions provided by the others at Alcatraz and by incoming names we occasionally picked up while listening to Hanoi Hannah which they generally played for us every evening. I continued to review it three times a day.

Each day I maintained a continuous vigorous exercise program conducted in the 4' x 4½' area available. I ran in place, did knee bends, arm stretches and hip twists. My broken shoulder and torn muscles gradually healed to a point where I could do a few mild half-hearted pushups. I tried new light exercises and would continue with them as long as I felt no pain. Whenever I was doing an exercise that brought pain I immediately stopped and switched to something else.

I had good wind from running in place and I felt I could make it to the 17th parallel if I could get out. My feet were toughened from callouses built up from running in place on the concrete floor. I started each day by running at least 2000 counts on my left foot at as rapid a pace as I could maintain.

During my Alcatraz confinement I was constantly bothered by sore kidneys and a tender liver. My eyes were yellow colored, and my skin bore a similar tint. My ears rang constantly. Occasionally this ringing was so loud that it interfered with my mental processes causing severe distraction. I was constantly plagued with diarrhea which often expanded into dysentery. I continually passed all types of small worms which bubbled in my loose running stools. My hair and beard had grown white and I looked twenty years older than my actual age.

We were in terrible straits, but the mutual support we gave each other communicating through the wall and under the door tied us together in an iron-like chain of resistance. Resist was the policy and resist we did. Stockdale and Denton were magnificent leaders. The rest of us were aggressive, obedient followers. I felt I could go through hell with these men. In fact that's exactly what we were doing day by day, hour by hour the entire time we were in Alcatraz.

Communications was our savior. From the beginning of our incarceration the Vietnamese had forbidden us to communicate with each other. Their goal was to keep us separated. Divide and conquer us one by one. Our goal was to follow the Code of Conduct, establish the chain of command, establish a mutual resistance posture, and survive as American fighting men to return home some day with honor. Whenever we were caught communicating, or even trying to communicate, we were severely punished. The periodic Vietnamese purges gave testimony to the seriousness they attached to the crime of communicating.

At Alcatraz we never stopped communicating. As each man at Alcatraz cleaned his personal convenience bucket with a stiff bamboo brush he would send his own personal message to one or all of the others. With the swish, swish of my broom I would often send a message like, "Hi JD, GBU," (Hi Jerry Denton, God bless you), to Jerry Denton, my former cellmate who was located in cell number 10, a fly-infested corner cell, that I knew must have been annoying to him.

Once a week we would wash our concrete floors with water and a stiff broom. At that time we could send long messages that were audible to all the POWs in Alcatraz. This required a good technique. We would mix up our sweeping with enough extra noises so that it didn't sound like any type of rhythmic code to the guards. To all of us who had devised and improved our clandestine communications methods, our efforts came through loud and clear.

Jerry Denton came up with a vocal cough code that paralleled our tap code. With this method we could cough, hack and spit slow messages. We had abbreviations for every type of quiz the Vietnamese held. Each man had an initial assigned to him. In this way he could identify himself and what was happening. Mine was M. If the guard came to my cell at any time and told me to dress for an interrogation I would cough a loud M, (3 coughs, pause, 2 coughs) followed by a Q, (a hack, pause, 1 cough). This meant Mulligan was going to a quiz. On my return I would tell what type of quiz it was by using the cough code, e.g., B.S., (Bullshit quiz), where nothing was going on, or B.I., (they wanted biography info which we never gave, of course). If a POW was receiving torture he would send TTR and alert his mates.

Stockdale and I could flash comm under our doors to Storz and Tanner so that we had good comm with the other building. I could thump softly with the heel of my hand and Stockdale could do the same. In this way we would comm right through the guard shack which was the empty cell between us. Denton and McKnight had a similar setup from their cells number 10 and 8 respectively. The other POWs had direct wall comm by tapping to each neighbor living on either side of him.

The Vietnamese couldn't stop our comm and to my knowledge had no idea of its extent or complexity. The guards harassed us continually about comm but they couldn't actually catch us. They were so uptight about comm that when Stockdale had some genuine nightmares and hollered out while sleeping they took him to quiz and threatened him with torture for comming. On one occasion they even beat him physically, misinterpreting his nightmares for comming.

With nothing to do in solitary we exchanged the details of our past lives. Gradually we knew each other intimately though for the most part we had never actually met one another.

The POWs in Alcatraz were the most proficient and aggressive comm men that I knew of in the entire POW community. Each in his own way would find some way to communicate with his fellow Americans. We considered communications absolutely essential for our own survival.

At Alcatraz when a POW had to sweep the courtyard he sent code. When we hung out our wash we snapped the clothes to shake off the water. The clothes snapping was in code. We could send code standing in the sun area by moving one foot, or one hand, and send a message to the other POWs watching. If we had a small hand fan we would fan ourselves, and send code. Communications, night and day in every way was what brought us together and kept us alive in Alcatraz; that and faith in God, our country and each other.

CHRISTMAS 1968
THE HANOI CATHEDRAL

Christmas morning I went to quiz with Mickey Mouse. He gave me a letter from Louise along with one from my folks and one from my brother John. I was coming up on three years as a POW and I had been allowed to receive three letters from Louise. It wasn't much, but it was more than a couple of the other POWs in Alcatraz had received. For some reason the North Vietnamese never acknowledged that Harry Jenkins and Howie Rutledge were alive and prisoners. Thus they never permitted either one to write or receive mail. They played this game with them until 1971 before letting them send and receive letters.

I was elated at hearing from home. Each bit of news brought me back into the world of reality from the never, never land of my existence in Hanoi.

We got better food at the noon meal and I gobbled down everything with gusto. At siesta I exchanged the news from my letters with Jim Stockdale and later on with Ron Storz who was in cell number 5 in the other building. Storz had received his first letter from home since his capture in April of 1965 and he was elated.

That night I was in leg irons under the mosquito net asleep when the guard came with Mickey Mouse. He removed the irons and I was directed to get ready to go out. Mickey Mouse looked at my blue pajama suit and decided it didn't fit the uniform of the day requirements. He went to Ron Storz's cell and borrowed a set of red striped clown suit pajamas, and gave them to me to put on.

Once dressed, I was immediately blindfolded, led through the courtyard, and placed in a vehicle. I had no idea what was happening but suspected it had something to do with a Christmas propaganda show. Mickey Mouse cleared things up when he said, "Mun, I take you to your Christmas celebration in the big Hanoi Church of the Catholics."

We moved slowly in heavy pedestrian, bicycle and vehicle traffic, stopping and starting every few feet. I could hear the impatient honking of the confused Asian transportation systems. A trolley car clanged several times and roared past us. I am in the middle of Hanoi, I thought.

On arrival, they led me from the vehicle, along a walkway and up a few stairs into a building. When they removed the blindfold I found myself standing in the corner of a large church. It was traditionally Catholic but had a heavily accented Asian architectural style. Besides the usual appointments like Stations of the Cross, pews, statues, and altar, it had a massive magnificent bright colored portrait of St. Francis kneeling at the foot of the Cross. This portrait hung directly behind the altar and was immediately the focus of attention for anyone entering the church. I had never seen anything so striking or so vividly beautiful. The impact of the scene was in stark contrast to the four bare blank walls which encompassed my daily existence.

I looked around and except for a few Vietnamese soldiers scurrying around, I saw no signs of any other activity. As I looked to the front of the church at the head of the left aisle leading to the main altar rail, I saw a huge Nativity scene, complete with large statues of men and animals depicting the stable at Bethlehem.

More Vietnamese came in, along with a good looking young American POW I did not recognize. He seemed in excellent physical condition. Mickey Mouse told me to remain in the corner and he went over to greet them.

I tried to tap code with my hand against my thigh when I caught the POW's eye. He looked at me strangely, finally figured out what I was trying to do and slowly shook a distinct no. Damn, he doesn't know how to tap communicate, I thought. Just my luck!

I heard a ruckus and looked over to see a dark looking American POW enter with a group of Vietnamese. He seemed to be some sort of celebrity and all the Vietnamese went over to greet him. I was wrong. One of his escorts was the infamous Major Buy, the Cat: the man who was running this show. I wondered about the American. They seemed to be too damn friendly towards him and he in return was the happiest looking POW I'd ever seen.

The young man I had tried to comm with was alone. No one was watching either of us. He looked at me and spoke softly but clear enough that I heard, "Tangeman, Plantation." I replied, "Jim Mulligan, eleven of us one block north of you in irons and in solitary." He nodded and said, "Are you all ok?" "We're ok," I replied.

Mickey Mouse looked at me and wasn't sure if I had been talking. He came over and said, "Don't communicate, keep sil-lent," then returned to the group around Cat and the smiling American.

Spying me alone in the corner, the dark looking POW told me by his eye movement that he had seen me. He continued his raucous behavior and put his arm around Cat like a long lost buddy. He maneuvered Cat so that Cat's back was directed at me. His hand was behind Cat's back. Damn, what a fink American, I thought in disgust at his actions of friendship towards the Vietnamese.

I was amazed when suddenly I saw his forefinger move in tap code. "Dick Stratton," I read. What a smart POW he is, I thought as I replied with my forefinger along side my thigh sending, "Jim Mulligan."

Cat was beaming at the obvious fawning attention he was receiving from Stratton and his own subservient army men. He pointed to the Nativity scene and indicated Stratton could pay his homage if he desired. Stratton walked the length of the aisle and knelt before the crib.

Cat directed the Vietnamese to their appointed positions. Mickey Mouse was returning to get me when Cat spied me and came over with him. "How are you?" he asked. "I am well, thank you," I replied as I bowed politely. "May I kneel at the crib before Mass starts?" I asked him. "Of course, you may go there now," he replied. I bowed and started down the aisle lickety split.

Stratton was kneeling in obvious prayer and was not aware of my coming. As I knelt next to him he was just about to rise. I held his left pajama pant leg to stop him from leaving. Looking straight ahead I blessed myself fervently and addressing the statues I said, "Eleven of us are one block north of the Plantation, in solitary and in irons. I'm Jim Mulligan. Rutledge, Jenkins, Johnson, Shumaker, Storz, Tanner, Coker, McKnight, Denton and Stockdale are with me. We are ok."

The Vietnamese cameramen were so impressed with my fervor that they put my whole conversation on film from their close-up shots taken while Dick Stratton and I were kneeling at the crib.

Stratton blessed himself, got up and was led off to a pew. I blessed myself, arose, and turned to face a fuming Mickey Mouse who was rushing down the aisle towards me. "You communicate, you communicate," he fumed. I gave him a look of innocence and amazement. "Oh no, I only pray to the Father on this Christmas celebration at the beautiful manger scene you have provided for me. Ask the men of your cameras that were filming as I prayed. They must know that I do not communicate. Ask them, they will tell you this is so."

Mickey Mouse was still angry but he wasn't sure, and besides he did not want to cause a major scene with so many reporters and photographers around. He pointed me towards a pew and I took my place as directed. Stratton was three pews in front of me by himself. I could see four other POWs in groups of two. All of us were well separated and spread out to prevent comm.

Father Ho Ti Binh was readying himself at the altar, which was suitably decorated with flowers for the occasion. I tried to pray but was distracted by the horde of Asian photographers and reporters who were milling around getting set up for the oncoming show. They were a crude group, smoking, fooling around and throwing their cigarette butts on the floor and stomping them out.

I heard something moving behind me and turned to see a POW take his place two pews away from me. It was Jerry Coffee. I recognized him from our encounter a year ago at the Christmas Mass held at the Plantation. Mickey Mouse motioned for me to turn around. "That is my friend from the East Coast Navy and I have not seen him for many years. Would you please let me say hello and tell him I received a letter from my wife. I know his wife and children and he knows mine," I begged. Mickey Mouse said, "No," but not firmly enough for him to dissuade me from further efforts. "Please, on the occasion of Christmas it can do no harm to you or Vietnam." He nodded a half hearted approval, and I quickly turned around, faced Jerry and said, "Jerry Coffee, Merry Christmas. I'm Jim Mulligan. How's your wife Bea and the children? I got a letter from Louise and my six sons. Did you get a letter? I am in the same state as last year. We are all ok. The eleven of us! Are you ok?"

"Merry Christmas Jim, I'm fine. I got a letter too. I've got it ok," and he winked indicating he understood my reference to the "Alcatraz Eleven."

"Enough, enough," said Mickey Mouse. "You speak too much to your friend." "Thank you sir," I said as politely as possible and turned my attention to the altar where Mass was beginning.

The photographers were rudely running helter skelter getting set up. Mass began and it was an utter fiasco. Everytime I saw a photographer zero in on me I tried to give some indication with a thumbs-up sign that I was ok.

I got up to receive Communion and later heard a Communist propaganda sermon which was given by Fr. Ho Ti Binh and translated into English by Rabbit. When Mass was finished I was whisked outside by Mickey Mouse, blindfolded and put in a vehicle which returned me to Alcatraz.

At my cell, Mickey Mouse made me remove the clown suit which he had the guard return to Ron Storz. He was quite angry with me and said, "Mun, tonight you have played the fool with me. You are a bad man. You violate the regulation of the camp. You communicate to your compatriots. You will be punished."

They put me in the irons, slammed the door and bolted me in. I thumped, "Christmas Mass at the Cathedral. C U TM," (see you tomorrow) to Stockdale.

I was unhappy about the filming which I was sure would be used as pure propaganda, but since I had been able to get the "Alcatraz Eleven" names out to Dick Stratton and communicate our state to Jerry Coffee I felt I had won a minor victory.

The next day I passed all the details of my downtown excursion to Stockdale and he passed it on to the other men in Alcatraz.

1969

THE TOUGHEST YEAR

In early January the Vietnamese accused Jerry Denton of comm and moved him to the quiz room in the main building behind the court-yard. They were working him over in order to get him to make a tape and read over the camp radio. He flatly refused, fighting them tooth and nail. Finally they tired of fooling around and rope tortured him badly. Late one morning we heard him screaming "Bao Cao" in agony and pain. I knew he was at the end of his rope, and I visualized what they must have done to him. I was so mad I refused to eat for three days until he was returned to his cell. Shortly before his arrival, they played a tape of Jerry reading something. He did a great job and messed it up completely. It was absolutely valueless.

I recognized his voice and knowing what they must have put him through, I felt deep sorrow. I didn't know what their game was but I knew something bad was in the air. They always seemed to start a torture program with Jerry Denton.

Suddenly every day for a week and a half, I was taken to an after-noon quiz with Slick and Mickey Mouse. Slick was trying to soften me up so that I would read over the camp radio. I constantly refused and he didn't use much pressure. He was following the good guy tactics to get me to cooperate. I was being pleasant but was not influenced by this effort. Mickey Mouse said in frustration, "Your friend Denton reads on the radio for us." I replied, "Bullshit, you tortured him badly and if you want me to read, you'll have to torture me the same way." Slick was appalled at my outburst. He tried to soothe things over and sent me back to my cell. I told Stockdale what they were up to. I felt I had won a victory and wouldn't be bothered about reading on the radio any more.

Late that night I suddenly awoke when I heard "Bao Cao" repeated several times from the other building. From the tone of the voice, I knew the caller was in bad shape. I arose and got to my peek-hole shuffling in my leg irons. Once in position, I looked out and saw a guard we called Sad Sack standing under the light, paying absolutely no attention to the Bao Caos which were increasing in amount and intensity.

I recognized Harry Jenkins' voice and it sounded like he was in bad shape. Harry had reported severe stomach pains several times the pre-vious two weeks and we were all concerned about him.

Sad Sack continued to ignore Harry's pitiful cry of "Bao Cao". I grew outraged and screamed at the top of my lungs, "Bao Cao, Bao Cao!!!", which was the Vietnamese phrase we were taught to say if we needed to see a camp officer in an emergency.

Sad Sack was enraged. He rushed to my door, opened the peek-in door and yelled, "No Bao Cao, no Bao Cao!" I faced him in a furious rage and yelled, "Bao Cao!" at the top of my lungs. Sad Sack smashed at my door with his bayonet three times. He would have killed me if he could have gotten in the cell. I knew he didn't have a key and I taunted him all the more by yelling, "Bao Cao!"

The other POWs were up and were in a rage. We all joined in yelling "Bao Cao" at the top of our lungs. It was a camp riot. Our spontaneous yelling and smashing at our cell doors broke the eerie silence that usually prevaded Alcatraz at this ungodly hour of the morning.

We quieted down only after we heard the English-speaking guard and officers, and knew that Harry would receive attention.

It had been a wild demonstration. All the pent-up emotion and fury of the last fifteen months in Alcatraz suddenly burst forth in one massive united outburst. We might be prisoners, but we weren't going to sit by idly while one of our members died of neglect. At Alcatraz, this was our finest hour. Each of us put ourselves on the line for our friend. Instinctively, each of us knew we would have to pay a terrible price for our actions. The North Vietnamese could not stand to lose face by such an uprising. They would make us pay dearly. For myself, I didn't care any more. "The hell with them," I said. "The second front has finally come to the middle of Hanoi where it belongs." I was keyed up but exhausted. I fell asleep with butterflies in my stomach wondering what would happen next.

We didn't have long to wait. In the morning, one by one we were led to quiz. They wanted us to make a tape and explain the events of the previous hours. To a man, we refused to tape or write anything. We put the blame rightly where it belonged, on Sad Sack.

We demanded medical attention. Collectively we had decided we should take a stand to make our position known. With our concurrence Jim Stockdale put us on a fast. No eating anything. This caught the Vietnamese by surprise and infuriated them. A day went by with no food taken from the tables. Each of us was quizzed again but we remained adamant on our position of no write, no tape. Also to a man, we demanded medical care for our sick men.

At dawn on 25 January, they came to Stockdale's cell, made him roll up his gear and moved him out of Alcatraz. Denton was now in command.

Later in the morning, they had a general inspection of each cell by the camp officers. The old doctor came with them to look us over. We had won our demand for medical care and Denton called off the fast at the noon meal. Our gain cost us Jim Stockdale.

At noon I elected to continue my fast. I had undergone the required number of hours to overcome hunger pains. I was ugly and mean as an irritated alligator and felt I could be at my best point of resistance by holding out on the food. Instinctively, I knew I was going to be punished for causing the riot.

When the tocsin rang for the noon siesta, the key guard came and told me to roll up my gear and get ready to move. I took my time, attended to the normal body reliefs and managed to use the cough code. I sent M MVG, meaning Mulligan's moving. I heard the reply of GBU, (God bless you) from Denton. I put on my socks, my short pants and short sleeve shirt, my winter sweater, and then put my blue quiz suit over them. I expected I would be beaten and I wanted as much clothing on as possible. Long ago I had learned that you kept as much clothing with you as long as possible when you expected to be tortured.

I found Slick at the quiz room, and I bowed politely. I maintained a subdued attitude which reflected repentance for my actions, which Slick said was the cause of all the difficulty in the camp, and the cause for great embarrassment of the camp authorities.

It was noon. I rejected his appeal that I tape or write an apology to the camp commander. Slick put me on the wall with my hands up as high as I could hold them. "You must stay like this till you do as I say," he said leaving the room. A guard was stationed to watch me carry out Slick's order.

I stayed this way until about six p.m. when the guard left to get some chow. My arms felt like they weighed a ton. I had been meditating and praying in this condition for five or six hours. Mostly I prayed for Stockdale and the trouble I had caused him. Maybe I could have done it differently, I thought. They'll come down hard on him for what I caused. But deep in my heart I knew I had done the right thing, done the only thing I could under the circumstances. The real villain is Sad Sack, I decided. If he did his job, Stockdale would still be here and I wouldn't be on the wall with my arms held up in the air.

I had a ten minute rest before a relief guard came and positioned himself to watch me. I was getting exhausted when Slick returned about eight in the evening. "You must write an apology to the camp commander and all this will be over with," he said. "All right," I said as I was at the point of exhaustion. "I'll write." He gave me pen and paper, told me to write and that the guard would deliver it to him.

I wrote, "I apologize to the camp commander for my actions in support of the sick American who needed medical attention. This event would not have happened if your guard on duty had done his job and reported to the authorities the American 'Bao Cao.' " I signed it with a scribble, J.A. Mulligan, CDR, USN.

The guard took it to Slick who returned immediately. "This will never do. You must repent, you must give yourself over to me and do what I tell you," he said. "That's it," I replied, "that's all I'll write."

"Then I must turn you over to my guards. They will persuade you to see the error of your ways. You cannot stand up against them, you cannot last," he cried vehemently. "Maybe I can't but I'll sure die trying," I replied.

"You fool! You fool! Do as I say before you are injured. No one cares about you. Your people won't care about this. Write! Give yourself to me and do as I say. Things will go much better for you here. This is the bad camp. We have a good camp where you can go. There are Americans happy there. Make it easy on yourself and cooperate."

"No! No!" I replied defiantly. "I won't write. The others here won't write. I don't care if no one else cares what I do. I care and that's all that counts." Pointing to the Alcatraz courtyard I said, "And they care too! What you do to one of us, you must do to all of us here."

"Then I leave you to my guards," he said and with a nonchalant wave of his hand, he was off into the night. I heard him talk softly outside and soon five guards came in the room. They put three sets of irons on my legs and made me kneel. Then they roped my wrists and arms behind my back, pulling them so tight I thought my chest would burst and my arms would fall off. They laughed and joked at my condition, taunting me in Vietnamese. I was getting weak and woozy. The pain from the ropes cut through my body and I shook all over. Then my finger tips went numb, followed by my hands, my wrists, my forearms and upper arms.

I was ready to swoon when Sad Sack gave me a vicious blow to the side of my head. I flopped over sideways. Cig Stealer gave me a kick in the ribs and I felt he had cracked them. Then they beat me about the head and body; dragged me about the room by my ears and hair. It went on and on and I couldn't pass out. These Oriental bastards are keeping me just this side of consciousness, I thought as I tried to roll with their blows. I don't know how long they kept this up, but it was a very long time. I began blubbering, "Bao Cao," but Sad Sack would say, "No Bao Cao," and I knew that he was getting even for the night riot and embarrassment I caused him.

I hurt all over and they wouldn't stop. I quit a hundred times and pleaded pitifully for mercy but to no avail. It was very late at night, a night I thought would never have an ending. I was pleading "Bao Cao" when Slick came in. "You cannot resist my guards anymore. You will do as I say, and write?" "Yes," I replied.

They took off the ropes and irons. A guard washed off my bloodied face with a large wet rag.

Slick brought the pen and paper, but I couldn't control my fingers to write legibly. Finally he gave up in disgust at my inability. He had a copy of a letter of apology which was typewritten. "Later today you will copy from this and sign it. Do you understand?" "Yes I'll do it," I replied in defeat.

"Now that you have come to understand the error of your ways, you must receive more punishment until later today when I return. You will not forget me," he said and left.

The guards put the three sets of irons back on and roped my arms in front of me so I couldn't move and left me sitting hunched over the rest of the night.

I was exhausted. I couldn't move and I hurt all over. In particular my chest gave me severe pains and I found breathing difficult as well as painful. I prayed for strength and forgiveness. Insane, I prayed to die. Finally, I flopped half over on my right side and half in a stupor and half in a nightmare. I wimpered and babbled in complete utter defeat.

When dawn came, the guards removed the ropes and irons. I was led back into the courtyard where they allowed me to empty and clean my bucket. I sent a broom message which said, "TTR F LTR OF APOLO-GY," (tortured for a letter of apology). I heard two coughs which meant someone had copied my message.

I was taken back to the quiz room where the guards held me while Sad Sack roped me terribly tight. My legs were in three sets of irons. My forearms were roped and I couldn't feel them in a few minutes. They sat me on the concrete floor, hunched me over and put a wooden pole behind my left knee over the inside of my elbow joints, and out the other side behind my right knee. I was bent over in a tight ball, sitting on the edge of my butt and my heels. The pain was awful. I half passed out and fell off uncontrollably to one side. The end of the pole hit the concrete, pivoted me and kept me from falling completely over. My arms burned, my body ached with pain. My brain was dulled from the terrible torture. I couldn't think. I couldn't even talk. I barely could muster up a weak "Bao Cao."

Sad Sack taunted me constantly. He showed me absolutely no mercy whatsoever. They kept me in this condition for more than an hour. I had given up. I couldn't stand the pain. I "Bao Cao'd" again and again but to no avail. He kept taunting me, and relished the sight of me squirming in pain. Finally a senior guard walked by, heard me and came in. "Bao Cao," he said to me. "Bao Cao," I replied.

He got Mickey Mouse to the quiz room. "Will you write for me, he asked?" "Yes, I'll write," I replied.

The guards removed the stick, ropes and irons. I sat at the desk and copied Slick's letter of apology. I was whipped and beaten down. I had lost very badly. Mickey Mouse looked triumphant at his latest conquest.

They took all my clothes and gear and left me in shorts and short sleeve shirt. The only other thing I had was my personal convenience bucket. I was exhausted and curled up on the deck and fell asleep. The mosquitoes ate me alive but there was nothing I could do to dissuade them. Late that afternoon, they brought me rice and seaweed soup. I ate it all. My fast was finished. I had already lost the ball game.

It was very dark, probably near ten at night when Mickey Mouse barged in and said, "You must write a letter like this one and ask for amnesty." He showed me a letter written and signed by another POW. From the tone of it, I knew the poor man had been tortured terribly.

"Write," Mickey Mouse said when I had finished reading it. "No," I replied. "I won't write."

He called out to Sad Sack and two other guards. Before I could get my wits I was roped and beaten viciously. I held out as long as I could, but finally had to give up. "Bao Cao, Bao Cao," I cried. Mickey Mouse came and said, "Will you write?" "Yes, I'll write," I answered and I wrote a letter requesting amnesty similar to the model letter I had been shown.

They kept me in irons constantly during my stay in the quiz room. I was cold and half eaten alive by the mosquitoes. Each successive day Mickey Mouse would come and make a demand that I write. Each time he demanded, I refused. He would have me beaten, rope tortured, and I would give in and acquiesce to his desires. He's trying to break me good, I thought. He's going to try to make me his slave.

Resist! Resist! I prayed for divine help to make me resist. But on he came, the relentless man on the attack. He had his opponent beaten and he wasn't going to quit until I gave him everything he asked whenever he asked.

"Write to President Nixon!" "No!" Torture! "Bao Cao!" "Will you write?" "Yes." "Write!" I did. I wrote to Nixon. "Write to *ENTERPRISE!*" "No!" Torture! "Bao Cao!" "Will you write?" "Yes." "Write!" I wrote to *ENTERPRISE.* "Write to your squadron. Write about NAS Cecil Field." "No! No!" Torture! Torture! "Write! Write!"

Oh God, when will he stop. I'm done Lord, I can't go through any more, I don't have enough guts to say no to him any more. It's been a week Lord and for the last six days every day he comes. I say no and I get tortured and I lose again. I'm a broken man. Lord, you've got to help me.

It was the noon siesta. My door rattled as the guard opened it. I shook uncontrollably. I knew Mickey Mouse was coming in to get me once again. I stood shaking in the leg irons, dreading to face him. Surprise! Slick entered with the key guard, Marty Mouthful. "Moo lig gun, I take away the irons. I permit you to wash and shave. Then you return your own room. Later today you will come back here and read to our camp commander the letter of apology that you have written for him. Do you understand?" "Yes, I understand. I will do as you ask."

Marty removed the irons and led me back to the courtyard where I was allowed to bathe and shave. I looked horrible with black and blue bruises and welts from the mosquitoes all over my body.

I poured cold water from the cistern over my filthy body and washed and washed and washed. The fresh air felt great. A heavy burden had been lifted from my mind. It's almost over, I thought. The letter of apology is just to save face for the camp commander and give him a reason to return me to my cell.

When I was shaved and washed, the guard had me put on my blue long sleeve pajama suit and took me back to the quiz room. Slick had covered a table with a large blue cloth which reached almost to the floor at the front and sides. The room had been swept out and the shutters were wide open, allowing an incoming breeze of fresh air. On the table were two ash trays and a shallow vase filled with cut flowers. Marty Mouthful bid me sit on the stool and he left to get Slick. I sneaked a fast peek under the cloth-covered table to see if it hid a tape recorder. I saw nothing and could see no wires anywhere in the room.

Slick entered with Slopehead the camp commander. I arose and bowed politely to them.

Slick handed me the letter of apology that he had written and which I copied after torture almost a week previous. "I have told the camp commander of your new-found good attitude. You have written many fine letters for us this past week," he said as he held a fistful of the material that they had tortured me to write.

"I see you have written asking our beloved Ho Chi Minh for amnesty. And you also write to your Navy compatriots, and to your new President Nixon. Oh, but what is this? You have written about your Florida base. I keep this myself to send to your government if your bad attitude should return," he concluded.

Blackmail, the son of a bitch thinks he can blackmail me with that bullshit story on Cecil Field. The only factual truth to that whole letter was the name of the field and that it had big runways. I smiled as my mind reviewed my subterfuges.

"You must read the letter to the camp commander. Now stand and read." I stood and read the letter of apology in a deliberate low and singsong voice. I didn't trust Slick. He might have a portable tape, I thought.

When I was finished Slick bade me to sit down, while the camp commander harangued me in Vietnamese, like a lecturing father towards a repentant son. Slick translated and I acted as contrite and repentant as possible as he ticked off a litany of my sins. At the conclusion, they made me promise I would no longer violate the regulations of the camp. With fingers crossed I promised I wouldn't.

"He is going to de-iron you and your comrades soon," Slick said. "Many good things are going to happen to all of you."

They dismissed me and I returned to my cell to find the purge was on. Rutledge was gone and Denton was moved out right after I moved back.

DEATH OF UNCLE HO

That spring one by one the Vietnamese ran a torture program on the men at Alcatraz. After my torture ordeal I was happy to be back in solitary in my cell. Stockdale was gone and I was all alone in my building. Each day I would tap visually under my door to Ron Storz and Nels Tanner. They would keep me informed on what was going on with the rest of the POWs in their cell block.

Rutledge and Denton and Jenkins were tortured for amnesty letters. Then suddenly this Vietnamese program was dropped, and Denton was told by Mickey Mouse that we would be POWs for at least two more years. Mickey Mouse was wrong. Though we didn't know it then, we had four full years still to go before we would be repatriated.

As a result of our camp uprising and Jim Stockdale's sacrifice, the medical conditions improved greatly at Alcatraz. The medic would generally come around two or three times a week to look us over and be available should we have a need for his services. The old French doctor came around once a month with a camp officer to look us over. The rest of the treatment hadn't changed. The food was a starvation diet. The guards continued to harass us about comm and anything else that came into their minds. The torture program was continued through to summer. One man would be replaced with another.

Each day I got news from Nels Tanner and morale messages from Ron Storz. Tanner was a Navy Lieutenant Commander who had been a pillar of resistance. After he was tortured he concocted a story about Clark Kent (Superman) which the Vietnamese swallowed hook, line and sinker. They were so impressed with the good propaganda they received from the Clark Kent story that they released it for publication in the western press. Any American reading the story immediately knew it was pure bullshit. When some visiting Americans told the North Vietnamese what Tanner had pulled on them, they came down very hard on him. More than anything else the Vietnamese didn't want to lose face publicly. Tanner had caught them cold, and they were furious.

Ron Storz was an Air Force Captain who had been shot down in late April 1965. He was actually captured in the demilitarized zone at the 17th parallel when his chute drifted him into that area. Ron was a strong family man and had a wife and two children. He had come to Vietnam in late August 1964. From the beginning Ron Storz gave the Vietnamese fits. He refused to bow or even act generally polite to his Asian captors. He was always in the middle of the communications rings we employed. At Little Las Vegas, he was instrumental in putting paper messages with the tap code in the plates of rice so that when a new POW got his rice dinner he also got a copy of the tap code. Storz was a very tall, good looking young man, though by 1969 his frame was only covered with loose hanging skin.

I was alone in the small three-cell building. He felt it was his obligation to be in constant communications with me in order to keep up my morale. Every day after bathing and washing our clothes, Ron and I would exchange info by flashing the palm of our hands in the small opening under the cell door. We used the standard POW tap code, the only difference being that this was a visual method of communications whereas the normal tap code was by audio comm.

Storz filled me in on his entire life, and I in turn did the same for him. We had a lot in common. He had done a tour of duty at Pease Air Force Base in New Hampshire, not too far from my hometown of Lawrence, Mass. I was very familiar with that area, and the North Shore of Massachusetts, as my folks had retired to a home in Ipswich. Storz loved Gloucester and Cape Ann, and told me that if possible he would like to retire there. Daily all he thought of was home and wife and children and someday returning to Cape Ann to retire. In the spring of 1969 I got to know Ron Storz very well. We had similar hopes and aspirations. We were both strong family men; our wives and children were the center of our lives. Though I had never met Ron Storz, or even ever had a chance to speak directly with him, or grasp his hand in friendship, I knew he was my kind of guy.

In late April I had to undergo another torture scene. One noon after chow and before siesta I was taken to quiz with Mickey Mouse in the main quiz room. He wanted me to fill out a biography. "No way," I said. Mickey Mouse played games and kept me on the wall all afternoon holding my arms up. When the guard assigned to watch me would sneak off for a respite I would lower my arms for as long as possible, only raising them when a guard was at the cell entrance.

About nine that night Mickey Mouse got serious and decided to play rough. He gave me over to two guards. They put two sets of irons on me and went to work. When they were in the midst of their activities a passing Vietnamese water girl stopped to watch the goings on. She seemed very pleased to see me at the mercy of the guards. At her urging they in turn put much more into their efforts. I "Bao Cao'd" for help and to say I quit but they wouldn't pay any heed to my pleadings. She was joined by another female and together they watched while the guards beat me unmercifully. I was in bad shape when suddenly Mickey Mouse arrived. On seeing him the girls beat a hasty retreat and the guards were left to continue without their female audience.

I wrote my memorized false biography to fulfill Mickey Mouse's requirements. He was angry at my resistance. When I had completed the form he had me put in double irons with only my shorts covering my torso. I was left in this condition, bruised, half naked and bleeding from the punishment that I had received. I collapsed in a heap on the concrete floor and tried to sleep while hordes of Vietnamese mosquitoes ate me alive. The next morning at an early hour I was returned to my cell and another POW took my place in the quiz room to be tortured for his false biography.

Storz seemed to be going off the deep end in early May. He was the thinnest man in camp and he was having problems eating what food they gave him. He couldn't keep it down. We were all worried about Ron but there was little we could do to help him except try to raise his morale.

The Vietnamese completed their biography push on most of the men, and then picked up a new tactic by putting Bob Shumaker in the quiz room on a stool where they made him sit for days on end. No sleep was permitted. When he fell off the stool they punished him and returned him to a sitting position on it. After a couple of weeks Shumaker was finally returned to his cell. They immediately replaced him with Nels Tanner. They repeated the same tactic with the stool on Tanner. He was gone for two weeks when Sad Sack made a large whip out of stiff reed vine. He tied a knot on the end and attached the other end to a homemade handle. When he was finished the other guards crowded around to see his handiwork. I could see them nod their heads in approval as I peeked through my tiny observation hole.

Sad Sack and a couple of the other guards took turns cracking the whip against the low brick wall in front of my door. I had a pretty good idea what they were going to do with that whip. Nels Tanner returned the next day and told how the guards stripped him naked, threw him on the concrete deck and whipped him mercilessly until he couldn't stand it any longer. I hated those little bastards, remembering the glee they showed while practicing with the whip.

Storz and I had a signal to call each other up for flash comm. Each day after the mid-morning meal of rice and pumpkin or seaweed soup he would smoke a cigarette. I would check under my door to see the guards' position and if it was clear, I would rattle the top of my personal convenience bucket. This was the signal for him to look out under the door and comm with me.

I was on my knees checking the courtyard looking under my door on 25 May 1969. Just as I was about to rattle my bucket cover to get Storz's attention I heard a loud crash coming from his direction. When I looked over to him I saw his outstretched arm halfway out the opening under his door. He didn't move a muscle. He had passed out cold and slammed his head against the door.

The guard was sitting in the guard shack reading in the next cell to me. When I called "Bao Cao" to get his attention he came to see what I wanted. I said that I had heard someone in the other building say Bao Cao. He indicated that I was hearing things and should go to sleep. He slammed the peek-in hole shut. I got on my knees, looked under the door at Storz and he was still in the same position, out cold.

I hollered, "Bao Cao, Bao Cao," and the guard came again mad as hell. When I tried to explain, he ignored me. Another guard came running to find out the reason for the Bao Cao. When I said I heard Bao Cao from the other building he looked in that direction and spied Storz's arm sticking out from under his door, still and lifeless. They slammed my peek-in door shut and went running to Storz. When they finally got his door opened, I could see that he had fallen forward, hit his head on his door and was still out cold. One of the guards went running out of the yard for help. The other just looked at Storz.

I cough coded "NT" for Nels Tanner and he looked out under his door to see what I wanted. I flashed him the news that Storz had passed out and was still out cold.

The courtyard was soon filled with guards and officers. Two medics and the old doctor came and rushed helter skelter. I don't know what they did, but finally they lifted Storz to a sitting position. I could see his glassy eyes. He didn't know who he was or where he was. I estimated that he had been out cold for at least ten or fifteen minutes.

They gave him a shot and he seemed to regain his senses. From the actions of the old doctor and the medics, I concluded Storz had something seriously wrong with him. Later he was taken to the quiz room for several days. There he received some type of intravenous feeding or transfusion.

When they returned him to his cell he seemed unsure of what had happened or what was wrong. It was the beginning of a long hot summer for Ron Storz. One which would see him deteriorate more and more each day.

The Vietnamese became very upset about something and for a month we didn't see any Vietnamese officers in the compound or have any quizzes with them. The guards seemed to increase their security measures by doubling up on duty assignments. They conducted many surprise and thorough room and body searches as if they were afraid that we were about to pull off some sort of caper.

While in Alcatraz I worked many hours to make small holes from which I could see clearly throughout the courtyard. I always made these at my eyeball height when I was standing tiptoe. This prevented the guards from seeing through them, because they were so much shorter than the average American. I plugged my peek holes with lint and soap when they weren't in use. To further confuse the Vietnamese I would make peek holes that they could find during the room searches. They would find these holes and block them up again warning me not to make any more. I played this game the entire time I was there, and they never were any the wiser. Over time, my peek holes were so sophisticated that I could go from one to another and track anyone visually who was within view in our courtyard.

Ron Storz was taken away on 29 June and moved to the main quiz room. His health was failing, and he was in poor mental spirits. The morning before he was moved out he flashed to me, "If something doesn't happen to me soon, I don't think I'll be able to make it through the summer."

When he was gone I was more lonesome than ever. I could still flash safely with Nels Tanner and he kept me up to speed on the news from the other POWs. The hours seemed to drag on longer and longer and my morale was at a new low point. Here I was a POW for more than three years, and I couldn't see any light at the end of the tunnel.

I kept my daily routine going at a good pace. My name bank repetition never slowed down to less than three times a day. I did as much exercise in my cell as I felt was valuable. I prayed with fervor and asked the Lord for the strength to survive. Lord, was I lonely.

Jerry Denton was running the camp in the usual hardline manner. Since Alcatraz was occupied only by hardliners his task was a relatively easy one. Though most of us at Alcatraz had never met one another, we forged a team bond of resistance, like a family of close brothers. We suffered the mutual agony of solitary confinement, leg irons, torture, abusive treatment and inhumane living conditions. These hardships only served to weld us into one steel chain with each link connected to the others and a part of the whole. My respect and admiration for the other men in Alcatraz grew daily. We might have our own personalities and individual differences, but when it came to living up to the Code of Conduct and resisting the brainwashing and torture efforts of the Vietnamese, we were united as one man.

We were collectively appalled at a tape made by two senior officers which the Vietnamese were playing for all the camps. The senior man was putting out a lot of bullshit about the war. He flatly indicated that the Code of Conduct didn't apply in Vietnam. At Alcatraz we were enraged at this type of fink behavior by senior POWs, and vowed we would investigate them and prosecute them when we got out.

This fink tape was the first indication I had that some men were not following the Code of Conduct. It really bothered me to think that some of our people were being duped by the North Vietnamese propaganda efforts, and more disgustedly, some of them were not living up to their commitments to follow the code. These few POWs were moral pygmies.

One day in July the Vietnamese camp radio came on in the afternoon. Slick made an excited and hurried announcement. We were to wrap up our gear and prepare to move quickly. We were to follow the directions of the Vietnamese soliders and not cause trouble. This is it, I thought. We must be getting ready to move out of Hanoi and head for home.

I sat all keyed up ready to go and nothing happened. They fed us the usual bowl of rice and pumpkin soup. I gobbled it down hoping it would be my last meal in Vietnam. It was dark when the guard came and told me to unwrap my gear and go to bed. "Bullshit," I said as I remained adamant, sitting firmly on the rolled up bed containing all my gear. The go-to-sleep tocsin rang and I held to my position. He said we were going to move and by God I'm going to move, I thought.

Slick came in the middle of the night after another guard reported that I wouldn't put my net up and go to sleep. "Moo lig gun," Slick said, "put up the net and go to sleep. No one here is going to leave this camp. The situation has changed; the river will rise no higher." A damn flood evacuation. That's all that it was. I went to sleep more frustrated and disappointed than I had been since the first day of my capture.

In late August the Voice of Vietnam radio broadcast mentioned that Ho Chi Minh was ill and in the hospital. Each day a report would be given concerning his latest condition. Early September came and suddenly I heard the strains of a new song I had never heard before. It was some sort of a ballad, quite melodious, and centered its theme on Ho Chi Minh. I'll bet he's dead, I thought.

They played the same song over and over again. The rifle guards and key guard were suddenly in full-dress uniform. The Vietnamese officers were in full uniform, and as usual, without any rank insignia to show their position in the army's hierarchy.

Slick made an announcement over the camp radio announcing the death, "of our beloved leader, President Ho Chi Minh." He went on to say that the POWs must cause no difficulties.

It was a time of tension in Hanoi. I could tell by the way the guards gathered quietly and secretly in the compound area. They had stashed some booze and a pipe which they filled with black pellets and lit. Passing the pipe and the bottle around, they seemed half in a stupor of mourning and half in celebration. I couldn't tell which.

A few days before the funeral at Ba Dinh Square I heard the exchange of small arms gunfire in the vicinity of Alcatraz. It continued through the night and into the next day. The night before the funeral oration I heard what appeared to be thousands of people rioting in the streets. Shots rang out in the distance and the mob seemed to grow noisier and more out of control. They seemed to be coming to Alcatraz as they moved closer and closer. Finally the noise subsided when someone spoke using an amplifier system. When the talk was finished, the noise of the mob increased, then slowly subsided as they moved off in the direction from where they had come. I often wondered if Hanoi was close to revolution during this time, or if the mob were coming to pay their respects to the captured Americans held in Alcatraz.

We were close enough to Ba Dinh Square that I could hear the band playing and then the voices over the amplifier system. I felt that whoever would give the funeral oration would be the new leader in North Vietnam.

My own feeling was that the Party First Secretary Le Duan would be the new man in charge. I wasn't surprised to find out a week later that indeed Le Duan had given the funeral oration, and was the new Uncle to replace Uncle Ho.

When the speech was finished, I heard the roar of MIG jets as they flew low level directly over the camp and Ba Dinh Square. The cannon fired several bursts of respectful salute before the guard on duty realized what was happening. He'd been sitting under the banana tree on guard duty, but mostly daydreaming. About the third roar of the cannon he stood erect at attention, faced westerly in the direction of Ba Dinh Square, and remained rigid until the roaring of the cannon ceased. I could hear the strains of the new ballad to Ho Chi Minh slowly fade out in the distance. Then there was an ominous silence. The guard about faced and slowly sat down on the chair under the banana tree. I could see that he was weeping uncontrollably. He hunched over, holding his rifle butt down on the ground and lowered his head onto his forearms. I could see him sobbing and for a few moments I felt sorry for him.

Poor little bastard, Uncle Ho's dead. The center piece of his country and life is gone and, he doesn't know what to do or what will happen. You poor leaderless bastards. I wonder what in hell is going to happen to all of us now that Ho is gone. Things can't be much worse than they are right now, I mused.

BACK TO THE HILTON!

In the third week of September it became obvious that major changes were in store for the POWs. I had a quiz with Slick and he was so friendly and charming that I couldn't believe it. "Many good things are soon going to happen to you," he said again and again. At its conclusion he gave me two bottles of vitamin pills and two pairs of socks which he said had been sent by my wife. It was the 17th of September. I rapidly calculated I could take two vitamin pills a day and run out at Christmas time. I went back to my cell, and discovered that Ron Storz had been moved into Jim Stockdale's old cell while I was gone. I was elated at this turn of events. I had missed Storz during his absence the previous three months.

We tapped incessantly that day. Ron wanted to know all the Alcatraz news and all about the North Shore of Massachusetts. I was pleased to be able to comm directly with him and to be able to pass him the info he wanted.

Things were certainly looking up and I expected a rapid change in our treatment. I told Ron about my new socks and he said his feet were freezing. I tapped that I'd leave him a new pair of ski socks on the clothes line with my wash and that he could pick them up when he hung his own clothing out to dry the next day. He was extremely happy to get such an unexpected gift.

Ron had been sick and had not been able to eat all his food and keep it down. Nels Tanner and I agreed that we should make every effort to urge him to eat more of his food. We badgered him every day on this point. He kept assuring us that he was eating all his food and feeling much better. Nels and I were pleased at the results of our efforts with Ron. We were worried about his poor eating habits and felt his health would improve if he would eat all the Vietnamese gave him.

Our efforts received a serious blow in mid-October when one morning Ron Storz was ill and the guard had me empty out his personal convenience bucket. When I lifted the lid to dump the contents I found Ron had thrown away almost all of the food he had been given the previous day. I couldn't believe my eyes. He had eaten almost nothing, if he had eaten anything at all. Furthermore, he had told the both of us that he had eaten all of his food for both prior meals.

I told Nels as soon as I could flash comm with him. Ron was caught red-handed and he was embarrassed. We coaxed, pleaded, urged and begged him to eat more. He in turn always assured us that his appetite was improving. In fact it wasn't and his condition worsened as time went by.

In mid-October we began to receive more food. The Vietnamese brought us bread and tea in the early morning. Our noon and late afternoon diet also improved. They began giving us more bananas. We even received granular sugar and bread on a plate for breakfast. The vitamins and the increased food immediately improved my condition.

With the turn of events I felt our release couldn't be too far away. We began to receive more outside time to sit in the sun. The guards seemed to suddenly go out of their way to insure that one POW would get to see another POW. One guard who knew that I had lived with Jerry Denton at the Hanoi Hilton indicated that I should look into Jerry's cell on my way back from emptying my bucket. I looked in and said, "Hi Jerry." He was as surprised as I was. "Hi Jim," he replied as I was off to my own cell. Nothing like this had ever been permitted before. Something big surely was up.

I wrote a letter home on 25 November giving the instructions to Louise on how to send a Christmas package. I'll probably be home by then, I thought.

When December arrived I began my usual Advent preparation for the coming Christmas. I was feeling better and had much to be thankful for. The increase in food was working wonders for me. My strength increased daily. I didn't even mind the chilly fall air that drifted into my cell. I long ago learned that food is more important than clothing for body warmth. Each day I ate absolutely everything they gave me, every grain of rice, every drop of soup.

The camp had a new commander. He was a man called Frenchy, by Denton and the original group of POWs back in mid-1965. I had seen him only once or twice since my incarceration and I had no previous contact with him. Frenchy had a get acquainted quiz with me. Slick attended and helped Frenchy over the rough spots with his English. "Good things are going to happen" was the theme of the quiz.

On December 9th in the afternoon the Vietnamese told us to pack up our gear and get ready to move. Frenchy came to Ron Storz's cell and tried to get Storz to roll up his gear and move. Storz said no he wouldn't move without me. He was so upset that he yelled at Frenchy driving him out of the cell. Ron immediately thumped on the wall, "Don't believe him, don't believe him; we are not going to move."

I was rolled up and ready. I neatly scratched Jim Mulligan 20 March 1966, CDR. USN here 25 Oct. 1967-9 Dec. 1969, on the walls in a couple of places to let any other future occupants know that I had been kept there.

Frenchy finally got tired of trying to get Ron Storz to move out. He had the guard lock Ron's door. I tapped to Ron and told him to eat his food and ask for a cellmate. He asked me to see his wife if I got out and I asked him to do the same. Late in the afternoon as the sun was setting they started to move the guys out. I kept tapping to Ron until they were at my door. "GBU CU later," and a series of dots. (God bless you, see you later). It was the end of my last transmission to Ron Storz. "GBU," he replied. To my knowledge this was the last contact any American ever had with Ron Storz. Nine of us left Alcatraz that day, and he was left behind, all by himself.

They blindfolded me and put me in a vehicle. I was sure that I was heading for home. This is it! It's finally over! I thanked God for letting me survive Alcatraz as we bumped our way along Hanoi's noisy streets.

When they stopped the vehicle and led me out I felt sure I'd be at the airfield. They led me along by the arm, and finally stopped, removed the blindfold and pointed for me to go through a doorway. My God! I couldn't believe my eyes! I was back at the Hilton, getting ready to walk into the Stardust. They pushed me in and put me into cell number 1 and slammed the door shut.

25 November 1969

Dear Louise, boys, folks and all

I received your previous packages (first time on 21 January 1969 second time on 17 September 1969).

I've been informed by the camp officers that this year the D.R.V. Government will again allow families of U.S. captured pilots to send Xmas packages.

In order to help packages arrive fast and in perfect condition - no breakage or spoiling due to transportation or weather you should follow these procedures:

1. Everyone is allowed to receive only one package and not exceeding 3 Kg (approx. 6 lbs. 6 g).

2. Following items are allowed: Dried food stuffs, tonics in pill, tablets or capsules. Tobacco together with pipe (no cigarettes). Personal articles, soap, tooth brush, paste, handkerchief, wash towel, underwear, scarf, pullover, gloves, and socks.

3. Food and medicine stuffs must be packed in hermetic and solid containers. Tonics must be packed in original containers from manufacturers. Attention - above procedures should be strictly followed otherwise packages will not reach.

All my love and Merry Xmas.

James Alfred McGilligan

Mrs. Louise M. Mulligan
905 Kemper Drive
Virginia Beach, Virginia 23454
The United States of America

You bastards! You can't do this to me! I'm suppose to be going home! I couldn't believe it! I wouldn't accept it! Not Stardust! You bastards! I was completely unglued, coming apart at the seams and mad as hell. The tears were running down my cheeks in frustration and disappointment.

Then the coughs came. D for Jerry Denton, H for Howie Rutledge, J for Harry Jenkins, and then the rest, Johnson, Shumaker, Tanner and finally myself. Missing were Coker, McKnight and Storz.

We thumped the walls until the noise reverberated throughout the building. We hacked and coughed in our secret way until we had pinpointed each man's location in each cell. We were all angry! We didn't give a damn about the Vietnamese! We didn't give a damn about their stupid regulations or their stupid guards and officers! We communicated boldy and openly and could be heard over the entire Las Vegas area.

The guards tried to quiet us but to no avail. Finally I heard a Q for quiz. It was Denton. One by one we were told to dress for quiz and were hauled off to face our old nemesis, the Bug. On my way out of my cell I bumped into the Cat who was standing in the hallway wearing civilian clothes. "You must obey the regulations of the camp," he said. "Bullshit," I replied as I was led past him to the quiz room.

Bug was clearly upset. "You make noise and you violate regulations of the camp," he yelled. "You're damn right," I replied. "This is a new camp for you, and you must follow strictly the regulation of the camp authority," said Bug. "Bullshit, it's the same damn place I left over two years ago! The same damn place, and even the same damn cell," I lied.

Bug lectured me on improving my behavior and decorum. "You must be polite, you must be polite," he yelled. I stared him down in disbelief. Can this really be happening to me?, I wondered. Not caring a damn about any of his threats, I just stood there. Finally he waved me away with a flick of his hand. "Return your room. Return your room. Keep silent," he ranted. I went back to my cell, dejectedly made up my bunk, and went to bed.

I had emptied my bucket and was returning to my cell the next morning when I came face to face with Cat. He was in full khaki uniform without any insignia. I bowed politely as my brashness of the previous evening had worn off and I didn't want to push my luck too far. "Good morning sir! Are you the camp commander here?" I asked as I bowed politely. "Yes, I have volunteered to be the commander of this camp. There are many bad crims," and he stopped in mid sentence, "there are many Americans here that I will be in charge of" he said. I bowed and proceeded on my way.

Cat's status had certainly changed and his demeanor had also. I guessed that the POW policy was changing due to the new regime, and Cat was the fall guy for the Vietnamese's past sins toward the American POWs.

The Alcatraz gang immediately began comming with anyone we could when we were taking our daily bath. Commander Bill Lawrence was in charge, though he wasn't the senior man. Jim Stockdale was senior but was living with a POW who wouldn't allow him to communicate. We soon learned that most of the men in this camp were rolling along. That is, the Vietnamese had, by threats and torture gotten them to go along with the camp propaganda program. Many of them were reading over the camp radio and writing articles for some camp magazines. One of the magazines was called the *"New Outlook"* and it was filled with propaganda. I was appalled when I first saw and read a copy that Bug gave me as an example of how some of my compatriots were obeying the regulations of the camp and had come to see the error of their ways. After a careful reading I could see that some of the stuff was written tongue in cheek and some of the drawings in the cartoons contained spoofs which were evident but not easy to pick out at first viewing.

Stardust had excellent communications. Each of the Alcatraz men did his best to communicate with other POWs from the other sections of Little Las Vegas. I was able to tap extensively with John McCain and Bill Lawrence, and was able to get a good amount of news on what was going on with the others. At noon siesta we passed all our info to Jerry Denton who was in cell 6.

Howie Rutledge, our master communicator, was in cell 2 which bordered on the main entrance to Stardust. He was able to track the guards' movement in and out of Stardust by a shadow as it passed over the rat hole located at the bottom right hand corner of his cell. Each of us would clear the area near us by getting on our knees and looking under the door. If no guard was seen inside Stardust we would cough code a C for clear. Howie Rutledge would then monitor the rat hole, and we were absolutely safe from the snooping guards. The system was ingenious and worked flawlessly. We thumped loudly so that the wall reverberated. When a man thumped his message all the others could hear him.

The Vietnamese knew what was going on and they were furious. They couldn't catch us and furthermore couldn't really do anything to stop us.

The Stardust key guard was the sharpest Vietnamese guard I ever met. We called him Hawk because he seemed to have eyes in the back of his head. There was no putting anything over on Hawk. His room and personal gear searches were meticulous. He seemed to treat me very fair. He spoke only a little English. His movements were quick, efficient and correct. He gave you eveything when you were supposed to get it. You always got what was prescribed for you, nothing less and certainly nothing more.

Early on I decided that I would be as expeditious with my personal chores like washing, laundry or emptying the bucket as I could in order to help Hawk get through his POW housekeeping duties. He appreciated my efforts and though he never bent the rules one iota, his attitude was one of compassion if not of friendship.

Cat had me to quiz and informed me he was allowing Denton to write a letter to Stockdale. Jerry had already passed this info at siesta comm time so it wasn't news to me. Cat asked if I wanted a roommate and I immediately said, "Yes, I want to live with Denton." He dangled this possibility, dependent of course on our mutual behavior with an admonition to, "follow correctly the regulations of the camp." I replied that if the Vietnamese regulations followed the Geneva Accords on POWs there would be no conflict. Surprisingly Cat didn't go into his usual harangue of threats of torture for failure to follow his directions. I felt instinctively that Cat had lost his power for some reason, and I thought the reason had something to do with Uncle Ho's death and the policies of the new regime. At quizzes with me the Cat was actually meek and mild. Furthermore, he had developed an obvious eye twitch which indicated he was under some pressure. His demotion to the position of camp commander further substantiated my belief.

Except for Storz, the Alcatraz gang was reunited in Vegas. Coker and McKnight had been put in the Mint area with John Dramesi, an Air Force POW who had escaped overnight the previous spring. Jim Stockdale was in the Golden Nugget area with a cellmate who was running scared. The rest of us were solo in Stardust.

The Cat asked me if I knew any of the men in camp. I replied I had seen Stockdale and John McCain from a distance. "How is Stockdale?" I asked Cat. "He is tres tranquile here in this camp," Cat replied of his old nemesis. "I saw him limping badly in the courtyard," I retorted. "My doctors will give him an operation," he answered. Bullshit I thought silently. Stockdale isn't about to let you bastards mess him up any more than you have already.

"Do you know McCain?" asked Cat. "No, not personally. We have been stationed at the same airbase some years ago and I know him by sight. How is his health?" I asked. "He is well," Cat answered. "Someday it may be possible to visit with him and see for yourself. Would you desire this?" "Yes," I replied. "I'd like to meet him, or any other American POW here."

The quiz continued and Cat repeated over and over that on the coming holiday of Christmas we would receive special food that he was having prepared for us. Finally he dismissed me to my room. I returned more convinced than ever that his teeth were pulled. No more threats of torture. No more screaming. Things certainly were in a state of change.

On the 23rd of December I was suddenly moved into cell 6 with Jerry Denton. Once in the cell we bear hugged and pounded each other's backs. Lord it was a happy day. You never really appreciate human companionship until you have been deprived of it.

We had lots of catching up to do since we were separated in early October of 1967. I looked Jerry over carefully. He had aged ten years since I last lived with him. My God, I thought silently, what are they trying to do with us?

I prayed that night in thanksgiving for being with Jerry again. Both of us prayed that the other men from Alcatraz would soon have roommates. Solitary confinement was something we all detested. God it's hard to live alone, I mused as I said a silent prayer for Ron Storz and the others.

CHRISTMAS WITH JERRY DENTON

Early Christmas morning Jerry and I were led by Hawk to the Vietnamese game room. It was fully decorated for the Christmas Holy Day with a tree and a Nativity Scene. Bug beckoned us in and after a brief display of friendly banter asked us to read the info posted on the walls and look at the pictures they had put up for display.

It was a massive propaganda effort. The pictures were filled with fawning visitors from the U.S. and all types of written material from the Communist and anti-war movement press. One picture that fascinated me was labeled the "Peaceful and Patriotic Catholics March in Militant Solidarity." There was eighty-year-old Father Ho Ti Binh holding a sign and leading the parade. It was a price he had to pay if he wanted to be able to continue to minister to the needs of his flock.

It was all propaganda. The North Vietnamese once again openly displayed their inability to separate Holy Days from politics. I was more convinced than ever that they held nothing sacred and that they would pervert everyone and everything to their own political advantage. I had no respect for Communism. The longer I was around it, the more I grew to hate it. It was composed of an insidious, self perpetuating minority whose corruption became more obvious. I felt sorry for all the do gooders and well wishers they were duping throughout the world. They will use everyone and everything to their own advantage. Anyone who doesn't really understand this is living in a dream world. They are slaves to themselves and their advancement to political domination and they want to enslave everyone else to their Communist way of thinking. The integrity of the individual means absolutely nothing. Communism is the greatest hoax ever perpetuated on mankind. I was sure that when the events of Vietnam finalized themselves in the annals of history, the true colors of the Communist experiment would be clear to everyone.

There was a tremendous amount of activity in the camp area for many hours prior to the noon meal. The cooks, water girls, off duty guard personnel, as well as camp officers, were running helter skelter in a beehive of activity all connected with the Christmas meal. Steaming hot coffee heavily laced with sugar was the first item to appear. Each of our cups was filled to the brim. We downed it with immense pleasure. Coffee, heavy black French style coffee; how I loved every drop of it. When the Hawk came around smiling to give refills, I knew that the good treatment had finally arrived.

We were into our second cup of coffee when Hawk opened the cell door. There stood Cat in full khaki uniform, insignia-less and very excited. He rushed to the adjacent food storage shelf, grabbed the two biggest plates, added more food to them and personally handed one to Jerry and one to me. "Feast yourselves, eat, eat," he implored. He dashed out and came in with two large bowls filled with a clear noodle soup made of heavy meat broth. He was grinning from ear to ear. "Eat Denton, eat Moo lig gun," he said approvingly as he caught our ravenous glances. We bowed politely and said, "Thank you Commander," to him as he left to supervise the rest of the feeding.

With tears in our eyes we said grace aloud, and asked the Lord to take care of our wives, children and parents back home. Then we dug in and attacked those wonderful edibles. I am sure that the piece of turkey on that plate was more meat at one time than I had seen altogether since my capture. I had forgotten how real meat looked and tasted. There were potatoes, carrots, cabbage, some sort of lettuce and other unfamiliar greens. I worked over everything till my plate was bare. Then I started on the soup determined to finish it no matter what the cost. My stomach growled in response and I emitted several loud burps. The Hawk happened to be looking in when I burped and he smiled with glee. I learned later that it is a Vietnamese custom to burp loudly as a sign of approval and appreciation for a good meal. On this day, I was only burping in response to overeating. For a while I didn't think I'd be able to get everything down. However, I persisted until nothing was left on my plate or in my bowl.

It truly had been a feast fit for a king. Cat had out done himself in dishing out the goodies, and I wondered what reasons caused him to have such a sudden change of heart. I wasn't sure of anything except that the improved treatment was a sign that as POWs we had finally turned the corner. From that time onward, until my release, more than three years later, I would continually search out and find good signs which I interpreted to mean that release was close at hand.

Jerry and I were too excited to nap that day. We gazed at each other's family pictures and read and reread the brief letters we received from our wives. The new era had included mail from home. I noticed that my wife was limited to six lines, which had been the format of my earlier letters. Well, six lines were better than no lines so I had a lot to be thankful for.

Late in the afternoon we were taken to a quiz with Bug. To my astonishment he had an array of goodies that had been sent by our wives. I got some freeze dried coffee, toothpaste, vitamin pills and a package of multiflavored life savers. Jerry got coffee, some Bob Hoffman protein pills, soap and some chocolate breakfast drink. We couldn't believe our eyes. Just seeing these creature comforts from home was enough to almost bowl me over. I had forgotten that such a variety of things existed in such an array of beautiful packages.

Late that night, after the tocsin had clanged, we heard the singing of familiar Christmas carols coming from the game room. We surmised correctly that it was another propaganda demonstration of The Peaceful and Patriotic Christians at Christmas designed for the benefit supposedly of the Protestant members of the POW community.

Certainly all of the good signs were here and visible at Christmas. As a born optimist I was convinced that the end was coming soon, and I'd be repatriated to my wife and children. I had a lot to be thankful for. Foremost was being with Jerry Denton once again. Solitary confinement had taken harsh tolls on my mental health. I used to say to myself constantly, "If you stay alone long enough you'll turn out to be wacky."

Living with Jerry brought a great sense of normalcy back into my life. Jerry and I were very close. We had shared the horrors of Alcatraz and we had survived the various torture programs and communication purges they had thrown at us. As I looked at Jerry, my joy of being with him was marred by a deep sadness. I felt the full impact of our incarceration whenever I looked at his emaciated body and his deep sunken eyes covered with heavy gray eyebrows. Since our previous sojourn as cellmates, Jerry had visibly deteriorated and aged. There was no question that his physical condition had gotten much worse. He was but an empty shell of the man I first knew aboard *U.S.S. INDEPENDENCE* in the early sixties. He was in one way more than half dead. My God Jerry, what have they done to you, I thought silently. Yes what have they done to us, as I realized that I myself, and the others from Alcatraz were all in a similar condition.

But there was another side to Denton. Behind that frail aging physical body was an indomitable spirit of courage, with a will to resist, to suffer uncomplainingly all the consequences of leadership that were thrust upon him from that position. He possessed a compassion for his fellow compatriots that never faltered. The duress of these years in Hanoi had tempered him as it had tempered the others who had shared the nightmarish burden. He was now a man of great moral courage and personal integrity. Above all else, he was a man of complete faith. He knew what he believed in, and he would die for those beliefs if necessary, without a wimper or a regret. The Communist Vietnamese could break his body but they could never break his soul. He had given his all and daily he gave his all as he lived according to the Code of Conduct. Aristotle would have understood him, would have agreed with him, and would have respected him. Jerry Denton was now truly a virtuous man.

Right after Christmas when we had established good camp communications, Jerry assumed formally the duties of senior ranking officer in Little Vegas. He had been permitted to write to Jim Stockdale, who was rolling along as a result of his prolonged isolation after being removed from Alcatraz the previous January. Stockdale was further hampered by a "nervous nelly" cellmate who threatened to turn him into the Vietnamese if he attempted to communicate with the other POWs in the camp.

Jerry understood where Stockdale was at for he himself had been there before as had the other senior officers from Alcatraz. He immediately established a policy of command succession based on the rolling along theory which he expressed as follows:

If the senior ranking officer in the camp cannot perform his duties as POW camp commander because he is under too much pressure from the Vietnamese, he will pass the responsibilites of leadership down to the next senior man. This command succession would be passed down the chain of command according to rank until a leader was found who was sufficiently unhampered by the Vietnamese to permit him to function effectively. Thus any SRO (Senior Ranking Officer) if he was ineffective, due to heavy Vietnamese pressure, could pass the lead to his successor without fear of criticism from the POW community.

"I'll pass the lead back to Stockdale just as soon as he gets his situation under control," Jerry said. "In the meantime, if the Vee get to me, Harry Jenkins is next in line, then you, then Howie Rutledge, and then back to Bill Lawrence," he instructed, passing over a few officers who were senior to those just mentioned but who had never assumed the mantle of leadership in the camps when things were going rough.

1970

STARDUST!

When Denton took control of Vegas, his first directive to the camp was to implement Stockdale's policy from Alcatraz of no write, no tape, and no read on the radio.

In Little Vegas at that time, the Bug had gathered in the Desert Inn a group of senior officers whom he was exploiting. Each day some of these men would be led to read Vietnamese propaganda over the camp public address system. On their way to the taping room, they would have to walk past the Stardust area. The Alcatraz men living in cells next to the walkway used every device to get these men to stop reading for the Vietnamese. They went so far as to verbally address them as they walked by. "Don't read, stop reading," they would say loud enough for the passersby to hear. One Alcatraz man fashioned a sign which said, "Don't Read," which he surreptitiously held up for them to see as they passed by.

With these tactics and Denton's direct orders which were now being passed at bathing by notes as well as being sent by tap code and cough code, all the men at Little Vegas, except three, stopped doing anything for the Vietnamese.

Bug was furious! In a very short time, Denton and his Alcatraz gang brought to naught a year of his previous torture and harrassment efforts. His propaganda programs were stopped dead in their tracks and he knew who was responsible for this sudden turn of events.

Bug had his roving patrol guards harass us at every opportunity. One in particular we called Big Ugh, for big and ugly, was more obnoxious than the rest. One morning as we received our breakfast, he told Jerry to take an extra piece of sugared bread. When Jerry did this, Big Ugh became furious, ranted in Vietnamese, slammed us back into our cell and left in a huff. A few minutes later Hawk came to take Jerry to quiz. When Jerry had left, another guard came and took all of Jerry's gear. Jerry was gone and I was back in solitary once again. I passed the word of Jerry's departure, and Harry Jenkins took command.

Each day every man in camp looked for signs of Denton's whereabouts, but it was all to no avail. He was nowhere to be found. A week later, just as I finished eating breakfast Hawk opened the door and in walked Jerry.

They had stashed him in a small cell behind the kitchen area where we couldn't see. He had received all types of verbal abuse and harassment but no physical abuse. "They've lost their teeth Jim, they obviously can't bite us any more," he said as he described the previous week's events. He assumed command and passed his conclusion to the rest of the men in the camp.

Though the Cat had lost his teeth he remained undaunted in his efforts to exploit us. His cajolery and tricks were to no avail. He had many quizzes each day as he endeavored to get Bug's propaganda effort back on track.

Jerry's primary objective was to get Cat to give every man a roommate, and then permit us to live according to the Code of Conduct. Everytime one of the POWs went to a quiz with Cat or Bug he would push for these objectives.

For some reason Cat was getting more nervous by the day. He had a visible facial and eye twitch and his hands shook uncontrollably as he smoked his cigarettes.

Tet came and on the evening of that big celebration I had a quiz with Cat. He poured me two shots of brandy, as he pried me for information regarding Denton's desires for the camp. I replied that Denton wanted no man kept in solitary confinement and wanted all the POWs to be able to live according to the Code of Conduct. "He wants us to be able to live as human beings, and according to our Code of Conduct, and if you permit this I am sure there will be no trouble in this camp," I replied matter-of-factly time and again as he kept addressing the same question.

When I returned to my cell and fully assessed Cat's performance I was convinced that he was working under tremendous pressure. I reported the quiz to Jerry and concluded with, "Cat's coming unglued; for some reason or other they've got him on the spot." The next day Jerry had a quiz with Cat and he came to the same conclusion.

After dark that night, I was taken to a quiz and given some of the goodies from home that Louise had sent: coffee, vitamins and soap. I also received a huge beach towel which was brilliantly decorated with a red, white and blue pattern. She sent me a flag, I concluded. Also I received another brief six line letter. I was sitting facing my quiz master, when they brought in John McCain. McCain was obviously startled at the turn of events. When he came next to me we shook hands, and exchanged identification. "Jim Mulligan. John, how are you feeling?" I asked. "Ok." he replied. At the beckoning of the quiz master, we sat on the stools provided. I looked McCain over closely. He was in poor physical shape. His limp was accompanied with a grimace, which indicated pain. "I got some stuff from home and a letter from my wife," I bantered. He seemed extremely nervous, sort of quivering from tension, yet in complete control of himself. He put his hand on my left leg and tapped quickly. "What in hell is going on?" Just then Hawk took a position at the door observing John. John couldn't see him, so I pushed his hand from my leg and said, "Denton was concerned about your health and they decided to let me see you. I'm glad you are feeling ok." John was still nervous at the event transpiring. "It's ok," I said and winked with a nod to the door so he'd know a guard was watching him.

After a few generalizations the quiz master said, "You have seen for yourself McCain is in good health, and now it is late and you must return to your rooms." We bowed and left, escorted in different directions to our respective cells. Back in the cell I reported everything to Denton. The next morning at bath, I received a frantic tap message directly from John McCain to be passed to me. "Tell Jim Mulligan not to do that quiz bit again," John rapped. "Roger, roger, I was just as surprised as you were," I tapped back.

In the weeks following, one by one Cat gave all the men still in solitary cellmates, until finally we only had two men in camp that were still solo. Lieutenant Colonel Sam Johnson came from Alcatraz and was fast approaching three consecutive years alone. Another Air Force man, Ted Guy, came from the Plantation and was also in solo. We had little info on Ted Guy and could not get comm with him.

My POW name bank expanded rapidly ever since arriving at Little Vegas in the Hanoi Hilton on 9 December. In addition to all of the new names I picked up from the Little Vegas head count, John McCain added a large number of new names that he had acquired at the Plantation. Other men contributed names from their contacts and by early spring my name count was more than three hundred.

Keeping track of the names was a primary assignment for me. I did all in my power to verify and retain each name I ever heard and the circumstances surrounding it. We learned of Dramesi and Atterbury's escape and immediate recapture the previous spring. Dramesi was with Coker and McKnight in the Mint, but Atterbury was nowhere to be found and hadn't even been seen since his recapture.

Bob Shumaker, a clandestine communicator par excellence, developed a secure note drop system and gathered huge amounts of information which he passed to the rest of us in the Stardust. In addition, he passed Jerry Denton's directives word for word to the rest of the camp.

Communications was the key to the POW resistance effort. We were able to establish contact with everyone but three senior officers in the Desert Inn who openly were collaborating with the North Vietnamese. They were just ignoring all the efforts we made to contact them.

At exercise Jerry and I had numerous opportunities to see and communicate with these men. However, they resisted our advances and went on their merry way, making tapes, reading over the radio and writing propaganda for their captors. Neither Jerry nor I could believe the good physical condition they were in. One of them was called the movie star by us. He looked like he stepped out of a health magazine. When compared to the living Zombies from Alcatraz he looked like he came from the twentieth century while we came from the tenth.

The Vietnamese went out of their way to insure that the rest of the POWs saw for themselves the good treatment these collaborators were getting. Almost every day we would see special food, fruit and often bottles of beer delivered to them for their consumption.

I was appalled at their behavior and felt that their sudden conversion to an open anti-war policy was more the result of their present circumstances in Hanoi than their new found dedication to peace. In spite of our disillusionment with them, Jerry ordered that we continually try to bring them back into the POW fold, help them live according to the Code of Conduct and above all else openly forgive them for their breach of faith in their country and fellow POWs. While we didn't make any progress with them in all of 1970, our efforts were the groundwork which led to the reconciliation of one of them a year later.

The Vietnamese were gradually improving our treatment. Almost every day we had a chance to exercise in the fresh air. We also were able to play ping pong and French pool in the areas provided. Jerry would trounce me terribly at ping pong and I would generally win at pool. Our competitive natures often got the better of us and we argued vehemently about the outcome of the various games.

Outside exercise gave us plenty of opportunity to communicate with other POWs. Jerry was a communication mastermind. When he did exercises he sent them in code. He tapped his foot in code so that other POWs kept behind a bamboo screen separator could see the foot movement and pass his message from the exercise area to the Desert Inn, Thunderbird or Golden Nugget areas.

I was Jerry's clearing man and I spent all my time checking on the whereabouts of the officers and guards while he was going through his communication procedures. Each day we had more info and each day he made policy to be followed in the camp. His leadership and direction were exemplary in all aspects. He never stopped communicating.

We had come a long way at Little Vegas since our return from Alcatraz. Except for the two men in solitary, everyone had a cellmate. Except for the three defectors, our resistance posture was firm and our behavior in accordance with the Code of Conduct. The main person responsible for this condition was Commander Jeremiah Andrew Denton, Jr., U.S. Navy, the acting senior ranking officer in the camp.

THE VEGAS HUNGER STRIKE

In mid spring the Vietnamese moved in young newly trained English-speaking guards to act as turn keys in the various sections of Little Vegas. Hawk moved up to a management position and monitored their performance rendering guidance and assistance whenever he thought they needed it. Stardust obtained a young man in his early twenties whose English was clearly superior to most of the Vietnamese we had been in contact with. He was for the most part bookish and more friendly than our previous turn keys. He made an effort to engage Jerry and me in open conversation, trying out his new found skills in English. He treated the Stardust gang almost as human beings. His schoolmaster decorum prompted Bob Shumaker to name him Icabod. One of his contemporaries working the Desert Inn was named Parrot because of his language proficiency. A sleepy eyed mumbling English-speaking turn key working the Thunderbird was named Magoo by its inhabitants.

There were obvious changes going on in the camps, and with our treatment. Outside time for exercise was increased. Our meager diet was definitely on the upswing. It wasn't much to brag about, but it was better than what we had been receiving previously. Each day we had breakfast. The Vietnamese even began to give us hot water at breakfast so that we could have a cup of coffee from the freeze dried instant coffee that most of our wives were sending to us on holidays, and later on in each monthly package. They let the men in each cell play French pool and ping pong in the areas provided.

Shumaker took advantage of this situation by establishing secure hiding places for note drops which allowed him to pass and receive volumes of information. He found places to hide notes behind light switches and other obscure places. The notes were tied by threads taken from clothing and then dropped in some hole to be left dangling well hidden but secured by a piece of dry soap. If you didn't know exactly where a note was hidden, you'd never find it. One day as Jerry and I were playing pool, a note fell out of an overhead light area and landed in the middle of the pool table. A guard was in the room with us but didn't see it fall. Jerry quickly palmed it and finished the game in a cold sweat. We were still subject to surprise room and body searches; consequently we were always careful with our notes. In this case when we got back to our cell, we inspected the note but couldn't decode it because Shumaker's code writing was too small for us to distinguish.

The notes were always written in code in either tic-tac-toe or a version of semaphore and later on in versions of the clock code. These three methods of encoding messages were the product of the expertise found in the POW communication system. Bob Shumaker's efforts helped to bring the Alcatraz gang up to speed on the events transpiring in the other POW camps during their 26-month isolation in Alcatraz.

Bug never let up on his efforts to intimidate and coerce us. While we had many quizzes, they were unproductive for him. We flatly refused to make any tapes, read on the radio, or write for a camp paper he had been running called The New Outlook. The New Outlook for Bug was one of complete frustration. His entire propaganda program was in a shambles. Except for the three finks living in the Desert Inn, his total propaganda productive effort was zero.

All of the Alcatraz gang except for Sam Johnson, had cellmates. I lived with Denton. Shumaker was with Tanner, Rutledge with Jenkins, and Coker and McKnight were together in the Mint with John Dramesi. Stockdale was living in the Thunderbird completely frustrated by the actions of his "nervous nelly" cellmate who threatened to turn him in if he communicated. Only Ron Storz was missing. We had not seen or heard from him since we left Alcatraz. I prayed for him each day, hoping against hope that he was in a Vietnamese hospital recuperating.

In May, Jerry had enough of Cat's promises of roommates for everyone. Sam Johnson and Ted Guy were still solo. We discussed the problem extensively in Stardust, and finally Jerry decided to force the issue by putting all the camp POWs on a hunger strike. Though there were some objections to this tactic, I and most of the others agreed that we should take this drastic action.

As was his usual desire, Jerry Denton began the fast first. I followed the next day. The remaining men in Stardust and then the rest of the camp followed in the order that he had carefully worked out and prescribed. In four days, the entire camp was participating in this effort.

The Vietnamese were wildly upset. They couldn't fathom our actions. Bug went crazy with quizzes and threats. Cat was almost unglued. A pale shell of his former self, he was shaking and twitching obviously completely out of control. After a quiz with Cat, I told Jerry Denton that I thought Cat must have a terminal illness.

Just as suddenly as he started the fast, Jerry called it to a halt. The Vietnamese began moving men to different cells. Ted Guy disappeared from camp. Coker, McKnight and Dramesi were moved to Stardust. Stockdale was made to move solo into the Mint. It was a welcomed relief from his previous situation. Things settled down quickly and we resumed our previous docile routine of outside time and exercise. At its conclusion Cat suddenly disappeared, never to be seen again by any of us in any camp. Only Sam Johnson's condition didn't change. He stayed in the same cell solo.

A week later, just after siesta, the guard came and unexpectedly opened Johnson's door and brought him to cell 6 where Jerry and I were living. Icabod opened our cell door and there stood Sam. He was emotionally overcome as Icabod bid him enter our cell. "The camp authorities permit you to visit with your friends," Icabod said. Sam pulled himself into rigid attention, saluted Jerry and said, "Lieutenant Colonel Sam Johnson reporting for duty, Sir!" Jerry returned his salute and we both grabbed him and hugged him, pounding him on the back in joyful reunion though we had never ever previously met. The tears were running down our cheeks. Even Icabod seemed to be filled with emotion. "You will visit today for an hour," he said as he closed the door.

I can't adequately describe that emotion-filled scene. Sam had been in continuous solitary for the past three years. For months Jerry and I were concerned about his mental stability. We both knew what it was like to be at the edge of mental despair for we had both been there ourselves. Jerry had never stopped worrying about Sam for one second. Now it was over. The solitary was broken and Sam would become, with human companionship, a whole man again. Who knows if the fast helped or not?

For myself I choose to believe that it did, that it rocked the Vegas camp sufficiently to get rid of Cat and get Sam out of solo, and forced new shuffles that were to our benefit.

In their panic to look for a fall guy to blame for calling the fast, the Vietnamese falsely settled on Jim Stockdale as the perpetrator and quickly whisked him out of the camp and stashed him behind the kitchen in a dank little cell called the Hole of Calcutta. We didn't know where Stockdale actually was, but Jerry guessed correctly about it right from Stockdale's departure. "Those bastards have blamed Jim for this and I'll bet they've got him stashed where I was last January," he said correctly.

When Bug came to the door and subsequently at quiz, Denton told him that he, Jerry Denton, ordered the camp fast. Not wanting to lose any more face, Bug refused to believe him. "Tell Bug I called the fast," he instructed as I was off for a quiz. I did as he instructed but to no avail. Bug chose to ignore me.

Stockdale was missing for about a month when suddenly he was moved into the Stardust and kept solo. He was still reeling from the oppressive heat of Calcutta and rolling along writing some junk for the Vietnamese. Bug was up to his old tricks and harassed Stockdale at every turn.

Jerry polled the Alcatraz guys and we unanimously agreed that Stockdale should do absolutely nothing for Bug. We tapped him a collective message saying we were behind him one hundred percent, but that from this time on he should not do anything at all, no matter how dire the threats of torture.

Stockdale told us everything that had happened to him since he was whisked away from Alcatraz in January of 1969. It was a terrible tale of a terrible ordeal and we all felt guilty about causing him those pains. As our leader at Alcatraz, he had paid the full price for our medical well being. Now we wanted to make amends and we could only do it by pressuring him to adopt a resistance posture, which if we were wrong, would only lead him back into a worse condition than he had left. It was a terrible dilemma but we had no other choice. We voted and Jerry passed to Jim, "In Stardust the policy is no read, no write, no tape."

When they took him off to quiz, we prayed fervently for him. In some hours he returned and tapped, "Heavy threats." He continued to resist all of Bug's harassments and finally Bug just quit. One day when Johnson, Shumaker and Tanner were talking, the guard opened their cell and there stood Stockdale. Except for Ron Storz, the Alcatraz gang was together, with cellmates. Soon even visiting between cells was being permitted. We had come a long way from the previous summer when all of us were more dead than alive.

At first the Vietnamese let Howie Rutledge and Harry Jenkins visit with Jerry and me. This expanded and we were allowed to bathe, exercise and eat together. They separated us at siesta and at night. We were in seventh heaven. Whenever we were together, we never stopped talking.

Our game time at French pool and ping pong became so competitive that we were openly getting very obnoxious with one another. Jerry would become completely frustrated when Howie walloped him in ping pong. Jerry would in turn wipe me out completely. I would in turn wipe out Jenkins. At doubles, Jerry and I would come out even with Howie and Harry. (No thanks to either Harry or myself for we were both lousy, but he had more bad days than I did.)

In pool it was the reverse. Harry was top dog and I was pressing him close. Howie and Jerry evened it out at the bottom of the heap. In pool doubles, we came out even, the eventual winner being determined by whether Harry or I came home with the lucky final shot. We fought like kids, but in our hearts we had more respect for each other than we dared show.

Harry Jenkins and Howie Rutledge are two of the finest men I'll ever know and I would go through hell with them any time. Later on as I had the opportunity to get to know the rest of the men of Alcatraz, I would have the same feeling. I always considered myself lucky to be with them, and often times at night as I prayed and reflected, I thanked the Lord for letting me be a member of the Hanoi Starting Eleven when the goings-on there were at their toughest.

Jerry Denton began acting strangely. It started in late spring and got worse as the weeks passed by. He had been a POW for almost five years. I was convinced he was becoming irrational and losing control of his senses. The reason for this irrationality was a dumpy short Vietnamese water girl we named the Tank.

Jerry became convinced that the Tank was his way out of Hanoi. If he cultivated her friendship she would somehow lead him out to freedom. He began to actively solicit her response by smiling at her whenever they came face to face. In these rare instances, he would bow graciously, move out of her way and even be so gallant as to open the door to Stardust where she could deliver the water in company with her equally ugly counterpart whom we had named Tuffy. From our cell, we could see the water girls moving in the kitchen area or alongside the Stardust walkway. Jerry would cough every time he saw the Tank. After a couple of weeks she would respond with a cough. Pretty soon all Denton was doing was coughing everytime he even suspected Tank was near. Then he would imagine a wild escape. His plans were complex and he was so convinced that he even had a contingency plan in the event he and Tank were fleeing south and the rest of us were suddenly released. He wanted me to lead a flight of A4's to look for him. This would let him know it was ok for him to come out of hiding. This was the damndest time of our living together. Jerry was driving me nuts. I in turn, with my negative responses, was completely frustrating him. For a while I thought he was actually losing his mind and one day when he was at quiz and I was alone, I tapped this feeling to Shumaker. I damn near died a few days later when Tank unlatched our door while she was delivering water. Jerry was now more convinced than ever of the success of his plan. Hawk and the other Vietnamese guards, however, had different ideas. They had gotten wise to Jerry and Tank's constant cough signals. I'm sure she was reprimanded for she suddenly ceased all activity, and openly scourned Jerry's overtures. One day as she and Tuffy were passing near us, she actually reprimanded Jerry in sign language, indicating by her gestures that he was a bad man. The saga of Jerry's water girl escape plan ended, sailing off into oblivion as he had more pressing business to attend to running the camp.

In Hanoi, the POWs had a saying, "no one ever died from a toothache; they only wished they did." Along with many other POWs, this adage was very appropriate to Jerry's circumstances. In late winter, he developed a visible abcess which swelled up and then reduced itself almost like clockwork. Normally on Monday, it would begin to give him serious pain. It would swell up on Tuesday and Wednesday and he would be utterably miserable and sick. Thursday it would begin to rescind. Friday he felt better. Saturday and Sunday he was his normal self. Then on Monday the cycle began over again.

It was the damndest sequence of tooth trouble I'd ever seen, and it prevailed into early summer. In spite of the pain, he never let it interfere with his running of the camp.

The Vietnamese, though aware of his condition, did nothing to help improve it. To my knowledge, he only received one aspirin during the many months he suffered. Finally in early summer, Jerry was taken to a quiz and told he would see a dentist soon. A few days later, Icabod came and led Jerry out to meet the dentist. The dentist was a woman and when she saw Jerry's condition, she explained she would have to cause him pain when she cleaned out the abcess.

She dabbed the abcess with cotton soaked with novacaine. All the Vietnamese guards and officers watched. One said, "You must suffer Denton." Jerry gripped the chair and never let out a sound as she dug in and cleaned the abcess. The Vietnamese were disappointed that he didn't yell or scream. There were many little incidents that he had caused for which they wanted to get even. To their chagrin he never cried out and hence never gave them any satisfaction. When he returned, he looked and felt one hundred percent better. He had little trouble with that tooth for the remainder of his stay in Hanoi. The lady dentist had done her job well.

MARKING TIME

In the summer the Vietnamese suddenly began to bring in prisoners by pairs from other parts of the Hanoi Hilton to Las Vegas so that they could have exercise and use the game rooms. After much effort by holding up signs in their cell window so the passing POWs could see them, Jenkins and Rutledge were able to identify Robbie Risner and the four Air Force colonels, Flynn, Winn, Gaddis and Beam. These men were living somewhere in either the Heartbreak Hotel or New Guy Village section of the main Hanoi Hilton. Though we had them identified, try as we might, we were unable to get any direct communication link to them.

The big red, white and blue decorated towel that Louise sent me was my pride and joy. Each day after bathing, I would hang it prominently on a line to dry. Bug became irritated and would have the towel reversed so that the colors wouldn't show. We jousted for months over the towel and which side was showing when it was hung to dry.

One day after I hung the towel with colors showing and while still at exercise, I saw an unfamiliar Asian busy whitewashing the baths. He kept glancing up at Jerry and me being careful to stay out of the view of the ever watchful guards.

Suddenly when the guards left the area momentarily, he stood at rigid attention and saluted my towel. "Me Thai," he said. I sent him a thumbs-up and said, "We Yanks." He went back to his work quickly when the guards returned.

Chai Charn Harnavee had been captured with the U.S. civilian pilot Ernie Brace very early in the war. He was the most magnificent looking Asian I had ever seen. His huge muscular body seemed in excellent shape. In a comparison of Asians, physically he was twice the man of any Vietnamese I'd ever seen. The Vietnamese seemed to openly resent him for his appearance and they worked him like a pack horse. Though we had little contact with Harnavee at this time, he would become at a later date an important cog in the POW camp communication wheel.

Bug and I had never seen eye-to-eye about anything from the first time we ever met. He was a boorish, belligerent, threatening North Vietnamese who delighted in turning his guards loose on the POWs in the old days of torture prior to the treatment change in late 1969. Even now at quiz, we were hostile towards each other, each openly contemptuous of the other. My continued bad attitude bothered Bug. In particular, one habit I had drove him up a wall. It centered around my light blue pajama suit. This piece of apparel was to my knowledge one of a kind in the POW complex. The other POWs had either khaki or more probably the numerous red and gray striped clown suit to wear at formal quizzes. My unique blue pajama quiz suit had one special addition none of the other POW suits had. Low on the long sleeve blouse were two outside pockets. I was in the habit of keeping my hands warm and relaxed in those pockets. One day at quiz, after months of frustration watching me stand nonchalantly before him with my hands in my pockets, Bug almost burst a blood vessel yelling at me, "Take out your hands! You are impolite." He made me stand in the corner and then he went to the doorway and began screaming in Vietnamese. Hawk arrived on the run followed by Icabod and Parrot. After an exchange in Vietnamese with his guards, Bug sat down behind the desk. Parrot said, "Mun, you must stand at attention before our camp officer. We are now going to depocket you." I snapped to attention before Bug. Hawk took out his pocket knife and proceeded to cut off both pockets. When Hawk was finished, Icabod said, "Bow and return to your cell." I complied, did a sharp about face and marched with a full military gait to my cell. The whole damned affair was a comic opera from start to finish. Bug honestly felt that by cutting off my pockets, he had put me into military disgrace. Once again his devious Asian mind was too much for me to fathom.

The North Vietnamese had a big celebration on their National Day in September of 1970. It climaxed that night with a fireworks display which lasted for several hours. From our cell Jerry and I could see the myriad of colored explosions high in the air north of us. We couldn't see anything but the high altitude bursts, but from the "oohs and aahs" that emanated from some female viewers looking out from the top windows of the main building in the prison, we concluded that it truly must have been a magnificent spectacle. The fireworks, we learned from Radio Hanoi, were provided by Communist China in honor of North Vietnam's National Founding Day. I can honestly say that during my lifetime, I had never seen any firework display which even remotely came close in magnitude to this one.

It's a helluva war when the citizens of Hanoi, living in a country fully at war, can have such a big beautiful unhampered celebration while we POWs just sit incarcerated and frustrated, I thought silently.

With the end of the bombing north of the 20th parallel, the war had ceased to be a reality for me. This one fact was the bitterest pill I had to swallow each day. I was convinced that I'd never be released until some drastic pressure was placed on Hanoi itself. Sometimes I felt that the war could drag on for a hundred years. I was a loser in this situation. I felt sorry for myself and the other POWs but I felt sorrier for our wives and children. I couldn't imagine the effect this prolonged separation would have on them, but I was sure that it would cause many family and personal crises. I had been in Hanoi for fifty-four months as of September 1970. This was far longer than I had ever been in one place, longer than high school, longer than college, longer than World War II. We are stuck on top dead center in this war, I concluded. I prayed constantly that something would happen to change this situation, but deep in my heart I couldn't see any quick change to my status.

The pressure for the most part was off. Each day we met with Howie and Harry. Together we bathed, exercised, ate and visited. In spite of our somewhat improved living conditions, mentally we were becoming more frustrated as time passed on. Flare-ups of temper, unnecessary arguments about inconsquential events, and little irritations brought on open verbal hostility. Like it or not, we were getting cabin fever. Howie and Harry had never received any mail and were not allowed to write home, while Jerry and I were now receiving and writing home six line monthly letters. Other groups that were paired together were experiencing the same frustrating problems that we were undergoing.

In late October, Jerry passed the lead back to Jim Stockdale and Jim took over running the camp. In a brief time Robbie Risner was moved back into Vegas, and because he was the senior man he relieved Jim.

Vern Ligon was senior to Risner so he took over the reins of leadership. The four colonels were moved into the Mint. Though we tried every available method known to us, we were unable to establish a communication link-up with them.

In November, the Vietnamese brought in a flock of the sorriest looking turkeys I'd ever seen. They made sure that all the POWs had an opportunity to see firsthand the feast they would be preparing for us for the holidays. Half were killed for Thanksgiving and the rest saved for Christmas.

Icabod brought us the dead turkeys and the four of us had the job of plucking the feathers and cleaning them prior to their being cooked. It was a belly full of laughs for us as we attacked this chore with a determined dedication. Howie and Harry had in their youth experienced some on-the-job farm training, and were stuck with Jerry and me, the two inept city slickers who didn't know one end of a turkey from the other. Not wanting to waste anything, the Vietnamese gave us whole dead turkeys with legs and heads still attached. When we completed our plucking, they took them, feet and heads included, and threw them into the pots for cooking. A couple of days later we had stringy turkey, rice, some vegetables and some clear noodle soup for the main meal of our Thanksgiving dinner.

Hanoi was quiet late at night. Except for an occasional misguided rooster who anticipated the dawn a few hours too early and aroused his answering compatriots for awhile before they would all quiet down and go back to sleep, we heard no noises. In the early dawn the rooster calls would be answered, and then joined by the noises of moving vehicular traffic as the city awoke and slowly began to move into its daily routine. I often awoke long before dawn and would lie on my bunk reminiscing about home and family and hundreds of people and things I longed to see again. Sleep came hard for me at this time. Slow to sleep and fast to awaken. All day and all night I thought, Lord, You've got to get me out of here.

I was in this state of self-pity one night some hours after the ringing of the night tocsin, when suddenly I heard a long rumble off in the distance. The noises increased and I could hear AA guns shooting. Then SAM missiles were fired. The camp came alive with nervous chattering Vietnamese who were running helter-skelter in the yard. "It's a raid. By God, it's a raid!" I yelled to Jerry who was still half asleep. We listened and heard the ack ack fire. The very earth shook from the big guns or bombs that were going off. In the distance I could faintly hear the roar of jets. We're back in the war zone, I thought. That can't mean anything but good news for us. Suddenly, just as quickly as it had begun, the event ended. Everything returned to a quiet stillness except for the chattering Vietnamese. They sounded worried and this in itself was a good morale builder.

The next day the Alcatraz gang reviewed the previous night's activities. Stockdale, with his usual brilliant assessment, concluded correctly that it was a snatch. "The U.S. came in to get some POWs," he told us. We prayed they were successful in this effort.

In December at various times, we heard some Yanks singing off in the distance. The men in the Thunderbird were able to determine that a large group of Yanks had been moved into a section of the camp that we knew very little about. Something was up and we wondered what it was leading to. Again Stockdale figured it out correctly. "The Vee have moved some Yanks in from the outlying camps," he said. "Probably a direct result of the raid we heard in late November."

We had excellent direct comm with all of Vegas. Stardust was hooked up with the Desert Inn by direct voice comm down the alleyway. The Desert Inn went directly to the Thunderbird. Thunderbird went to Golden Nugget. Only the Mint containing the four Air Force colonels, (Flynn, Winn, Gaddis and Beam) was not in the system.

Some innovative things had been happening to comm. One night Jerry and I were listening to the camp radio when suddenly we heard some static which came out in tap code. Commander Chuck Gillespie had figured out a way for an entire camp comm system by using the camp's own radio system. The Vietnamese wised up to this and began monitoring our squawk boxes so Gillespie's effective system was short-lived. Comm was still a sin with the North Vietnamese and we didn't want to push our luck too far. Besides, Shumaker's note drop system was working in a completely secure and effective manner.

Harry Jenkins, a gadgeteer par excellence, liked to rattle the Vee's Cage. Every once in a while he would send a message to the other POWs which said, "The phantom electrician will strike again tonight." That evening Harry would short out the entire camp electrical system by crossing the wires in his room light. This would cause at least a half hour of wild confusion before the trouble would be remedied and the lights returned to normal.

The Vietnamese showed us outdoor movies that summer and fall. Some were war propaganda films and some were classical productions. "A Midsummer Night's Dream" was one of them.

The Vee kept the POWs separated by erecting the usual blanket barriers which they began first using in the summer of 1966. At the outdoor shows, we could see the stars and the heavens. One night I happened to focus on an orbiting satellite which crossed the heavens from left to right. About ninety minutes later it reappeared. "It's got to be one of ours," I told Jerry. "I'll bet they are taking pictures of us with it."

At quiz the next day, Bug harangued me about the American anti-war propaganda movie shown the previous evening. I told him about the orbiting satellite and suggested that the U.S. was watching the camps in Hanoi with this method of surveillance. "You should pay more attention to the movements in the sky than the movie," I said. "The U.S. is not bombing Hanoi, but some day when it does, you will understand why our satellites in orbit are focusing on Hanoi." I could see that Bug was bothered by my comments and I continued on. "You must know that some day Hanoi will be destroyed by our bombers. Now it is quiet like the calm before the storm." He became enraged, put me in the corner and had me sent back to my cell. His eye twitch was worse than ever. My irritating verbal arrows must have struck home and caused him some concern. Being able to needle Bug when he had lost his power to physically punish me was one of the few joys I had. I was, of course, always careful not too carry things too far. I had long ago learned that if a Vietnamese lost face, he would insure that some form of retribution would be inflicted on the perpetrator.

The Vietnamese followed their usual routine for the Christmas Holiday. They decorated the Auditorium game room with a tree and crib and covered the walls with numerous propaganda pictures depicting the glorious victories in their People's War of Liberation in the South.

Jerry and I received some items from gift packages that had been sent by our wives in November. Normally we got vitamins, toothpaste, soap, some high protein pills, coffee and chocolate breakfast drink. For some reason, Jerry and I received very few items out of the total that were sent to us while other POWs would get twenty or more items per gift package from home. In addition to our goodies, we each received brief letters and a few pictures.

I could hardly believe the change in my sons. They were growing into young men. The long hair on most of them was a sight that I found difficult to accept. I didn't know what was going on with my youthful family members, but the pictures made me feel very uneasy. Jerry found a similar situation. We lamented about our inability to have any direct influence on the lives of our children.

The Christmas meal was not as impressive as the one served by the Cat the previous year, but it was far superior to our normal meals. We had much to be thankful for. This was my sixth Christmas away from my wife and children, and though my personal situation had improved since the early years of captivity, I found myself suffering increased mental anguish at the permanency of my situation.

I longed for freedom, for the comforts of my wife and children, my parents, relatives and friends. I longed for my country, that beautiful land of abundance so much taken for granted and so little appreciated by those millions enjoying its benefits. We human beings often put a true value on someone or something only long after we have lost the comforts they provided for us. I vowed constantly that if I ever was returned to freedom and my loved ones, I would never again take it or them for granted. Christmas was once again here and gone. Maybe next year, Lord, maybe next year, I prayed, as I fell off saddened into another lonely night's sleep.

TOGETHER AT LAST!

The 26th of December was an ordinary, quiet day, not much different from the many hundreds of similar days that preceded it. Jerry and I were lolling around on our bunks shooting the breeze and waiting for the night toscin to ring, announcing to us once again that one more day of imprisonment was over with. Suddenly the quiet of the camp was interrupted by the hectic movement of the entire camp guard force, kitchen personnel and officers. Jerry peeked out the barred window overlooking the walkway and kitchen area. "It must be some sort of move, Jim," he called down to me. "I can see the water girls and cooks moving dishes from the main area and taking them out to the main entrance towards Heartbreak Hotel," he continued.

In a short while, the girls came and removed all the dishes from Stardust. We got word from another cell that they saw POWs leaving the Vegas area heading for the Heartbreak Hotel and the New Guy Village section of the main prison. It wasn't too much longer before Icabod came and had all of us in Stardust roll up our gear in preparation for a move.

Section by section Vegas was emptied. The Alcatraz gang was the last to be moved out. We were led out human chain style, one behind the other holding our gear wrapped up in our reed sleeping mats, and following the man ahead of us. Guards were stationed on either side of this human line. We moved out, slowly shuffling along and weaving erratically. Once I made the left turn out of Stardust into the walkway heading towards the main building, I lost all sense of direction. Try as I might, I could not keep track of the various turns. I had no idea where I was or where I was going, until I found myself in the Hanoi Hilton's main courtyard.

The guards and the other Vietnamese members of the camp seemed to be in a very jovial and congenial mood. Once I stumbled and I felt a firm hand grasp my shoulder and help me regain my balance. A voice said, "Go easy, Mun," and I recognized Parrot as the man who had come to my assistance.

We walked a long way in this manner and were finally led into a building. I could hear the slamming of cell doors as other men were once again being incarcerated. The faint hope I had been nursing, that somehow this could be our final move to freedom, faded quickly when I was pushed through a door. Jerry and I were standing next to one another in a small 7'x7' cell with two bunks and a barred window covered with heavy wire. "We will bring you the rest of your belongings later," Icabod said. He left us there, closed and bolted the door and was on his way.

We each took a bunk. Jerry tapped to the room adjoining him. I tapped to Fred Crowe who was with Al Brady in the cell next to my bunk. In a matter of minutes we found out that almost all of the senior POWs had been moved to this building. We feigned innocence when Icabod quickly peeked in before opening our cell door and delivered the remainder of our personal gear which had been wrapped in our blankets for easy transport.

When Icabod left, we continued our comm. We had just completed establishing the room line up when the building was invaded by a group of Vietnamese I had never seen before. Icabod opened the cell door and three men came in. One began a body search of Denton, another started in on me and the third seemed to supervise.

It was the most detailed check I had ever seen. They inspected every part of my body: my mouth, ears, nostrils, anus, between my toes and underneath my feet. They checked my hair, under my armpits, my testicles and between my legs. I didn't know what they were looking for, but I'm sure that if I had been trying to hide something on myself, or in that cell, I would have been caught cold.

When the body search was finished, they inspected in detail every square inch of the cell. By the time they were finished I had decided that they must have been professional police and intelligence men who were actively looking for something in particular. I didn't have any idea what it was, but the Vietnamese must have considered it extremely important, for they had obviously used their top personnel.

It took a long time before they completed checking everyone. When it was over we turned in, exhausted by the night's activities. We had no idea what was going on, but whatever it was it would be a welcomed change to the vegetating we had been undergoing in the Stardust for more than a year.

The following day we had a normal routine except for exercise time. We ate, washed our clothes and bathed. The remainder of the time was spent in our small cells.

When darkness came that night the Vietnamese guards came, unlocked all the cell doors, told us to wrap up all our belongings and go out into the courtyard. In minutes we were gathered in one group. The guards seemed pleased about our new found freedom as we introduced ourselves to one another. I met men whose names I had learned from my shootdown onward, but whom I had never even seen or spoken to. We were overjoyed at this sudden turn of events, and our emotions were running high.

A Vietnamese officer spoke and told us we were going to be permitted to live with our compatriots in a large room. We were then led out of our walled courtyard and into the main yard to the large doors which were the entrance to Building Number Seven.

When the doors were opened, we entered the room which already housed about twenty-seven Americans. Our arrival was the signal for wild celebration, as old friends greeted former cellmates and campmates.

Jerry and I put our sleeping gear next to each other so that we would remain close. On the other side of me was Commander Ken Coskey whom I had known on the U.S.S. INDEPENDENCE in the early sixties, but whom I had never seen or been in contact with during my stay in Hanoi.

The Alcatraz gang immediately joined together. I finally got to meet Jim Stockdale, Nels Tanner, George Coker and George McKnight in person. It was a wonderful reunion. Being in one room with forty-five other Americans was overwhelming.

After greeting my Alcatraz friends, I went around the room and met each of the other men. It was a wonderful experience. For the first time since I'd been in Hanoi, I felt like a human being again. The lack of human companionship had been a heavy burden for me. When I was once again with a group of fellow Americans, this fact became more evident.

At the night's tocsin we raised our nets and said a collective prayer of thanks for our new found living conditions. I lay awake most of the night, tossing and turning. The excitement of the earlier move was just too much for me. Jerry and Ken Coskey were in the same condition, resting on either side of me. Our quarters were cramped, but none of us minded it one bit. Compared to solitary confinement, or two men to a cell, our new found environment was heaven on earth.

1971

THE CHURCH SERVICE REVOLT

The days went by all too fast. Everyone was on a physical exercise program. Many of the men who had not been injured went through a very strenuous exercise program. Others, injured like myself, had developed a program suitable to their particular needs. When we were allowed outside to bathe and exercise, most of the men ran laps from one end of the yard to the other. I can still see Jim Stockdale, one leg completely stiffened from the injuries he received and abuse they imposed on him, running lickety-split like a man on a peg leg. Stockdale gave no quarter and pushed himself to the utmost. He's a man of dogged determination, I concluded, observing him closely; a real leader, a proud American and a dedicated Navy man.

We spent our days catching up on what had transpired in all of the various camps. Each camp had its own story to tell. These tales filled in the gaps of POW history. Our communications network between buildings was excellent. A covert escape committee, whose leadership and composition was not known by the senior leaders, was quickly established and began to develop an escape plan.

Harry Jenkins led a group that began drilling a small communications hole between the thick walls separating Building Six and Seven. During the actual drilling an elaborate clearance system was established to protect Harry and his crew from the prying eyes of curious guards.

The room was divided into flight groups which took turns handling the disbursement of the food we received. We had clean up duties and the room was kept shipshape by the duty clean up flight.

We named this new area Camp Unity. It contained 342 American prisoners, three Thai prisoners and a South Vietnamese POW pilot we named Max.

We were missing J.J. Connell, Ken Cameron, Ron Storz and a man who had been driven into complete insanity. We made every effort we could to get the Vietnamese to give us info on these men. We asked the Vietnamese to move them in with us so we could care for them. Our efforts were completely fruitless, and they were never seen or heard from again. Later the Vietnamese acknowledged that they had all died.

For some unknown reason, the Vietnamese became upset when each room held a non-denominational Sunday Worship Service. Bug ranted and raved and flatly refused to permit any type of group worship.

The top seniors held a conclave, and discussed what action we should take. Most were undecided. A few wanted to accommodate Bug and not make an issue of the church service. If we push the Vietnamese on this they will retaliate and we'll be back in solitary or small cells again, they rightly concluded. I took the exact opposite viewpoint.

"This is a moral point. It is our fundamental right as human beings to have a worship service. As Americans we have no other choice but to meet the Vietnamese head on in this issue. Yes, we will lose this battle, but we will have won the war morally, right here in the middle of Hanoi. Besides, they can't punish everyone so they will concentrate on the leaders. This action will only weld Camp Unity into a single unit. As the senior room it is our duty to take the lead and hold fast to our beliefs. No other choice is available to us," I concluded. When the discussion was finished the consensus was to go full speed ahead and conduct our normal religious service on Sunday.

We held our service on Sunday 7 February. Risner, Rutledge and Coker led the service, conducted scripture readings and a homily. Though the Vietnamese attempted to interrupt the service, we saw it through to conclusion. When it was finished, the three men who had prominent roles in it were removed from the building and taken to a quiz. Later they were moved into a Heartbreak Hotel cell. To show our defiance we sang the Star Spangled Banner at the top of our lungs. The Vietnamese were up in arms. At bedtime that night, we sang American patriotic songs and chanted, "This is Building Number Seven, Number Seven, Number Seven, this is Building Number Seven. Where the hell is Six?"

The chant picked up and reverberated throughout the camp till we were down to Building Number One. The Vietnamese were in a panic. Officers and guards were running pell-mell in all directions. There was an audio riot going on right in the middle of Hanoi by the irate and emotional POWs and the Vietnamese didn't know what to do about it. Finally things quieted down throughout the camp and we drifted off to sleep.

They lost face, and we'll pay the price tomorrow, I said silently to myself. But it was worth it, every damn word and song. We had vented our anger, and in so doing, we had stood up for our rights. It was our proudest hour as a group.

Next day when Risner, Rutledge and Coker were not returned, the hardliners, led by Jerry Denton put the camp on a hunger strike. Ligon, Stockdale and Denton were promptly moved out. Jenkins became senior ranking officer. Bill Frank was next senior, then myself. Jenkins took the camp off the fast Wednesday as we had made our point.

We knew that Risner, Rutledge and Coker were in Heartbreak Hotel, but we had no idea of Ligon's, Stockdale's and Denton's whereabouts.

Thursday night, February 11th, Building Seven had a celebration for Bob Shumaker. It was his sixth anniversary as a POW. He had been captured on 11 February 1965. The Vietnamese became upset at the frivolity and interrupted the concluding ceremonies by having Jenkins and me dress for quiz. Once outside our building we were hauled to the quiz room. Bug ranted that we would be severely punished for our actions. When he was finished we were blindfolded and marched off into the night. The guards punched and pummeled me as I staggered onward, half falling and stumbling, but not actually losing complete control of my balance. When we entered a building, I coughed a loud "M" for Mulligan. Immediately I heard a cough code reply "D" for Denton. Harry coughed a "J" for Jenkins and we got a roger "R" reply from Denton.

They took off the blindfolds and locked us into leg stocks and left. I was bruised and hurting, but otherwise wasn't in bad shape. Harry Jenkins was in a similar state.

To the tune of "I'm Back in the Saddle Again," I crooned softly to Harry, "We're back in the irons again." Our honeymoon living in a large group was finished and we were undergoing a rapid reversion to the bad treatment policy.

BACK IN THE IRONS AGAIN

Harry and I were flat on our backs secured in leg stocks. The building became quiet as the guards left us and returned to the main camp area. We were reviewing the events of the night when I heard Jerry Denton moaning. He was obviously sick. I called out to him, "What's wrong Jerry?" He replied that he was sick and in leg stocks. He reported that Stockdale and Ligon shared one small bunk and each had one leg secured in the leg stocks.

"Harry and I are in stocks in the next to last cell," I reported. I then told them what had happened since they had been removed from Building Seven. I completed my audible report when I heard a strange voice speak up and say, "Who are you guys?"

I replied, "I'm Jim Mulligan. Harry Jenkins and I are in leg stocks here. Denton, Stockdale and Ligon are in leg stocks near you. Who are you?" "Colonel John Flynn," he replied. "Dave Winn is with me and Norm Gaddis and Jim Beam are in the next cell. We aren't in leg stocks."

It was our first direct comm with The Bulls, as we had named the four Air Force Colonels who were the senior men in Hanoi. Jerry exchanged a few sentences with Colonel Flynn then had to quit when we heard a guard come in through the gate into our courtyard.

I didn't sleep much that night. The stocks were small and held me rather rigid so that I couldn't turn. Being flat on my back was quite uncomfortable, but it was a condition that from past experience I knew I could adjust to. In the past I had found that physical restraint was more of a mental frustration than a physically painful experience. Over a prolonged period of time it was a debilitating influence on the body, and would result in extreme weakness. The human body just seems to wind down when it cannot move naturally. For months I had been bothered by kidney pains and this condition seemed to worsen as soon as I was made immobile by the restraining leg stocks.

Harry and I were lying flat on our concrete bunks shooting the breeze the next morning when the Vietnamese moved prisoners into our adjacent cell. When the guards were gone, I heard a faint rapid call up on my wall. I replied, "JM" and he sent, "HR," for Howie Rutledge. In machine gun manner he brought me up to date on what he and his cellmates had undergone since leaving Building Seven. He was with Robbie Risner and they were not in stocks.

Howie had the well deserved reputation of being one of the best communicators in the POW system. If there was a way to communicate he would soon find it out. That morning he discovered that by peeking out his window, he could keep track of the guards as they entered and left our courtyard. When the siesta period arrived he was able to observe the guard leave our courtyard area. While he cleared, Robbie Risner began to verbally communicate with us.

It was a foolproof system. Once the area was cleared of guards, we could just talk down the hallway to each other. When Robbie Risner assumed the job of maintaining the clearance, Howie began to pass all the history of POW confinement in Hanoi to the Bulls. Jerry Denton alternated with Howie, and in a matter of days Colonel Flynn and his fellows were brought completely up to speed.

Since capture, none of the colonels had ever been in contact with the POW system. In fact they knew almost nothing about our communication methods. They couldn't tap, flash, didn't know the cough code or any of the other codes we used for written communications. Rutledge's and Denton's briefings opened up a whole new world for them.

The Vietnamese moved Max Dat, the South Vietnamese pilot, into our building, and the three Thais were put into a cell adjacent to him.

Max had long been a part of our system. He was invaluable because he could overhear the Vietnamese soldiers as they talked and he would pass on what they said to us. He enjoyed good relations with the three Thais, and he got them working for us full time. The Thais were working as trustees throughout the camp, cleaning up and doing odd jobs assigned by the Vietnamese. They kept a watchful eye on everything going on in camp and reported it to Max, who in turn reported it to Howie Rutledge. The intelligence data provided by the four Asians was of great value and played an important part in the functioning of the POW Wing which was formed as soon as Colonel Flynn took over the reins of leadership.

Within a week's time Howie Rutledge made contact through the shower wall with another roomful of POWs and was able to establish through them a direct communcations line to the entire camp.

One by one the Vietnamese removed the men from leg stocks; however, Harry and I stayed locked in tight till the last day. We had been flat on our backs for thirty-eight days. Each day one of us was allowed out of stocks to empty our personal convenience buckets. We alternated this privilege as it meant we could get some movement for our bodies. They let us bathe once a week. This meant we were free to move for about fifteen or twenty minutes. The remainder of the time was spent flat on our backs.

Harry was a great guy to go through this ordeal with. He had the ability to recall the plot of any movie he had ever seen. In addition he had memorized numerous poems and entertained me by reciting them. The "Cremation of Sam McGee" and the "Shooting of Dan McGrew" were two of his favorites. He seemed to know a thousand verses from a thousand songs. Harry was a born entertainer and storyteller. He kept my spirits up every day.

The longer I was restrained the worse I felt. My kidneys were causing me a great deal of difficulty, but I didn't let this on to Harry. Long ago I had decided that physical ailment would be the routine in Hanoi and that the less said about it the better off we'd all be. With this in mind I always tried to cover up any physical problems I might have. Some POWs had already developed the reputation of making too much out of their ailments. I noticed that the men who were sickest generally said the least about their condition. For my part I tried to take the same posture.

On 20 March there was a big move. Every cell in Building Zero was filled. They came and took Harry and me out of stocks. I was so weak I couldn't handle my own gear, so Icabod wrapped it up and carried it out. I was led to cell Three and told to enter. Inside were three men from Building Number Seven: Commanders Bill Lawrence, Chuck Gillespie and Dan Daniels. Harry went into cell Four with Stockdale, Denton and Rutledge. When things quieted down we established a completely secure comm system, and found out that the top seniors were being kept in this building.

Living with Lawrence, Gillespie and Daniels was a great joy. Our 7' x 7' quarters were cramped but the company was enjoyable. In their own way each of them was a remarkable man. Over the little more than three months we lived together, they were a great source of comfort to me. Dan Daniels and I had served together in Pensacola during the late fifties and we had many mutual friends. Bill Lawrence and Chuck Gillespie seemed to know every east coast naval aviator that I knew.

They were all remarkable men, highly intelligent with great retentive memories. They had been in contact with numerous POWs and had a wealth of info for me from both the outside world as well as from the POW community.

The awesome loneliness of Alcatraz and the twenty-six month vacuum from reality it produced suddenly dawned on me. My God, I'm years behind in what's going on with the POWs. I can't imagine how far behind I am on what's been going on in the world, I thought silently to myself.

It took me some weeks before I began to get my normal strength back. The restraint of 38 days in stocks had taken more of a toll on my health than I had realized. My three cellmates did everything to make my life as easy as possible. They shared the chores of clean up and in general left me little to do. My health was deteriorating. My kidneys always bothered me with a lingering dull ache which never seemed to go away.

The comm in Building Zero was excellent. We developed a full set of guidelines which was passed to all the men in camp. Colonel Flynn was the POW camp commander. Commander Jim Stockdale personally authored the rules and regulations, which were put into our memory banks and then passed word for word to the rest of the men in the camp.

Each cell in Building Zero was working on some particular project. My cell was assigned to keep track of a group of POWs who were openly collaborating with the Vietnamese. We labeled them the "Outer Seven". Four junior rank men were being led by the three seniors who had been making propaganda for the Vietnamese back in Little Vegas. We tried unsuccessfully to get them back in the fold ever since we became aware of their activities. They ignored all our efforts then, as they were continuing to do now. Each day we had intelligence reports on their activities from the other men in the camp as well as from Max and the three Thais who were keeping them under close observation.

On Sunday 6 June we celebrated Jerry Denton's twenty-fifth wedding anniversary at our church service which was led by the Wing Chaplain Chuck Gillespie. I recited a poem that I had written for the occasion for my old cellmate and closest friend in Hanoi. Lieutenant Colonel John Finlay concluded the ceremony by whistling The Anniversary Waltz as beautifully as I have ever heard it. I prayed long and silently for Jerry and Jane. I prayed that Louise and I would be together on our twenty-fifth anniversary, 14 October 1973. The years are passing us by, I thought silently and sadly; I wonder when it will end?

The following week we all caught a severe case of pink eye which traveled through the camp like wildfire. The Vietnamese responded to this epidemic by treating us with drops of onion water which to my knowledge did absolutely nothing for our condition.

Three of the Bulls, Flynn, Winn and Gaddis were suddenly moved out. Robbie Risner was the new SRO and camp commander of Unity, which, except for the "Outer Seven", had been welded into one firm mass of resistance against all the Vietnamese propaganda efforts.

In late June, the Vietnamese made another shuffle and I was moved into a cell with my old friends Harry Jenkins and Howie Rutledge. Howie slept on the floor in the 7' x 7' cell midway between our concrete bunks. We had a tremendous amount of rain that summer and the roof leaked in such a way that the water found its way to the overhead light and then dropped onto Howie. Howie had to abandon ship a couple of times due to the heavy rain. Since the Vietnamese would never repair the roof this situation called for some decisive action.

Harry came up with a brilliant idea. He made a collection boat out of a handkerchief and bamboo sticks, and he attached this to the light bulb so the water running from the bulb would now run into the cloth collector.

At the low end of the boat he tied a group of woven strings which he had pulled from his blanket. The string went in an arc from the ceiling to a rat hole at the foot of Howie's bunk. When it started to rain Harry lubricated the string with water from his jug. As the torrent of rain continued the water rushed to the light bulb, then into the collector boat and then down the string and out the rat hole and into the back walkway.

Harry's Rube Goldberg rig worked perfectly. From outside the cell it looked as if the water was just falling from the ceiling and going into an arc and then out the rat hole. At first the guards were befuddled by the contraption. They came into the cell to see what kind of black activities we had been up to. Parrot and Icabod couldn't believe their eyes. They even got the Vietnamese officers to come and see Jenkins' waterworks at work. To the Vietnamese this was a fantastic feat of engineering, but to Harry Jenkins it was just another way to solve a problem.

THE OUTER SEVEN

From the very beginning of the POW experience in Hanoi, compassion and forgiveness was the rule that prevailed with regard to POW conduct and behavior. For the most part over the years, the Code of Conduct had been zealously followed. Deviations from The Code were relatively few and mostly minor in nature. Some infractions were caused by a misinterpretation of the rules or else by Vietnamese trickery and others due to the frailty of human weakness. Jerry Denton constantly demanded that every POW maintain a high degree of trust in his fellow POW, no matter what the appearances of the situation indicated. Jim Stockdale authored the policy that it is neither American nor Christian to nag a repentant sinner to the grave. The stated policy for years for offenders of the Code of Conduct was simply this: please return home to our fold, all is forgiven.

In Vegas, for almost a year, we constantly tried to get the three senior officers who were collaborating openly with the Vietnamese propaganda effort to cease and desist their efforts and come back into the resisting POW community. We were always rebuffed by them. They seemed to be enjoying their relative freedom and the fine treatment that they were receiving. Compared to what was happening to the rest of us, they were living the lives of the country club set. They received special food, alcoholic beverages and often were seen to leave Vegas at night to go for a touring excursion through the city.

In early summer of 1971, the Vietnamese had gathered together the seven POW deviationists, and moved them into building eight. The constant efforts we made to communicate with them finally paid off and a direct audio link was established down the back alley. Immediately the policies of the wing were sent verbatim to them. Personal messages of encouragement were sent from the many friends and acquaintances they had in the Hanoi POW community.

In Building Zero it was my job to keep track of the "Outer Seven" and their activities. Each day during the noon siesta we held a formal briefing for our SRO Robbie Risner. I made a daily report on the status of the "Outer Seven", and what luck we were having in our efforts to win them back into the fold.

Since the three seniors were from the Department of the Navy, (two Navy men and one Marine), Jim Stockdale, the senior Navy officer in Hanoi, sent them a personal message telling them to write nothing, meet no delegations, make no tapes and accept no early release.

Two of the seniors replied that they actively opposed the war. The third senior replied that he was in general agreement with Jim Stockdale. Our communication team was able to determine from the juniors of the "Outer Seven" that for the most part the entire group was in general not obeying the Code of Conduct.

For some weeks Colonel Risner continued to make overtures to the dissident group asking them to return to the POW fold. He received a rapid favorable response from one senior and the four junior men. The other two seniors remained adamant, and refused to deviate from their line of collaboration with the Vietnamese.

Finally after exhausting all efforts at reconciliation with the two seniors, Colonel Risner officially informed them, and the entire camp, that they both were relieved of all military command authority. The remaining five members of the "Outer Seven" refused to cooperate with the Vietnamese and were reconciled with the entire POW community.

I was proud of the way Robbie Risner and Jim Stockdale handled the entire situation. Their actions reinforced my belief in the fairness of the military system, which continued to exist even in the harshest environment imposed by Hanoi.

In addition to these two senior officers, only two other men in Hanoi were relieved of military command. Both the result of severe emotional instability caused by the rigors of their incarceration. Considering the lengthy time element involved and the terrible conditions, I was pleased with the overall POW performance as loyal Americans and loyal military men.

I felt sorry for the two bad apples we had uncovered. Both of them had been career military men. They had wives and children back home who would suffer more deeply than these men themselves would. I felt strongly that Hanoi was no place to get religious about the Vietnam War. I thought about Ron Storz, J.J. Connell and Ken Cameron who, to my knowledge, were still paying the price for remaining loyal. In my mind I could still see the Navy defector running in place at bath number one in Vegas in Jan. 1970. He wouldn't communicate with me. He looked worried and in bad health, a far cry from his Marine counterpart. When I first saw the Marine defector that January, he looked to be in tiptop physical condition. He looked so good that Jerry Denton and I called him the movie actor. We often tried to communicate with him while in Vegas, but he would ignore us completely and refuse all of our overtures.

The philosophers say that war polarizes men and brings out the best in some of them and the worst in others. Vietnam would be no exception to this rule. Hanoi was the place where a man's moral character and personal integrity would be well tested. Here virtue would really be its own reward. We aviator POWs could never be winners in the normal sense of that word. But in the real meaning of life, where a man suffers for what he believes in, and perseveres through adversity when no one is watching, or no one even cares, we aviator POWs could and did rise to the occasion, so that one day all could "return with honor". All but two that is!

THE WING COMMANDER AND STAFF

As fall began in 1971, the Vietnamese made another of their sudden shuffles. Stockdale, Denton, Jenkins, Rutledge, myself and Jim Hughes were moved out of Building Zero down to the small compound of Building Eight which we later code named Blue. On our arrival at our new quarters we met Colonels Flynn, Winn and Gaddis who had been moved out of the Camp Unity area some months previously.

It was a glorious day for us. We would have a considerable amount of freedom living in our own little compound. In addition, the Vietnamese had made the tactical error of putting the top seniors in one place. Only Robbie Risner was missing, and he was still running the camp as SRO from Building Zero.

We immediately established a Wing Staff which would assume all the responsibilities for running the camp. Colonel John Peter Flynn, code name Sky, was the senior man in camp and assumed the position of Wing Commander. Jerry Denton assumed the responsibility of Wing Operations. Jim Stockdale was in charge of Intelligence Operations and the updating of wing policies which we had code named Plums. Howie Rutledge headed Wing Communications. The rest of us assisted in the usual staff work required to run the Wing. Harry Jenkins and I worked directly with Howie to produce the various coded messages that we had to send to the rest of the camp.

Our living conditions were very good in Building Eight. Jenkins, Rutledge and I slept in one cell that connected directly with Stockdale, Denton and Hughes. The six of us were always together whenever we were locked in the cell. Directly opposite us the Vee had put Flynn, Gaddis and Winn in one cell. We could talk directly from our cells to their cell and we were always in direct open communication with each other. Between us was a corner room where the Vietnamese installed a crude wooden table and a couple of benches. The nine of us ate our meals together in this room.

Our daily routine was quite standard. Each morning the guard would let the nine of us out of our respective cells. We would get hot water and a light snack for breakfast. Then we took turns bathing and washing our clothes after our exercises were completed. We stayed in the courtyard all morning until after we had eaten our noon meal. Then as siesta time came we were locked into our respective cells.

After siesta we had more outside time, until after the late afternoon meal was completed, when we would again be locked in for the night. Compared to our previous existence it was like living in a country club.

Once again I was overwhelmed by being with so many different human beings. Solitary confinement had left its impact on me, much deeper than I had ever expected. It was a welcome relief to be with people that I had never known before. My social circle in Hanoi had for the most part been generally limited to the Alcatraz Gang. There was little that we didn't know about each other. At times the closeness that we had developed over the years during the harsh treatment days became a hindrance to us in community living. The years of frustration would show through on more than one occasion, and we would engage in petty rivalries like a bunch of kids fighting about nothing in general. These sudden outbursts of temper were, to my knowledge, quickly forgotten and put into proper perspective and chalked up to the cabin fever we were all experiencing from the prolonged enslavement we had already undergone.

I immediately discovered that I liked "The Bulls". John Flynn was a large, strong man who gave the physical appearance that he had played in the line for the Chicago Bears. A year previous when Jerry and I first saw him in Vegas, we called him the football player. Despite his appearance of being only a physical man I soon found John Flynn to be one of the most mature, compassionate and understanding men that I had met in my years of military service. He was a dedicated leader whose personal stability brought a great deal of sanity into an insane environment.

John's sidekick, Dave Winn, had one of those easy going personalities that I could accommodate to in minutes. Dave was an openly friendly man, sincere with deep convictions, yet one who would never show hostility no matter what the circumstance. Norman Gaddis possessed a super keen mind with perfect recall. Norman, I could tell, was an indefatiguable worker. No matter what the task, he would see it through to successful completion. I can honestly say that I liked them all, right from the first meeting, and I considered myself fortunate to be living in daily contact with them.

The remainder of our group, except for Jim Hughes, were part of the Alcatraz Gang. Hughes was a loner who had lived with Stockdale in Vegas, but who had been primarily responsible for Stockdale's inability to run that camp. He had witnessed a horrifying, emotional experience early in his capture, and had been more or less rolling along in fear ever since.

In spring of '71 he had suddenly become a radical and had caused considerable trouble to the Vietnamese. Finally they moved him to Building Zero and then into Blue, where I'm sure they felt the senior Americans would help keep him in line. I felt sorry for Hughes. Right from the first meeting in Building Seven it was apparent to me that he was having more severe emotional problems than the rest of us. In Blue I tried to establish a rapport of friendship, but failed as he withdrew more and more into his own personal fantasies.

Jim Stockdale was the senior naval officer. We called him CAG in deference to his position of Carrier Air Wing Commander. Stockdale was the most politically attuned military officer I had ever known. He had a brilliant mind, and was liberally educated. He was the antithesis of the military mind stereotype I had grown accustomed to serving with. Stockdale was a striver. I was convinced that he had the abilities needed and would push himself to the utmost to reach the top. I was also convinced that Jim Stockdale was a fighter who would always find a way to come out a winner, even in Hanoi. He was a first class intellectual superior to any one else I knew in military service.

Jerry Denton, the second senior Navy man and my long time cellmate when we both were not in solitary, was Stockdale's Naval Academy classmate. Jerry was a true believer. I never knew a man who had as deep a faith in God as Jerry possessed. He was a man of conscience who made clear distinctions between right and wrong. He had proven himself during the harshest days in Hanoi, when he assumed the mantle of leadership and directed the POW resistance effort against propaganda exploitation. Though Jerry and I could fight like cats and dogs or like twin brothers, we had developed a deep and lasting friendship from the mutual hardship and torture that we had shared together. I could honestly say that I knew more about him than any other person in the world, and he in turn, would say the same about me. We are the closest of friends.

Harry Jenkins and Howie Rutledge completed the roster of the men in Blue. Harry was a wonderful innovator and a man who could not only figure out what needed to be done, but also the way it could be accomplished. Howie was a master communicator as well as an indominable resister to all of the North Vietnamese propaganda exploitation efforts. They became fast friends ever since they lived in adjacent cells at Alcatraz. Later on in Vegas they had been mated up together and were inseparable from that time on. They formed the main communication team which directed all the Wing policies to the Squadrons.

Life in Blue was a wonderful respite from the harsh conditions we had known in earlier years. The food improved greatly in nourishment and taste over what we had previously. The war was stuck on top dead center, but now the Vee seemed to want to keep the prisoners alive and improve our overall health. We received adequate medical attention and some dental care for those who needed it. The Vietnamese gave us immunization shots to help ward off some of the more prevalent diseases found in that part of the world.

The biggest and best improvement was the new freedom that we enjoyed in our daily routine. Being able to mix freely and interact with eight other human beings was the best therapy I could receive. My mind seemed to become more alert and the mental pressures of years of solitary confinement were pushed into the past as each day I discovered something new and wonderful about my associates.

In the past, I had dedicated a good part of each day to meditation and prayer. It was an exercise, that more than anything else, helped to sustain me through those terrible years of utter loneliness. On more than one occasion during those years, I felt that I would lose my mind completely, but everytime I reached that point of despair, the Lord seemed to suddenly find some way to help me through my difficulties.

Each Sunday the men in Blue held a joint Ecumenical Church Service. It was a thoroughly planned affair under the guidance of Colonel Norman Gaddis who acted as our Chaplain. We sang an entrance hymn, said the Pledge of Allegiance followed by readings from a Bible, and a prepared homily given by one of the nine of us who had volunteered to accept this assignment. We rotated the homily duty each week. We broke bread and took Communion using water in place of wine. We meditated and said a Communal Prayer before we sang the final closing hymn. When the service was completed, we shook hands and wished each other well with a "God bless, have a good week".

I can honestly say that these Sunday services conducted in the barred cell where we normally ate our meals were some of the most moving and genuine religious experiences that I had ever experienced.

We were military men, but we were also God-fearing men. Each night before retiring to our respective wood pallet beds and mosquito nets, we said a communal good night prayer, recited the Pledge of Allegiance and sang a chorus of Taps which went something like this: "Day is done, gone the sun, from the earth, from the sea, from the sky, rest in peace, valiant men, God is nigh."

The Vietnamese were not happy with our religious services or with our good night ritual, but other than the occasional grousing of a guard who urged us to, "Keep sil-lent", they didn't bother us.

As it happened, John Flynn, Jerry Denton and I were three Roman Catholics who lived in Blue. Each afternoon, during our outside time following the noon siesta, we would go to the barred room and hold a daily Mass. John and Jerry would alternate the duties of celebrant. I would get the bread and water so we could take Communion and also I would schedule the time of the event and keep track of who would be the celebrant. It was a brief service without singing or homily but closely paralleled to a standard Mass celebrated by Roman Catholics in all parts of the world.

Our daily Mass became more meaningful for me as time went by. It seemed to bring an aura of peace into my life, and I looked forward eagerly to joining John and Jerry in our own daily communal prayer and Communion service.

Our daily eating routine began in the morning when we were given hot water to mix with any freeze-dried coffee we had received as gifts from home. These packages came first on a bi-monthly basis, and then on a monthly schedule. The coffee received was put into a community pool and parceled out in a manner that would allow us to make it last through the month or until we received the next packages. Since coffee was my main vice, the others put me in charge of doling it out equitably whenever the hot water was provided in the morning or afternoon. It was a chore that I relished and the Vietnamese regretted. My temperament is such that when the Vietnamese guards were careless and didn't deliver our hot water promptly I would immediately bellow, "Bao Cao" at such a volume as to bring them running. They soon discovered that life would be much quieter if the hot water for coffee was delivered to Blue promptly. Except for a few occasions of tardiness, where upon I took immediate vocal action, the problem was eliminated.

Our normal life was a far cry from times past. The Vietnamese began taking precautions to protect our health. One of the new benefits was the sterilization of our eating dishes and utensils. Each morning and afternoon, prior to the main meals, they brought us a bucket of scalding water to sterilize the eating equipment. Normally we paired off in twos to handle the chore of soaking the dishes and then putting them on a rack to dry prior to use. After the meal was finished, the same pair did the dishes using cold water and the standard inferior Vietnamese lye soap. Another pair cleaned up the eating area, wiped the table and benches as well as washed out the concrete floor with buckets of cold water. These housekeeping chores were always diligently performed both for health reasons as well as for personal comfort.

Long ago each of us had been amazed at the dirt the Vietnamese tolerated in their buildings and once given the opportunity to keep our station clean, we maintained cell and personal cleanliness with a vengence.

I never felt clean from my first moments in Hanoi. In Blue each day, at the earliest opportunity, I would strip naked and douse myself with buckets of cold water, soap myself as best I could and then rinse off completely. I wasn't trying to become a member of the Hanoi Polar Bear Club, but I'm sure that on many cold winter mornings when I went through this ritual, some of my cohorts in Blue must have thought that I had lost my mind.

The days always went fast in Blue. We had much work to do writing the POW camp policies and then passing them by coded messages to the rest of the camp. I assisted Howie and Harry, our chief communicators. They had developed a secure coded system that required diligent attention to detail to get out messages correctly. It was called reverse slide and sent more or less like this:

A message had a coded date which told the day of the week. The code was up 1 for Monday, up 2 for Tuesday, up 3 for Wednesday, down 1 for Thursday, down 2 for Friday, down 3 for Saturday and down 4 for Sunday.

If the letter was code dated Monday, for each letter of the alphabet in the message, we would send the letter succeeding it, e.g., for the word "ALL" we sent "BMM". The people getting the message would get "BMM" on Monday and go down one letter to read, "ALL" the word we sent. To decode a Tuesday message, the receivers had to go back or down 2 letters, e.g., a "C" would be decoded as an "A", etc. To further complicate the system and insure even more security, the message was written out and encoded on the floor of our cell using soft stone for chalk. When the encoding was completed the message would be transferred to paper beginning at the end of the message and working forward. It was coded in groups of three letters to a group, and eleven groups to a line. Howie and Harry used tic-tac-toe, or the clock code, or semaphone to write the message on paper. Reverse slide was really a very sophisticated way of sending a top secret message. It went up or down according to the day of the week. It was sent backwards in groups of three and it was written in one of three code systems. With the diligence and effort put into this system, we were able to feel that none of our messages would be decoded if they were intercepted by the Vietnamese.

The credit for this sophistication and for the success of our extensive clandestine codes must go to Howie Rutledge and Harry Jenkins who worked patiently to perfect them. I spent many hours daily assisting them, encoding outgoing messages and decoding incoming ones. Each message presented a mental challenge and helped to sharpen our stagnant minds. Our communication effort enabled the Wing to function almost as efficiently as the normal administration facilities available back home. It was truly a marvel which the Vietnamese always completely underestimated, and were never able to comprehend in even the slightest manner.

PASSING STONES

As Thanksgiving approached we knew we would receive a meal out of the ordinary. The Vietnamese came through with extra meat, a good wholesome soup laced with vegetables and meat broth, some hot sweet syrupy coffee, but that was it. It was no extravaganza but was better than average. We held our communal religious Thanksgiving service in the barred cell where we normally took our meals. It was truly a meaningful experience.

I had spent many sleepless hours the previous night thinking of home and family, of Louise and our six sons and the last Thanksgiving we had spent together in 1964. Seven Thanksgivings had come and gone and I was no closer to being with them than I was on the first one apart. "Lord, when will it end? When will it end?" I pleaded as I yearned to be home. Home seemed like such a long time ago to me. I felt like I was left hanging in a perpetual state of limbo, but I knew down deep in my heart that somehow I must hold on. Never, never, never give up. Keep the faith and someday this will pass and I'll be free again, a whole man and hopefully a better man than when I came to this hellish place.

But though I was saddened by my mental retreat to my family and better times, I finally took hold of myself and forced myself to see my own situation as it presently existed in Blue. I truly had much to be thankful for. The good companionship of my eight cohorts, the relative freedom I had compared to the solitary of times past, the lack of torture, the improvement in food and medical care. Yes, I have much to be thankful for, I thought as I lay flat on my back wrapped in a homemade sleeping bag made out of two rust colored Vietnamese army blankets.

I thought of my friends in Blue and mentally composed the following poem which I would recite to them at the Thanksgiving church service.

When Thanksgiving Comes

When Thanksgiving comes,
   the place I should be
is sitting at home,
   with my own family.
Giving thanks to the Lord
   for the good things of life
for the wonderful food, for my children,
   my wife.
But here in Hanoi
   where my pickin's are lean
with my plate mostly bare
   and the soup mostly green
and with little of comforts
   and not much to do
I thank the good Lord
   for giving me you.

The next day at our service, I recited it slowly with all the sincerity that I possessed. It wasn't much, but it came from my heart and each man took my hand and said thank you when I had finished.

Winter's winds arrived in late November and icy blasts fluttered through the open barred windows in the walls and over the cell doors. We always ate quickly because the chilly wind would make the food cold, and even less appetizing than it normally was.

Our daily routine had settled down and we were kept quite busy making policy for the camp and keeping track of what was going on with all of the squadrons. Max Dat, the South Vietnamese pilot, and the three Thais, were doing a great job delivering our messages to the rest of the camp, and bringing their return communications back to us. Additionally, we had developed a thumping capability on our back wall which would put us in direct contact with Robbie Risner and the remaining seniors in Building Zero.

Since the distance between us was about fifty feet, we needed an exotic clearing system if we were not to be caught. Harry Jenkins once more came up with the answer. He managed to get a small piece of glass from one of the shaving mirrors. He attached this to a stick and made a periscope which allowed him to look down the alleyway to see if any of the guards were hiding there.

The clearance system became so secure that Howie Rutledge could talk out the back window while Harry cleared the alleyway. I would get near our door and clear the front part of our exercise area. The Vietnamese were never able to catch us communicating, and for the most part were oblivious to our efforts.

Jim Stockdale came up with an idea which allowed Blue to develop one-way direct communications with the squadrons located directly opposite us on the other side of Camp Unity courtyard. We had a vent pipe in the roof of our toilet facility. Jim's idea was to use a long stick and send code by raising and lowering the stick. We got the Thais to leave us a stick when they were cleaning the courtyard. Then we set up a code time schedule when we would send code in the blind to our compatriots on the other side of the camp. Right from the start the system worked beautifully. We used it for many weeks, before the Vietnamese discovered our latest black activity.

Howie was sending code one day, raising and lowering the stick. Suddenly he felt a tug. He held on, looked up and was eyeball to eyeball with a Vietnamese guard. Howie pulled the stick away from the Vietnamese and we all immediately retreated to our sacks. We had been caught and the jig was up.

Though the system had been working very effectively for many weeks we decided to bluff the Vietnamese and confess to them that they caught us in the very act of communicating the first time we ever tried this method. They accepted our explanations quite readily. Howie Rutledge was removed and told he was a bad man engaged in black activities. In a short time he was returned to us none the worse for wear. By telling the Vietnamese that they were too smart for us we allowed them to save face. This was an excellent tactic which made them feel like professionals. The end result was we did not get tortured and the Vietnamese guards felt they had our comm efforts completely under control.

I had been suffering from a kidney problem for many months. It had cropped up seriously the previous March when I was in stocks for thirty-eight days. I never told anyone that I was having kidney problems but I was having a fair amount of pain and occasionally felt much worse than normal. In mid-December I had a few days where I just felt bad. I took to my sack and slept more than usual, I ate my soup, but skipped most of the rest of the food.

We were in the middle of the siesta period. Rutledge and Jenkins were completing a comm message. I awoke with a terrible urge to urinate. I hit the bucket at full speed half afraid I would wet my pants before I could begin to pass urine. I had a full head of steam up as the hot urine flowed with much more pressure than was normal for me. Suddenly I felt like I was passing large ball bearings. Two of them rolled down my urinary tract and popped out into the bucket. A third came rumbling down and came to a full stop just prior to my passing it. The urine flow stopped and I started to pass a lot of blood.

Damn, I said to myself, I'm stopped up and bleeding. Jim Stockdale noticed I was having a problem and asked, "What's wrong?" "I can't believe it Jim," I replied. "I just passed two stones and I've got a third one stuck at the head of my penis. I can't pass any more water and the stone won't move and to top it off, I'm bleeding."

I can truthfully say that I was scared to death of my predicament. The bleeding slowed to a trickle in a few minutes. I was beside myself with anxiety as I tried to assess my situation. I was feeling badly and slept for a short while as the others showed their concern and wondered about my condition.

On awakening I lay on my bed and pondered my options. I had few choices. Either I could tough it out and hope for the best, or else I could throw myself at the mercy of the Vietnamese and beg for some medical attention. After much reflection, I settled on riding it out. I decided that I should force myself to drink an enormous amount of water. Hold off from urinating as long as I could, build up a full head of steam and then let go and hope everything turned out all right.

I followed my decision to its completion and drank about three quarts of hot water, then waited for an urgent urge to pass it all. I held off as long as I could. Finally when I felt I would get my back teeth floating, I advanced to the bucket to give it one massive try. I pushed with all my might but nothing happened. I was blocked up completely. A little blood oozed out and a drop of urine followed. I tried again in bitter pain physically, but suffering even more emotionally at the thoughts of my plight. Suddenly everything let go. Out popped the stone into the bucket followed by a hot stream of urine mixed with deep red blood. I kept the pressure up and the stream going until I had completely evacuated my bladder. The sweat was pouring down my brow. I was exhausted. The pain faded away as my anxiety was completely relieved. I fell into a deep sound sleep. When I awoke hours later I had to urinate. I approached the bucket with some apprehension, but when I immediately passed a normal stream without difficulty, my mind was once again put at ease. In the next few days I felt better than I had in years. I felt inwardly that a good part of my prior poor health must be attributed to the kidney stones, which had caused me difficulty since my early days at Alcatraz in late 1967.

I said a prayer of thanks, and once again reaffirmed my belief that in his direst straits man will do what he has to in order to survive and that man's body is, in itself and of itself, a wonderful healer.

In a couple of weeks Christmas was coming and I had already received a wonderful gift, my improved health.

The camp was preparing for Christmas. In Blue we heard of the choral groups and church services that were being planned by the various squadrons. Norman Gaddis began working up a special service. He asked Howie Rutledge and Harry Jenkins to come up with a Christmas song sheet. These two members of the Southern Baptist religion seemed to know the words for every hymn that I had ever heard. They sat for hours writing verse by verse. It was a tribute to their memories, and to the many hours they had spent in religious services during their early childhood days.

When Christmas came we got a special meal of turkey, a salad and soup. They even served us beer and some strong rice wine and one by one, we went to the quiz room to receive gifts from home and letters from our families.

I received many pictures of my boys and I was appalled at the length of the hair on most of them. One picture of Louise really hit home. I could see that she was deeply hurt. Her eyes looked like those of a wounded animal begging to be put out of its misery. She had fought the good fight for many years but now she was reaching the end of the rope. She needs me just as I need her. Somehow I've got to get home before it's too late. How much can you ask one woman to bear? Six sons and more than six years of separation. The years are beginning to take their toll on her as they have already taken their toll on me. I prayed! More than anything else I prayed for Louise and that she could hold on till I came home. And that picture! How I hated it! It tormented me! Yet I couldn't resist looking at it. It haunted me, and I felt so helpless, yet so guilty. Look what I'm doing to my wife, I said over and over again mentally to myself. Then in my abject sadness I prayed, prayed that somehow something would happen and something would change. And suddenly it did. A few days after Christmas we heard of new bombing raids and a few new POW names from the infamous Hanoi Hannah, our only link to the outside news.

1972

The New Year was upon us. Another election year. Years ago at Alcatraz, we had each selected a date for release when we thought we would go home. I recalled Jim Stockdale taking February 1973. "After the next election," he tapped, "then we'll be going home and not before then." That was in early 1969 — as the eternal optimist I thought him out of his mind. I took June 1969 as my release date. The winner would get to call the date and place of the Alcatraz reunion. So far we had all lost but Jim Stockdale. His selection would turn out to be prophetically accurate.

THE BOMBING RESUMED!

The New Year arrived and with it came a few scattered names of new POWs which I immediately added to my POW name memory bank. Since I first began memorizing POW names back in April of 1966 my routine never varied. I mentally recited the entire list three times daily almost like a prayer ritual, first on arising, then at the mid-day siesta and finally on retiring.

When the new names began coming in, I had already locked in some three hundred fifty-three names of living POWs. In addition I had info on scores of others who had died or been killed on shootdown. I kept everyone alphabetically but decided that the 1972 shootdowns would require a separate accounting, so I began a separate list just for them.

Except for the routine of running the camp, our staff work at Blue was mostly completed. Time was hanging heavy on our hands more and more as the newness of living together gradually wore off.

Colonel John Flynn asked me to see if I could work out a combination educational and entertainment program that we would put into effect each night after we were locked in our cells and before the night tocsin.

I scheduled each man to talk on his area of expertise. During the entire year we had a wondeful series of lectures and discussions on a great variety of topics which ranged from our own detailed personal biographies to a series of movies brought to us by our favorite storyteller Harry Jenkins. Harry could remember the cast and theme of every movie that he had ever seen. Howie Rutledge opened up the world of dog racing and gambling at Las Vegas. Jim Hughes covered the world of Wall

Street and margin accounts. John Flynn took more than a week to cover a detailed in-depth study of European table wines. Norman Gaddis explained the mystifying ways of pushing papers through the Pentagon Puzzle Palace in Washington. Jim Stockdale's expertise was on Greek and Roman philosophers. Jerry Denton covered the world of electronics and Navy blimps. Dave Winn told of his many great outdoor adventures in the wilds of Canada and the raging waters of rivers that he rafted on. My specialty was national politics and the workings of Congress. We eagerly looked forward to these entertaining lectures. Each man took a deep interest and put in much preparation so that the entire series was very professional.

Collectively we investigated many natural phenomena by observing the moon, the sun and the stars. We made a sundial and after much effort were able to come up with a compass rose showing true and magnetic north which we inscribed on our concrete courtyard. Each day we saved scraps of bread and when things quieted down we would feed the birds. At first only a few birds dropped into our courtyard, but soon they grew into a flock as we increased our output of food and established a feeding time.

The Vietnamese moved Max Dat and left the three Thais living alone next to us. Harry Jenkins developed a tool and worked diligently until he bored a hole through the brick wall separating our toilet area from them. We now could pass our communication notes easily and safely.

Howie Rutledge became friendly with the Thais and began teaching them English. It was amazing the great amount of progress he was able to make with them. Through his efforts they soon had a very good working knowledge of the language, and our communications link with the camp became even more effective.

Max Dat and the three Thais had trustee status and performed much of the housework, cleaning and minor repairing of the Hanoi Hilton's Camp Unity area. Because of this they were able to pass to the Blue Staff a great deal of important camp intelligence information.

Max would listen to the Vietnamese guards and officers, and then would pass the contents of their conversations to us. This info was invaluable to us, and allowed us to anticipate many of the moves the Vietnamese were going to make in the camp.

The new POWs who had been recently captured in late 1971 and early 1972 had been briefed in survival school that they should try to get their names out to the world press. All of them were photographed and most made innocuous statements which we could easily see through. Occasionally one of them would make a tape which would be played over our camp radio. Since they didn't show up in Camp Unity we surmised that they were being kept at the Zoo with the remaining members of the "Outer Seven" and another group of mostly junior officers who had been moved there from Unity the previous summer.

One day in April, the air war, which, according to Hanoi Hannah had been gradually escalating, burst forth into full bloom right in Hanoi. On Sunday the 16th the U.S. conducted a massive air strike on Hanoi. We cheered as we viewed the attacking planes winging their way into the targets, shooting missiles, dropping bombs and dodging Vietnamese counter fire.

The SAM sites were firing from all over the area, and we watched as most of them went awry from the vigorous electronic warfare counter measures that the attackers were employing.

We saw two planes take direct hits and explode in a fiery blast high in the sky. From one victim we saw two chutes open and drift slowly downward to the south. I didn't see anything come out of the other plane as it plummeted earthward with black smoke and fire bellowing from it. I said a prayer for the attackers, and a prayer of thanksgiving that once again the war had finally moved off top dead center. How ironic, I thought. It's almost six years to the day since the first American bomb had been dropped on Hanoi proper. That event had occurred on Sunday the 17th of April 1966. I was in New Guy Village as a recently captured prisoner then. Before the air war was over, I would find that I was in Hanoi for every American bombing raid there, from the very beginning to the final end.

On this initial raid, as the air war resumed, we could see a remarkable difference in the weapons employed and the tactics used by the United States airmen.

The Vietnamese had installed a radar close to the edge of the Hanoi Hilton. Midway during the attack we heard the swish of an incoming missile as it passed close and low overhead. It went off with a blast near the main building. Smoke filled our area and pieces of metal ricocheted around our courtyard. One of them bounced off the courtyard wall into our cell and off a wall and finally came to rest after it hit Jim Stockdale's leg. He picked up the hot piece of metal and gave it to our resident weapons expert Howie Rutledge. Howie had done a tour of duty in China Lake where our new Navy air weapons are developed. In seconds Howie said, "It's from a shaped charge that we had in our shrike missile, and used to destroy acquisition radars on flack and missile sites."

Finally the attack was over. We could see black billowing smoke to the west and it looked like an oil storage area had been hit. The Vietnamese guards had cheered on several occasions and we knew that in addition to the two planes downed south of us that more were probably downed out of our area of vision.

The all-clear siren rang. The guards were in an uproar and very belligerent. They had grown accustomed to safety ever since Johnson's move which stopped the Hanoi bombing back in March of 1968. They ran around the courtyard picking up pieces of metal from bombs or flak exploding near our area. For almost an hour afterwards we saw all sizes and types of electronic countermeasure chaff float slowly to the earth near us. This explained much of the wild erratic SAM missile behavior we had observed coming from the defending Russian SAM sites.

We all felt jubilant at the sudden turn of events. After years of languishing as forgotten men in Hanoi we had something concrete to hang our hopes on.

At the evening meal we critiqued what we had observed from the three cells we occupied, and we established areas of responsibility for covering future raids. Jenkins, Rutledge and myself would cover the southern half of the sky from our rear cell windows. Stockdale, Denton and Hughes would cover the north and as much of the east as they could see and also clear our courtyard area and gate for incoming guards. Flynn, Winn and Gaddis took responsibility for the southwest to the north area.

We were prepared for future incoming raids. Once again we felt like we were active military men. If we couldn't fight we could at least get as much intelligence information as possible on the new air war.

We wondered about new POWs but we didn't have long to wait. That very night Hanoi Hannah had a taped statement from one of the downed airmen.

The staff in Blue put out a policy to all the other POWs in camp which basically said, "Play it cool and don't provoke the guards." We were concerned that the sudden turn of events in the air war might bring on Vietnamese retribution against the POW community as it had in previous years.

A NEW AIR WAR

The resumption of the air war over Hanoi put the guards on edge and the Vietnamese officers in panic. On several occasions during raids, Fox, one of the former camp commanders came to our courtyard and voiced his disapproval of them to us. Because of our excellent clearing procedures neither he nor the guards were able to catch us observing the raids from our designated observation posts. The Vietnamese wanted us to sit on our bunks during any raid, and would get upset if they caught a POW in any place other than the designated one.

In early May, Max Dat and the Thais pulled a great intelligence coup when they reported to us they overheard the Vietnamese guards talking about a major move of POWs from the camp which would be occurring in the immediate future. They reported that a large group of POWs and accompanying guards would be moved close to the China border. We sent out a top secret message alerting the entire camp and directed the men who would be moved to follow the policies as they had been implemented under Colonel Flynn. We wanted to insure that the mantle of leadership and responsibility would follow the procedures that we had prescribed.

On the night of 13 May after dark, we heard a shuffling of feet as the movement began. The men had to pass close to Blue as they made their way out of the Camp Unity area and through Heartbreak Hotel to the waiting trucks. We heard several "MVG" cough code letters which to our trained ears meant "moving."

The next day we took a head count in Camp Unity and found that 209 men had been moved. The Thais and Max came up with the name of a city, Lang Son, and we felt we had the move pretty well pinpointed.

The raids increased in intensity and number as the summer moved on. Newly captured POWs were generally moved into New Guy Village and Heartbreak Hotel adjacent to Unity. The Thais and Max delivered their food which was prepared in our area. They were able to pass written info on notes placed in the rice and in return get names of the new men. Generally the names would be inscribed on the backs of the returning rice plates. Also Hanoi Hannah obliged our name bank by issuing names and statements as soon as possible after a man was captured.

Following their initial incarceration in New Guy Village or Heartbreak the new men would be moved to the Zoo where our two senior defectors were stashed.

Soon the numbers of POWs increased at the Zoo and a few of them began to actively resist the new Vietnamese propaganda effort. Some of these dissidents were moved to Building Seven which for a time was isolated from the rest of us. Once again Max and the trusty Thais came through, and established a safe communications link which enabled us to pass them the POW policies. When we got our first glimpse of the new POWs we were thunderstruck. They seemed so young and had so much long hair, sideburns, beards and moustaches. They were a far cry from the military appearance that most of us had been accustomed to during our careers. The men on the staff in Blue considered the newly arrived POWs a motley looking crew if ever there was one. We were in for a rude awakening when we received a long message which the Thais picked up from the hidden cache we called a mail drop. It contained all types of news from home including the new service regulations pertaining to hair style, sideburns, beards and moustaches.

We were starving for news. The new POWs proceeded to send us info on all current events, military pay and promotion info, sports, etc. ad infinitum. The changes in American morals and life style they described were almost too unreal to believe. Deep in my heart I had known that I had gotten off the world when I was captured in March of 1966, but until now I had no idea of just how far behind in everything I had fallen.

With the air war once again moving at top speed and with the imposition of the blockade of the seaports, we all felt that somehow we were on the final leg of our journey.

The new bombing tactics amazed us. The night low level attacks by the Air Force F-111's and the Navy A-6's seemed to terrorize the Vietnamese camp personnel. Generally the planes would roar in and drop their weapons before any flak could be fired or missiles launched. Often times the only defense was the fruitless spattering from a few hand held rifles hoping for a lucky hit or firing just to reinforce their own defenseless inadequacy.

For the most part that summer things were quiet in Camp Unity. We received a few live immunization shots for some of the prevailing diseases. The food was nothing to rave about but much more adequate in taste and content to that which we received prior to 1970. Medical care was available and some long-time injuries even received current attention by sudden trips to the hospital at night. These were all good signs that the light at the end of our tunnel would soon become a reality.

Jane Fonda and Ramsey Clark visited Hanoi. Both were given a tour of the Zoo and were allowed to meet with a small select group of POWs headed by our two senior defectors. Naturally everything they said was put on tape and played for us to hear over the camp radio.

In one way I honestly felt sorry for Fonda and Clark. I considered them well intentioned do-gooders who were being duped and exploited at every turn by the fawning Vietnamese Communists. In another way I hated them for their phony concern for the poor and downtrodden. I was convinced that neither of them had wanted for anything their entire lives and, in fact, had been raised smack in the middle of the lap of luxury. I was also convinced that they didn't have an ounce of common sense between them. There might be a lot of things wrong with the U.S. war in Vietnam but for the POW part of it, ours was an honest effort in a basically just cause. Fonda and Clark in the short run would only muddy the POW waters in Hanoi. In the long run they would ultimately have to account for behavior which, if nothing else, aided and abetted our enemies, and caused us by their visits to suffer more mental and physical anguish than was our usual want.

I had long ago in my early years learned to distrust the shrill yells of those self-appointed saviors who occasionally rise to the forefront in a free democracy. I never made any distinction whether they came from the political right or political left. I have never had any taste for either the George Wallaces and Joe McCarthys or the Jane Fondas and Ramsey Clarks. To my way of thinking they are equally dangerous to the American way of life.

I would have preferred however, that those dissidents of the left remain at home in the U.S.A. where they rightfully enjoyed the privilege of opposition rather than come to Hanoi and give mock testimony that everything in the U.S. is bad. Anyone who thought that the slightest iota of freedom existed in Hanoi for the North Vietnamese people certainly didn't recognize the realities of the existing situation in that city.

Yes, they turned my stomach with the lies they were handing out. I was sure that the abject subjugation of the Vietnamese people by the Communist political regime would ultimately be visible to all in the later annals of history. I felt sorry for all the Vietnamese people. Given an opportunity in a free society I felt they would do very well. Under Communism they would develop like a colony of ants, millions united as one going absolutely nowhere and doomed to a life of mediocrity. I am convinced that the world's greatest material development had been achieved not by political direction but by the economic results of human effort in a free society. I feel that history shows that in free societies economics dominates politics, whereas in totalitarian societies the exact opposite prevails. Hanoi is living testimony to the latter's inadequacies.

The air war continued, and the so called Paris Peace Conference dragged on and on as it had for years. We spotted several SAM sites located south of us and watched closely as the U.S. made pinpoint attacks to put them out of commission. The Vietnamese installed new rapid firing anti-aircraft guns close to the camp, and these also were soon singled out for attack by American aircraft. One day during a raid as I looked out the south window, I saw the shadows of incoming rockets. They landed a short distance outside the prison walls and were followed by large explosions which scattered debris over the Hanoi Hilton and blew in some of the closed doors from the concussion waves. When everything settled down, the raids continued but the flak sites were silent and the SAM sites fired no longer on that day.

The air war was truly different now. Obviously the U.S. had introduced many new sophisticated weapon delivery systems. Often when a SAM site fired, we would see seconds later incoming missiles that roared through the sky, leaving vapor trails as they zeroed in towards their newly acquired SAM targets.

In spite of all the American successes we still painfully observed some of our losses. Whenever an American plane took an obvious hit we could hear the Vietnamese guards cheering. Many times some of our lookouts would be able to observe the falling plane. We always watched closely for parachutes which meant the possibility of another POW survivor.

Our POW name list grew as the months passed by. Since the bombing began the previous December, I had added over seventy new POW names to my bank when the end of September arrived. The rate of capture was approaching the levels we experienced during 1967. The only significant difference was the bombing of the Hanoi area seemed to be much more intense. We felt that our losses now were proportionately much less than they had been earlier in the North Vietnam air war.

In September the Vietnamese began blaring their propaganda to us that another group of American anti-war saviors would be visiting us.

The Wing had established a firm policy against the fink release program that the Vietnamese had initiated. In order to stop any further propaganda exploitation of us by such releases, Colonel Flynn had decreed that no one leave without his permission.

In addition to the men in the Camp Unity area of the Hanoi Hilton, we knew that there were other POWs at the Zoo, the Plantation, and other areas in the Hanoi area. We sent the policy out but we were not sure that all the other camps had it. We felt that with the air war going at full force and the Paris Peace talks still meeting, there was a good chance for a fink release.

Our suspicions were confirmed when one member of the American Peace Delegation in Hanoi was the mother of a POW who had until the recent past been one of the "Outer Seven." We expected that in spite of the Wing policy, of which he was aware, he would rationalize his way clear of this proviso and fly home to the States with his mother. He lived up to his established reputation, and took his departure with two of his cohorts, both recent 1972 shootdowns.

It was ironic that these men left so easily when languishing in our camps were other POWs who were critically injured, ill and who had borne the brunt of captivity for seven years or longer.

Of the twelve men who had received early release at Hanoi only one had been authorized to go. That man was Doug Hegdahl, a Navy seaman, who had fallen or been blown from his ship during a night bombardment attack and who had kept himself afloat till capture by passing North Vietnamese fishermen. Hegdahl had been primed to return with names of POWs and tales of the atrocities we were subjected to at the hands of the Vietnamese. He was always a highly respected member of the POW community. The others earned their way home early in one way or another and, of course, must face up to this reality for the rest of their lives.

THE MUSEUM TRIP!

The North Vietnamese were always eager to play tapes over the camp radio made by anti-war Americans. Over the years we had been subjected to the propaganda put out by a wide variety of dissenting Americans, many of whom saw fit to visit Hanoi where they poured forth their anti-American venom.

The latest delegation to arrive was no different from the others in this respect. A few days after their arrival, one of the American females made a tape glorifying the exploits of the North Vietnamese. During her casual vocal meanderings she mentioned how privileged she felt to have been shown the Hanoi War Museum. She said she felt all the POWs should be given the opportunity to visit this museum which she said was filled with remnants of downed American planes and pictures of American atrocities caused by the American bombing.

When I heard this I said to the others, "The next thing you know the Gooks will be dragging us downtown to the War Museum. What a great idea for a propaganda stunt, and just think they got it from some dumb American broad who was shooting off her mouth."

The next night we heard men leaving the camp through Heartbreak Hotel. In the morning we got a flash intelligence message saying a small group of men had been taken to the War Museum. The Blue Staff immediately put out a policy to the camp which said, "Actively resist being taken to the museum." That night the Vietnamese came to one of the squadrons to take the men on the museum tour, but the POWs refused to dress or to leave. Stymied in this effort the North Vietnamese backed off without making trouble. The next morning when we heard of the squadron's successful resistance, we in Blue were elated. Hang tough and actively resist going was the message we sent through the camp that noon.

The night of 25 September after dark when we were locked in our cells, the guards came and took Colonel Flynn to quiz. We heard him scuffle as he left through Heartbreak. In minutes they came for Colonel Winn, then Colonel Gaddis. From the commotion outside our courtyard we could tell that they were forcibly being moved. It's the damn museum trip, I thought.

Next the guards opened our cell door and told Denton, myself and Rutledge to dress for quiz. Stockdale, Jenkins and Hughes would be left behind.

Jerry had his clown suit on and wouldn't leave. The guards overwhelmed him and dragged him outside. I refused to dress so they pounced on me, dragged me outside the gate and forcibly put a quiz suit on me. I fought them off as long as I could, but it was a losing battle. The sheer numbers of them overwhelmed me. They half carried and half dragged me through Heartbreak Hotel and through the long courtyard of the Hanoi Hilton to the main entrance next to New Guy Village. They kicked and punched me all along the way. I was skinned and bruised, but fought on as best I could getting a limb free and returning wild blows and kicks of my own. I took ten in return for each lick I got in. The Vietnamese were wildly angry, getting revenge for the bombing and all the hates they had built up since the torture period had ceased two years prior.

They dragged me out the main gate and across the sidewalk to a waiting bus. Jerry Denton had just been forcibly placed inside and I was next to follow. Kicking, fighting and cursing all the way I was finally violently deposited in a seat and held there.

The last man in was Howie Rutledge. He wasn't even dressed and had his shorts on. They were knocking the hell out of him. When everything settled down there were six POWs in the bus accompanied by twenty-six North Vietnamese and a bus driver.

I had never been moved in Hanoi without being blindfolded and I was not prepared at all for the sights of the city that I saw on this trip.

I was startled to see that the Hanoi Hilton was located downtown in a heavily populated urban area. There were thousands of Vietnamese all over the place, on the sidewalks, in the doorways, and on the streets. Traffic consisted of bicycles, carts, wagons, some army trucks and a few military staff cars. At each street intersection there were security guards and police traffic directors.

Most of the light came from small cooking fires in the doorways of buildings. I could see hundreds of these surrounded by small groups of Vietnamese huddled together around the fires like bands of Boy Scouts on a cookout.

The buildings looked drab and unkempt. The Vietnamese had no preventive maintenance. The whole damn city looked like it needed a good cleaning and painting. I saw a few factories working but all had obviously been the targets of American air strikes. The accuracy of the attackers was amazing, for each factory had sustained direct hit damage yet the surrounding buildings looked untouched.

After winding our way through the streets for some minutes, we came to a stop in front of an official looking building.

The Vietnamese hauled us out, dressed Howie Rutledge, and led us into the museum for our guided tour which would be narrated by Parrot, one of our English-speaking camp guards. We moved more or less in the manner we left our cells, mostly two-by-two with Flynn and Winn leading, followed by Gaddis and Denton. Rutledge and I took up the rear.

The Wing objective had always been for the POWs to resist exploitation as much as possible, and when no longer able to withstand the Vietnamese onslaught, to fall back to a posture where we would do everything to spoil their show.

I felt sure the Vietnamese would film us with well hidden cameras so I held my head down and refused to look at any displays. Parrot tried to get our attention but we refused to cooperate. This angered the guards accompanying us and they used roughhouse tactics to get us to cooperate. This only resulted in more of a commotion.

Howie Rutledge began cursing and yelling at the Vietnamese and I joined in with him. When the guards did anything more physical to us we yelled and cursed. Soon we were being dragged, pushed and shoved from one display to another. Parrot droned on, but you could barely hear him because of the uproar Rutledge and I were causing.

We were all doing our best but fighting a losing battle. They dragged us on and on using more and more force, twisting arms, pulling ears and hair, sneaking in punches to the sides of our rib cages to get us moving.

It was an exhausting experience, but my adrenalin was up so I fought on. I did everything I could to spoil my part of the propaganda show. Finally as we neared the end of the building I spied a group of Vietnamese officers watching the whole episode in rapt attention. I couldn't believe my eyes. One of them was the notorious J.C. or Dum Dum as he had been later known at the Zoo.

When they dragged me past this group, I stopped, pointed my finger at J.C. and shouted as I moved towards him. "I remember you. You people haven't changed. You're the same barbarians. You're still doing the same things you were doing at the beginning."

J.C. sneered in recognition as the guards hauled me away. Next we were led into a movie where they attempted to show us a propaganda show. I closed my eyes and put my head down. They put a guard in each seat on either side of me and two guards behind me. They forced my head up and pulled my hair and twisted my ears in an effort to get me in a good photographic posture. When they let go I would hide my head and turn away repeating my former resistance tactics. I hollered, swore, sweated and fought through the entire show. I could hear Rutledge causing one helluva commotion.

It wasn't a movie, it was a riot. I felt sure that there was no way the Vietnamese could get any good propaganda pictures of me. If they wanted to show me watching a show with four guards holding my head up by my hair and ears, it was ok with me. Finally the show was over with and the lights came on and we were dragged out to the bus.

It was a quiet ride back. I hurt all over. I had been skinned from being dragged and the skin burns were starting to be painful now that my adrenalin had worn off. Even more than the pain, the fear of what would happen to me next completely overcame everything else that had happened. We had fought the Vietnamese in public and I was convinced that once they got us back in the Hilton there would be hell to pay. In the past any time a POW had caused the Vietnamese to lose face, he would receive special attention in retribution for his being impolite.

I was shaking inwardly with fear when we arrived at the main gate. The guards led us singly back into the courtyard and towards Heartbreak Hotel. I felt sure we would each be put in solitary and then tortured for our bad behavior that night. I was surprised when we were led through the Hearbreak hallway, and then into the Blue courtyard and put back in our cells.

Flynn, Winn and Gaddis were locked into their cell and the guards left without ever showing any overt hostility. Denton and Rutledge and I briefed our three other cellmates on the night's acitvities. We were dead tired and we hurt all over, but we had the knowledge that we had done our very best to spoil the museum propaganda effort.

The next morning Parrot led in a group of medics who promptly began painting and bandaging our numerous skinned and sore areas. Times had certainly changed from the bad days of years gone by, when we would have been severely punished for our bad behavior.

On 27 September 1972 the three latest fink releases left for home. I was glad that they took with them the American bitch that had caused our museum troubles. On more than one occasion in the past, a big-mouth American female visiting Hanoi had caused us to be mistreated. I should not have been surprised that even by September 1972 things hadn't changed much.

THE B-52s!

In October the bombing stopped and peace was at hand. Conditions improved greatly in the camp, but things for the seniors in Blue didn't change much except in one major manner. We suddenly had a new cellmate. Colonel Joe Kittinger, U.S. Air Force, captured in May of 1972, joined the nine of us.

He had been leading the resistance movement as the senior man in Building Seven and had caused the new shootdowns to give the Vietnamese fits. The North Vietnamese probably rightly felt that he would cause a revolution in the camp if he were allowed to mix and mingle with the others.

Joe Kittinger is a colorful man who had a fascinating career as an Air Force flyer. Among his many exploits he once had been trained in a high altitude balloon program and had bailed out of one from over one hundred thousand feet of altitude.

Kittinger was my ace in the hole. As the Education and Entertainment Officer in Blue, I had exhausted all avenues of interest from its occupants. Joe Kittinger was a new face with all kinds of news and stories from home. I promptly scheduled him to give a one-hour lecture every night on anything he wanted to talk about. He saw our plight for up-to-date news and outdid himself every night as he kept us on the edge of our bunks listening to his personal escapades or his recital of current world events.

The peace overtures were on-again off-again and for our part, we really couldn't see any changes except once again there was no bombing in Hanoi.

We were approaching Advent and the coming of Christmas once more. I was saddened with self-pity once again. My last Christmas at home with my family was in 1964 and here it was 1972, some eight Christmases later. My boys were grown up. One had married the previous June. Life was passing me completely by and there was nothing I could do about it. Except for Kittinger, who was the new guy on our POW street, the others seemed to be quite subdued like myself. We old timers were slowly running out of gas. It was getting to be one helluva long lousy war for us.

In late November I wrote the rough of my Christmas letter home. It was a chore that had become more difficult as the years passed by.

I felt inadequate trying to help keep my family's spirits up. My written words seemed meaningless. My family seemed far removed from my reality and at times I felt they were just another hallucination from my own minuscule mental world. Their pictures, however, confirmed their existence. They were mine and I theirs, and as long as we breathed it would be that way. But it was sad. Just to think of them was sad. My morale was reaching its lowest depths as the sheer weight of the passing years had worn me down. Lord, You've got to get me out of this place before I lose my mind completely, I prayed silently over and over again, night and day.

It was the night of December 18th. We were locked in our cells almost ready for sleep. A few minutes earlier Joe Kittinger pulled the string attached to a stick holding up a large wash bucket. A rat had gone under it to get the bread he left as bait. Down came the bucket with a crash and another Asian rat was trapped and at the mercy of the great white hunter, Colonel Joe Kittinger. Since he had joined us, rat hunting had become a ritual and he caught one almost every night. The following morning we would club it to death and give it to the Vietnamese guards who marveled at our expertise in rat hunting.

It was chilly. Winter comes fast in Hanoi. The winds blow mostly from the northeast. I was getting ready to raise my mosquito net and was looking forward to enjoying the warmth of all my clothes in the home-made sleeping bag I had stitched together, using my two Vietnamese Army blankets. The wind was whistling in through the barred window over the cell door and blowing out the south cell window directly behind me.

All of a sudden the wails of the air raid warning siren echoed through the camp. Just another low level night recce plane to see if we are still here, I thought silently as I unraveled my net and began raising it. The lights went out and we were plunged into darkness. I looked out the south window scanning the black sky to see if I might catch a glimpse of anything.

Suddenly the missiles from the SAM sites began to roar off into space. One, two, three I counted from one site as they climbed heading north. From the southwest I saw more missiles leap skyward heading in the same general direction as the first group.

Then all hell broke loose, and I heard the rolling thunder of massive strings of bombs going off in the distance. The earth shook violently and the building reverberated wildly. The sky turned white. Glowing missiles were flying in towards the SAM sites that had already fired a few moments earlier. It seemed like every anti-aircraft gun in Hanoi was firing. The rolling thunder of bombs echoed and reechoed.

"It's a B-52 raid Harry," I said to my lookout partner, Commander Jenkins. "Pack your bags. We're going home."

The flak unit just outside of the camp had new high velocity firing guns that peppered the sky. Suddenly a low level night attacker roared directly overhead and dumped a load of ordnance on them. The blast shook the building and firing from that site stopped.

The B-52 action was north of me and I couldn't see much of them. The defenses south of us were constantly under attack from low flying aircraft which roared overhead and into their targets. The white sky turned yellow as a B-52 was hit and exploded, then burned wildly as it fluttered down from high in the atmosphere. Night had turned into day. The strings of bombs came on and on and on. The earth rumbled, retched and shook.

We were jubilant! At last, after all these years of utter frustration, the United States had finally stopped fooling around and had pulled the plug on Hanoi. There's no stopping now, I thought. When the bombing ends this time I'll be going home at last. But as happy as I was I knew that above me Americans were dying in battle. I prayed for their safety and survival.

The heavens rumbled with the roar of the incoming B-52s as they came in a never-ending stream. I figured each one carried about 81 high explosive bombs and they usually flew in groups of three and dropped in unison. Two hundred and forty-three blasts milleseconds apart. They sounded like the burp of a rapid fire Gatling gun, only the noise was a thousand times louder. It must have been a terrifying experience for the North Vietnamese. Hanoi had never before felt the shock from all out bombing. From the beginning it had been conditioned to the gradual escalation of selective target bombing followed by a bombing pause. That type of bombing was a political arm twisting technique doomed to insure military failure. It was an extension of LBJ's Congressional arm twisting. The only thing wrong was that it wouldn't work. The Communists world fights to win. They like long drawn out engagements, and the only thing they truly respect or fear is absolute brute force.

Under the piecemeal bombing of the past, Hanoi could last forever. But now the brute force of total destruction was raining down all around them, and for the first time in the war they felt the shock of knowing that they and their capital city could be absolutely leveled if the U.S. so desired.

I wondered how long it would take before they reached some cease fire agreement. I was sure it wouldn't be long in coming. The ironic part of it all was that the U.S. could have initiated the same type of bombing at any time in the war from 1965 onwards. I remembered the Presidential campaign of 1964. The Executive Department kept Vietnam under such close control even the men on active duty in the military didn't know the scope of activities. Mr. Goldwater was right; either go in to win or get out of Vietnam. I was convinced that this night's B-52 bombing raid was just about seven or eight years too late in coming. My mind rambled wildly! What a terrible price we had to pay in men, money and materials because of this indecision. What a terrible price I paid and my family paid. But it's finally coming to an end. There is no way the Vietnamese government can stand up to this type of pressure on Hanoi. Besides the all out bombing is backed up by the blockade! They'll run out of ammo and missiles and they won't be able to be resupplied as they had been in the previous years. We are doing now what we should have done years ago.

I wondered what finally pushed the U.S. to take this action. They probably double crossed Nixon in the Peace Talks and now that he's in for another four years, he's going to finish the war off quickly. I wondered what happened to his secret plan to end the war which he had announced in the previous election of 1968.

My mind rambled on and on as I watched the battle in the heavens above me. I suddenly felt ten feet tall. For almost seven years I had been a loser in the POW skirmishes with the Vietnamese in Hanoi. I had been bent, broken, bloodied and humbled by them. I was at their mercy for almost seven years when they showed no mercy. I had lived like a caged animal. They had kept me in solitary for more than three and a half years, and the mental miseries I suffered there almost drove me insane. But I had survived. Through the grace of God and the best human effort I could make, I had fought the battle. And now I would soon be free. And when I was freed, I would go home head held high, ten feet tall. These poor bastards, when its all over with, they have nothing to look forward to except their own miseries.

The raid finally ended. The all-clear signal sounded and the lights came back on in the camp. A Vietnamese officer came around with the guard and checked our cell doors and courtyard. They were both totally subdued. Absolute fear was written clearly on their faces.

When they were gone we critiqued the entire raid. Each lookout sector gave a detailed report of what they observed in their areas of responsibility. The attacking Americans had lost a few planes. The massive fires in the skies could only be caused by the huge amount of fuel burning from downed B-52's. Secondary explosions from the bombing were still going off in the distance north of us. The sky flickered with yellow from the fires.

There was a stillness about the camp. The Vietnamese were thunderstruck and in shock. The full realization of the air war had finally come home to them. It was an eerie sensation that I had never before known.

I felt like a free man. The pent-up frustrations of the past years were gone, a direct result of this one massive raid. We had taken losses, but so had the Vietnamese. The missile sites had been struck, the flak sites hammered. Some of them were out of action.

I climbed silently between my blankets and gave a prayer of thanksgiving. I was lying quietly reviewing the meaning of this night's action. It had been incredible! Almost mind boggling! Even for a professional attack pilot like myself, the extent and scope of this bombing attack was hard to believe. Only a nuclear attack could be more devastating and destructive. I had heard it and I had seen it, but I still couldn't believe it. I was wondering what was going to happen next.

Suddenly in the distance I heard the wail of the air raid warning system faintly echo through the night. Two MIGS took off and climbed over head. The Hanoi sirens sounded. Two missiles launched from the southwest headed east as I stood at my lookout post.

Then the B-52's came again in a repeat performance of their previous attack. The targets were mostly east of us but much closer. I could hear the drones from the high flying bombers. They seemed to be passing almost over head.

Once again low flying attackers roared in on flak and missile sites. Some of them sped directly over the camp, and drew rifle fire from the guards in the main courtyard. The second raid seemed even more ferocious than the first. The earth shook and the building rattled from the shock of the explosions. For the Vietnamese it must have truly been Armageddon. The black sky once again turned white from the glare of exploding bombs, missiles and flak. A huge bon fire in the sky lit up the camp as a burning B-52 slowly settled earthward.

But they came on and on and on. Their bombs punishing the targets, scorching the earth and terrifying the populace.

I watched it all in complete calm, with satisfaction. I stood fearless at my lookout post feeling impervious to any injury. It was almost as if I were safe watching a war movie. My mind gobbled up the details of the action. I noted the location of the missile sites, and the direction of flight of on rushing missiles, and the number of attacks against the defenses.

The U.S. was pulling out all stops. Slowly the defenses began to crumble. One by one the SAM sites slowed until there was only an occasional response. Still the bombers came on. When the last one left, the outskirts of Hanoi were ablaze. Finally the all-clear sounded once again and we critiqued this second attack.

I went to bed once again and fell asleep contented in the knowledge that I was on the last lap before I would be going home. I said my prayers and reviewed my POW name bank. It had truly been a glorious night in Hanoi for me.

HANOI'S ARMAGEDDON!

The next day the camp turn keys rushed us through our bathing and clothes washing routine. They looked troubled. Fear was obvious in all of them. It was a new stage of the war and even they must have recognized it as a final one.

The weather was cool and clear. A brisk wind blew out of the north. Suddenly, just as we finished washing, the air raid alarm sounded. The guard rushed us to our cells and slammed the doors shut locking us in. As he left the courtyard, we took our lookout positions.

The air defenses exploded with launching missiles and booming flak. I saw incoming missiles arch towards the SAM sites and explode, raising a great cloud of smoke and dust.

I tracked the SAM missiles as they leaped high in the sky. Some of them turned wildly in erratic uncontrolled patterns. I could see the outline of tactical attack planes coming down through the contrail area as they made high speed approach bombing dives.

I counted twenty-four planes in two attack formations of twelve each. Two missiles still streaked towards them. One plane took a hit which immediately caused it to burst into flames. The smoke poured out as it came crazily to earth. The other missile missed and twenty-three planes came onward. They were in their dives going for the southwest SAM sites. Suddenly I glimpsed four separate attack planes in a shallow high speed dive about five thousand feet above the ground. Three missiles left the site and headed towards the main group. The four-plane division of F-4's pushed in and fired a salvo of rockets at the Russian-made SAM site. The rockets streamed towards the ground and the planes made a hard turn as they took evasive action from the high velocity anti-aircraft fire which was trying to track them. They were heading straight for me when they passed out of my vision, streaking towards the ground to escape missile and flak fire.

I looked back to see the main groups had split further apart. Obviously each had its own target. They launched rockets first, then kept pushing in until they were at a low level directly over their targets. Nothing happened as they sped off into the distance. I was perplexed at this turn of events when suddenly one of the retreating low level F-4's roared by and flew directly overhead on its way home to safety. Seconds later his three division mates roared by jinking and staying at roof top level.

I glanced back to the main attack forces, and they were out of sight, screaming on their way to safety at tree top level.

Suddenly bombs began to explode from where I had seen the SAMs launched. Delay bombs, I mused. They must have scattered them all over the launch area. There were too many explosions to count. In the next five minutes bombs kept going off.

I was watching the bombs explode when I heard the swish of an incoming missile pass low overhead. It exploded a couple of seconds later just outside the main Hanoi Hilton area. It must be a Shrike seeking a radar, I thought.

Shrapnel from the flak rained on our roof top and bounced in the courtyard and ricocheted off the stone walls. More planes were coming in at high level. I saw one burst into flame and then something fall. In seconds I heard the Vietnamese guards cheering. I scanned the sky closely and saw a parachute descending slowly into the Hell of Hanoi. After a while the raid ended, and the all-clear rang. The guards checked our area and seemed more nervous than ever.

At noon another raid came. In the afternoon a third and fourth raid followed.

The air defenses were being used on a sparing basis. Few missiles were fired. Flak sites would alternate shooting at the planes. The Vietnamese were figuring out that the Americans wanted to put out of action all the missile sites defending Hanoi.

It had been an exhausting day for all of us. That night we had two other B-52 raids identical to the previous evening. Each lasted well over an hour.

The air defenses of Hanoi responded with the same ferocity they had the previous night. New missile sites had been brought into play or old ones used. A ring of flak sites was located just outside the south wall of the Hanoi Hilton. The concussion from their firing shook our buildings. I could hear vehicle movement and Vietnamese shouting from the same area. Either they were putting Army defenses in place to prevent another Son Tay type raid for POWs or else they felt that the known existence of the Hilton could deter the U.S. planes from attacking so close to the major POW area.

The B-52's kept thundering in. Their massive string of bombs seemed like an endless chain of 4th of July firecrackers. The secondary explosions and fires gave testimony to the accuracy of their bombing.

The thought never entered my mind that a stray bomb would land in the camp. We felt relatively secure, for the location and purpose of the Hanoi Hilton was well known to the U.S. military airmen. Besides we felt we had an ace in the hole working for us.

In early 1971 when the POWs were first introduced into Camp Unity we watched the erection of a large TV tower just outside the northwest corner of the camp. It went up several hundred feet in the air and towered above anything else in Hanoi. The Vietnamese told us it was a gift from their fraternal brothers the Communist Chinese.

I had been exposed to some of the offset radar bombing techniques that were standard procedures used by attacking aircraft at night or in bad weather. To be most effective these techniques required a significant radar reflected target. One that was permanent, gave a positive radar return on the scope and one that couldn't be easily confused with other radar returns. The TV tower was just such a radar target and it was located right next to the Hanoi Hilton.

If nothing else, every B-52 up there knew exactly where the Hanoi Hilton was. It's the safest place in town, I told myself. I'll bet they are using the TV tower for their radar offset run to the target. A few days later a recently captured B-52 crewman passed us information that confirmed my suspicions.

The size and length of the raids amazed me. There must have been hundreds of aircraft involved. I wondered where the B-52's were coming from. Probably Guam, the Philippines and maybe from South Vietnam, I guessed. The logistics for this force must require a massive effort. I felt sure SAC (Strategic Air Command) had been preparing for years for this occasion. How ironic after all. For years the Carrier Navy Air Arm and TAC (Tactical Air Command) had borne the brunt of the air war effort in North Vietnam. Now SAC was coming to our rescue to finish the war. We couldn't have a better ally than the men in SAC. They were all professional airmen to the core. But they were human, and like ourselves took some losses. Surprisingly few, I thought, for the magnitude of their effort.

The sky stayed white from all the exploding ordnance. It would turn into a yellowish daylight whenever a burning B-52 fell earthward. It seemed to take them so long to fall. I guessed that they were attacking at a height of five or six miles. I wondered how many men were in each crew? I wondered how many would be able to survive and parachute to safety?

Finally the second night of B-52 activities was over. The all-clear wailed. We could see the sky flicker from secondary fires burning north and east of us. I could hear the movement of vehicles outside the south wall, as well as the shouts of the Vietnamese associated with them. I said my prayers, reviewed my names and fell asleep.

The guards were testy the next day. It was a different war now, and they were well aware of the change. They hurried us through our morning wash routine, obviously expecting an early air raid to interrupt us at any time.

Parrot was on duty. He'd been narrator at our museum visit fiasco, but had been embarrassed by the whole affair. Since I had known him over the past three years he had treated us quite fairly. I took one look at his face and I could tell he was scared to death. "Hurry, hurry, Mun. Wash quickly," he said to me. I got up from the washtub and walked over to him. "Parrot, I don't want to see you get hurt. Take my advice and do not go out of the camp. It's the safest place in Hanoi. Tell Hawk and Icabod also. You stay here in camp with us, and you will be safe from the bombs. They know we are here," I said pointing skyward. "Finish your wash quickly," he retorted and I returned to the washtub and completed my chores.

At mid-morning the tactical air attackers returned again; they were after the missile and flak defenses. Intelligence must have been good because I saw them head for areas that were the new sites the previous night.

I heard the roar of low flying incoming aircraft and I glimpsed a string of rockets pass directly overhead and fly into the area just outside the south wall. I couldn't see most of the planes but from their roar I guessed about eight were in that particular attack. They pumped a very large number of small rockets into the general area very close to me. They can't drop bombs because the flak sites are too close to the Hilton, I said to myself. As a professional military man, I was pleased with their performance. They are taking out the air defenses one by one, I thought as I scanned the sky for other incoming raiders.

The Vietnamese did not fire one SAM missile from any of the sites south of us that I knew were active sites. They are either out of action or else saving what they have for any further B-52 raids, I guessed.

The incoming attackers hammered away with their bombs, facing only flak and small arms fire in return. There were no Vietnamese cheers and I didn't see any planes in my area get hit, so I assumed they took no losses.

The raid ended as suddenly as it began. The all-clear sounded and Parrot and the kitchen help brought in the noon meal of rice and soup. He made us dish it out quickly and then we ate in our own cells. Because of the frequency of the raids, our daily routine was changed rapidly; no more communal meals for the ten of us in the barred room which had served as our dining area the past sixteen months.

The camp army personnel were tense and nervous. The officers seemed to recognize the urgency of their situation more than the guards. They would pop into our courtyard during raids to see that we were on our bunks. Our front clearance was excellent, and they never caught any of us at our lookout posts.

We had great camp communications. The Thais and Max suddenly had to bring more dishes and food to the Heartbreak and New Guy Village areas. They reported numerous new prisoners, and also that a large group of POWs had been moved into the Little Vegas area. We guessed the group came from the Zoo and Plantation.

The Vietnamese had isolated one of the old time POWs who was quite sick. They began moving newly injured POWs in with him. He was able to pass notes with the returning dishes via the Thais and they in turn fed the info to us directly in Blue. We got names, descriptions of injuries and much intelligence info on the extent of the B-52 raids.

Night and day the U.S. hammered at Hanoi. The missile defenses were being weakened by the attacks of tactical air incoming missiles that sought out a site everytime it launched a missile or turned up its acquisition radar.

The weather stayed good. We watched the daylight attacks and were able to identify numbers and types of the attackers and the targets they were after. After the first few days, air opposition by defending MIGS had vanished completely. Flak firing was noticeably reduced, and missile firing almost non-existent in daylight hours.

At night, defenses were more active when the B-52's came in. But each night we saw less and less anti-aircraft flak and missile opposition. The attacks never slowed one bit.

Each day and night they came in a never ending steam of death and destruction. Night was like day during B-52 attacks. The strings of bombs rained all around us; north, east, south and west as the B-52's ate up their targets one by one.

We could see the city proper was not being leveled. It did take damage from falling aircraft and bombs which never reached their re-lease point but that was beyond the control of the SAC professionals, and to be somewhat expected in such ferocious onslaughts against heavy air defense.

A hush seemed to come over the city and the usual vehicular traffic and street noises were conspicuous by their absence. Even the voices of the camp personnel were subdued. The shock from the massive bomb-ing attacks was taking hold. I wondered if the Vietnamese had evacuated the citizens of Hanoi to remote outlying areas. I concluded this was a remote possibility for the massive bombing must have come as a com-plete surprise to the nation's leaders. The peace talks had been going on and according to the news from Hanoi Hannah, there seemed to be some hope of solution. Yes, the massive bombing must have come suddenly as a response to a breakdown in the talks, and that would give little time for evacuation even if the North Vietnamese rightfully gauged the enormity of the new U.S. air effort against them.

The city was silent because its citizens were afraid. It was a city dominated from the sky night and day. It couldn't last much longer under the deluge of continuous attack. Something would have to give, and I was sure it would be the North Vietnamese government.

The last big raid came at night early on Christmas Eve. Then the U.S. took a twenty-four hour respite in honor of that Holy Day.

We had our full church service in the barred room late Christmas morning. It was complete with joyful hymns of the occasion, our patriotic prayer, the Pledge of Allegiance, and a beautiful homily. We broke bread together and wished each other well. We prayed for the early end of the war and a quick return home. It was a Christmas with real hope. The first one that I ever had in Vietnam.

Though not a feast, the noon meal was much better than normal. The soup was laced with meat and broth. We even had some fresh green vegetables. The camp personnel seemed relaxed and assured of a day of safety from air attack.

Promptly at noon an unmanned recce plane flew low overhead and turned directly over the camp. I just happened to be in the front window, and caught a full glimpse of it as it flashed by. "I guess they just want to make sure we're still here," I said to my fellow cellmates. It had come in so fast and so low that the Vietnamese didn't get a shot off at it, or even sound the alarm until it was on its way back home.

It had been a quiet day. We received some short six line letters from home in the afternoon. Later Icabod brought us some family pictures. The Vee had screened them but got them mixed up so we went through the pile he had in a box and took out those we could identify as ours.

I went to sleep shortly after the toscin rang and we had finished our nightly ritual by reciting the Lord's Prayer and singing our version of Taps. I wondered what the morrow would bring. Things had gotten so exciting since the 18th, the full impact of Christmas had been lost. I was too busy even to think of myself or my family. For the first time since my capture, I wasn't lonely. It's got to end soon, I told myself, and when it does I'll soon be on my way home.

The moaning of the air raid alarm woke me from my sleep. The B-52's were back on schedule after a twenty-four hour lay off. The earth shook and shuddered. The sky turned white. The flashes from the bombs illuminated the sky just southeast of us. It looked like the grand finale of the annual 4th of July fireworks display I had witnessed as a lad at the Municipal Stadium in Lawrence, Massachusetts. But this was no show. It was for real. These were real bombs, real planes, real targets, real missiles, real flak, real blasts. Real people were dying out there on the ground and in the air.

I was sure that short of Nagasaki and Hiroshima, the world had never seen any bombing of this magnitude.

Midway through the raid, it was clearly evident that the defenses of Hanoi were crumbling. Low level tactical aircraft attacked what few missile sites fired. The flak fire was half what it had been prior to Christmas. By God they are winding down. I'll bet they are running out of ammunition and missiles; and with the blockade there's no way they can be suitably resupplied. My mind wandered wildly from one thought to another.

We had a good communications link with the new POWs. Many of them were wounded or injured. They sent us excellent intelligence information.

In turn they were receiving the wing policies on POW behavior. My name bank increased at a rapid rate. The new list of 1972 arrivals was now over one hundred. In addition I held three hundred fifty-three good POW names from the old group in Hanoi plus some names of Army men and civilians captured in South Vietnam who were now in the north.

Our established wing policy for release had been in effect for some years. The release order would be sick and wounded first, then all other POWs in order of shootdown.

We even had a list of the sick and wounded for the longtime POWs. We had to do this because some of these men didn't want to accept a release priority because of their health. The Wing Staff and Colonel Flynn thought otherwise so we had the list made up by impartial Squadron Commanders. Thus if you were on this list you were going to go home at the first release and this was a wing directive.

We had become by the end of 1972, a very tight-knit military command engaged in a military operation. We all had designated responsibilities. The Squadron Leaders and seniors had the responsibility of preparing evaluation reports on each POW's performance, which would be a part of his official military record on return home.

The day after Christmas we got an urgent message from a newly arrived POW. He was a B-52 crewman who had been wounded before he bailed out of his burning plane the previous night. The message said, "Gooks suing for peace. Bombing ends in a couple of days, then war is over."

We were elated at this piece of info, and immediately reviewed the release policy. We instructed any POWs taken to quiz to be sure and state the exact release policy to the quiz master. We wanted the Vietnamese to know we were united on this issue.

The American raids continued to pound Hanoi day and night. The intensity of the B-52 effort never seemed to slacken. The Vietnamese in the camp were terrified and this was plainly evident for all of us to see.

Parrot half-joked that he wasn't going downtown this week on his day off. By now it must have been apparent to him and the others that indeed the Hanoi Hilton was the safest place in Hanoi.

The American planes drew almost no return fire as they raced around in clear daylight looking for targets. The B-52 raids at night were almost unopposed. Defenses were probably down to ten percent of what they had been at the beginning of the massive air offense on the 18th of December.

We had the last B-52 raid on the night of the 29th. It was as ferocious as the initial one on the 18th. Hanoi rumbled and groaned. A dying city brought to its knees. I saw no SAM missiles fired. Hanoi was virtually defenseless against air attack.

The 30th dawned bright and clear. The winter air was crisp as I took my daily wash by dousing myself with a couple of buckets of cold water I got from the cistern.

Our routine was not interrupted by any air raid warnings. There was a stillness in the camp that almost seemed like the calm before the storm. We waited all day and when nothing happened and there was no night raid, we knew that it was finished. Peace must be at hand, and we were about to come out of the tunnel of capitivity and enter the light of freedom.

I prayed thankfully that night, and reviewed in my mind the events of the past years. It was almost dawn before I fell asleep.

1973

The air war had stopped as suddenly as it had started. Almost every day we heard the supersonic boom from the high altitude recce that flew so fast nothing was ever fired against it.

The camp was quiet and the peace talks were back on. The guards recovered from the shock of the B-52 raids. They caused us no trouble. Everyone sensed that the war was about finished, and we would be leaving Hanoi soon.

LIBERATION AND FREEDOM

The North Vietnamese read the stipulations of the Peace Treaty to us in January and we knew that all of the POWs would be repatriated within sixty days. The following day the men in Blue were told to pack up their gear in preparation for a move. We said our goodbyes and awaited the movement.

Jim Stockdale, Jerry Denton, Harry Jenkins, Howie Rutledge and I were moved to Building Seven where we were joined by many of the early shootdowns. The Vietnamese were trying to divide the POWs into groups according to date of capture. Building Seven housed most of the senior and early shootdowns. It was a joyous reunion for us.

Most of the men were quite a bit younger than the men from Blue. They had established a daily educational and entertainment program to keep their minds active. Every night they had a movie where one of the group of movie experts gave the complete story for the night's movie. It was a refreshing experience. They even had an intermission break to enable us to have a drink, walk around or make a trip to the bathroom. They also had a polished choir which sang all the church service hymns in harmony and on key.

I spent hours talking to Jerry Coffee, Brad Smith, Ev Alvarez and the others whom I had been in contact with at one time or another, but actually had never met before. Living with these men was a joyful experience. As a result I felt better mentally and physically than I had since before I was first captured.

We were on our final wait and then it would all be over at last. I didn't even grow impatient. I knew the big day was not too far in the distance.

As usual the Vietnamese had problems trying to sort out the POWs. They moved some men to other camps at the Plantation and Zoo and then had to move them back to the Hilton once they discovered their mistake. This enabled us at the Hilton to have an exact run down of just where all the POWs were and who was in charge.

In early February they let all of the POWs in Camp Unity go out in the recreational area at the same time. I met many men whose names I had carried since their shootdown, but whom I had never met or seen before.

All the POWs were back in Hanoi from the China border camps. I learned the sad news that John Fredericks, the Marine sergeant who had first taught me the POW tap code in April 1966, had died the previous summer from an Asian disease when he was in the camp near China. The Vietnamese also told us that Ron Storz, J.J. Connell, Ken Cameron and Ed Atterbury had all died.

On the tenth of February they gave me a big bundle of letters and a batch of pictures from home which they had been withholding from me for some years. Though the news in them was outdated, it did give me the opportunity to have a better idea of what had gone on with my wife and sons.

On the night of 11 February, the first group of POWs scheduled for release was outfitted with going-home clothes and shoes. They gave us a ditty bag with soap, and toothpaste. It was a carry-all for the few personal belongings I would take home. Besides my personal letters and pictures I only took my drinking cup as a memento of that horrible place.

Sleep came hard for us that night. The excitement was just too much to take. We talked and joked and reminisced of what happened to us since we were captured. Finally exhausted, I turned in, said my night prayers and fell asleep.

The next morning when they came for us we lined up in order of shootdown. The sick and wounded would be first. The Vietnamese were well aware of the Wing's go home policy and they didn't do anything to upset it.

We had to wait in line in the main courtyard for the bus transportation to come. One of the men had to go to the bathroom so he went in to the New Guy Village facility. On the way back he saw two cell doors closed. He opened one and found a German nurse who was being held captive. In the second room he found the last captured American who had been a rear seat man and shot down in South Vietnam on the last day before the cease fire. The pilot of his plane did not show up as a POW, and was thought not to have survived.

Finally we boarded the buses and slowly made our way through Hanoi towards the airport. The trip was a far cry from the downtown trip to the Museum we had made the previous September.

The city was drab and in disrepair, showing the strain from a prolonged war. Some of the curious citizens half waved to us as we passed by. It was a half-hearted gesture which none of us saw fit to return. The main part of the city seemed undamaged from the massive bombing. It was a different story on the outskirts, however.

We crossed the river slowly on a pontoon bridge. I could see the main span of the permanent bridge had been dropped at the center by accurate bombing.

The outskirts were leveled for miles. It was truly an awesome sight. The ground was bare with tremendous blotches of bomb potholes. Whole sections of the primitive road structure had been destroyed. Hardly a tree was standing and those that were had been damaged and were leafless. The earth looked as barren as pictures of the surface of the moon I had seen.

Gia Lam airport was a disaster. Nothing was standing for miles around it. The area had borne the brunt of the B-52 effort.

The Vietnamese kept us for awhile in a building a couple of miles from the field while they waited for the American C-141's to land and pick us up. They offered tea and sandwiches, but we were too excited to partake of either.

Finally we heard the drone of incoming aircraft. Soon we saw a glistening silvery C-141 transport enter the pattern and land. A second followed it in minutes. The first and second buses left and headed for the ramp area at the makeshift tower.

I was senior man when we loaded the third and last bus. The entire trip from the Hilton to Gia Lam had been for the most part quite subdued. Little emotion was being shown. The shock of release finally being at hand was too much for us to handle. It wasn't so much the uncertainties of our future freedom as it was of the past memories which caused this stillness.

I looked at the scars on my wrists from the ropes and the gasoline. I thought of the torture, the beatings, the starvation and loneliness. The utter misery of solitary confinement. Alcatraz and all of its horrors flashed before me. I thought of them all. Rutledge and Jenkins; Johnson and Shumaker; Storz and Tanner; Coker and McKnight; Denton and Stockdale and myself. But mostly I thought about Ron Storz. And I was sad for him and his family and for all those countless others who wouldn't return. We had all done our very best. It had been a damn lousy war. More than most, in our hearts we knew it, because we had paid a terrible price.

This was the only good day I would ever have in North Vietnam, and it would only become good when I boarded that plane and flew out of this damn country. I had spent 2522 days here and I hated every damn one of them. They were firmly etched deep in my mind. I couldn't forget them even if I wanted to. They were as much a part of me as an arm or a leg.

In one way I had been a loser for all of those days, yet in another way I had much to be thankful about. For out of the miseries had come strength; out of the suffering, compassion; out of hate, love. If nothing else, I would come home a better man than when I entered there. Life would be more meaningful in every aspect from now on. Freedom, integrity, moral character had new and stronger meanings for me. I knew that I could face the future with faith and hope. I had learned firsthand that in life's darkest hours in Hanoi, God's grace had shone down upon me. In my heart I knew that during my captivity I had lost all the battles, but had won the war because I had done my best. I had paid the price. I had day by day put myself on the line for what I believed in. Alone and in solitary, when no one knew and no one cared, I and the others had fought the good fight. If nothing else, I cared, and they cared. There was no easy way. When the chips were down we did what we had to and we paid the price with physical and mental pain.

Now that it was over, we could go home with heads held high. We would walk erect as free men taking our rightful place in a free world. The man who appreciates freedom the most is the free man who has become a slave. We were leaving Hanoi, slaves no more.

Two planes left and I waited for the third to arrive. Finally it came, settled gracefully to the runway and made its way back next to the waiting C-130 which was serving as a Command Post for the operation.

The bus drove to the ramp area next to the makeshift tower. We unloaded in military fashion. Being senior I had them form in ranks of two. I was about to give the marching order when I spied the Vietnamese guard known as Hawk standing behind the bus in view of me, but hidden to the other Vietnamese and Americans. He smiled, snapped to attention and gave me a farewell salute. I returned it snappily and barked, "Left face, forward march," as we headed for the designated release area.

Hawk was tough but Hawk was fair. He had been with Jerry Denton and me ever since he brought us back from Alcatraz in December 1969, over three years previously. He's the only North Vietnamese I ever had any respect for. Now I felt sorry for him. The poor bastard, stuck forever in this God forsaken country, I thought as I put him out of my mind.

At the edge of the roped release area I gave, "Platoon halt." The area was covered with a makeshift canopy made out of an old parachute which was blowing and flapping from the wind. On my left was a table covered with a white cloth. Four Vietnamese sat behind it. One was Frenchy, the Camp Commander at Alcatraz when we left Ron Storz. I didn't recognize the others who obviously outranked him. Rabbit and Slick stood a few paces in front of the table facing us. Several rows of chairs were in a semi-circle behind the table and housed visiting dignitaries from the Communist leadership who were here to attend the release ceremonies. Among them sat Mickey Mouse, Bug, Lump, Rat, Dum Dum, Spot, Slopehead and others I had seen at one time or another during my incarceration.

Only the Cat was missing!

Rabbit started snarling instructions. I wanted to leap at him and smash him and the others. I couldn't stand them singly, never mind seeing them all at once. In a flash the remembrance of time past, those terrible times, caused a terrible anger to arise in me. Hate oozed out of my eyes and I could have killed them one by one.

Then he called out, "Commander James Mulligan." I said, "Here," and stepped forward and saluted the waiting American Air Force Colonel to whom I was being turned over. We shook hands and he passed me to

Captain Jim Mulligan being released at Gia Lam Airport — Hanoi, D.R.V. 12 Feb. 1973

an Air Force enlisted man who took my arm and led me towards the waiting C-141.

I was free! This was the moment I had been waiting for. I half ran towards the safety of the waiting C-141 when the fullness of the emotion of that happy time hit me. I started sobbing. The tears ran uncontrolledly down my cheeks. It was the pent-up sadness of 2522 days filled to the brim and finally bursting over.

I climbed the stairway to the plane aided by my escort and stepped aboard. I took the nearest seat, put my head in my hands and cried like a baby.

She sat next to me and put her arm around me to comfort me. "It's ok, Captain Mulligan," she said. "It's all over with, and we are going to take you home." I rubbed the tears away with my forearm, got my composure and said, "Thanks, I guess the excitement of this day has been a little too much for me." She was one of the flight nurses, maybe 28 or 30 years old. "You're the first American woman I've seen in seven years," I said. "It's been such a long time I forgot how beautiful they are."

She laughed and said, "It's my lucky day, too. You see this POW bracelet I'm wearing? It has your name on it."

I looked at the stainless steel bracelet and read its inscription. "Capt. James A. Mulligan, Jr. 3-20-66."

We'd heard something about the POW bracelets from the 1972

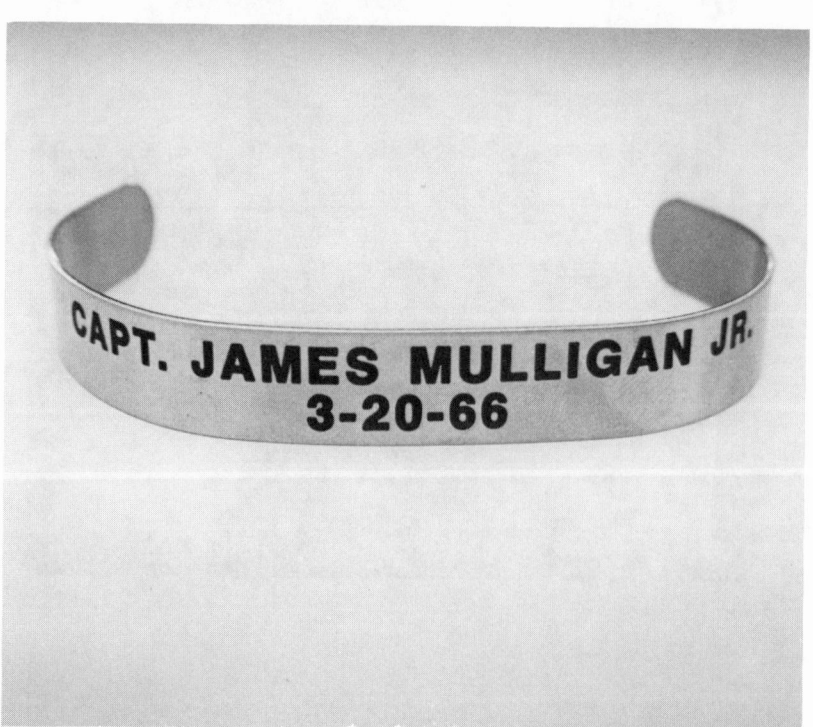

shootdowns. It was an effort the POW wives had made to get public opinion behind their movement. "Thanks for wearing it," I said, "I'm flattered."

Just then some of the other POWs were climbing aboard the plane. Like me, they were in tears and overcome by emotion.

I got up and made my way forward and was greeted by a man in civilian clothes. "I'm Captain Jim Mulligan," I said. "I'm senior man here, do you have any instructions?" "No Jim," he replied. "I'm Frank Sieverts of the State Department, and I have known Louise and your family for a long while now. I'll brief you on your family after we take off."

The last of the POWs were aboard and the engines were quickly started. We taxied out to the runway. The last tears had been dried and there was a strange silence from the emancipated. We were all holding our breaths as if time had stopped. Maybe it's a dream! Maybe it isn't true! It can't be! The thoughts flashed through my mind.

Then with a roar the take off roll began and we lumbered down the bumpy runway gaining speed toward lift off. We lurched into the air. "Gentlemen, we're airborne," the pilot said over the loud speaker system. The plane echoed with the cheers and yells of liberation. We were on our feet, pounding each other on the back, hugging the nurses, grasping each other's hands. It was pandemonium, and it lasted till everyone had greeted everyone else. "We made it! We made it! We made it!" Over and over! And over and over! "We made it!"

I took a seat next to Frank Sieverts. "Frank, I need a tape recorder. Do you have one? I'm a memory bank." "We're all set to go," he said as he pointed me towards a recorder and headset at the navigator's table.

I recited my memory bank of POW names A thru Z and passed as much information as I could under the circumstances. More detailed debriefing would have to come later on the ground.

I gave four hundred and fifty-nine names of known live POWs. When I finished I looked up and said, "That's it, Frank." "This info will be in Washington before we land in the Philippines," he replied.

The pilot announced that we were leaving North Vietnam and heading over the South China Sea. Again the tumultuous cheers rang out.

It was the happiest flight I'd ever have. I was completely overwhelmed. I said a silent prayer of thanks to the Lord.

Frank told me about Louise and how she had been the East Coast founder of the POW wives organization. How she had worked night and day on my behalf. How she had won the respect of the political establishment in Washington. "Louise had us all jumping through hoops," he said. "She just wouldn't give up on you. She's been to see everyone: Nixon, Kissinger, Haig, Scowcroft, Kennedy, Admiral Moorer, and the Joint Chiefs of Staff. When you find out the things she has done on your behalf, you'll be proud of her," he concluded.

As we neared the Philippines, Frank Sieverts came to me and said, "Jim, as senior man, you'll have to say a few words after you're on the ground." I sat and composed my thoughts. As I finished, the "fasten your seat belts" came on as we were on final approach for landing.

The door to the C-141 opened. I heard my name echo over a public address system. Then I stepped out into the Philippine sunshine before a cheering crowd of hundreds of Americans who were lined up behind a rope restraining barrier. Admiral Noel Gayler, Commander-In-Chief of the Pacific was at the bottom of the ramp to greet me. I was overwhelmed as I saluted and said, "Captain Jim Mulligan, United States Navy reporting for duty, Sir!" "Welcome home Jim, we're all proud of you," he replied, as he led me up to a microphone to say a few words.

The cheers from the crowd was an unexpected but pleasant surprise. They were genuinely wildly exuberant, and as happy about our being freed as we were. Hundreds of children of all ages were screaming and cheering and waving "Welcome Home" signs.

At the microphone I addressed them as follows: "It has been our privilege to serve you Americans these many years, and during this time our Faith in God, our country and our families never wavered." I went on to thank President Nixon and the American people for making this great day possible.

We boarded the bus and were taken to the hospital for our initial physical examination. As I was checked in a nurse said to me, "I just saw you on TV. You sounded great."

I didn't quite understand her and she saw my puzzlement. "Don't tell me you didn't know you were on TV," she said. "That's right, I had no idea about TV. I just thought I was speaking to the people at Clark Air Force Base," I replied. "Captain, you were talking to the world. You were talking to your wife and family and friends. Your arrival at Clark is being sent via satellite to TV stations all over the world. There's a replay coming up in a few minutes. Watch it on my set with me."

I couldn't believe my eyes when I saw the replay. "Lord I guess I have been gone a long time. I didn't realize that TV coverage was now world-wide. I guess there's a lot of new things I'll have to get accustomed to," I said to her. It was the understatement of the century.

THE FIRST PLANE HOME!

The security they placed on the POWs in the hospital made the security in the Hanoi Hilton look like child's play. They had us in the standard hospital uniform of the day, pajamas, slippers and robes. Nurses and guards were everywhere. We couldn't get off the floor because the elevator and staircase were off limits and under guard.

Each of the POWs was assigned his own personal military aide who would be responsible to assist him to go through his physical exam and help him get squared away with his military uniforms and personal needs. Lieutenant Commander Jerry Fogle was assigned as my aide.

Fortunately for me he had served a tour of duty as an aide to an Admiral so he knew how to get things done.

"What are your instructions Sir?" he asked after our initial introduction. "Jerry, I want to be on the first plane that goes back to the states," I replied. "You just keep me moving as fast as you can and make sure you see Captain Denton's aide and tell him to get moving. I want us to be together going home." "Yes Sir," he answered. "I'll get you moving as fast as possible."

It seemed like we milled around for hours visiting and getting to meet new shootdowns who were wounded or injured. We were all getting hungry. Most of us had eaten very little in Hanoi because we were too excited.

The delay in our feeding was due to the doctors. They were worried about our physical condition, and weren't sure what we should be fed. Finally common sense prevailed and they allowed us to go to the hospital cafeteria and eat whatever we wanted.

Soon we were escorted down to the cafeteria and formed a long line in the hallway. We were shielded from all contact with anyone not directly involved in our medical program. The nurses took no nonsense from us. We behaved like obedient children in a well run parochial school.

I was standing in line waiting for the cafeteria doors to open. I saw a door marked "Chaplain", eased it open and peeked in. I checked to see if I could sneak away from the nurse escorts. When they turned their backs I slipped in unnoticed and saw a man in an Army officers uniform in an adjoining room. "I'm Jim Mulligan, a POW," I said. "I'm looking for a Catholic Chaplain. "You've found him, Father MacNamara," he replied extending his hand. "It's been a long time away from Confession and Communion for me, Father. Very close to seven years." "How did it go with you and the Lord, Jim?" he asked. "Overall ok. I think I'm coming home a better man and a better Christian than when I went in. Years ago, back in Hanoi when I had been in solitary for a couple of years, I thought about the time that Christ healed the lepers and told them to go show themselves to the Priest. I vowed that if I ever got out alive I'd go show myself to the Priest at the first opportunity. The sign on your door beckoned me in to fullfill that promise."

"Would you like Communion, Jim?" "Yes Father, very much." He put his hand on my head, gave me absolution and brought me Communion. I put my head in my hands as I knelt in thanksgiving prayer for a few minutes. When I raised my head he indicated that I could be seated.

"Jim, you are coming back into a new world. It's a lot different from the world you left back in 1966. It's going to be very hard for you to accept many of the changes. Most of all you are coming back to a different Catholic Church. I want you to promise me that you won't make any hasty decisions. Give yourself time to adjust to it all. There has been a lot of upheaval in the country and in the church but things are beginning to settle down. I'll be saying Mass at 1215 tomorrow noon in the little Chapel across the hallway. Try to come. You'll find things very different,

Freedom at last — Clark AFB Philippines
12 Feb. 1973

but don't be shocked. We really have made a lot of very nice changes," he said.

"Thanks Father. I promise I'll go slow and I'll try to be at Mass tomorrow noon if my schedule allows."

I said goodbye, peeked out the doorway and saw the line just begin to move as the cafeteria doors opened. I was back in my place having not been missed. It was a good feeling. Absolution and Communion in such a brief time. I wondered about the changes in the church and promised myself I'd try to get to Mass to see for myself just what Father MacNamara was talking about.

I had forgotten what American food was like and was overwhelmed by the choices available to me. I settled for steak and eggs, French fries and two half pints of milk. Then I had a piece of apple pie and vanilla ice cream for dessert.

I devoured everything on the plates with such eagerness that I failed to notice a TV crew who were filming me dining for the entire world to see. I was filled completely and returned quickly to my hospital room so that I could begin going through the release physical examination.

My aide Jerry Fogle brought a Chaplain over to see me. He explained that the Chaplain had word from home and wanted to talk to me about my family.

"Jim, I have letters for you from your wife and children. Lots of things have happened to your family and relatives since you left. The letters will explain everything. But please sit down while I give you the sad news," said the Chaplain.

I sat on the bed. For sometime I had had a hunch that my father had died. I got the clue from a letter where Louise said she had visited my mother. Since Dad and Mom were always together I feared that she was trying to tell me that Dad was gone, but I wasn't sure.

"Jim, your Dad died while you were gone. Your Mom is fine," he said. "I half suspected that," I said, but the reality of the shock brought tears to my eyes. "There's one more sad thing I have for you, Jim. Your brother John died also."

I was stunned! John and I were very close. He was three years younger than I. I wasn't prepared for this. It was too much, and though I tried to restrain myself, I broke down completely. I stuck my face in a pillow and forced back the tears and sobs. "Damn! Damn! Damn!" I said in anger. I bit my lip and regained my composure. "Is that all the bad news?" I asked. "Yes," he replied as he handed me a stack of letters from Louise and my six sons. "Thanks Chaplain, I'm ok. I think I can handle things now." He left and I read each letter beginning with Louise's and then going down the line from number one son to number six.

The letters were reassuring, full of news and love. They were all waiting for me to come home. I reread them all, line by line, devouring each piece of information. My family was fine. It must have been terribly hard on them but they persevered through it all. And they were waiting for me with all their love.

Jerry Fogle came in. "Are you ok, Captain?" I nodded, "I'm fine,

Jerry. I had some sad news about my Dad and my kid brother. They died while I was gone. But my wife and sons are fine."

Jerry said, "We are moving fast. You can make a phone call home now if you're ready. I had to wait until you had seen the Chaplain and read your personal mail." "Let's go," I said and he led me to a room that had been set up for us to make phone calls.

The call went through immediately. I heard the operator say to one of my kids, "Is Mrs. Mulligan there? She has a call from Captain Mulligan in the Philippines." I could hear the pandamonium. "Mom, it's Dad!" he yelled. And she came on, "Jim, Jim is it you?" "I love you, Louise," I said. I could hear her cry with joy. "I'm fine, Louise. I have all the news. I got all your letters from you and the boys."

I talked to everyone. It was so dramatic, I couldn't contain myself. The tears rolled down my cheeks. When I had finished talking to Neil, my youngest son, I said, "Put Mom back on. Louise, I love you and I'll be home as soon as I can finish this physical. I'll call you tomorrow." We said our goodbyes and I hung up. I turned to my waiting aide and said, "Ok Jerry, let's get moving. I've got to get out of this place and get home." "Yes sir," he responded.

I got started on my physical right away that night. This would be a standard military procedure and I knew that I wouldn't be heading home until every square on my health form had been filled in and initialed off.

I managed to get a lot completed that night. When I returned to my floor, I visited with all my close acquaintances, especially Jerry Denton and the Alcatraz gang. We exchanged our sad news and consoled one another on our losses.

I had a hasty lunch the following noon and quickly made my way to the Chapel for Mass. It was so different; I was lost completely. I tried to follow and pray but the changes were all too distracting. Gone was the Latin, gone the prayers at the foot of the altar, gone the last Gospel and the closing Litany which I had learned in my earliest childhood. He gave me Communion and I drank from the cup, an experience I'd never had or seen before. Then it was over and I left confused and hurt. I rushed about my physical exam the rest of the day. In my mind I couldn't get rid of the apprehension I felt about my Catholic Mass experience. I don't know, I'll just have to give it a chance and wait and see, I said mentally.

The following afternoon I asked Jerry Fogle to find out how the schedule for the return-home flight would be set up. He returned quickly, stating that a Command Center was set up in the hospital and when the first POW was cleared for release they would inform the Command Center in Washington. The air lift planes would then be dispatched to begin the air lift home. "They don't expect to activate the plan for a couple of days," he added.

I looked over my physical exam sheet and quickly calculated I could have everything done by mid-morning the next day. Jerry and I conferred with the doctor assigned to me. "Release me now, Doc," I said. "I can't; you're not completed," he replied. "Look Doc, I can get the rest of this stuff done tonight and tomorrow morning. The Command Center won't activate anything until someone is formally released. The soonest any plane will be ready to go will be by tomorrow afternoon. If you wait till I complete in the morning I'll have to sit around for another day before leaving." He looked at me skeptically and hesitated about taking the big step. "Dial the Command Center, Jerry," I instructed my aide. "Come on Doc, you've got to release me now so we can get this operation started." Jerry handed me the phone. "Command Center, this is Captain Mulligan. My doctor wants to tell you something. Go ahead, Doc, tell them," I said, as I handed him the phone. "Captain Mulligan is cleared and ready to return to the United States," he said and hung up. "Thanks, Doc. My beautiful Polish wife and my six sons thank you too."

I sent my aide to see Jerry Denton's aide to let him know the news. "Tell him to keep Captain Denton moving" for I knew that my old cellmate was often prone to move a little slowly.

One by one they made up the list that night. I kept close tabs and finally relaxed when Jerry Denton's doctor cleared him for release and his name was added to the list. It would be a great trip home for both of us. Our families were living in Virginia Beach and we would be flown to Norfolk, Virginia and assigned to the Portsmouth Naval Hospital for our detailed physical, debriefing and rehabilitation.

We left Clark Air Force Base the following afternoon in a C-141, and flew all night, crossing the various time zones and the international date line.

On departure from Clark we received a royal send off from the cheering spectators who gathered to see us off. There was something about the spontaneity of the celebrations we received on arrival and departure. I couldn't quite understand them. I wasn't prepared for the sudden acclaim. For years the Vietnamese had been brainwashing us with the thoughts that back in the States, except for a few, no one really cared about the POWs. After hearing the anit-war Americans in Hanoi, and after seeing some of the anti-war movies, I tended to half believe that we were ear-marked as social outcasts.

But just the opposite seemed to be true. Everyone connected with Operation Homecoming seemed personally concerned for the well being of each of us. After suffering years of subjugation, humiliation, isolation, and degradation the sudden acclamation and kindness I received from everyone I met touched me deeply.

Obviously the Vietnam War had left a terrible scar on the average American. As wars go, it had been a real lousy war for all of us. Maybe the homecoming of the POWs was the only good thing to come out of that damn war. I certainly felt that our release was the first good thing the average American had to cheer about since the moon landing.

As long-time POWs we were certainly big losers. We didn't win anything in Hanoi from day one there till the day we left. Yet in spite of it all, we could return, heads held high. We knew what we believed in, even if half the country didn't. We had paid the price for being Americans. You could see it in our eyes and hear it in our voices. Our families had paid the price also. The country had a massive guilt complex about the war, and we were living testimony to its fruitlessness. So they showed us their thanks by the welcome home greetings at every stop we made. I was proud to be an American and even more proud of the American people, especially the youth. They really showed us their great compassion, and I was most appreciative.

We landed in Hawaii to refuel before continuing on our way home to the land of milk and honey. Throngs of well wishers lined the ramp area as we taxied in. We had a brief respite and reception in the field operations building while the plane was refueled. Many of us met some former shipmates we had served with at one time or another in years past.

We were kept under close scrutiny. Only a few senior military commanders and their wives were allowed to be part of the welcoming reception. A junior Intelligence Officer put a piece of paper in my hand. It said, Frank Overby. "Where is he?" I asked. He pointed to a hall door. "Out there," he replied. I rushed headlong to greet my long time friend and former roommate aboard the *USS PHILIPPINE SEA* in the late forties. A guard made a halfhearted attempt to restrain me, but then thought better of it.

He was on the other side of the door waiting. "Welcome home, Jim," he said as he spied me. The tears rolled down his cheek, and he put a bear hug greeting on me which left me breathless. "Thanks for coming, Frank," I said. "I'm leaving in a few minutes but when I got your note I had to break out and say hello." We had barely exchanged greetings and mutual remembrances to our wives and family when they called out to me that it was time to leave and reboard our aircraft.

The flight to Travis Air Force Base in California was restful and uneventful. I had figured out that I better get some rest, because we would be winging our way to the east coast and home with only brief stopovers. I slept like a baby from Hawaii until about an hour from California.

At Travis the crowds greeting us were bigger and more enthusiastic. We were met by Air Force General Daniel "Chappie" James, who had flown out from Washington, D.C. to accompany us on the rest of the trip home.

Chappie James, fighter pilot par excellence was an Air Force legend. He was a black American originally raised in Pensacola, Florida, who by dint of his military performance in combat, his hard work, natural ability as a leader and drive, had risen to the rank of General. He was an aviator's aviator. I couldn't believe that we were so important that a busy Air Force General stationed in Washington, D.C. could take the time to meet us in California and fly back east with us.

While the plane was refueled, Jerry Denton had to go to a press conference with the newsmen and I had to give a TV interview to newscasters in front of our waiting C-141 parked on the ramp. The stopover was as expeditious as possible. Soon we were winging our way east. Our next scheduled stop was Scott AFB in East St. Louis where we would leave our C-141 and transfer to a DC-9 which would drop three of us off in Norfolk before proceeding to Washington, D.C. with the remainder of the POWs traveling with us.

The west coast POWs left us at Travis and were assigned to military hospitals near their homes for physical evaluation and complete debriefing.

When we were airborne, Chappie James came and took the seat next to me. "Jim, you tell me about Hanoi and I'll tell you about your wonderful wife Louise's activities in Washington." I gave him a hasty run-down of POW life in Hanoi as I had experienced it. I could tell he was a compassionate man by the questions he asked and the concern he showed. When I concluded, he said to me as sincerely as I had ever heard anyone speak, "Jim, your wife Louise is truly a remarkable woman. She fought in the trenches of Washington, D.C. night and day for your return. She is a most respected woman by everyone on the Washington scene from the President on down. Believe me, she knows everyone up there and they all damn well know who she is and what she was fighting for. She said things in public that had to be said, but which military men on active duty were prohibited from saying. You will be real proud of her when you learn of the effort she made for you these past years." He went on to tell me how Louise had led the fight to go public on the POW issue. How she recited a poem at a big POW rally in Independence Hall entitled, "May Day, May Day, May Day" and how when she was through there wasn't a dry eye in that room. "She had me crying like a baby," said Chappie James. "And by God she was right. She said what we couldn't say. One time she told a group of Flag Officers that they ought to win the war and get you out or put their ranks on the line and quit. Another time she told the Joint Chiefs and a roomful of Flag Officers that if the U.S. continued to abandon their POWs that it wouldn't have any more credibility, and would never be able to put men in the field of battle again. She's a fighter Jim, and she never gave up. She's a wonderful woman."

When General James finished talking to me about Louise, I was overcome with emotional pride. I had no idea of Louise's activities and how she had become a nationally recognized spokesman for the POW cause.

In the past, Louise had been a typical Navy wife, concerned with her family and her husband. She was a quiet, private person, one who avoided publicity and the limelight. She was an excellent judge of character and had more common sense than anyone else I ever knew. I had difficulty envisioning her in Washington trading verbal blows with the leaders of the establishment. But I did understand one thing. Louise Mulligan would keep her family together, and do anything she thought necessary to help get her husband home. If that meant fighting in the political trenches of Washington, so be it, she'd be there. And God help those who were her adversaries, because above all else, Louise would tell it like it was and call a spade a spade.

We landed at Scott and changed planes. Now only those continuing on to Norfolk and Washington, D.C. were left. I couldn't believe the size of the crowd that greeted us. It was well after midnight and thousands of cheering Americans lined the ramp area. The wind was blowing and the weather cold. They moved us by bus from the C-141 to the DC-9 area. We were waiting for the DC-9. Thousands of people were showing their love and affection by waving signs and cheering. And we were being kept in a bus out of the wind, and out of their reach. "I can't stand it, Jerry," I said to Captain Denton. "Those people out there deserve more than to see us in a bus. I'm going out there." A medic tried to restrain me. "Open the damn door," I yelled to the driver and to the medic. "If I get pneumonia from meeting this crowd of well wishers it'll be worth it."

I plunged down the steps and ran to the cheering crowd and shook hands with as many as I could reach as I went up and down the ramp. The rest of the POWs followed me and the crowd went wild, particularly the kids. I couldn't quite understand the huge spontaneous welcome. The whole damn country must be glad we're back, I said to myself.

We were in the soup most of the way from St. Louis to Norfolk. I was getting butterflies in my stomach the closer we got to home. It had been a long flight from the Philippines to Hawaii, to California, to St. Louis and now to Virginia. It was a day of days. It was the Judgment Day and Day of Resurrection when I would be born again into a free world to be reunited with my wife and family, with my relatives and friends.

Suddenly the sky broke clear and the moon shone through. "We'll be landing shortly," the pilot announced and the "fasten seat belt" signs came on. I looked out the window and could see the puffy broken white clouds below and the reflection of the moonbeams on the black Atlantic. I recognized the lights from Virginia Beach, and I saw the outline of the Chesapeake Bay Bridge-Tunnel complex as we descended towards our destination. When the plane turned in on its final approach the sky was absolutely clear. I saw the outline of Pier 12; it was here I had bid Louise and my sons a tearful goodbye in October 1965 as I boarded *ENTERPRISE* on my way to combat in Vietnam. Louise was crying as she drove from the pier that fateful morning. In all my years of going to sea she had never cried, at least openly. I remembered saying to myself as I went up the gangway, "That's a bad sign." Then I gave my last final wave to her and my sons, arrived at the Quarter Deck, saluted the colors and stepped into what turned out to be an eternity.

We touched gently down and quickly taxied into the main ramp area. I couldn't believe the size of the crowd that was out there to welcome us. It looked like the entire Navy and the cities of Norfolk and Virginia Beach were there. Hundreds of children were carrying and waving signs. A band was playing. A group of police escort cars with flashing lights stood ready to lead the caravan that would whisk us to the Portsmouth Naval Hospital.

Jerry Denton, Paul Galanti and I would get off here. We disembarked, waved goodbye to our compatriots in the DC-9 who were pushing on to Washington, D.C.

We were greeted by Admiral Ralph Cousins and a host of senior officers. Each of us said a few words of greeting to the cheering crowd.

I could see my Louise and our six sons standing next to Jane Denton and her family. As soon as the official greetings were over, I rushed towards Louise and took her in my arms and we exchanged our first lingering kiss since the 24th of October 1965. We shed tears of joy, wordless, for a few moments, for the emotional reunion was just too much for us to handle. I cradled her in my arms as she sobbed softly. "It's ok Louise, I'm home. I'll never leave you again as long as I live." Then I greeted my sons one by one.

The great day had finally come, the answer to those thousand pleading prayers I made in Hanoi. Thanks, Lord. Thanks, Lord, I said silently as we boarded the waiting autos for the trip to the hospital while thousands of well-wishing cheers rang through the stillness of the night.

The reception accorded us was beyond my wildest imagination. It was a magnificent gesture from a concerned people in our land of freedom. Just as it was our POW day of liberation, so it was theirs.

For me the nightmare of Vietnam was finally over. Thank God! Freedom at last! I'm home!

Home with family — NAS, Norfolk, Va.
15 Feb. 1973

THE WHITE HOUSE

WASHINGTON

February 14, 1973

Dear Captain Mulligan:

No words can compensate you for the ordeal
you have passed through for your country.
The captivity you have undergone for nearly
seven years required a strength of faith,
patience and patriotism which can never be
fully comprehended by others. However, I
do want to impress on you the heartfelt
gratitude that I and millions of other
Americans feel toward you on your return
home.

Some things about America may appear to
have changed since your departure. That
is inevitable. But I can assure you that
there has been no change in the pride and
gratitude the American people feel for
what you have done, and the thankfulness
we share on your safe return.

Your splendid statement when you stepped
off the airplane at Clark made all of us
very proud of the men and women who have
served their country with such fidelity
and courage.

My sincerest wish is for your future
success and happiness.

Welcome home,

Richard Nixon

Captain James A. Mulligan, Jr., USN
Naval Hospital
Portsmouth, Virginia 23708

Louise   Jim

Portsmouth Naval Hospital

EPILOGUE

Forty-two months in solitary confinement gave me time to think and assess my place in life. Some lessons I learned are:

1. With God all things are possible. Matthew 19:20

2. Permissiveness is the corruption of Freedom.

3. Anarchy is the corruption of Democracy.

4. Immorality is the corruption of Morality.

A free democratic moral society has the right as well as the obligation to resist the incursions of those perversions which would lead to its destruction.

A free society requires order, discipline and moderation. Thus it follows that rights and freedoms demand corresponding duties and obligations from all citizens.

Man is an imperfect creature living in an imperfect world but he should always strive to be better than he is. In this struggle he should never, never, never, give up!

Jim Mulligan
May 1981

WU VABCH

NFA045(1037)(1-004319C029002)PD 01/29/73

ICS IPMWAWB WSH

ZCZCO2007 INTER USGOVT W WASHINGTON DC 94 0

PMS

MRS JAMES ALFRED MULLIGAN JR, DLR DONT PHONE

DONT DLR BETWEEN 10PM AND 6AM

912 FIVE POINTS RD

VIRGINIABEACH VIR

I AM PLEASED TO INFORM YOU THAT YOUR HUSBAND, C

ALFRED MULLIGAN, JR., USN, 033 14 9477/1310, WAS

ON THE LIST OF CAPTURED IN SOUTHEAST ASIA PROVIDE

GOVERNMENT BY THE GOVERNMENT OF NORTH VIETNAM. IT

THAT THE FIRST INCREMENTAL RELEASE WILL BE WITHIN

TWO WEEKS. YOU WILL BE NOTIFIED OF ANY ADDITONAL IN

CONCERNING THE RELEASE, HEALTH, AND WELFARE OF YOUR

CONFIRMS THE INFORMATION PASSED TO YOU EARLIER BY YOU

ASSISTANCE OFFICER.

VICE ADMIRAL DAVID H BAGLEY CHIEF OF NAVAL PERSONNEL.